Microsoft Power Platform Solution Architect's Handbook

An expert's guide to becoming a Power Platform solution architect and preparing for the PL-600 exam

Hugo Herrera

Packt>

BIRMINGHAM—MUMBAI

Microsoft Power Platform Solution Architect's Handbook

Group Product Manager: Alok Dhuri
Publishing Product Manager: Harshal Gundetty
Senior Editor: Ruvika Rao
Content Development Editor: Urvi Shah
Technical Editor: Pradeep Sahu
Copy Editor: Safis Editing
Language Support Editor: Safis Editing
Project Coordinator: Deeksha Thakkar
Proofreader: Safis Editing
Indexer: Subalakshmi Govindhan
Production Designer: Sinhayna Bais
Marketing Coordinator: Deepak Kumar and Rayyan Khan
Business Development Executive: Puneet Kaur

First published: July 2022

Production reference: 2290722

Published by Packt Publishing Ltd.
Livery Place
35 Livery Street
Birmingham
B3 2PB, UK.

978-1-80181-933-6

www.packt.com

For my daughter, Laura – thank you for being there. You made writing this book possible.

– Hugo Herrera

Contributors

About the author

Hugo Herrera is an experienced and versatile Power Platform and Dynamics 365 solution architect, with a track record of successfully implementing solutions on behalf of Microsoft and the global Partner Network. His hands-on approach to technical leadership brings teams together and gets them working to the highest standards, using industry best practices. He is an articulate communicator who engages with business owners and stakeholders alike, running workshops and presentations with large audiences for maximum effect. As a freelance solution architect, he works with financial institutions, global consultancies, government organizations, partners, and Microsoft to fulfill their business goals.

To all the editors who supported me through this journey, and especially my wife, Janni – thank you

About the reviewer

Tristan Shortland is chief innovation officer at Infinity Group, a UK-headquartered Microsoft partner, specializing in providing digital transformation services across the Microsoft stack. Tristan has worked with Dynamics 365 Customer Engagement for over 13 years, having started with Microsoft Dynamics CRM 3.0. During this time, he has worked in multiple roles, including consultancy, architecture, and presales, with both end users and Microsoft partners. In his latest role as chief innovation officer, Tristan is responsible for thought leadership, presales, and product development at Infinity Group.

Table of Contents

Preface

Part 1: Introduction

1

Introduction to Power Platform Solution Architecture

2

The Digital Transformation Case Study

Part 2: Requirements Analysis, Solution Envisioning, and the Implementation Roadmap

3

Discovery and Initial Solution Planning

4

Identifying Business Processes, Risk Factors, and Success Criteria

5

Understanding the Existing Architectural Landscape

6

Requirements Analysis and Engineering for Solution Architecture

7

Power Platform Fit Gap Analysis

Part 3: Architecting the Power Platform Solution

8
Designing the Power Platform Solution

9

Effective Power Platform Data Modeling

10

Power Platform Integration Strategies

11
Defining Power Platform Security Concepts

Part 4: The Build – Implementing Solid
Power Platform Solutions

12
Validating the Solution's Design and Implementation

13

Power Platform Implementation Strategies

14

Leveraging Azure DevOps for Power Platform

15
Go-Live Strategies

Part 5: Power Platform Solution Architect Certification Prep

16
Microsoft Certified: Power Platform Solution Architect Expert Certification Prep

Index

Other Books You May Enjoy

Preface

If you've been looking for a way to unlock the potential of Microsoft Power Platform and take your career as a solution architect to the next level, then look no further—this practical guide covers it all.

Microsoft Power Platform Solution Architect's Handbook will equip you with everything you need to build flexible and cost-effective end-to-end solutions. Its comprehensive coverage ranges from best practices surrounding fit-gap analysis, leading design processes, and navigating existing systems to application lifecycle management with Microsoft Azure DevOps, security compliance monitoring, and third-party API integration.

The book takes a hands-on approach by guiding you through a fictional case study throughout, allowing you to apply what you learn as you learn it. At the end of the handbook, you'll discover a set of mock exam questions for you to embed your progress and prepare for the PL-600 Microsoft certification.

Whether you want to learn how to work with Power Platform or want to take your skills from the intermediate to advanced level, this book will help you achieve that and ensure that you're able to add value to your organization as an expert solution architect.

Who this book is for?

This book is for solution architects, enterprise architects, technical consultants, and business and system analysts who implement, optimize, and architect Power Platform and Dataverse solutions. It will also help anyone who needs a detailed playbook for architecting and delivering successful digital transformation projects that leverage Power Platform apps and the Microsoft business apps ecosystem. A solid understanding of Power Platform configuration and administration, Power Automate processes, Power Apps portals, canvas apps, Dataverse plugins, and workflow capabilities is expected.

What does this book cover?

Chapter 1, Introducing Power Platform Solution Architecture, describes the solution architect's role, the general approach to applying best practices to solve problems, and a Power Platform architecture overview.

Chapter 2, The Digital Transformation Case Study, introduces the fictional case study used throughout the book.

Chapter 3, Discovery and Initial Solution Planning, discusses high-level business requirements and how to identify suitable solutions across the Microsoft stack.

Chapter 4, Identifying the Desired Business Process, Risk Factors, and Success Criteria, discusses options for running discovery workshops, performing high-level process and data modeling, and identifying automation opportunities. The chapter concludes with a discussion on balancing risk factors through mitigation strategies.

Chapter 5, Understanding the Existing Architectural Landscape, describes the enterprise architecture assessment process and how to identify external data sources and document the existing architectural structure and business processes.

Chapter 6, Requirements Analysis and Engineering for Solution Architecture, discusses effective requirements analysis and engineering, including the preparation, delivery, and post-requirement-capture activities.

Chapter 7, Power Platform Fit-Gap Analysis, describes the fit-gap analysis process, AppSource, third-party solution evaluation, proofs of concept, and the overall project scope definition.

Chapter 8, Leading the Power Platform Design Process, covers the design process from defining the architecture topology to detailed visual designs, prototyping, and data migration strategies.

Chapter 9, Effective Power Platform Data Modeling, discusses how to translate business requirements to visual data models, deciding factors for the integration or import of data, defining extensible Dataverse models, reference data strategies, table relationships, and overall data modeling best practices.

Chapter 10, Power Platform Integration Strategies, discusses various options for integrating Power Platform with on-premises and cloud-based systems and Microsoft 365 services. It then concludes with authentication and business continuity strategies.

Chapter 11, Defining Power Platform Security Concepts, discusses the core security model, implementing data loss prevention policies, Dataverse security, and defining access routes for external users.

Chapter 12, Validating the Solution Design and Implementation, discusses the design and implementation review process, compliance with security concepts, Power Platform API limits, and options for resolving automation and integration conflicts.

Chapter 13, Power Platform Implementation Strategies, discusses the configuration of environments and tenants, optimizing the output of Power Platform teams, and effective test strategies.

Chapter 14, Leveraging Azure DevOps for Power Platform, describes the use of Azure DevOps for application lifecycle management.

Chapter 15, Go-Live Strategies and Support, discusses go-live strategies, preparation, and the rollout of Power Platform solutions into production.

Chapter 16, Microsoft Certified: Power Platform Solution Architect Expert Practice Exams, discusses the benefits of being a Microsoft Certified Power Platform Solution Architect, how to prepare for the PL-600 examination, PL-600 prep questions, recommended reading, and final thoughts.

To get the most out of this book

This book assumes general knowledge of the configuration and administration of Power Platform applications. The PL-200: Microsoft Power Platform Functional Consultant and PL-400: Microsoft Power Platform Developer exams cover the ideal base knowledge required for this book.

Any errata related to this book can be found at `https://github.com/ PacktPublishing/Microsoft-Power-Platform-Solution-Architect-s- Handbook`.

Download the color images

We also provide a PDF file that has color images of the screenshots and diagrams used in this book. You can download it here: `https://packt.link/D9wUs`

Conventions used

There are a number of text conventions used throughout this book.

Bold: Indicates a new term, an important word, or words that you see onscreen. For instance, words in menus or dialog boxes appear in **bold**. Here is an example: "**Append To** – Grants users the ability to associate a record from another row (for example, from the account record, associate existing contacts to the account)."

> **Tips or Important Notes**
> Appear like this.

Get in touch

Feedback from our readers is always welcome.

General feedback: If you have questions about any aspect of this book, email us at customercare@packtpub.com and mention the book title in the subject of your message.

Errata: Although we have taken every care to ensure the accuracy of our content, mistakes do happen. If you have found a mistake in this book, we would be grateful if you would report this to us. Please visit www.packtpub.com/support/errata and fill in the form.

Piracy: If you come across any illegal copies of our works in any form on the internet, we would be grateful if you would provide us with the location address or website name. Please contact us at copyright@packt.com with a link to the material.

If you are interested in becoming an author: If there is a topic that you have expertise in and you are interested in either writing or contributing to a book, please visit authors.packtpub.com.

Share Your Thoughts

Once you've read *Microsoft Power Platform Solution Architect's Handbook,* we'd love to hear your thoughts! Scan the QR code below to go straight to the Amazon review page for this book and share your feedback.

https://packt.link/r/1-801-81933-5

Your review is important to us and the tech community and will help us make sure we're delivering excellent quality content.

Part 1: Introduction

This section introduces the solution architect's role in Microsoft Power Platform implementations. After completing this part, you will have a high-level understanding of Power Platform's capabilities and how it benefits from the Microsoft 365 and Azure ecosystem. This section contains the following chapters:

- *Chapter 1, Introducing Power Platform Solution Architecture*
- *Chapter 2, The Digital Transformation Case Study*

1
Introduction to Power Platform Solution Architecture

Microsoft Power Platform solution architects have functional and technical knowledge across the Microsoft cloud ecosystem and other third-party technologies. This chapter introduces the solution architect's role, the Power Platform, and the broader Microsoft stack. You will be taken through a journey covering the hands-on approach used to apply best practices, solve problems, identify opportunities, and increase the value of the customer's investment in Microsoft solutions.

In this chapter, we are going to cover the following main topics:

- Laying the foundations for great solution architecture
- Understanding the solution architect's role
- Power Platform architecture overview
- The Microsoft cloud-based ecosystem
- A hands-on approach to solution architecture

By the end of this chapter, you will be equipped with the tools and context to propel you through the activities and scenarios in the chapters to come. You will also gain an awareness of the various components and moving parts that make up Power Platform implementations of varying sizes and complexity.

Laying the foundations for great solution architecture

The advent of cloud-based solutions has brought forth the era of scalable, highly performant, and secure business applications. Planning, designing, and building great Power Platform solution architecture requires the consistent application of a set of principles. Each organization and solution is unique, and while a single solution design pattern does not exist, the following nine concepts will help you lay the foundations for a great Power Platform solution architecture:

Figure 1.1 – The pillars for great solution architecture

Now, let's outline these nine key concepts for great Power Platform solution architecture.

The security concept

Data is the crown jewel of most organizations. The **security concept** encompasses every aspect of the implementation. You define the authentication strategies, identify network vulnerabilities, and management of secrets, certificates, and other credentials. These activities will result in effective perimeter control for your solution.

The definition of a solid security concept will do the following:

- Provide the client with confidence in their Power Platform investment.
- Expedite the implementation and configuration of the solution.
- Reduce the risk of data breaches in production environments.

Through access control, you will also define the level of access that the internal users will be granted. In the chapters that follow, you will learn how to define a security concept that ensures data is placed only in the hands of the right users.

Empowered users – the cloud citizen

The Power Platform provides a wealth of features, allowing users to extend the base implementation. A great architecture blueprint will be cognizant of these user-accessible features and plan for these to be used as part of the user's daily activities. The Power Platform design will define guardrails to safely empower users to build their components, allowing them to achieve greater productivity through a synergy between the base implementation and user-created enhancements.

In the use case scenarios that follow, you will learn how to define Power Platform guardrails to safely empower users.

Compliance

Privacy and trust requirements vary greatly, depending on the industry, geographical location, scope, and nature of the implementation. Data retention policies and access request channels are defined to comply with local and international regulations.

In this book, you will explore the Microsoft Trust Center tools and capabilities to locate certifications for the components that make up the solution architecture.

Maintainability and supportability

Power Platform solution architects design solutions that leverage the inherent functionality available within each Microsoft component. Making use of the standard functionality within the various Power Apps, Dataverse, and the wider Microsoft ecosystem, configuring and customizing these components are the first implementation point of call. Custom development is considered only when all other options have been exhausted and implemented within the bounds of supported customizations.

Following the configure-first approach outlined and thorough documentation of the implementation build, a solution architect defines the implementation principles and best practices for the teams to follow.

Availability and recoverability

Organizations have expectations regarding the uptime and availability of their critical systems and business applications. As a part of the initial phases of the solution design, these requirements are identified and mapped to Power Platform product capabilities. Solution architects understand the availability and recoverability features within each component in the implementation, and design integrations with retry strategies and fallbacks to prevent the transient faults from impacting the solution.

In the following chapters, you will explore the features available within each Power Platform component, define recoverability strategies, and design integration patterns that benefit from a high level of fault tolerance.

Performant and scalable solutions

Users expect business applications and portals to respond within a specific amount of time. Successful Power Platform solutions take these expectations into account and are designed to perform within the customer's requirements. Solution architects document these performance requirements and translate them into actionable implementation tasks. Considerations such as Dataverse capacity planning, integration response times, Power Automate throughput, and Power Apps portal user experience are considerations during the solution architecture process.

In addition to performance, the solution architect plans for the dynamic allocation of resources to scale with changing demands on the system. In the following chapters, you will work through the planning of efficient resource allocation to maximize performance while optimizing costs.

Implementation and operation efficiency

A solid monitoring architecture provides a platform for the detection of faults in the solution before they happen. Monitoring strategies also provide visibility over the usage of resources. Administrators can visualize how efficiently the solution is performing and make adjustments where needed.

In the upcoming chapters, you will learn how to plan effective monitoring solutions to facilitate the efficient operation of the Power Platform systems.

Cloud delegation

The Power Platform and the wider Microsoft cloud-based ecosystem present the opportunity to delegate the responsibility for the setup and maintenance of the management of the underlying platform. Solution architects have greater freedom to focus on the implementation architecture, compared to on-premises solutions, which require careful consideration of hardware and software capabilities, constraints, and ongoing administration overheads.

In the chapters that follow, you will learn how to shift the responsibilities to the service provider, leveraging the Microsoft support infrastructure.

Balanced design decisions

Applying the aforementioned key solution architecture concepts will result in the creation of a scalable, performant, and secure Power Platform implementation. Adhering to these pillars of architecture attracts a cost, be it financial, increased project implementation timescales, or operational agility.

Throughout this book, you will learn how to balance the cost of employing these key concepts versus the benefits to the organization using the systems. You will learn how to initiate discussions with key stakeholders to agree on the goals that are most important to the organization and balance these with the cost/benefits associated with each pillar for great solution architecture.

> **Note**
>
> Look out for the *Applying the pillars for great architecture* sections, as these are hands-on applications of each of the nine pillars discussed previously throughout the activities covered in the upcoming chapters.

Understanding the solution architect's role

The Power Platform solution architect's role is to harness their technical knowledge and functional expertise to chart a path for the implementation team, navigating risks, issues, and changes to make the implementation a success. The solution architect is in constant dialog with the project stakeholders, project managers, and development and implementation team members to ensure the project's vision is achieved.

The following diagram illustrates the key activities a solution architect engages in on a typical Power Platform implementation:

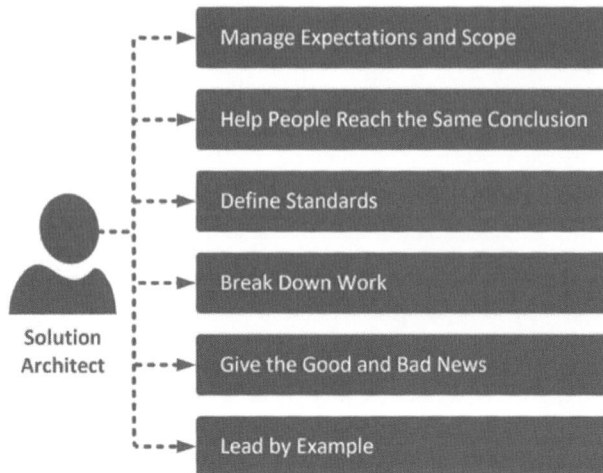

Figure 1.2 – The solution architect's role

Managing expectations and project scope

A solution architect is responsible for ensuring project requirements are actioned. When requirements inevitably change throughout a project, the solution architect manages the change in scope, assesses the risk and impact these changes would bring to the build, and sets the right expectations regarding timescales for implementation. When *scope creep* occurs, the solution architect reviews the change, breaks down the new requirements into tasks, and communicates an action plan to the project managers, stakeholders, and the development team, thus preventing unexpected impacts on the project budget and implementation timeline.

Managing expectations and project scope is one of the key activities performed by a Power Platform solution architect and ensures that nothing is over-promised or under-delivered. The chapters that follow provide practical examples for successfully managing project scope and customer expectations.

Defining standards and implementation guidelines

As a solution architect, you will be responsible for defining the development and implementation standards that will help Power Platform consultants and developers build high-quality supportable solutions. Development standards define the technical approach, conventions, and controls expected from the implementation team, and provide a template for the Power Platform solution.

Defining clear implementation standards helps boost the build teams' output capacity by providing a foundation for the customization of each aspect of the Power Platform, from table and column-naming conventions to advanced integration patterns, peer reviews, and coding standards. In the chapters that follow, you will learn how to define implementation standards that bring new team members up to speed faster and propel your implementation.

Breaking down work into implementable tasks

Organizational requirements are captured in the early stages of a Power Platform project and throughout the various phases of implementation. For these requirements to be implemented in harmony with the overall solution, they are broken down into tasks that the various implementation team members can perform.

Through the use of task management and sprint planning tools, such as Azure DevOps, solution architects analyze these requirements and related user stories, design a blueprint for the implementation, and create tasks that are later assigned to the implementation team members. Having an awareness of the various technical skillsets that make up a Power Platform implementation team, tasks are created to address each aspect of the organizational requirement.

In the chapters that follow, you will work through sample scenarios, and learn how to divide implementation work into discrete pieces of work to match the technical and functional skillsets of a build team.

Leading by example

Having defined the project development standards and designed a blueprint for the Power Platform solution to be implemented, solution architects proceed to lay the foundations for the implementation, helping team members build the solution from the ground up. Junior team members requiring additional attention during the early stages of the project are guided by the solution architect, providing a cushion to handle development issues, and making sure the project timescales are achieved by boosting the overall output for the team.

Helping people reach the same conclusion

During the various phases of a Power Platform project, team members will have varying opinions on the best course of action when implementing customer requirements. The solution architect listens to the options proposed by team members, project managers, and stakeholders, to ascertain the value contribution to the project. It is the solution architect's job to convey the best solution for the various problems and tasks that come up during the implementation.

Achieving harmony and the cooperation of the implementation team is achieved by creating an environment in which discussions can take place, weighing up the pros and cons, and clearly explaining why the solution blueprint put forth is the best way forward to achieve the current and future organizational requirements. Solution architects do not assume all team members have the same level of technical expertise. They aim to raise the team's awareness of the benefits the solution design brings to the implementation by highlighting use cases where specific implementation strategies have been successful in the past.

In the coming chapters, you will work through several scenarios where these negotiating skills will come into play, helping the project become a success.

Giving good news and bad news

Everyone enjoys giving people good news. There will be times during the implementation of business applications and portals when unexpected complications arise. This may be in the shape of new technical constraints, changes to the licensing model resulting in additional costs, or the deprecation of product features. A solution architect is responsible for the timely management of these issues, researching solutions to mitigate risks, and communicating the best course of action to the customer or project stakeholders.

In the chapters that follow, you will work through a sample implementation scenario that requires just this type of intervention to ensure the successful completion of a Power Platform project.

This section described the general activities and responsibilities solution architects take on during a typical Power Platform implementation. In this book, you will work through these activities to help cement their understanding for application in future projects.

Power Platform architecture overview

The Power Platform architecture comprises four key components, the environments and tenants that host these components, and the security capabilities used to control access.

Before delving into the Power Platform components, it is important to understand the data management framework that underpins the majority of Power Platform implementation. Dataverse is the foundation of most Power Platform implementations and is the first topic for our architecture overview.

Dataverse, the foundation of Power Platform data-based applications

Dataverse is a configurable business application data store with advanced processing capabilities and the foundation of most Power Apps-based solutions. Previously known as the Common Data Service, it consists of a relational database made up of tables and fields. Dataverse is configured using a graphical user interface (the Solution Explorer), and a wide range of processing capabilities, APIs, and security features. Dataverse includes a wide range of integration, security, and business process logic features.

The following diagram illustrates the key Dataverse components and interactions:

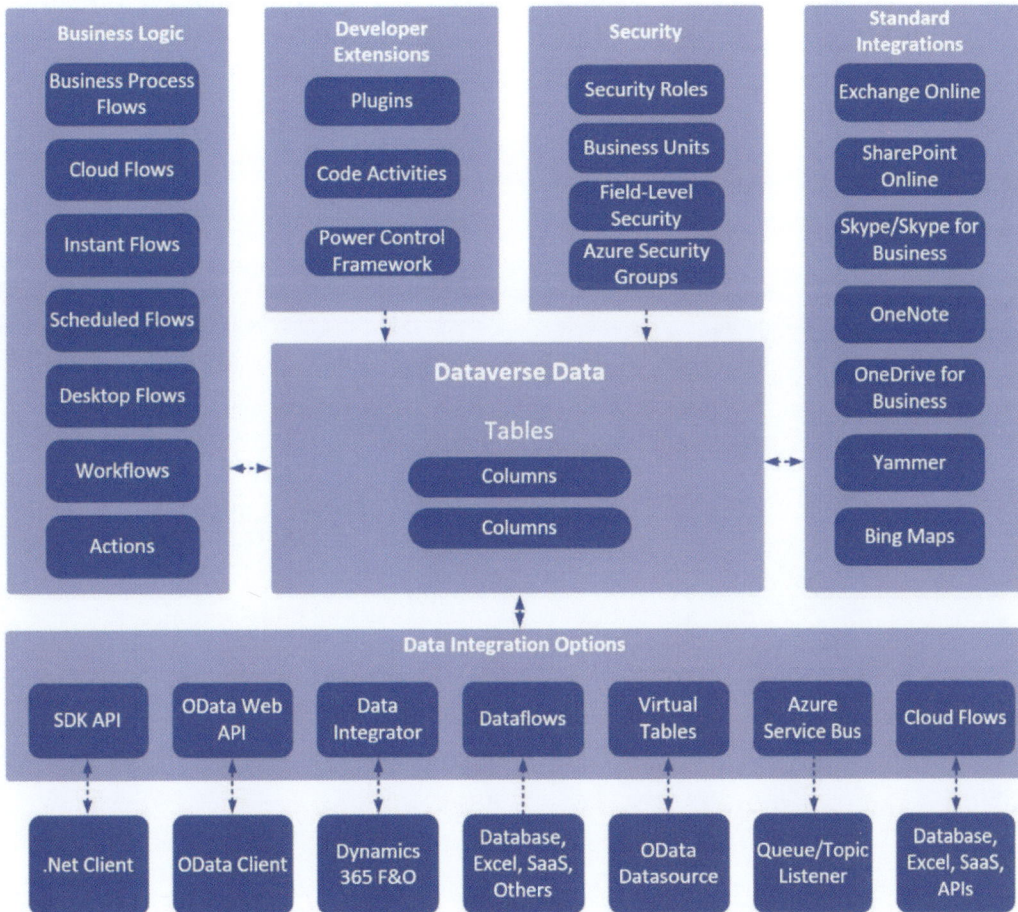

Figure 1.3 – Key Dataverse components and interactions

The flexible and configurable nature of Dataverse, combined with the wider Power Platform capabilities provides a unique opportunity to solve business problems for a virtually unlimited set of use cases. In the chapters that follow, you will learn how to design Power Platform solutions that make the most of Dataverse's capabilities.

> **Further Reading**
>
> Please follow the documentation link (`https://docs.microsoft.com/en-us/powerapps/maker/data-platform`) for further information on Dataverse capabilities and configuration options.

The four key Power Platform components

The Microsoft Power Platform is made of up four key components, each delivering powerful capabilities on its own; combined, they provide a compelling framework for the creation of advanced business applications. The four key Power Platform components are as follows:

- Power Apps
- Power Automate
- Power BI
- Power Virtual Agents

An overview of each of the four Power Platform components follows.

Power Platform component 1 – Power Apps

Power Apps makes up one of the five key components within the Power Platform architecture. Model-driven apps, Canvas apps, Power Pages, and Power Apps Portals are the four types of applications available via this low-code/no-code Power Apps framework. All Power Apps are managed via the `https://make.powerapps.com` portal, which is illustrated in the following screenshot:

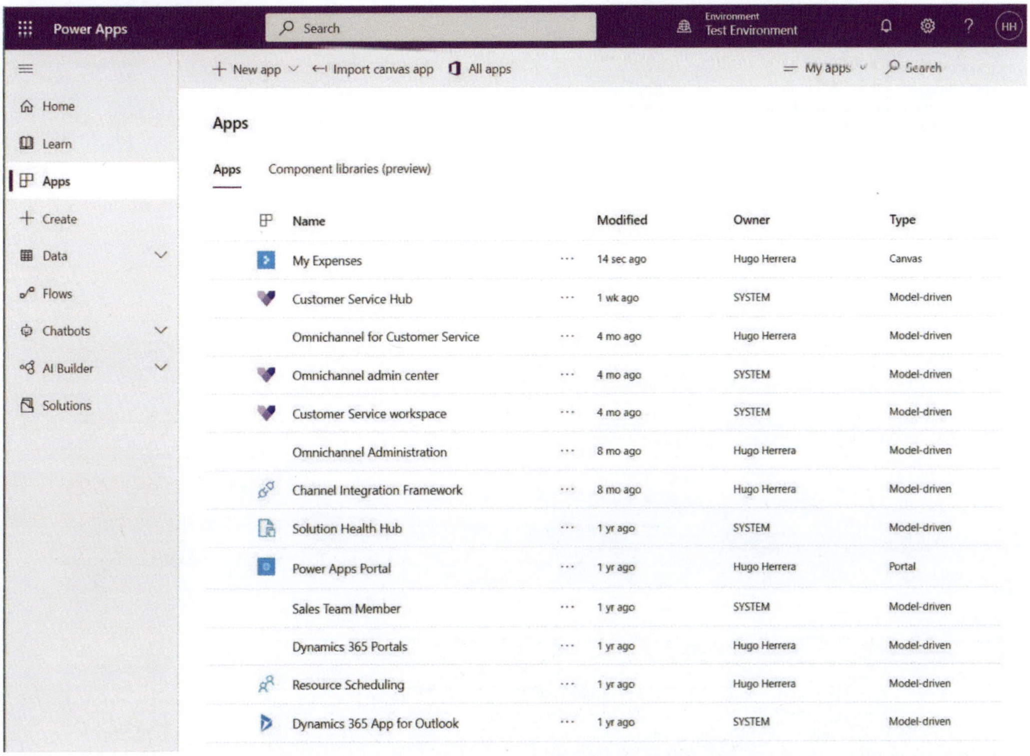

Figure 1.4 – Screenshot listing Power Apps in a Power Platform environment

A summary of the three different types of Power Apps available is as follows:

- **Model-driven apps** are a key component of a Power Platform implementation. They are the user-facing portion of a Dataverse database. The following figure illustrates a simple model-driven app (top) and the corresponding model-driven app editor (bottom):

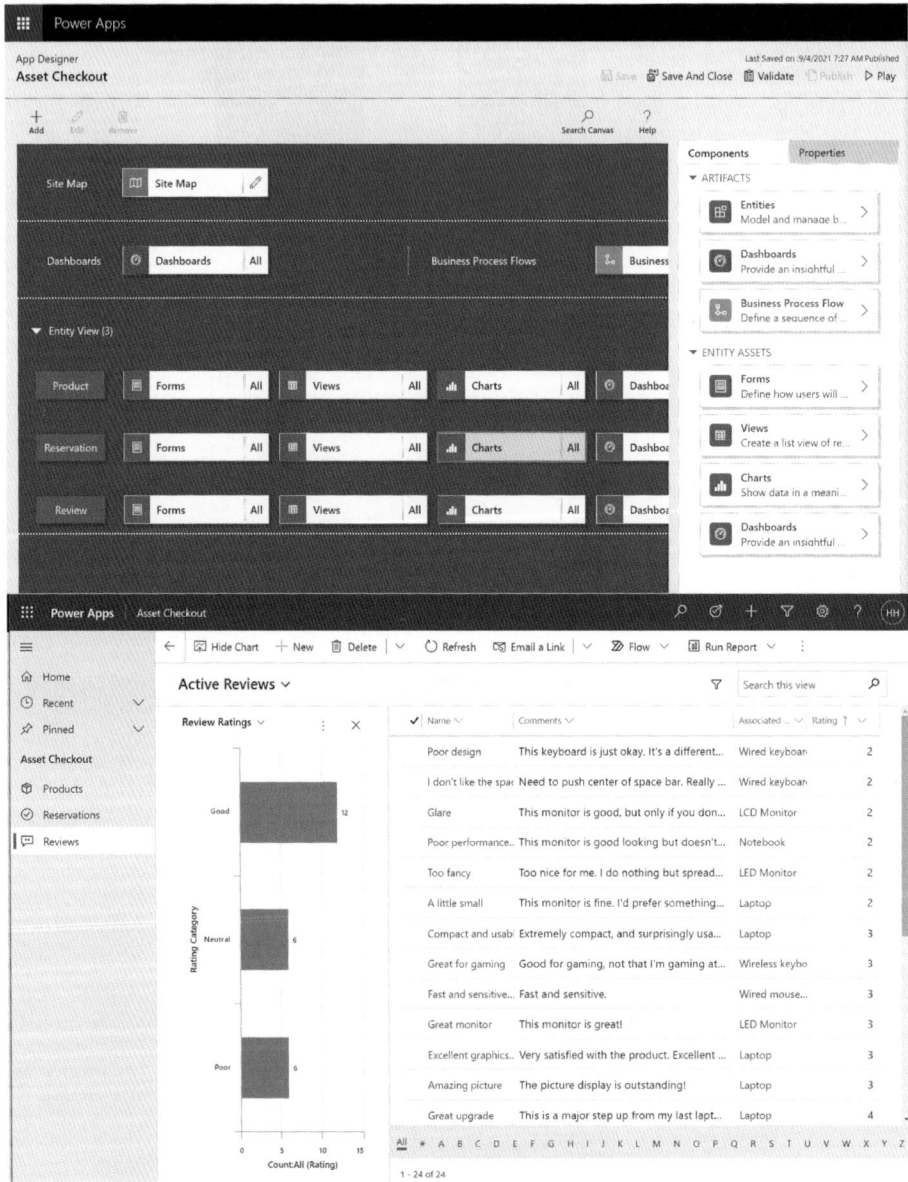

Figure 1.5 – Screenshot of a model-driven app next to its editor page

Web and mobile users interact with model-driven apps through the web or dedicated mobile applications. The diagram that follows presents a high-level architectural view of the component:

Model Driven Apps
Architecture Overview

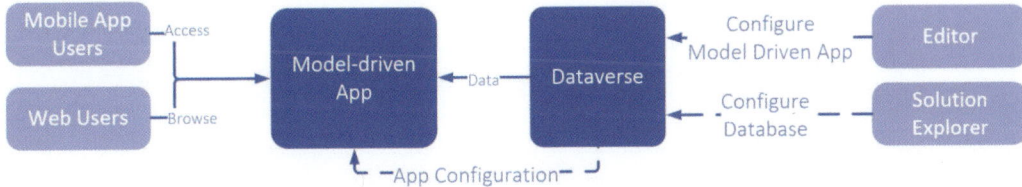

Figure 1.6 – Model-driven apps architectural overview

- **Power Pages** are internet-facing websites that leverage Dataverse capabilities to present a rich and customizable web experience. The administration section includes default templates for typical requirements such as customer service, partner management, employee self-service, and community portals. These default templates may be extended, or complete custom portal applications may be created depending on the organization's requirements. The following screenshot illustrates the Power Pages editor:

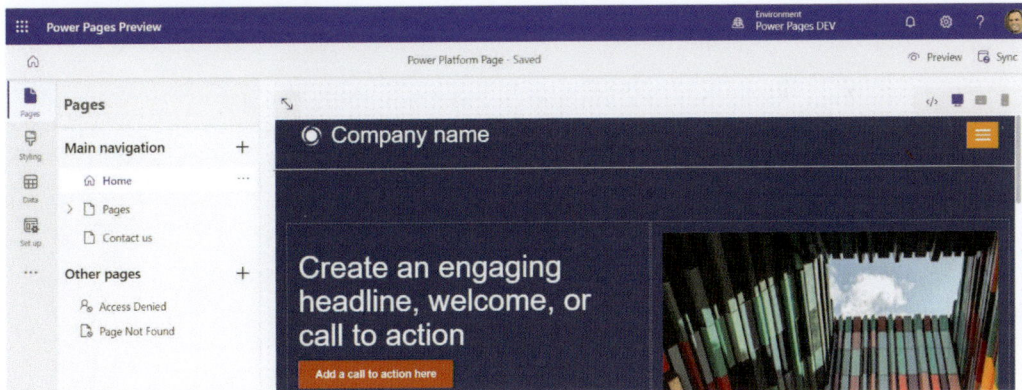

Figure 1.7 – Screenshot of the Power Pages editor

The diagram that follows presents a high-level architectural view of the component:

Power Pages
Architecture Overview

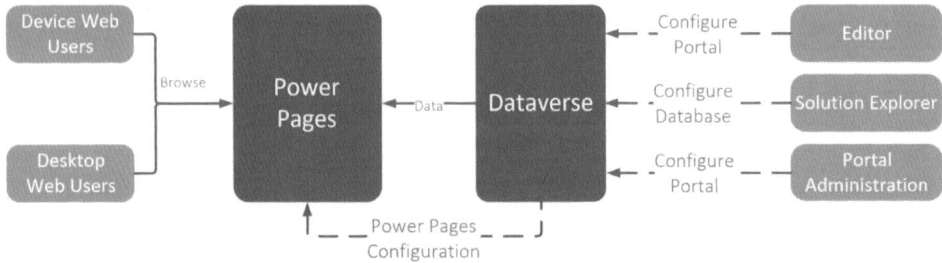

Figure 1.8 – Power Apps portal architectural overview

Power Pages are an evolution of Power Apps Portals, providing a superset of the Portals capabilities, including new low-code capabilities and out-of-the-box templates.

- **Power Apps Portals** are the predecessors to Power Pages, providing the same core functionality but lacking the additional templates and low-code editor capabilities afforded by Power Pages.

- **Canvas apps** are **user interface** (**UI**)-centered applications that can be used standalone or embedded into other Power Platform applications. They may be connected to a Dataverse database or other data sources to present a fully customizable UI for interacting with the underlying data. The screenshot that follows illustrates a sample canvas app and its editor:

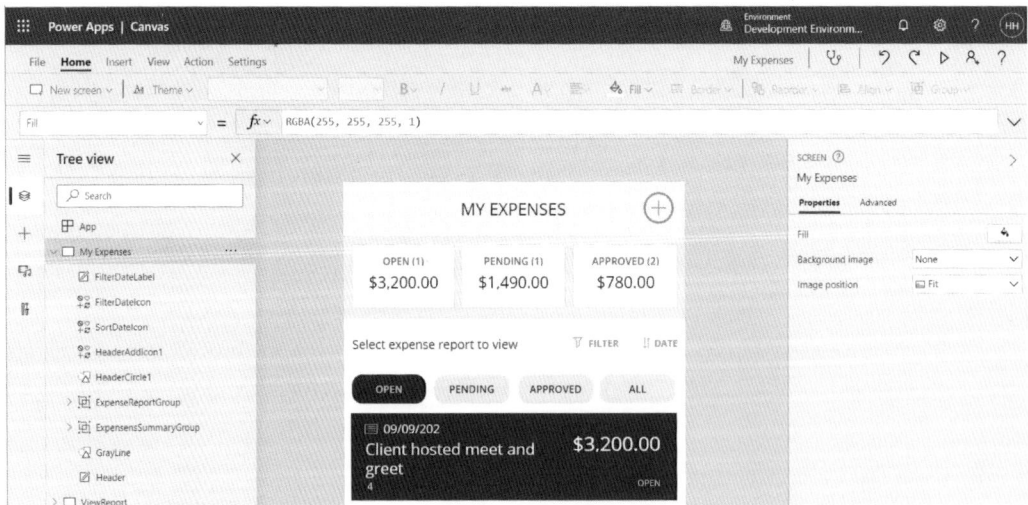

Figure 1.9 – Screenshot of a canvas app editor

All three Power Apps use Dataverse as an underlying platform and data source. The administration of usage of Dataverse databases is discussed in detail in the following sections and chapters.

> **Note Regarding Canvas Apps**
>
> The usage of Dataverse is optional within canvas apps, as these applications may be solely connected to alternative data sources, such as OneDrive or SharePoint, without the need for a Dataverse database.

The diagram that follows presents a high-level architectural view of the component:

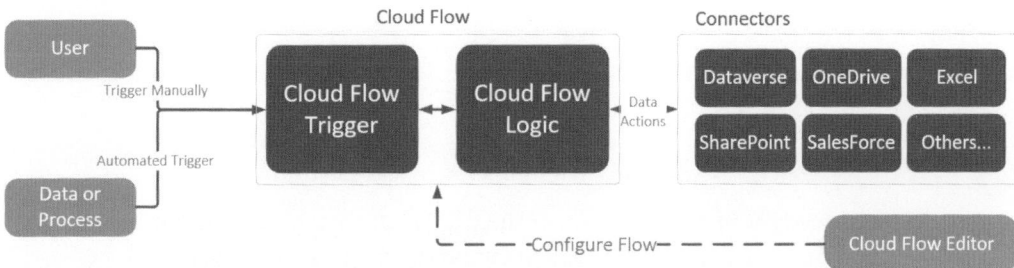

Figure 1.10 – Canvas Apps Architectural Overview

In the chapters that follow, you will learn how to design leading-edge business applications that benefit from the extensible and rapid development afforded by the three Power Apps.

> **Further Reading**
>
> Please follow the documentation link (`https://docs.microsoft.com/en-us/powerapps/`) for full details on Power Apps capabilities.

Power Platform component 2 – Power Automate

Power Automate is another key component within the Power Platform architecture. It provides a no-code/low-code solution for business process automation.

- **Cloud flows** provide a graphical user interface to build advanced business logic to suit exacting organizational requirements. Integrations with other Power Platform applications and external third-party systems are achieved through an easy-to-use point-and-click editor.

The following screenshot shows a simple Power Automate cloud flow being edited:

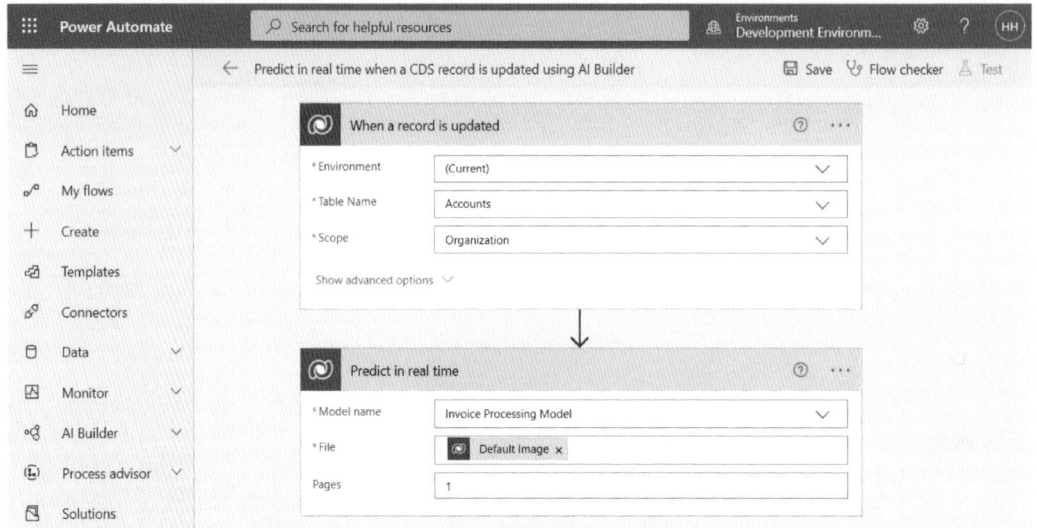

Figure 1.11 – Screenshot of the Power Automate cloud flow editor

The two key components of a cloud flow are the trigger (the action that will initiate the process) and one or more actions that will be executed when the flow runs.

Cloud flows may be triggered manually (for example, a user presses a button) or automatically (a record is created). There is a wide range of cloud flow triggers available. The key Dataverse triggers are as follows:

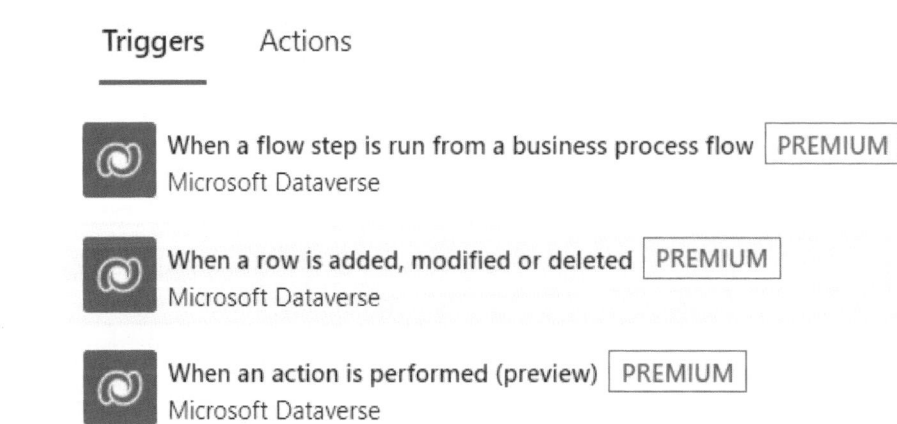

Figure 1.12 – Cloud flow Dataverse triggers

The wide range of available cloud flow actions provides solution architects with a powerful toolset for the automation of business processes and rapid integration with several Microsoft services and third-party APIs. A full list of Power Automate connectors is documented on the Microsoft documentation page titled *Connector reference overview ()*.

The screenshot that follows illustrates a subset of the actions available when using the Dataverse connector:

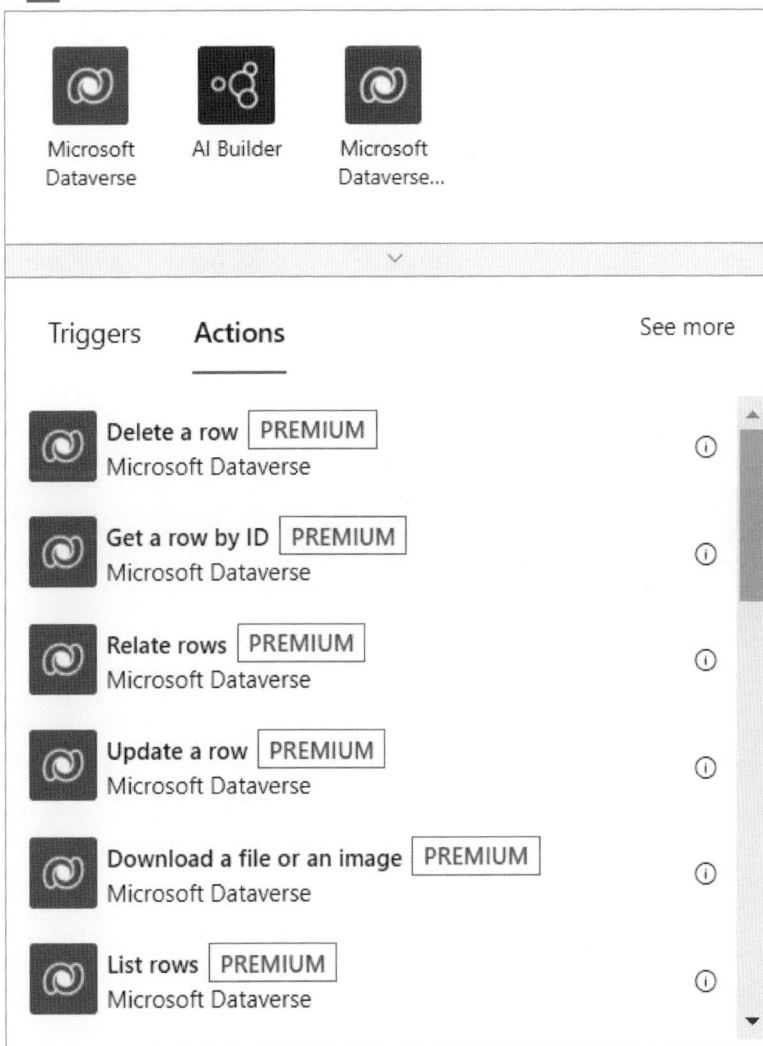

Figure 1.13 – A selection of cloud flow Dataverse actions

The diagram that follows presents a high-level architectural view of the component:

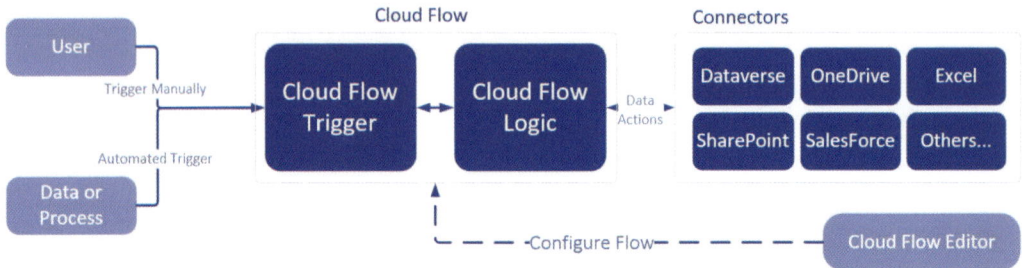

Figure 1.14 – Cloud flows architectural overvie

- **Desktop flows** are designed to automate rule-based tasks on a user's workstation. They provide a wide range of conditions and actions that interact with UI elements, Excel files, web browsers, and various other systems typically available in a user's workstation.

  The following screenshot illustrates a simple desktop flow being edited:

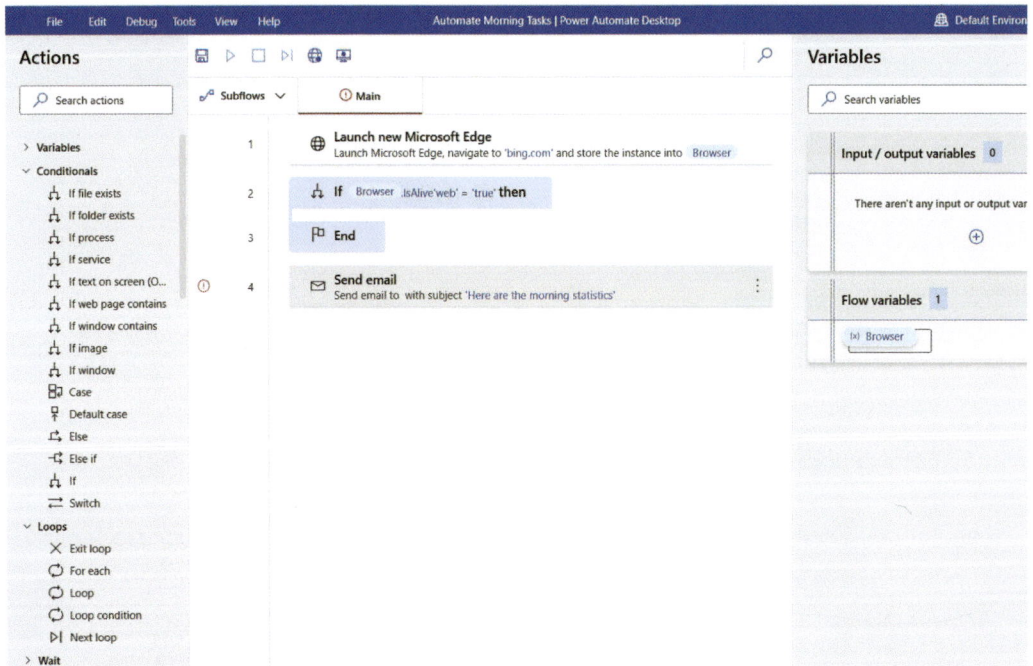

Figure 1.15 – Screenshot of the desktop flow editor

Cloud flows and desktop flows provide a rich toolset for business process automation. In this book, you will learn how to create architectural blueprints that leverage this powerful toolset.

> **Further Reading**
>
> Please follow the documentation link (`https://docs.microsoft.com/en-us/power-automate/`) for detailed instructions on the creation and administration of Power Automate flows.

Power Platform component 3 – Power BI

The third Power Platform component discussed in this book, Power BI is an analytics and reporting framework that connects to various data sources, to present high-impact visuals. Advanced data visualizations can be quickly generated from multiple data sources and presented through a range of software services. The diagram that follows presents a high-level architectural view of the component:

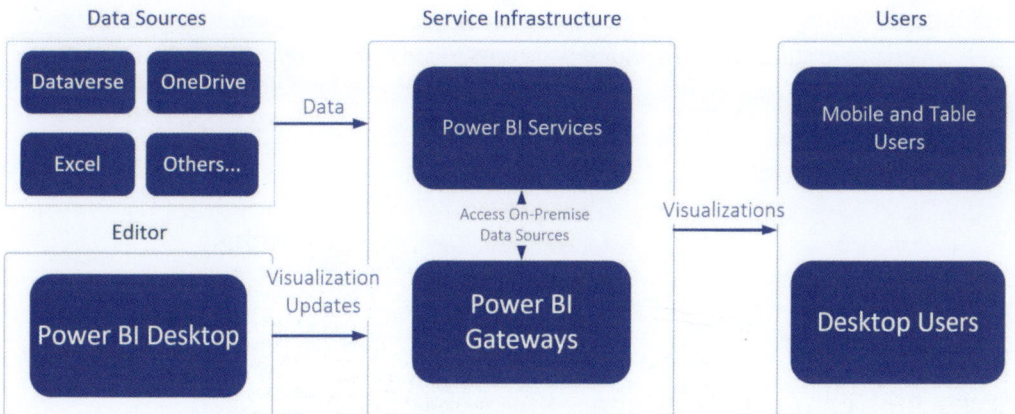

Figure 1.16 – Power BI architectural overview

Power BI reports are edited using either the Power BI desktop app or the web version of the report editor. The following screenshot presents a Power BI report in the process of being edited:

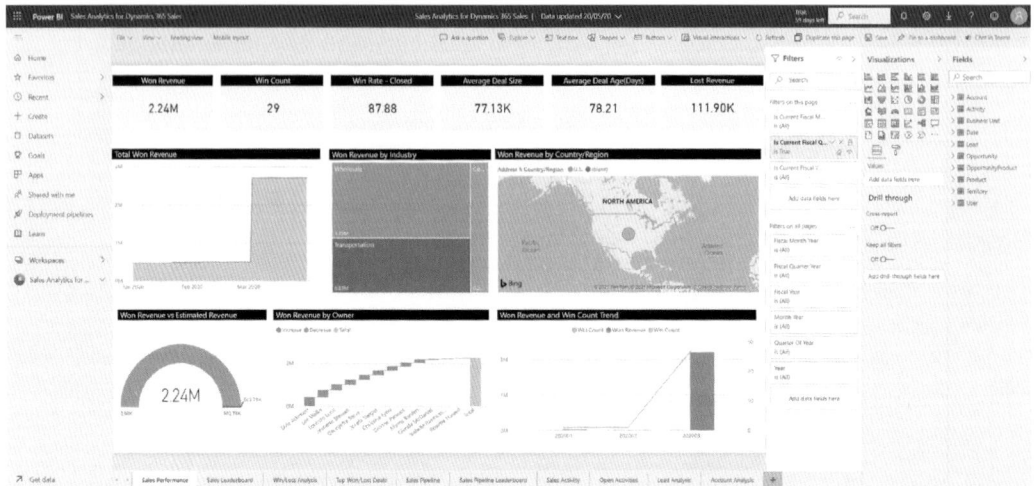

Figure 1.17 – Screenshot of the Power BI report editor

Working through the implementation scenarios discussed in this book, you will learn how to plan and design Power BI-based solutions to solve an organization's most complex reporting business requirements.

Further Reading

Please follow the documentation link (`https://docs.microsoft.com/en-us/power-bi/`) for detailed information on Power BI capabilities, data modeling, development of Power BI reports, and best practice guidance.

Power Platform component 4 – Power Virtual Agents

Organizations streamline costs and provide their customers with a responsive user experience using Power Virtual Agents. Users interact with the platform through various channels, including web chat and SMS messaging, benefiting from advanced routing capabilities.

The following screenshot illustrates a Power Virtual Agents chatbot test facility:

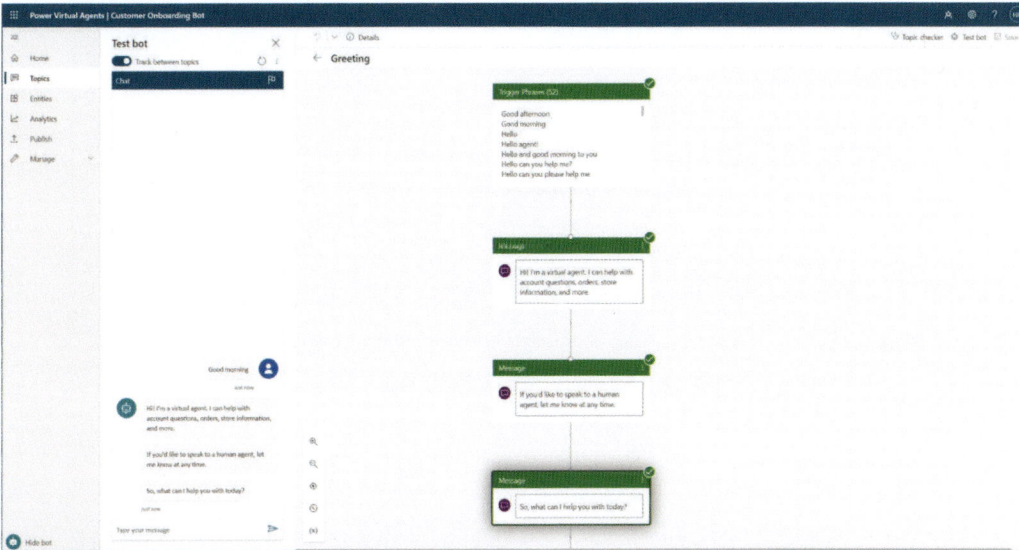

Figure 1.18 – Screenshot of a Power Virtual Agent being tested

Power Virtual Agents can be embedded within websites and deployed to entities including Facebook, Slack, Twilio, email, and mobile apps. The following diagram provides an overview of the Power Virtual Agents architecture:

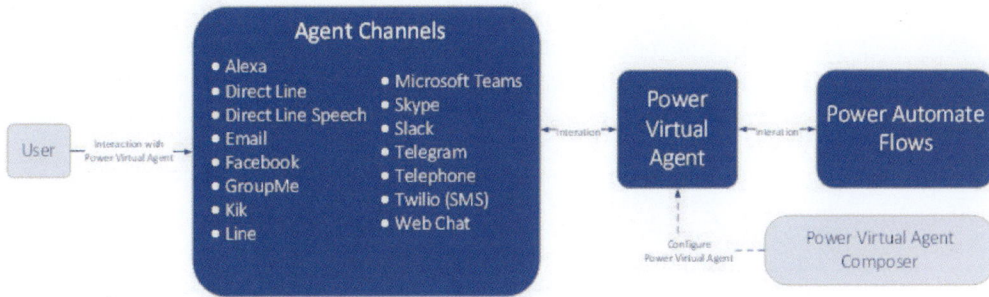

Figure 1.19 – Power Virtual Agents architectural overview

In this book, you will learn how to define customer interaction strategies that leverage the cost-saving and operational benefits of Power Virtual Agents.

> **Further Reading**
>
> Please follow the documentation link (`https://docs.microsoft.com/en-us/power-virtual-agents/`) for step-by-step guidance on the creation of Power Virtual Agents.

Other Power Platform building blocks

The previous sections described the four key Power Platform components. These components are underpinned by two additional building blocks:

- **Data connectors**

  Data connectors facilitate integrations between Power Platform components and external systems, solving previously complex integration problems with just a few clicks. Connections to Dataverse, SQL databases, SharePoint files, and various other sources of data are easily accessible through the use of data connectors.

  > **Further Reading**
  >
  > Please follow the documentation link (`https://docs.microsoft.com/en-us/connectors/`) for further information on available Power Platform connectors and their capabilities.

- **AI Builder**

  A pivotal tool in the Power Platform arsenal. AI Builder provides a no-code solution for the creation of AI-powered automation processes.

  > **Further Reading**
  >
  > Please visit `https://docs.microsoft.com/en-us/ai-builder/` for full instructions on using the AI Builder for Power Automation, Power Apps, and other Microsoft services.

In the coming chapters, you will navigate through the use cases for these two building blocks, and design architectural blueprints to maximize an organization's investment in the Power Platform and the wider Microsoft ecosystem.

Environments and tenants

Power Platform applications exist within an environment. In turn, environments are hosted within a Microsoft tenant. A Power Platform environment is made up of the following components:

- **Name**: A textual label for the environment
- **Location**: The geographical region where the data and configuration will be stored within Azure data centers
- **Admins**: The users that will administer and configure the environment
- **Security groups**: Controls that define who can access specific data records and application features
- **Apps**: Model-driven apps, portals, canvas apps, and other applications that exist within the environment
- **Flows**: Power Automate components that implement business process and integration routes
- **Bots**: Power Virtual Agents chatbots that are configured to interact with users
- **Connectors**: Identifies the connections that have been configured for Power Platform and external systems
- **Gateways**: Components that allow the integration with on-premise applications
- **Dataverse**: An optional Power Platform component and data store instance used by various Power Apps, such as model-driven apps

The following screenshot presents a typical set of development, test, and production Power Platform environments:

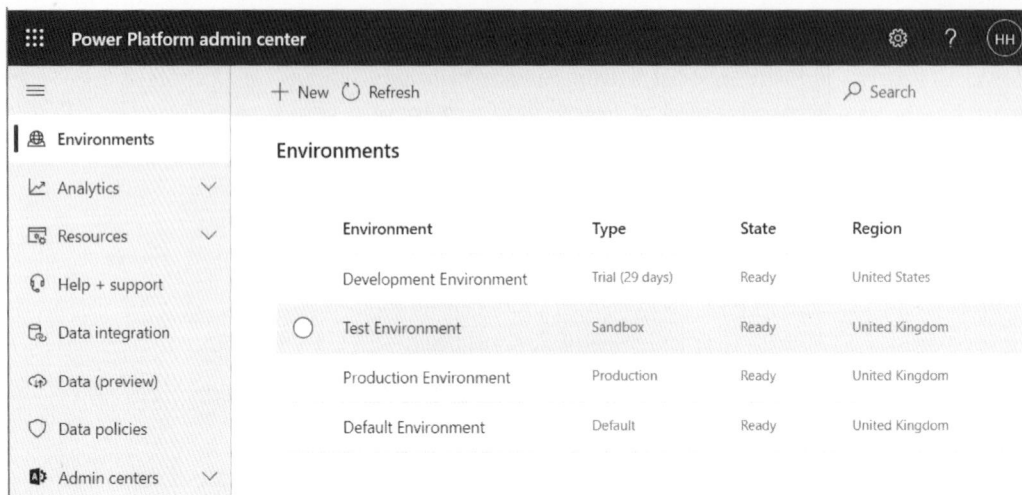

Figure 1.20 – Screenshot of a Power Platform environments list

Multiple environments may be created to support the development and release cycles. A typical Power Platform implementation includes development, test, and production environments. They may all be hosted within the same tenant or spread across a multi-tenant architecture. In this book, you will learn how to decide on the best environment and tenant strategy to achieve the organization's goals.

> **Further Reading**
>
> Please follow the documentation link (`https://docs.microsoft.com/en-us/power-platform/admin/environments-overview`) to review the options available when managing Power Platform environments.

Security

The security of data hosted within a Power Platform environment is enforced through the following layers:

- **Azure AD**

  The cloud-based Active Directory solution. Users are configured for access to specific resources, assigned security groups, and authentication policies.

- **Licenses**

  Assignment of licenses to Azure AD users grants them access to specific
  Power Platform applications, providing an additional access security layer.

- **Environments**

  Assigning security groups to Azure AD users sets them up for access to the
  applications within environments associated with those security groups. An
  additional security layer for Power Platform applications and data sources.

- **Data loss prevention policies**

  Data loss prevention policies define the types of connectors and inbound/outbound
  data privileges afforded to users of Power Platform applications.

- **Security roles**

  Security roles provide granular control over the data tables and columns stored
  in the Power Platform Dataverse. They further control access to specific features
  within Power Platform applications.

- **Encryption**

  Power Platform applications benefit from the encryption of data both in transit
  and at rest.

The various security features and considerations will be discussed in more detail in the
upcoming chapters, where you will learn how to define a security concept document to
satisfy an organization's strict requirements.

Power Platform application life cycle management

Application life cycle management (**ALM**) is a set of disciplines through which Power
Platform projects can be defined, implemented, deployed, and operated through a
controlled framework. It is a cyclical set of activities and processes through which Power
Platform requirements are captured, broken down into tasks, developed, tested, and
deployed. Once deployed, the operation of the system is managed and monitored, and the
next cycle is optimized based on lessons learned.

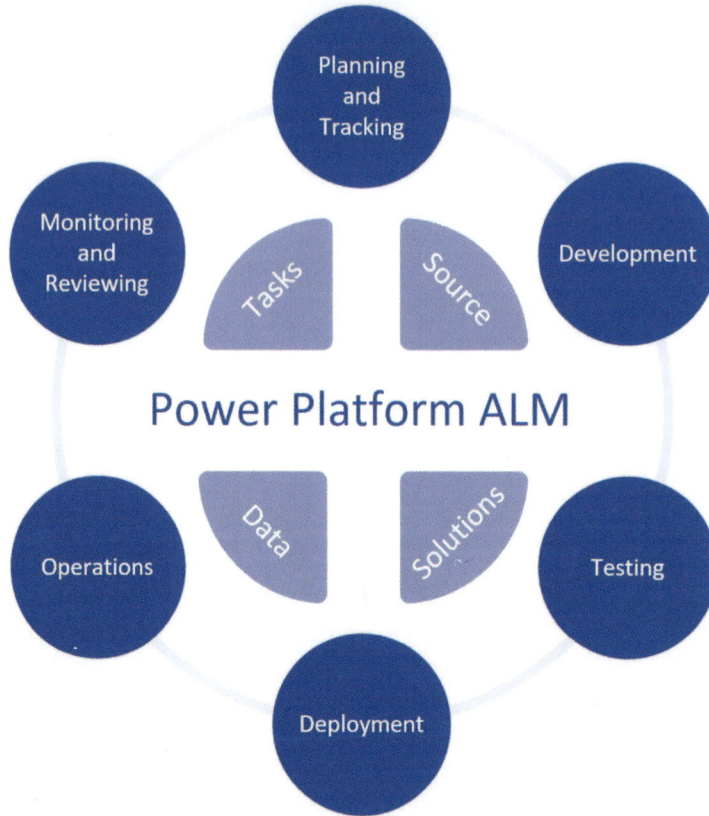

Figure 1.21 – Power Platform ALM activities and key components

ALM is the key to the success of any Power Platform project. In the chapters that follow, you will work through a set of practical scenarios, configuring Azure DevOps to manage the life cycle of a Power Platform project, configuring task management, source control, build, unit test, and automated deployment pipelines, and monitoring capabilities.

The Microsoft cloud-based ecosystem

The Microsoft cloud-based ecosystem caters to a wide range of business needs. Solution architects are aware of the capabilities afforded by this rich set of business applications and resources. In this chapter, we will review Dynamics 365 business applications, Microsoft 365, Azure, and AppSource.

Dynamics 365

Several Dynamics 365 applications are based on the same DNA as Power Platform model-driven apps. The following Dynamics 365 applications use Dataverse as the backbone for their data storage and business logic processing capabilities:

- **Dataverse-based Dynamics 365 applications** – Dataverse is the foundation for the following applications:

  - Dynamics 365 Sales

  - Dynamics 365 Marketing

  - Dynamics 365 Field Service

  - Dynamics 365 Project Operations

- **Other Dynamics 365 applications** – The following Dynamics 365 applications also provide a rich feature set outside the confines of the Dataverse framework:

  - Dynamics 365 Business Central

  - Dynamics 365 Human Resources

  - Dynamics 365 Finance

  - Dynamics 365 Supply Chain Management

  - Dynamics 365 Customer Insights

  - Dynamics 365 Commerce

  - Dynamics 365 Customer Voice (uses Dataverse to store configuration and operational data)

> **Further Reading**
>
> Please visit `https://docs.microsoft.com/en-us/dynamics365/` for full product documentation on all Dynamics 365 applications.

Microsoft 365

Microsoft 365 is the ubiquitous office application platform. Power Platform solutions leverage the capabilities of Microsoft 365 to present a complete solution for most business needs.

The key Microsoft 365 applications discussed in this book are as follows:

- Exchange
- SharePoint
- Office applications (Word, Excel, Outlook, OneNote, Teams, OneDrive, and Microsoft Forms)

> **Further Reading**
>
> Please visit `https://docs.microsoft.com/en-us/microsoft-365` to review the documentation on the Microsoft 365 suite of applications and services.

AppSource

AppSource is a vital resource for Power Platform and Dynamics 365 solutions beyond the standard Microsoft feature set. Solution architects leverage the applications and extensions found in AppSource to fill functionality gaps. Applications are available for instant download and installation onto your Power Platform environment.

In the use case scenarios discussed in this book, you will learn how to use this valuable resource.

> **Further Reading**
>
> Please visit `https://appsource.microsoft.com/` to access the full range of AppSource business applications and extensions for Power Platform and Dynamics 365.

Azure

Microsoft Azure provides a wide range of cloud-based components that are used to extend the Power Platform beyond its functional boundaries. Solution architects analyze organizational requirements and map the implementation to Azure components when the Power Platform feature set does not fulfill the project goals. The key Azure components used in typical Power Platform implementations are listed here:

- Logic Apps
- Functions
- Azure SQL
- Web Apps
- Data Factory
- Application Proxy
- Data gateways

In the upcoming chapters, you will learn how to run a fit-gap analysis for business requirements, decide when to leverage Azure components, and define a secure architectural blueprint that combines Power Platform with Azure capabilities to build a successful Microsoft-based solution.

> **Further Reading**
>
> Please visit `https://docs.microsoft.com/en-us/azure/?product=compute` for detailed documentation on Azure components referenced in this book.

A hands-on approach to Power Platform solution architecture

By providing best practice guidance and laying the foundations for the implementation, solution architects lead by example. They complement and enhance the technical capabilities of the delivery team, resulting in team output that is greater than the sum of the individual members. The following diagram illustrates the support, documentation, and tools a solution architect may provide to the various project teams and individuals:

Power Platform Solution Architecture
A Hands-on Approach

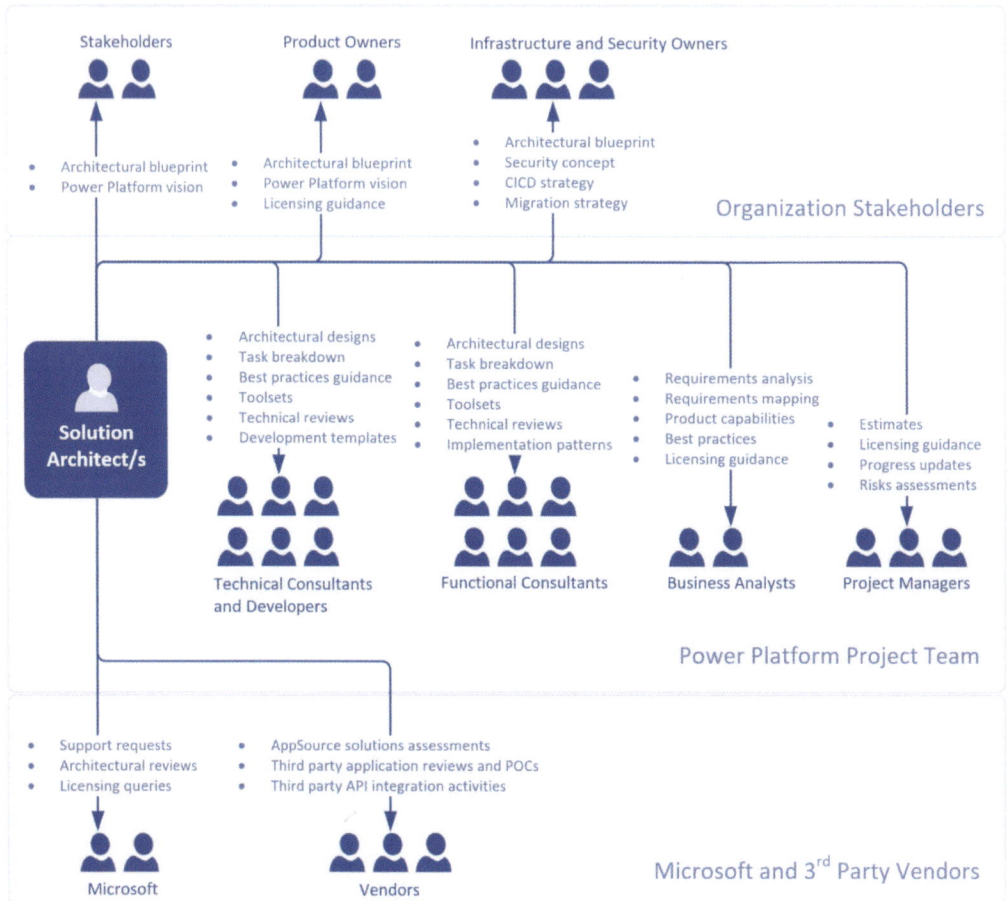

Figure 1.22 – Illustration of a Power Platform solution architect's hands-on role and responsibilities

Solution architects interact with a wide variety of teams during a Power Platform implementation, and will typically provide hands-on support to the following individuals:

- **Supporting technical consultants and developers**

    Technical consultants and developers working on a Power Platform implementation benefit from access to high-level technical blueprints and detailed designs. The blueprints provide a clear direction for the technical implementation. Standardized toolsets, source control strategies, development templates, and a **continuous integration and deployment (CI/CD)** framework will help guide the implementation using a common and consistent approach.

- **Supporting functional consultants**

  Functional consultants benefit from design documentation in the same way as technical consultants. When provided with functional implementation templates (for example, Power Automate design patterns and Dataverse table best practices), consultants benefit from a consistent approach to Power Platform configuration and implementation, resulting in a maintainable and more closely aligned solution with published best practices.

- **Supporting business analysts**

  Solution architects work hand-in-hand with business analysts to understand the product capabilities and licensing constraints, shaping the requirements and success criteria for the project. Solution architects provide a guide to Power Platform's best practices to steer the requirements towards solutions that are supportable and suited to the platform's capabilities.

- **Supporting project managers**

  Solution architects facilitate the smooth running of a project by providing estimates and progress updates to project managers. Risks to the project are presented to project managers alongside solutions and options to mitigate those risks.

Using a hands-on approach, solution architects provide project team members and stakeholders with the toolsets and information required for a successful Power Platform implementation.

Summary

This chapter introduced the nine pillars for great solution architecture, described the architect's role, and provided an overview of the capabilities and features available within Power Platform and the wider Microsoft cloud-based ecosystem. Understanding the capabilities and features available within the Power Platform framework and associated Microsoft services will help find the most optimal solution during the design process. The pillars for great architecture will, in turn, guide the decisions and actions taken throughout the project, resulting in a secure, cost-effective, supportable solution that solves the organization's problem.

The next chapter introduces our sample case study used throughout this book's Power Platform implementation case study.

OneDrive for Business is a data storage service and is not one of the channels that may interact with a Power Virtual Agent as standard.

Further reading

For further information on the components discussed in this chapter, please visit the following documentation pages:

- *Dataverse*: https://docs.microsoft.com/en-us/powerapps/maker/data-platform/

- *Overview of creating applications in Power Apps*: https://docs.microsoft.com/en-us/powerapps/maker/

- *Power Apps model-driven apps documentation*: https://docs.microsoft.com/en-gb/powerapps/maker/model-driven-apps/

- *What are Power Apps portals?*: https://docs.microsoft.com/en-gb/powerapps/maker/portals/overview

- *Powe Pages:* https://powerpages.microsoft.com/

- *Power Apps canvas apps documentation*: https://docs.microsoft.com/en-gb/powerapps/maker/canvas-apps/

- *Power Platform connector reference overview*: https://docs.microsoft.com/en-us/connectors/connector-reference

- *Power BI*: https://docs.microsoft.com/en-us/power-bi/

- *Power Virtual Agents*: https://docs.microsoft.com/en-us/power-virtual-agents/

2
The Digital Transformation Case Study

This chapter introduces Inveriance Corps, a large financial services organization with a clear mandate, to streamline business operations through the digital transformation of its core legacy systems and processes. Security of its data and processes is paramount to this organization, which prides itself on its successful customer data protection track record. In this chapter, you will learn about the current state of the organization's infrastructure, and the range of requirements requested by this theoretical customer, which are reviewed and applied to use case scenarios throughout this book.

In this chapter, we are going to cover the following main topics:

- Introducing Inveriance Corps, the legacy organization with a vision
- The organization's infrastructure and processes, as-is
- Inveriance Corps' vision of the future

By the end of this chapter, you will learn to read high-level requirements, anticipate potential problems, and understand the architectural and organizational structure referenced throughout the implementation life cycle presented in this book.

Introducing Inveriance Corps

Established in the early 1970s, having weathered the stormy 1980s financial markets, and the 2000s ups and downs, Inveriance Corps is a fictional organization and the focus of our digital transformation efforts. It is a financial services organization and a leader of the industry with a legacy to live up to, and legacy systems and processes underpinning the business.

The organization has grown through organic expansion and several acquisitions. The board of directors has come to the realization that times have changed. To continue to lead in today's world will require a thorough digital transformation of its systems and business processes. You are being tasked with leading that journey. The goal is to take stock of the current infrastructure and business processes, and consolidate and streamline the solution architecture, paving the way for increased revenue, reduced costs, and enabling further expansion.

The three revenue streams at Inveriance Corps are as follows:

- Personal insurance products
- Commercial insurance products
- Financial consultancy services

The organization has 40 offices across the world, with headquarters in Chicago and main offices in London, Tokyo, and Singapore. Multiple acquisitions over the years have resulted in multiple systems performing the same function across business units.

Understanding the architecture as-is

Inveriance Corps has three business units, each having dedicated marketing and sales teams. Each business unit has a network of partners supporting sales and delivery activities.

The following diagram illustrates the three business units:

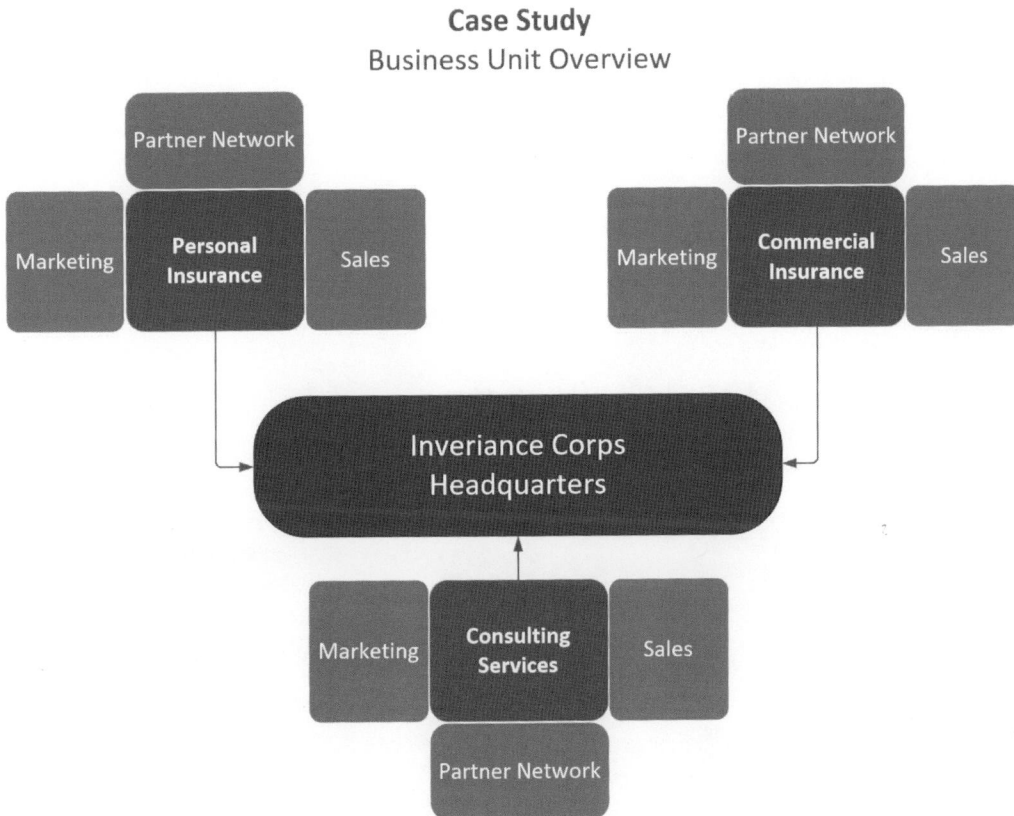

Figure 2.1 – Inveriance Corps business unit structure

Each business unit has a separate product catalog, CRM system, and invoicing platform. These systems are connected to the company headquarters via manual processes and data transfers. The following diagram illustrates the architectural overview of the organization's core systems:

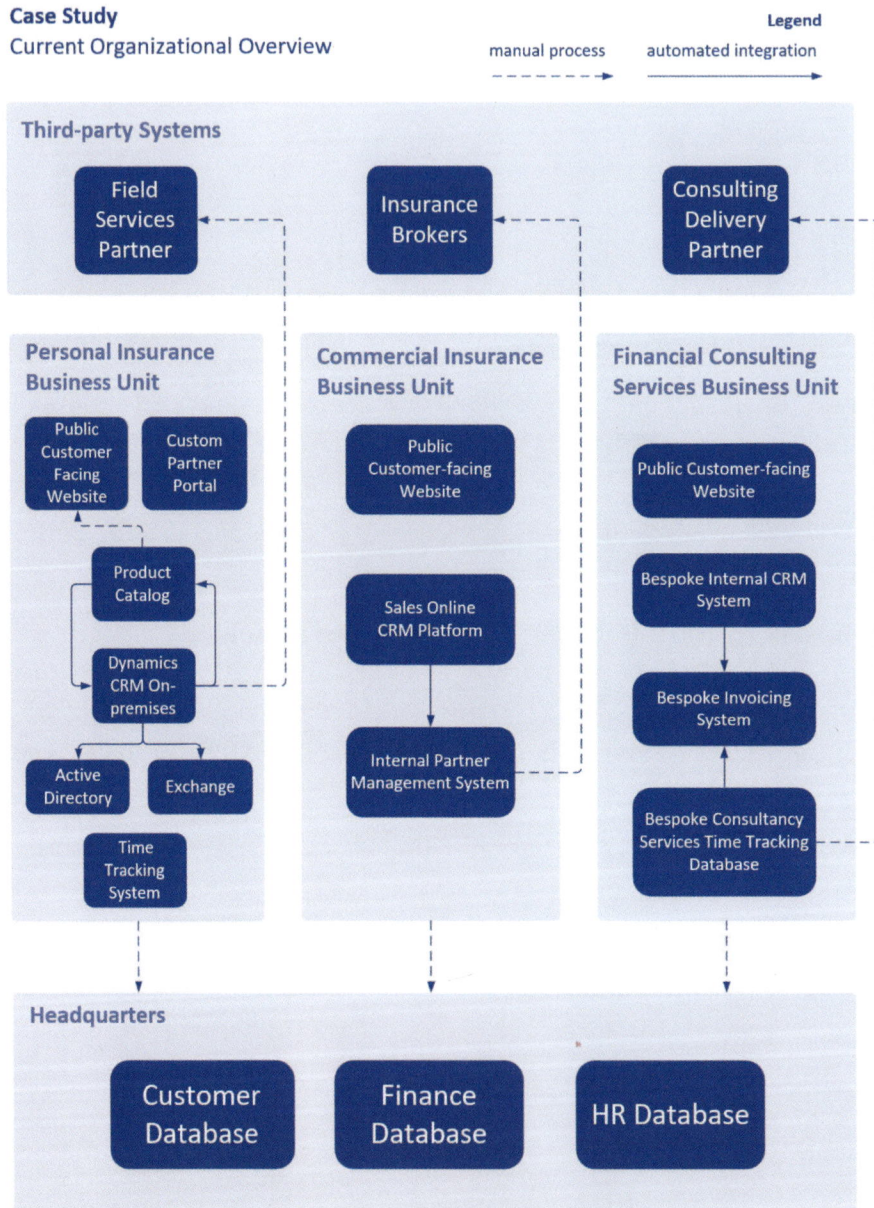

Figure 2.2 – Inveriance Corps architectural overview as-is

Each business unit also currently manages its own sales, CRM, and finance systems. They integrate with head office central systems mostly through manual updates. The various business units, mostly gained through acquisitions, share few resources between them.

Understanding the to-be architecture

Managing the multiple disparate systems across the three business units results in high maintenance and support overheads. Communication across business units is time-consuming and cumbersome as each uses its own CRM, sales, and finance systems. Manual processes dominate all three business units to varying degrees.

The mandate is for the transformation of the organization's business processes into a single cohesive organization, supported by a single set of core systems supporting all three business units.

The core system will deliver the following functionality to all business units:

- A directory of all staff and users within the organization
- A centralized customer relationship management database
- A centralized partner management platform
- All business units to use the same sales, service, and field service (where applicable) platform

The goals of the digital transformation exercise are as follows:

- Reduce system maintenance and support costs.
- Open business opportunities through cross-business-unit collaboration and data sharing.
- Increase sales through responsive and streamlined product offering portals.
- Improve customer experience through a centralized and dedicated support platform.
- Enable expansion by consolidating operations.
- Improve conversion rates by automating the customer onboarding journey for all business units.

The following diagram illustrates the desired systems architecture overview at Inveriance Corps:

Case study
Desired high-level architecture overview

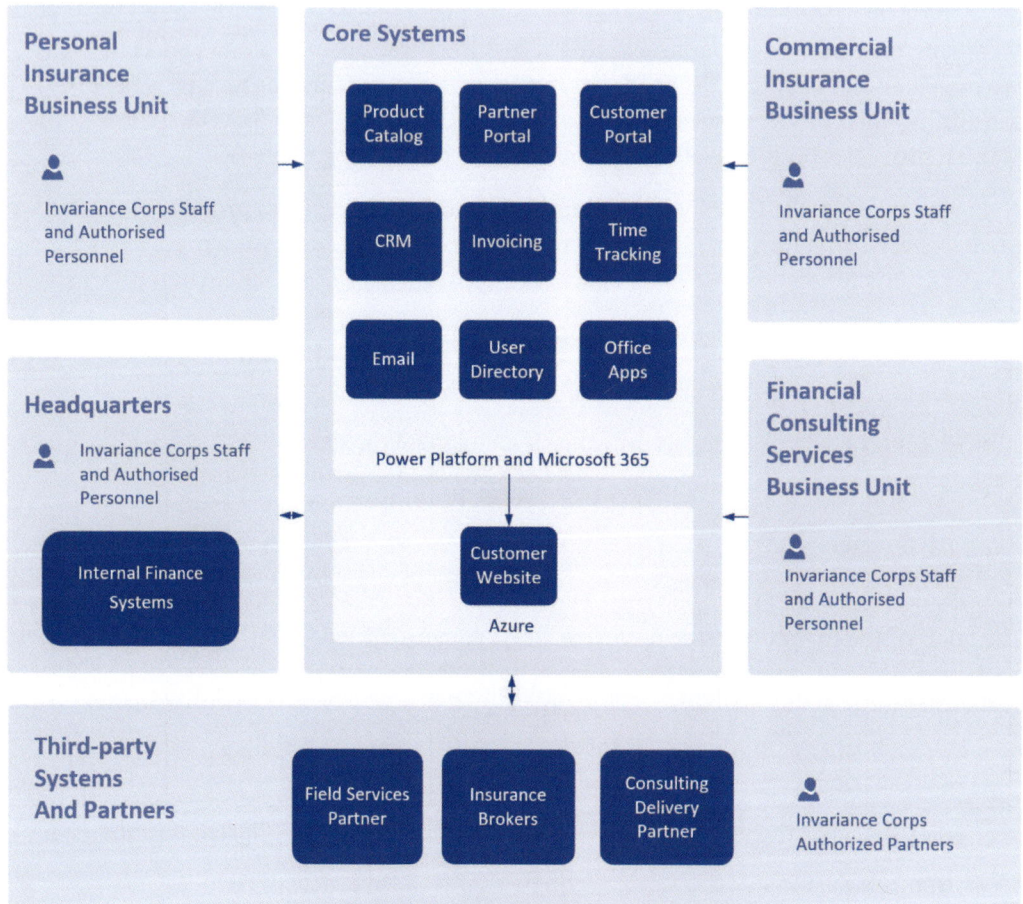

Figure 2.3 – Inveriance Corps architectural overview to-be

The following table lists the core systems that make up the desired to-be architecture:

System	Description	Personal Insurance	Commercial Insurance	Investments	Financial Consulting
Active Directory	Active Directory managing access to various business applications	●	●	●	●
Product Catalog	Central repository for all products sold by the organization	●	●	●	●
Partner Portal	A public-facing portal used by partners to manage sales and service delivery	●	●	●	●
Consultancy Delivery	Consultancy project delivery platform used to manage in-house and partner consultancy service delivery, time tracking, and billing of services				●
CRM	Central customer database and relationship management platform, used by the organization to track product sales, service delivery, and case management across all business units	●	●	●	●
Field Services	Controls field service operations for insurance validation activities and consultancy delivery services	●	●		●

System	Description	Personal Insurance	Commercial Insurance	Investments	Financial Consulting
Marketing	Platform used to manage marketing campaigns and conversion to sales	●	●	●	●
HR Database	List of all staff members and contractors working for the organization	●	●	●	●
Time Tracking	Tracking of activities across the business units for consultancy services and other non-billable field operations	●	●		●
Invoicing	Invoicing of commercial insurance, consultancy services, or financial products		●	●	●
Email	Centralized email platform to be used across all business units	●	●	●	●
Office Applications	SharePoint, Teams, Excel, Word, and other office applications	●	●	●	●
Customer Website	Public-facing website integrated with the organization's core systems product and services catalogs	●	●	●	●
Internal Finance Systems	Finance systems	●	●	●	●

Table 2.1 – High-level list of desired business systems

With this, we have understood the current and future architectures.

Summary

Inveriance Corps is an organization with a pressing need to initiate a complete digital overhaul of its business processes and organizational structure to thrive and remain competitive. In this chapter, we have laid out the case study that will be used throughout the exercises in this book. With a high-level understanding of their current architecture and a clear mandate to consolidate resources, we are now at the starting line of the organization's digital transformation journey.

In the coming chapters, you will analyze the organization's architecture and individual systems in detail, perform a fit-gap analysis against the Power Platform, Dynamics 365, Microsoft 365, and Azure platforms, and create a blueprint to deliver Inveriance Corps' vision of a centralized business, and take that vision right through to fruition.

Part 2: Requirements Analysis, Solution Envisioning, and the Implementation Roadmap

This section discusses how to plan the implementation; analyze the organization's current process, solutions, and systems to identify the risk factors and success criteria; capture the requirements; and perform a fit-gap analysis to match these to Power Platform solutions for a successful implementation. This section contains the following chapters:

- *Chapter 3, Discovery and Initial Solution Planning*
- *Chapter 4, Identifying the Desired Business Process, Risk Factors, and Success Criteria*
- *Chapter 5, Understanding the Existing Architectural Landscape*
- *Chapter 6, Requirements Analysis and Engineering for Solution Architecture*
- *Chapter 7, Power Platform Fit-Gap Analysis*

3
Discovery and Initial Solution Planning

The solution architect's planning role steers the technical direction at the very early stages of a project. The purpose of the discovery phase is to research business needs to define the scope of the project and manage the uncertainty that exists in the initial stages of implementation.

In this chapter, you will lay the foundations for a successful Power Platform implementation. You will learn to perform an effective high-level analysis of organizational business processes, apply a digital transformation vision to Microsoft Power Platform components and third-party solutions, and about the effort required to migrate to an organization's Microsoft-based vision of the future.

In this chapter, we are going to cover the following main topics:

- Understanding high-level business requirements
- Identifying applicable solutions within Microsoft Power Platform
- Identifying applicable solutions within the wider Microsoft cloud-based ecosystem
- Leveraging AppSource apps, third-party applications, and other solutions
- Estimating the migration effort

By the end of this chapter, you will have learned how to match Microsoft capabilities to business requirements and pave a roadmap for a successful go-live migration, navigating through our case study at Inveriance Corps at each stage.

Discovering the business and its needs

The discovery phase is an opportunity to collect information about a project. It provides an early glimpse of the key project risks and the best route to help a business achieve its goals. Reviewing publicly available information about the customer will help the delivery team prepare for the discovery sessions and set the scene for the implementation.

Pre-discovery research

Organizations tend to have a wealth of information publicly available. Pre-discovery research sets the delivery team one step ahead during the discovery phase. This preview of the organization's products, services, locations, and public sentiment will make the upcoming discovery sessions more productive. The delivery team will be prepared with the right questions to get the information needed to build a picture of the organization's goals and the best way to achieve them.

Solution architects and pre-sales team members use the information readily available to them to build a picture of an organization. The following diagram illustrates the key sources of information used during the pre-discovery phase:

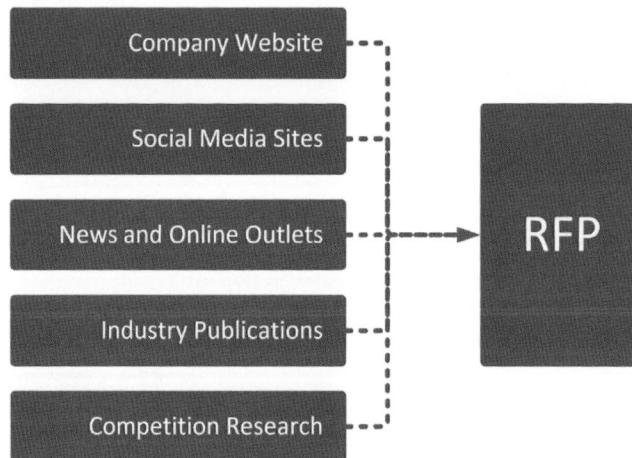

Figure 3.1 – Pre-discovery information sources

The key pre-discovery information sources and their benefits are described in the following subsections.

Company website

The company website is an organization's window to the world. The company's website presents a unique and concise source of information listing its products and services. It also tends to provide a view of the geographical spread of operations and the location of the company's headquarters.

Researching the company website is likely to yield some or most of the key information listed here:

- **Company brief**: A general understanding of the company's purpose, mission, size, and foundation, used to gauge the scope and scale of a digital transformation exercise.

- **Names of C-suite individuals**: Awareness of who the chief executive, financial and technical officers are (CEO, CFO, and CTOs) will significantly facilitate the discovery conversations.

- **Products and services**: Understanding the company's key sources of revenue will guide the discovery phase and the overall implementation.

- **Geographical locations**: Knowing where the staff and facilities are located presents a unique opportunity to draft the organization's current architecture.

- **Company size**: Knowing the number of staff members and offices provides an understanding of the scope of the digital transformation that will be required and an estimate of budgets that could be available for implementation.

- **Business units**: Business units or divisions within the organization may sometimes be apparent within the company website (for example, multiple websites for different business units or companies within a larger company group).

- **Mergers and acquisitions**: The company website may announce any recent mergers or acquisitions, which would help further expose the company structure and solution architecture.

- **Public-facing portals**: Company websites often include a route to any existing public-facing customer portals, be it for self-service case management, account management, or other features. Previewing any existing customer portal provides early insight into the current infrastructure and vendors involved.

> **Note**
> Large organizations with multiple acquisitions or groups of companies may have more than one company website and possibly a main group site. Reviewing all the related company websites will help build the bigger picture and understand the scope for a digital transformation project that spans entities within a group.

Social media sites

A company's social media presence provides another angle through which an organization can be understood. Reviewing the company's interactions with its customers and the public will help identify pain points to be addressed and successes to be nurtured.

Researching a company's social media presence will help understand the following:

- **Customer pain points**: Areas with scope for improvement regarding their customer interaction strategy.

- **Public success points**: Areas to be celebrated and leveraged during the digital transformation project.

- **Fans and casual associates**: Individuals and organizations that interact with the company in a positive manner.

- **Key players' online profiles**: Reviewing the CEO's online presence and other key stakeholders on social media sites such as LinkedIn will help understand their backgrounds and motivations.

- **Mergers and acquisitions**: Announcements made on social media sites will provide an understanding of changes in an organization and thus their solution architecture.

News and online outlets

News articles and online encyclopedias provide yet another perspective on an organization and shape the public perception of a company. Additionally, online encyclopedia sites tend to provide a concise brief of a company's background, structure, and history. Researching news articles related to an organization will provide a view of the following:

- **Delicate topics**: Recent pain points highlighted by news outlets should be noted and treated delicately or omitted altogether during discovery conversations.

- **Market speculation**: Market motivation and future movements predicted in news articles help complete the bigger picture for a company.

- **Company brief**: Online encyclopedia sites tend to provide a concise brief of a company's background, structure, and history, which may sometimes be missing from the company's website.

Industry publications

Having a high-level view of any white papers and other publications will garner insights into the company's key competencies and technical maturity, thus allowing a solution architect to plan accordingly and pitch a solution that matches the company's capabilities. Reviewing these documents may provide an insight into the company's areas of expertise and technical capabilities.

Competition

Understanding a company's key competitors means the delivery team can gauge the company's offerings and customer interactions and provide an insight into what the market leaders are doing right.

Researching the company's competitors will help to benchmark against the competition. A typical example would be a bank's new customer onboarding journey, where the steps carried out by a competitor's new business onboarding website are compared to understand improvements that can be made to gain an edge over the competition.

Request for proposal

A **Request for Proposal (RFP)** is sent out by an organization that requires a solution to be implemented. It is often distributed to multiple suppliers and tends to be a formal document. Its purpose is to describe the customer's problem so that multiple vendors can propose a solution, and the customer selects the vendor that most closely matches technical and budgetary expectations.

Solution architects review RFP documentation to identify the following information:

- **Key areas of importance to the customer**: Identifying areas of focus in an RFP document provides a glimpse into the mindset and key points to be addressed by any incoming solution architecture. Suppose an RFP is concerned mainly with security concepts. The focus of the RFP indicates security is paramount to the customer's success criteria, while an RFP focusing on a cost-effective delivery and operation of a system would suggest that a lower-cost solution architecture is more important.

- **The current architecture/problem**: RFPs often provide an overview of extant solution architecture and pointers to the desired target solution. This information is invaluable, as it provides the first set of requirements that the customer has dictated. This early glimpse gives solution architects a preliminary idea of how a solution could be structured and whether the customer's budget is aligned with their expectations.

Case study – pre-discovery research

In the case study being presented in this book, Inveriance Corps has issued an RFP to multiple Power Platform solution providers, including yourself. From this RFP and other publicly available information sources, we will complete the pre-discovery research checklist, as shown in the following table:

Key area	Pre-discovery results	Source of results
Company brief	Established in 1975, Inveriance Corps is a financial services organization, providing insurance and consultancy services. IT reached a turnover of $10 billion in the last fiscal year and profits of £1 billion.	• Company website • Online encyclopedia
Names of C-suite individuals	CEO – Jane Dawson CFO – Michael Jefferson CTO – Laura Danielson	• Company website • Online encyclopedia • Social media
Products and services	Personal insurance products Commercial insurance products Investment products Financial consultancy services	• Company website • Online encyclopedia
Geographical locations	The organization has 40 offices across the world, with headquarters in Chicago and main offices in London, Tokyo, and Singapore.	• Company website • Online encyclopedia
Company size	Staff totaling 40,000 worldwide	• Company website • Online encyclopedia
Business units	Three business units. The core business deals in commercial insurance, acquisitions bringing in personal insurance, and an expansion into financial consultancy services.	• Company websites • Online encyclopedia

Key area	Pre-discovery results	Source of results
Mergers and acquisitions	Acquisition of personal insurance company two years ago. Acquisition of an investment products company 10 years ago.	• Company website • Online encyclopedia
Public-facing portals	The personal insurance business website directs customers to a public-facing **My Account** page and case management facilities. There is a custom-made portal built PHP. The personal insurance business website directs partners to a portal. The technology stack appears to be classic ASP. NET.	• Company website
Customer pain points	Long response times to customer queries Difficulty opening an insurance services account	• Social media sites • News outlets
Public success points	Customers are satisfied with the level of cover and the responsiveness of their insurance services.	• Social media sites
Fans and casual associates	Small businesses and contractors see Inveriance Corps as the go-to place for business insurance.	• Social media sites
Key players' online profiles	Jane Dawson, the CEO of the company, has a background in sales and marketing, and has worked at Inveriance Corps for the last 2 years. The CFO, Michael Jefferson, works across the insurance business units. The CTO, Laura Danielson, has a background in software engineering and telecommunications.	• Social media sites

Key area	Pre-discovery results	Source of results
Delicate topics	A data breach in 2020 resulted in 2 million customer records being exposed and regulatory body fines in four countries.	• News outlets
Market speculation	Analysts expect Inveriance Corps to boost commercial insurance operations through an improved product catalog and new customer onboarding facilities.	• News outlets
White papers and other publications	White paper – delivering financial consulting services	• Industry publications
Benchmarking against the competition	Edge over the competition – delivery of claims and coverage of products. Scope for improvement – a new customer onboarding journey, as competitors have the edge in terms of speed, drop rate, and aesthetics. An integrated and easy-to-use onboarding journey is requested in the RFP received from the customer.	• Company website • Competitors • RFP
The current architecture/problem	Manual processes dominate all three business units to varying degrees. Communication across business units is time-consuming and cumbersome as each uses its own **customer relationship management system (CRM)**, sales, and finance systems. Each business unit also currently manages its sales, CRM, and finance systems. They integrate with head office central systems, mostly through manual updates.	• RFP • Company website

Key area	Pre-discovery results	Source of results
Key areas of importance to the customer	• Improving information security is key following the security data breach of 2020. Protection of customer and operational data is mentioned throughout the RFP. • Transformation of the organization's business processes into a single cohesive organization, supported by a single set of core systems supporting all three business units, with a focus on the following: • Improving conversion rates by automating the customer onboarding journey for all business units. • Reduce system maintenance and support costs. • Open business opportunities through collaboration across business units and data sharing. • Increase sales through responsive and streamlined product-offering portals. • Improve customer experience through a centralized and dedicated support platform. • Enable expansion by consolidating operations.	• RFP • News outlets • Social media sites

Table 3.1 – The results of pre-discovery research into Inveriance Corps

Preparing effective discovery questions

The pre-discovery information sources described in this section will help you define the questions designed to gain the insights needed for an effective digital transformation strategy and solution architecture blueprint. These well-informed questions will also resonate with the organization and its stakeholders, conveying a deep understanding of the customer and their needs even before the first coffee meeting is over.

From the pre-discovery research checklist compiled in the previous subsection, we understand that customer and operational data security will be foremost in the stakeholder's mind, given the previous data breaches at the organization. From this insight, we would formulate the following example question:

> *One of the requirements is for an improved customer onboarding journey. When implementing a public-facing portal, would you want prospective customers to have the option of resuming a previously started application using strong customer authentication?*

The answer to this question would help shape the project's architectural blueprint and security concept. The customer would also be made aware that you consider the security of their systems as important as they do.

The following question would provide insights on the scope of the consolidation part of the project, particularly when it comes to using a centralized CRM system across business units:

> *What are the different locations and types of CRM databases used across the business units, and would you consider a phased approach to consolidating your customer data?*

The answer to the preceding question would help define the architectural blueprint for a Power Platform-based solution and draft the migration strategies that could be used to achieve the company's goal of a centralized CRM system.

In short, having reviewed all the pre-discovery information available, you will want to prepare a set of questions that do the following:

- Provide a high-level understanding of the scope of the project (that is, implementation of a new system, replacement of legacy components, or integration with existing software).

- Identify the types and locations of databases, directory systems, portals, and other components relevant to the project.

- Define the level of security and compliance required.
- Identify the key stakeholders for the project.
- Instill confidence in your understanding of the organization's needs and your ability to deliver on these.
- Allow you to outline the current topography and draft an architecture blueprint for the proposed solution.

Running the discovery phase

Having completed the pre-discovery research checklist, you will initiate the discovery process. Your role as a solution architect will schedule the following activities to define the project scope:

- **Meetings**: These may be formal or informal, and either in person or via online conferencing facilities. There will typically be an initial meeting to discuss the best approach to make the best use of time for all parties involved, where you will become familiar with the stakeholders and get an answer to a number of your pre-discovery questions. You will then have an understanding of the types of interactions that will be required, the individuals and roles involved in each session, and the schedule.

- **Workshops**: A targeted session designed to gather as much information as possible from the participants. Workshops usually cover a specific area of the solution. Working with the company's stakeholders, you will identify the roles and individuals best suited to attend each workshop, depending on the subject, expertise, and relevance to the individuals in attendance. Depending on the breadth of the project, multiple workshops that are run over various locations may be required to gather sufficient information for the project.

- **Email communications**: While meetings and workshops provide instant interaction with stakeholders and subject-matter experts within the company, several questions and answer sessions will likely need to be carried out via email.

- **Online collaboration**: Depending on the willingness and technical capabilities of the company staff members, collaboration on discovery and requirement documents could be performed online. This activity can significantly expedite the documentation of customer requirements, current architecture, and proposed solutions through a series of interactive document authoring and commenting cycles.

- **Surveys**: A set of questions can be distributed to stakeholders or staff members using various services within the organization. Surveys can provide an insight into the challenges faced by the company and provide a voice to an otherwise quiet user base through anonymous responses.

- **Job shadowing**: This activity allows for detailed analysis and understanding of the users you hope to help as part of the project. Through active listening, targeted questions, and thorough documentation, job shadowing will allow you to clearly understand the pain points experienced by the active user base.

Achieving the aim of discovery goals

The interactions listed in the previous subsection will provide a platform upon which you will be able to fill the gaps and answer the open questions from the pre-discovery research. Each workshop, meeting, and internal document you review will get you closer to defining the following:

- The customer's data architecture

- The customer's organizational structure and business units

- The current software and applications in use

- The problems and pain points the customer is looking to address

Defining the success criteria

Once you have identified the various pain points, challenges, goals, and aspirations that the company has for the future, you will be able to document these and put forward a solution that addresses each of these concerns.

Documenting the success criteria is done at a high level by listing the key actions and outcomes that will result in the overall project being successful. Establishing and documenting these requirements and how they will be satisfied will pave the way to a successful Power Platform implementation.

Case study – a discovery outcome and project plan

Having completed the discovery meetings and workshops, you are now fully versed with Inveriance Corp's requirements. You also have a high-level understanding of the systems currently in use. The following diagrams describe the high-level architectural overview of the organization's current systems, as discovered during the workshop sessions for each business unit.

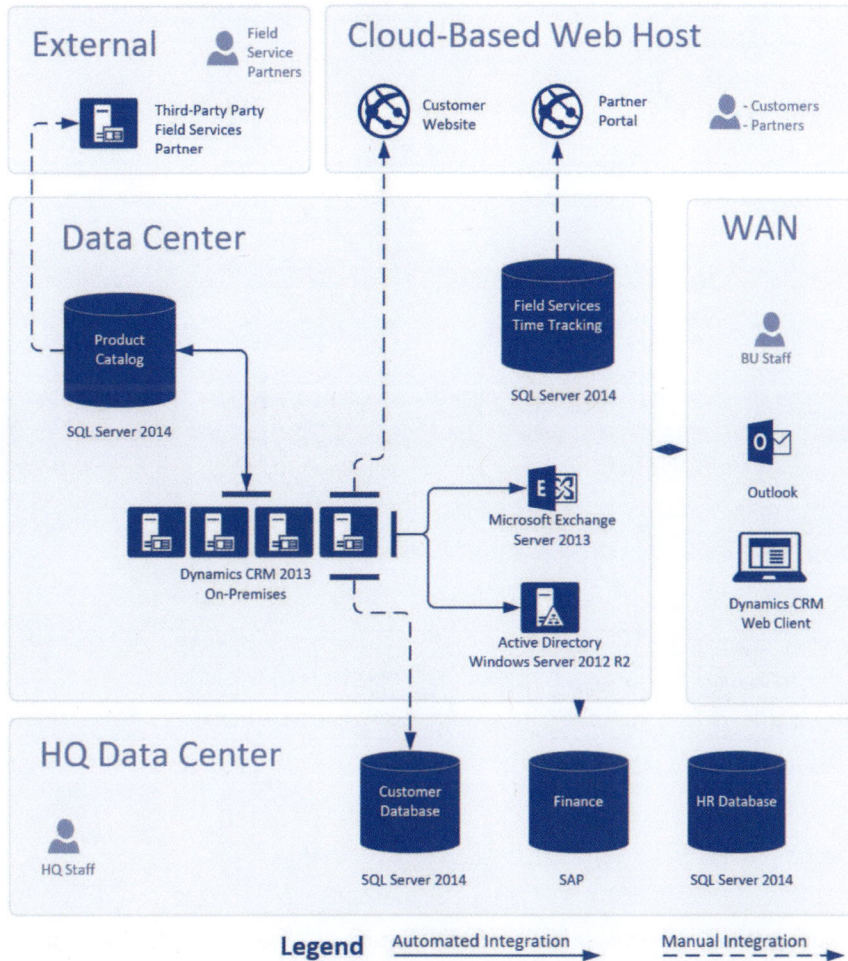

Figure 3.2 – Current architecture overview for the personal insurance business unit

The Commercial Business Unit has a separate set of architectural components, illustrated in the following diagram.

Current Architecture Overview

Commercial Insurance Business Unit

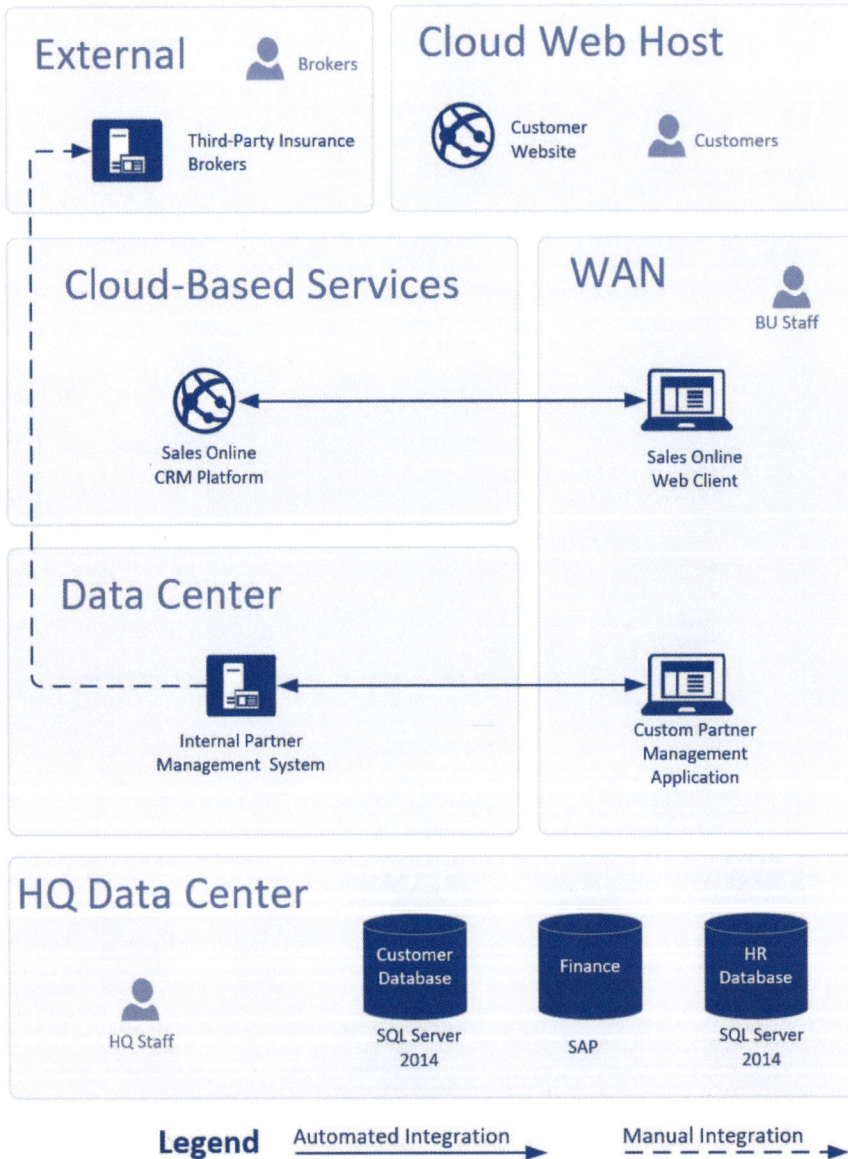

Figure 3.3 – The commercial insurance architecture overview – the as-is diagram

And finally, the Financial Consulting Services Business Unit has its own set of systems identified in the following diagram.

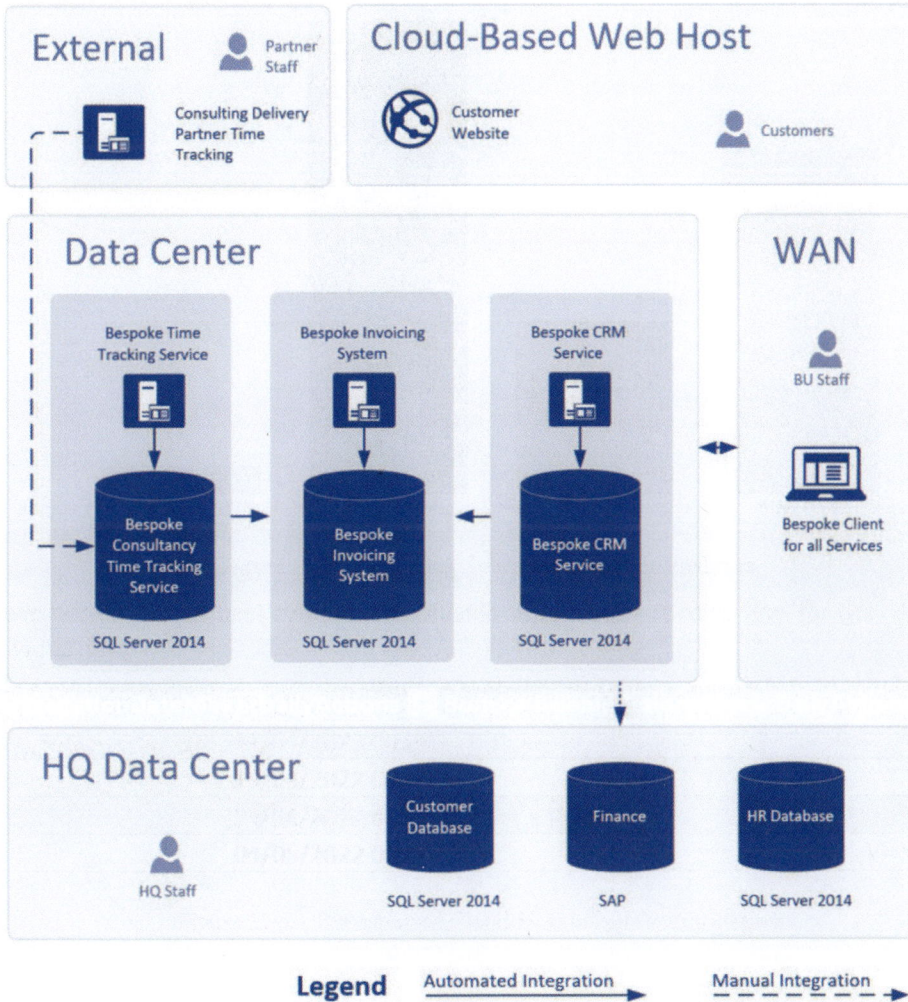

Figure 3.4 – The commercial insurance architecture overview – the as-is diagram

Managing the multiple disparate systems across the three business units results in high maintenance and support overheads. Communication across business units is time-consuming and cumbersome, as each uses its own CRM, sales, and finance systems. Manual processes dominate all three business units to varying degrees.

The mandate is for the transformation of the organization's business processes into a single cohesive organization, supported by a single set of core systems supporting all three business units.

The core system will deliver the following capabilities to all business units:

- A directory of all staff and users within the organization
- A centralized customer relationship management database
- A centralized partner management platform
- All business units to use the same sales, service, and field service (where applicable) platforms

The goals of the digital transformation exercise are the following:

- Reducing system maintenance and support costs
- Opening business opportunities through collaboration across business units and data sharing
- Increasing sales through responsive and streamlined product offering portals
- Improving customer experience through a centralized and dedicated support platform
- Enabling expansion by consolidating operations

Proposed architecture overview

The discovery sessions have identified a need to consolidate disconnected systems across the three business units. Having reviewed the architectural landscape, we are now ready to present an initial high-level blueprint for the digital transformation exercise at Inveriance Corps. The following diagram illustrates a high-level blueprint that leverages Power Platform capabilities, aiming to achieve the organization's goals of a centralized architecture for resource sharing:

Proposed High-Level Architecture Overview

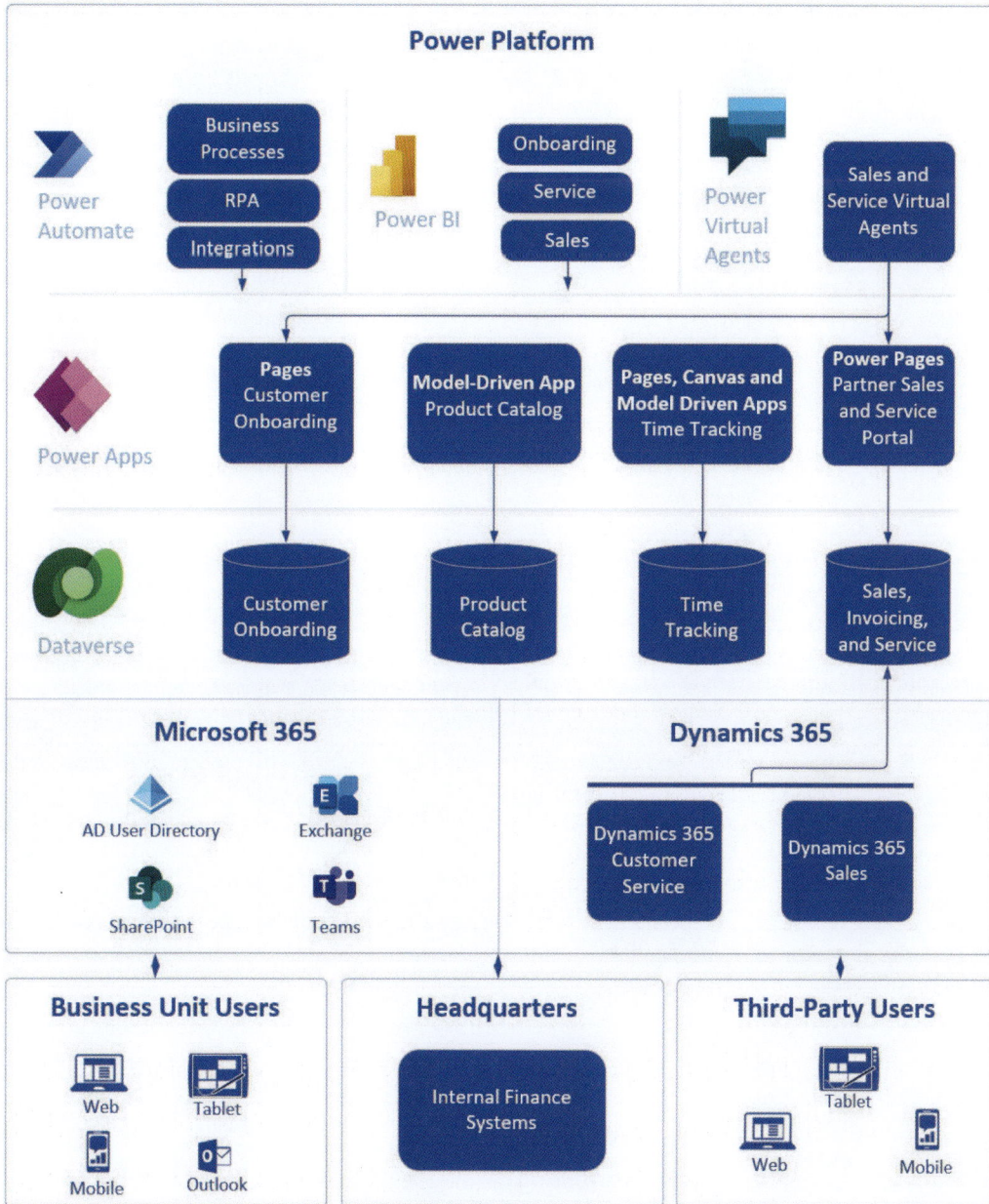

Power Platform

Power Automate
- Business Processes
- RPA
- Integrations

Power BI

- Onboarding
- Service
- Sales

Power Virtual Agents
- Sales and Service Virtual Agents

Power Apps
- Pages Customer Onboarding
- Model-Driven App Product Catalog
- Pages, Canvas and Model Driven Apps Time Tracking
- Power Pages Partner Sales and Service Portal

Dataverse
- Customer Onboarding
- Product Catalog
- Time Tracking
- Sales, Invoicing, and Service

Microsoft 365

- AD User Directory
- Exchange
- SharePoint
- Teams

Dynamics 365

- Dynamics 365 Customer Service
- Dynamics 365 Sales

Business Unit Users
- Web
- Tablet
- Mobile
- Outlook

Headquarters
- Internal Finance Systems

Third-Party Users
- Tablet
- Web
- Mobile

Figure 3.5 – Diagram for the proposed architecture of Inveriance Corps

The following table describes the areas and components referenced in the proposed architectural blueprint:

Area	Components used	Description
User directory	– Azure **Active Directory (AD)**	Active Directory manages staff access to various business applications. Uses the default Microsoft 365 AD.
Product catalog	– Dataverse – Model-driven apps	A central repository for all products sold by the organization.
Partner sales and service	– Dataverse – Power Pages – Power Virtual Agents – Power BI	A public-facing portal used by partners to manage sales and service delivery. A Dataverse backend supports Power Pages. Power Virtual Agents provide partners with guidance if required.
Customer portal	– Dataverse – Power Pages – Power Virtual Agents – Power BI – Power AI	A public-facing portal used for onboarding new customers across all lines of business. Users are also able to submit queries, cases, and manage their accounts. Power Virtual agents provide guidance and routing to customer service agents. Power AI supports ID recognition to expedite the onboarding process.
Sales, invoicing, and service	– Dataverse – Model-driven apps – Dynamics 365 Sales – Dynamics 365 Customer Service – Power BI – Power Automate	A central customer database and relationship management platform, used by the organization to track product sales, service delivery, and case management across all business units. The dashboard and chart features within model-driven apps will be complemented by more advanced Power BI reports. Power Automate will be used for business process automation, RPA, and integration capabilities throughout. The sales and customer service capabilities in Dynamics 365 will further enhance the standard Power Platform offering.

Area	Components used	Description
Time tracking	– Dataverse – Canvas apps – Model-driven apps – Power Pages – Power Apps mobile	The tracking of activities across the business units for consultancy services and other non-billable field operations. Power Pages and canvas apps will provide various means of logging time entries, while the back-office staff can leverage the reporting and data management capabilities within model-driven apps.
Microsoft 365	– AD – Exchange – SharePoint – Teams	The proposed solution takes advantage of core Microsoft 365 capabilities, including the previously mentioned AD for staff members. Incoming and outgoing emails will be provided by Microsoft Exchange. Power Apps will take advantage of standard integration with SharePoint's advanced document management facilities. Teams will be integrated and used by model-driven apps to promote collaboration across teams and business units.
Headquarters, business units, and third-party users	– Web client – Power Apps mobile – Dynamics 365 mobile – Outlook	Internal staff members and external partners will be able to access Power Apps assigned to them. Standard web clients will be complemented by Power Apps mobile applications, Dynamics 365 Mobile, and Outlook.
Internal finance systems	(existing component) – Power Automate	The existing internal finance systems will be integrated using Power Automate for low-volume transactions. Higher volume integrations may require a dedicated integration component, such as Azure Data Factory or Azure Logic Apps.

Table 3.2 – The Inveriance Corps high-level digital transformation to-be component description

Identifying applicable solutions within the Microsoft Power Platform and the wider Microsoft Cloud-Based ecosystem

Having defined the company's high-level digital transformation requirements, you are now ready to start matching these up to Microsoft capabilities. Solution architects list the components that make up the desired solution and identify the corresponding Power Platform features that best address the requirement.

Case study – matching Inveriance Corps' requirements to Microsoft solutions

In this book's case study, we will proceed to match the customer requirements to Microsoft solutions as follows:

Requirement	Requirement description	Current systems	Matched to	Implementing team
User directory	AD managing staff access to various business applications. A centralized user directory to be used by all lines of business and head office.	AD on-premises and SQL-based staff-member databases	Azure AD	Microsoft Azure team
Product catalog	A central repository for all products sold by the organization	Dynamics CRM 2013 on-premises, an Access database, and Excel spreadsheets	– Dataverse – Model-driven apps	Power Platform team
Partner portal	A public-facing portal used by partners to manage sales and service delivery	A custom ASP.NET portal	– Dataverse – Power Pages – Power Virtual Agents – Model-driven apps	Power Platform team
Customer portal	A public-facing portal used by the customer to submit queries and cases and manage their account. Also used for onboarding new customers across all lines of business.	A custom ASP.NET portal and a custom PHP portal	– Dataverse – Power Pages – Power Virtual Agents – Model-driven apps – Power AI	Power Platform team

Requirement	Requirement description	Current systems	Matched to	Implementing team
Sales, invoicing, and service	A central customer database and relationship management platform, used by the organization to track product sales, service delivery, and case management across all business units	Dynamics CRM 2013 on-premises, SalesForce, and a bespoke on-premises system	– Dataverse – Model-driven apps – Dynamics 365 Sales – Dynamics 365 Customer Service – Power BI – Power Automate	Power Platform team
Time tracking	The tracking of activities across the business units for consultancy services and other non-billable field operations	SQL databases with custom applications, and Excel spreadsheets	– Dataverse – Canvas apps – Model-driven apps – Power Pages – Power Apps mobile	Power Platform team
Internal financial services	The invoicing of commercial insurance, consultancy services, or financial products	SAP	Not applicable. The existing financial services systems will remain as they are. Integrations using Power Automate will be implemented as required.	Power Platform team
Email	A centralized email platform to be used across all business units	Exchange on-premises, Lotus, and an ISP-based email server	– Microsoft 365 Exchange	Microsoft Azure team

Table 3.3 – The requirements mapped to the Microsoft solutions

Leveraging AppSource apps, third-party applications, and other solutions

Microsoft AppSource provides extensions to the standard Power Platform and Dynamics 365 product capabilities. As part of the discovery phase, you will make use of this resource to fill any gaps in the Microsoft solution's feature sets.

AppSource components are available for review via `https://appsource.microsoft.com/`. The rationale behind using an AppSource component to fulfill organizational requirements is as follows:

- The standard Power Platform functionality does not fulfill a requirement.
- It is not possible to adapt the requirement to match the Power Platform feature set.
- One or more AppSource components exist that fulfill the requirement.
- The AppSource components have been trialed in a proof-of-concept, demonstrated, and rated internally to confirm their fitness for purpose.
- The vendor has been identified as a company of sufficient repute to satisfy organizational procurement requirements.
- The vendor has confirmed support for future updates of the Power Platform.
- The licensing and maintenance costs are aligned with the project's budget.
- The cost/timescales for developing a custom solution to fulfill the requirement are too large, making the AppSource solution a better option.

Following the preceding assessment steps, you will then be in a position to make the most informed decision, selecting the component that best fulfills the project's needs, even if it means developing a custom solution in-house when suitable AppSource components are not available.

> **A Pillar for Great Architecture – Build and Operation Efficiency**
>
> The decision to use an AppSource component will often have an impact on the overall project implementation times and the ongoing operational efficiency of the production environment. To that end, you will review AppSource solutions to ensure they deliver these benefits. You will quantify the expected build-time gains, ongoing costs, and support prospects for AppSource solutions by trialing these components and communicating with the vendor's sales and support channels to ensure the component meets the overall needs of the organization.

You will now.

Case study – matching Inveriance Corp's requirements to AppSource components

Inveriance Corps has stated a requirement for their customer onboarding portal. The requirement is as follows:

> *Back-office agents will be able to offer customers currently browsing on the onboarding portal a co-browsing experience, where the agent can see the customer's browser window contents, allowing them to guide the user through the onboarding application process. The customer may also be able to communicate with the customer via a web chat and accept the co-browsing invitation from the agent.*

As part of the third-party assessment process, we will proceed to review the solution. The following table lists each of the review steps and the outcome of the review for this particular requirement:

AppSource component assessment		Notes	Result
1	The standard Power Platform functionality does not fulfill a requirement.	No co-browsing is available in the Power Pages or related components.	✓
2	It is not possible to adapt the requirement to match the Power Platform feature set.	The requirement is fixed and mandatory.	✓
3	One or more AppSource components exist that fulfill the requirement.	Identified the Power Co-browse component from AppSource as a potential candidate.	✓
4	The AppSource components have been trialed in a proof-of-concept, demonstrated, and rated internally to confirm their fitness for purpose.	A vendor demo and a trial solution have been installed, demonstrated, and proven to work as required.	✓
5	The vendor has been identified as a company of sufficient repute to satisfy organizational procurement requirements.	Confirmed with the customer.	✓
6	The vendor has confirmed support for future updates of the Power Platform.	Confirmed by the vendor via their online literature.	✓
7	The licensing and maintenance costs are aligned with the project's budget.	Confirmed licensing costs with vendor and customer.	✓
8	The cost/timescales for developing a custom solution to fulfill the requirement are too large, making the AppSource solution a better option.	Developing a co-browsing solution would not be feasible within project timescales.	✓
Outcome – the AppSource component is the best option to fulfill the requirement.			

Table 3.4 – The third-party solution review checklist

The outcome of the review process identifies the Power Co-browse component as the best solution to fulfill the customer's requirement. The procurement process for the AppSource solution is initiated for inclusion in the build.

Estimating the migration effort

Once you have defined the high-level requirements and matched these to Microsoft product capabilities, you can gain an understanding of the effort required to migrate from the current architecture to Power Platform. You can estimate the migration effort by considering the following:

- The volume of data to be migrated
- The structure and format of the data to be migrated
- Access the source data
- The level of data processing required during migration
- Potential API throttling that may impact the migration, depending on the throughput required
- Production downtime considerations and the level of risk mitigation required

At this early stage in the project, it would suffice to understand the migration strategy at a high level. You will want to consider the acceptable length of time for key systems to remain offline, the rollback requirements, and mitigation through gradual migration from legacy systems where possible.

We will now work through the case study at Inveriance Corps, sizing the Power Platform migration effort for the organization.

Case study – sizing the migration effort at Inveriance Corps

Having reviewed the various components identified during the discovery sessions, identified the proposed target systems, and performed a high-level analysis of the migration considerations, you are now in a position to estimate the effort required. The following tables describe a high-level strategy and rough estimates for the migration of Inveriance Corp's legacy systems to a consolidated Power Platform architecture:

User Directory - Migration Estimates

Migrate from	Migrate to	Strategy
AD on-premise, SQL HR database	Azure AD	A phased migration moves one business unit at a time, using AAD Sync for the AD on-premise and bulk user import of the users located in the HR database.
Sizing		
Volume	50,000 users	M
Structure and format	Single AD, custom SQL database	XL
Access to source	Require proxy and firewall access for outbound data.	L
Processing required	HR data requires normalization	L
Throttling considerations	N/A	S
Production downtime considerations	Aim to minimize downtime through a phased approach, risk identified.	XL
Overall Sizing		
A complex migration to Azure AD for three business units and the headquarters.		XXL

Product Catalog - Migration Estimates

Migrate from	Migrate to	Strategy	
Dynamics CRM 2013 on-premise, Access database, Excel	Dataverse and model-driven App	A phased migration, one business unit at a time, using Dataflows and/or Power Automate, and manual imports into Dataverse.	
Sizing			
Volume	1,000 records		M
Structure and format	Hierarchical data, each business unit has a different format and source type		L
Access to source	Accessible offline		S
Processing required	Normalization into a consolidated product catalog		L
Throttling considerations	Low volume		S
Production downtime considerations	No downtime expected		S
Overall Sizing			
A low-risk migration that can be carried out using offline data.			L

CRM - Migration Estimates

Migrate from	Migrate to	Strategy	
Dynamics CRM 2013 on-premise, Salesforce, bespoke on-premise system	Dynamics 365 Customer Service	Initial bulk import of data from Dynamics CRM 2013 to Dataverse followed by delta updates via an on-premises Power Automate data gateway or Dataflows. Following a similar strategy for bespoke systems, and finally Salesforce.	
Sizing			
Volume		100,000 cases, 900,000 customer records	XL
Structure and format		Varies depending on the source system, complexity identified	XL
Access to source		On-premises systems require proxy and firewall access, online system provides an API	L
Processing required		Normalization into a consolidated product catalog	L
Throttling considerations		Dataverse API throttling expected, require use of bulk import mitigation	L
Production downtime considerations		Downtime expected during migration window	L
Overall Sizing			
A complex migration that will require data normalization and cleansing.			XXL

Time Tracking - Migration Estimates

Migrate from	Migrate to	Strategy	
SQL databases and custom applications, Excel spreadsheets	Dataverse, model-driven apps, canvas apps, Power Pages. May consider Dynamics 365 Field Service, Dynamics 365 Project Operations.	Bulk import into Dataverse, potentially using Dataflows and/or Power Automate and an on-premise data gateway. Migrating each business unit in turn.	
Sizing			
Volume	100,000 time entries		L
Structure and format	Varies depending on the source system, complexity identified		XL
Access to source	On-premises systems require proxy and firewall access, online system provides API/export		L
Processing required	Extensive normalization into a consolidated Dataverse time tracking tables will be required.		XL
Throttling considerations	Low level throttling may need to be mitigated using bulk import		S
Production downtime considerations	Downtime expected during migration window		L
Overall Sizing			
A complex migration that will require data normalization and cleansing.			XL

Table 3.5 – High-level Power Platform migration estimates

With the migration effort now sized, you can then translate the estimates into timescales for the migration. The time estimates must consider the implementation team's size, skillsets, and any other considerations that may impact the migration effort. The migration sizing exercise provides early visibility over the impact on production facilities, allowing decision-makers to steer the project based on these considerations.

Summary

Having completed the high-level requirements mapping exercise and defined a draft migration strategy, you now have an understanding of the organization's current architecture, the motivations behind the push for digital transformation, and a base blueprint for achieving the organization's goals.

In the next chapter, you will delve deeper into the organization's requirements to define the business processes and identify the risk factors and success criteria to facilitate a smooth digital transformation journey.

4

Identifying Business Processes, Risk Factors, and Success Criteria

A **business process** is a sequence of actions performed by a group of stakeholders. In this chapter, you will learn to identify an organization's high-level business processes and opportunities for streamlining and automation, considering the associated risk factors. You will also learn to recognize and formalize an organization's key success criteria to drive the **Microsoft Power Platform** implementation.

In this chapter, we are going to cover the following main topics:

- Conducting high-level discovery workshops
- Understanding an organization's key success criteria
- Facilitating understanding through high-level process and data modeling
- Identifying automation and optimization opportunities
- Balancing risk factors through planning and mitigation strategies

High-level process and data models provide an important early glimpse of the level of complexity of a project and provide a single vision for the processes involved. Initial high-level business process optimization plans serve as the first step toward achieving the added value that an organization expects from a digital transformation exercise. Understanding the project risk factors and success criteria will help steer the business and architectural decisions toward the desired outcome.

The purpose of the high-level process discovery exercise described in this chapter is to set the scene for the Power Platform implementation project, providing a unified vision and understanding of the scope of the solution. The details of the requirements will be discussed in the chapters that follow. Each of the topics discussed in this chapter will be illustrated through our fictional case study scenario at Inveriance Corps to provide tangible examples for each activity.

Conducting high-level discovery workshops

Solution architects plan and conduct discovery workshops, asking relevant questions to gain an understanding of the success criteria, high-level business processes, and data models within an organization. The following diagram illustrates the three stages of a discovery workshop:

High-Level Business Process and Data Modelling Workshops

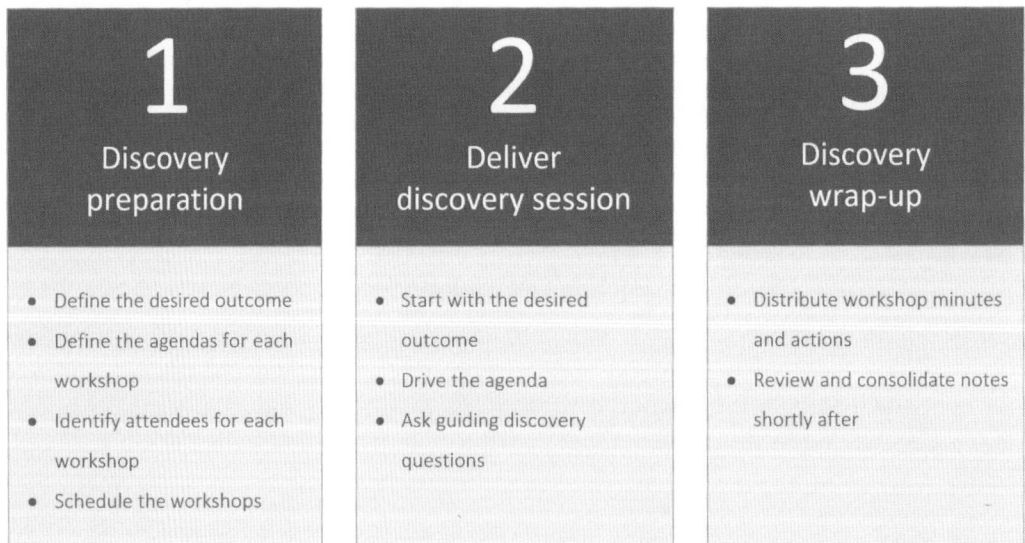

1 Discovery preparation	2 Deliver discovery session	3 Discovery wrap-up
• Define the desired outcome • Define the agendas for each workshop • Identify attendees for each workshop • Schedule the workshops	• Start with the desired outcome • Drive the agenda • Ask guiding discovery questions	• Distribute workshop minutes and actions • Review and consolidate notes shortly after

Figure 4.1 – The three steps to conducting discovery workshops

The first step to a successful discovery phase is planning, which is the subject of the following section.

Preparing discovery sessions

As a solution architect, you will work with key stakeholders, project managers, and other interested parties to plan discovery sessions.

Planning activities can be broken down as follows:

- **Define the purpose and desired outcome for the discovery sessions**

  You will define a high-level goal and desired outcome for the discovery exercise and each workshop or session. Depending on the scope of the project, a single discovery session may be sufficient. As a solution architect, you will decide the number of sessions and the topics for each discovery session to ensure all areas of interest are identified.

- **Define a clear agenda for the discovery sessions**

  A clear agenda provides direction to the discovery sessions. Depending on the project scope, you may wish to have a single discovery session to cover all areas of the implementation, or split the discovery phase into multiple workshops, each focused on specific areas of the organization or the solution.

- **Identify attendees and stakeholders**

  Having defined the agenda for each workshop session, you will identify the individuals (or roles within the organization) whose input is required during the discovery session.

- **Schedule the discovery sessions**

  Having identified the agenda and attendees, it is time to schedule the discovery sessions. You will work with the company project owners to find a suitable place and time for the sessions.

Delivering discovery sessions

Having prepared the discovery sessions in advance, you are now ready to start delivering the workshops. One of the first things you want to do is set the scene by setting out the desired outcome from the workshops and reviewing the agenda.

- **Start with the desired outcome**

  Stating the desired outcome at the start of the discovery workshop will help keep everyone in the room on the same agenda.

- **Drive the agenda**

  It is important as a solution architect to ensure the items on the agenda are covered and guide the discussions to ensure that the business processes and data models on the agenda are covered during the session.

- **Asking discovery questions**

  You will typically ask a set of questions during discovery sessions to understand the high-level business processes and data models within the organization. The following set of questions will help initiate a conversation regarding the high-level business processes:

  - What are the core activities that are visible to the customer?

  - What other activities and operations are performed by the company to support these core activities?

  Asking these types of open-ended questions will open the discussion, leading to a more detailed explanation of the actual business processes.

- **Making use of whiteboards and other visualization tools during discovery sessions**

  Discovery session attendees will be able to follow the more complex nuances of business processes when using visual aids such as whiteboarding or diagram tools. You might also encourage interactive collaboration on a whiteboard or diagram, allowing the subject-matter experts to draw out their understanding of the current processes and data stores.

  Taking advantage of illustrations and diagrams during a requirements conversation will lead to a deeper understanding of the requirements and bring everyone in attendance up to speed quicker, while keeping everyone on the same page during the requirements-capture exercise.

The post-discovery session wrap-up

Following a discovery session, you will want to review any notes, diagrams, whiteboarding sessions, and any collateral information shortly after the completion of the workshop, while they are still fresh in your mind. These are then translated and refined into discovery documentation for review during the requirements-capture and design stages of the project.

At this point, you will also want to distribute any meeting minutes or actions captured during the sessions to keep the momentum built as part of the exercise.

Understanding the organization's key success criteria

Having a clear definition of what constitutes a successful project will pave the way for a successful implementation. A clear vision for an organization's goals steers the implementation to fulfill that vision.

A key part of the discovery phase is to list the organization's key success criteria for the project. These may have been drawn up at the early stages of the engagement. Key stakeholders within the organization will have defined their expectations from the Power Platform digital transformation project. As a solution architect, you will be responsible for ensuring that these key success criteria are understood and recorded so that they may be used as a compass steering the implementation.

Organizations often have a clearly defined idea of what their success criteria are. You may at times need to ask relevant questions to engage the key stakeholders and project owners. The following set of questions will help initiate a conversation. The answers to these questions can then be used to define the key success criteria for the project:

1. What are the key benefits you would like to see from a Power Platform implementation?

2. How would you quantify the benefits you expect to gain from this project?

3. When would you like to see the desired results from this implementation?

   You will need to adjust these questions, nuanced with the context gained from your understanding of the organization's high-level architecture. The more targeted question that follows could be used to understand the organization's success criteria for a Power Apps Portal implementation:

4. There is currently a high dropout rate from your current customer onboarding process. What conversion rate would you like to see from your new customer onboarding portal?

The answers to these questions will often need to be tempered, grounding them with what would be technically feasible from the Power Platform solution. The organization may express their desire for a 0% dropout rate in their customer onboarding process, while in reality, it would be virtually impossible to force 100% of customers to complete an application process of any length.

In the chapters that follow, you will capture detailed requirements for the solution, defining success criteria for each area of the solution. For now, we will focus on the overall success criteria for the project. The activity that follows illustrates how the success criteria can be drawn up for the digital transformation project in our fictional case study at Inveriance Corps.

Case study – reviewing the key success criteria at Inveriance Corps

Engaging with key stakeholders and project owners in initial discovery meetings, you have asked the key success criteria identifying questions, leading you and the organization to a better understanding of the desired outcome from the project.

Leading the conversation with the "what," "how," and "when" questions listed earlier in this chapter, you now understand the success criteria for the digital transformation project at **Inveriance Corps** to be as follows:

- Reducing system maintenance and support costs by 20%

- Increasing sales by 30% through responsive and streamlined product-offering portals

- Opening business opportunities through collaboration across business units and data sharing

- Improving customer experience through a centralized and dedicated support platform

- Increasing conversion rates from 50% to 70% through a streamlined customer onboarding journey for all business units

Some of the success criteria will be based on broad assumptions of how the organization operates, its internal costs, and overhead. While the organization originally expressed a desire to increase conversion rates from 50% to 95% for their new customer onboarding portal, a high-level review of their onboarding process led you to believe that the dropout rate is not wholly within the control of the technical implementation, and a more realistic 70% conversion rate was agreed.

While success criteria may evolve, particularly when working within an agile environment, it serves as a guiding compass for the implementation. The list of key success criteria can now be recorded in the early chapters of a project proposal and documentation to solidify the overarching project goals.

Facilitating understanding through high-level processes and data modeling

During the discovery phase, you will run interactive sessions with an organization's stakeholders and subject-matter experts, review any existing documentation, and ask questions that will lead to an understanding of the current business processes and data structure that supports the organization's operations.

Detailed requirement capture and analysis are discussed in the upcoming chapters of this book. In the early stages of the project, you will look to understand the high-level business processes and data models so that you can build a frame of reference for how an organization currently operates. The output from this discovery exercise will be used as the context and structure for the upcoming requirement-engineering exercises in the chapters that follow.

The benefits of high-level processing and data modeling are as follows.

The benefits of a high-level process and data models

Power Platform projects benefit from high-level business processes and data models in the following ways:

- Models facilitate a single vision for a project and the underlying processes.
- The development team and stakeholders will gain a deeper understanding of the business processes through model diagrams and visual process representations.
- Models reduce ambiguities when reviewing the nature and complexities of various business processes.
- Power Platform implementation is fast-tracked through a shared understanding of current and desired business processes and data models.

High-level models of existing processes and data are drawn up during the discovery phase. In the following sections, you will work through our case study at Inveriance Corps to draw up high-level models for the organization.

Modeling the high-level business processes

During the discovery workshops and Q&A sessions, you will learn about the current business processes within an organization. Business processes may be categorized as one of the following two types:

- **Core activities**: These are the primary processes and activities that are part of the company's goals and the value offered to customers.

- **Supporting processes**: These are other activities that support the purpose of the company and its core activities, but they are not visible to the customer.

Asking questions that lead to a differentiation between core activities and supporting processes will help you draw up a high-level process model that reflects current business operations. Asking similar questions during the discovery workshops will also help you draw up a high-level business process model that fulfills the organization's aspirations and goals for the digital transformation project.

Case study – modeling existing and proposed business processes

During the discovery workshops with our case study project at Inveriance Corps, you identified core activities and secondary processes for each of the four business units by asking the following questions:

- What are the core activities that are visible to the customer?

- What other activities and operations are performed by the company to support these core activities?

The answers to these questions allow you to draw up the following high-level business process models for each of the four business units:

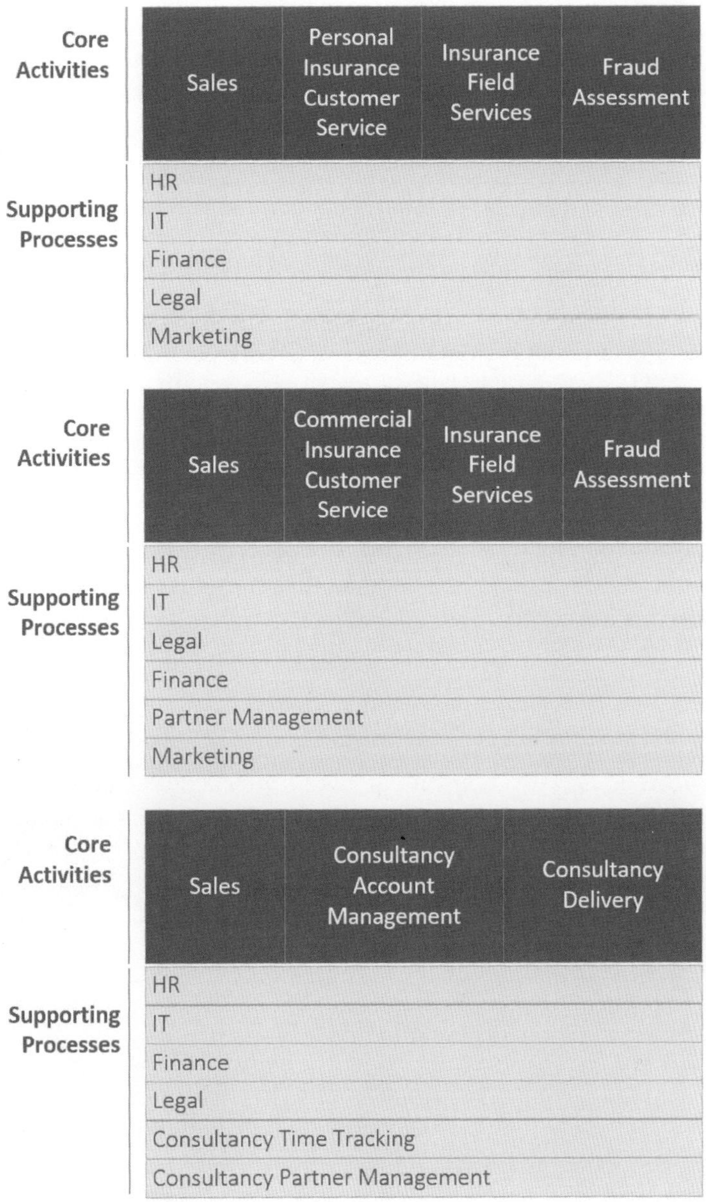

Core Activities	Sales	Personal Insurance Customer Service	Insurance Field Services	Fraud Assessment

Supporting Processes	HR
	IT
	Finance
	Legal
	Marketing

Core Activities	Sales	Commercial Insurance Customer Service	Insurance Field Services	Fraud Assessment

Supporting Processes	HR
	IT
	Legal
	Finance
	Partner Management
	Marketing

Core Activities	Sales	Consultancy Account Management	Consultancy Delivery

Supporting Processes	HR
	IT
	Finance
	Legal
	Consultancy Time Tracking
	Consultancy Partner Management

Figure 4.2 – The high-level model of the current business processes at Inveriance Corps

As part of the discovery phase, you may propose a change to existing processes to fulfill a customer's goals. In our case study, Inveriance Corps seeks an optimization of their disparate business processes, replicated across business units to streamline operations, reduce costs, and energize growth. Having reviewed the current business processes, we can identify key optimization and resource sharing areas.

Core activities such as sales, customer services, field services, and fraud assessment can share resources and systems across business units. Secondary processes such as HR, IT, finance, legal operations, marketing, and time tracking can also be centralized, thus providing Inveriance Corps with a consistent approach to managing these activities.

> **Pillars for Great Architecture – Implementation and Operation Efficiency**
>
> When reviewing the current business process model and systems that support it, it is evident that the customer service process is a candidate for improving operational efficiency. Each of the four business units runs a separate customer service and case management system in isolation. Applying the *implementation and operation efficiency pillars for great architecture*, a centralized cloud-based case management solution based around Dynamics 365 Customer Service would provide the operational efficiency and cost-effectiveness the organization seeks from the digital transformation project.

Having reviewed and identified the key areas for digital transformation, we can draw a proposed high-level business process diagram that consolidates similar activities performed across business units.

The following diagram illustrates the proposed high-level business process model:

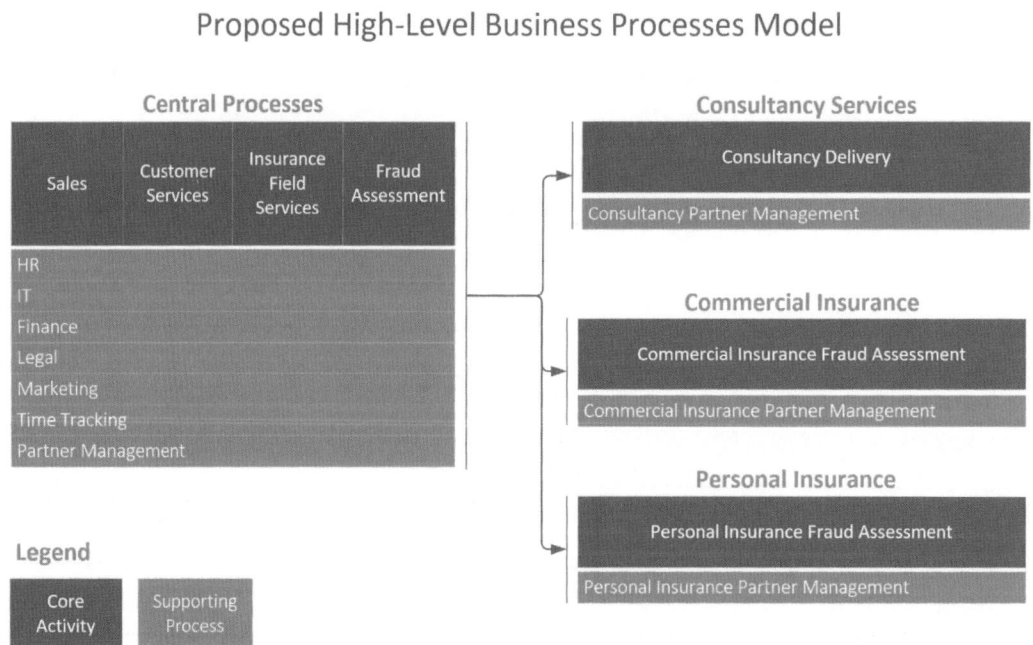

Figure 4.3 – The high-level model for the proposed business process structure at Inveriance Corps

When proposing a change to business processes, it is important to highlight the benefits afforded by the change. The following list outlines some of the key benefits derived from the proposed high-level business process model:

- Reduced customer service overhead when transferring customers between business units, reducing operation costs by 20%.

- Reduced customer service operational costs when using a central cloud-based case management solution across business units, increasing customer satisfaction and the call resolution rate by 50%.

- Individual business units can focus on and improve their core activities and competencies.

- Improved data quality from the reduction of manual data transfers to and from company headquarters.

- Improved visibility over overall company finances using a central system, reducing invoice errors by an estimated 30%.

The high-level process models drawn during the discovery phase are a starting point that will facilitate the detailed design phase to come.

High-level data models

While detailed data models are usually drawn up during the design phase, it is often useful to identify the core data items used by an organization and the location of these data stores. A high-level data model will facilitate discussions during discovery workshops, providing a visual representation that aids understanding. These high-level data models will be later used to kick-start data modeling activities during the design phase.

Case study – a high-level model of the existing data structure

During the discovery workshops with our case study project at Inveriance Corps, you identified the key pieces of data stored within the personal insurance business unit. The following diagram illustrates the data stores identified during the discovery sessions:

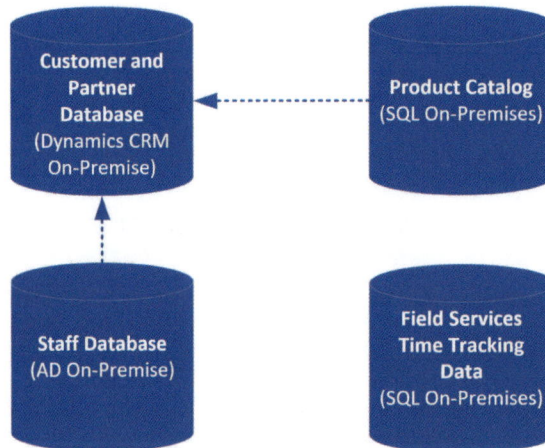

Figure 4.4 – The high-level data model for the personal insurance business unit

Now let us understand how to identify automation opportunities and process optimizations.

Identifying automation opportunities and process optimization

During the discovery workshops, you will review an organization's business processes and identify areas that would benefit from optimization. While drawing high-level diagrams for the key business processes, you will be able to identify opportunities for automation. Legacy systems often involve the manual processing of data. That is where the automation capabilities within the Power Platform framework come into play. You will seek to identify areas of the current business processes suitable for automation.

Let's take the example of a new customer onboarding journey, where prospective clients navigate onto a company website or portal and enter their personal and business details to apply for a product offered by the organization. During the discovery workshops, you may learn that the onboarding process involves a set of manual steps, as illustrated in the following diagram:

Example High-Level Process
Current Customer Onboarding Journey

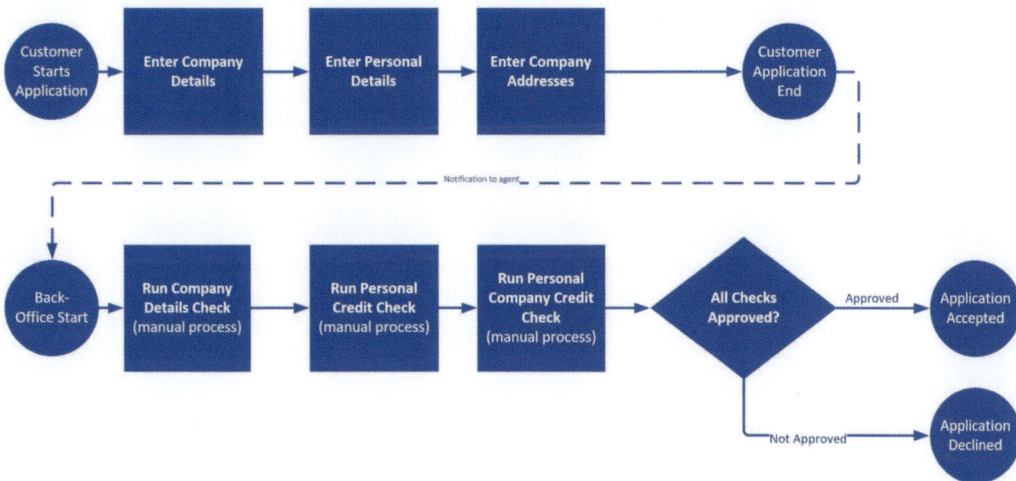

Figure 4.5 – Manual steps in the onboarding process

You analyze the high-level onboarding process and identify the opportunities for optimization, seeking to automate the manual checks carried out by the back-office agent after the customer has completed the application. If the checks can be performed automatically and at the time the customer enters the data, the end-to-end application timelines will be greatly reduced, and the prospective customer can become an actual client at the point they have completed the application.

The optimized business process can then be transformed to match the following diagram:

Example High-Level Process
Automated Customer Onboarding Journey

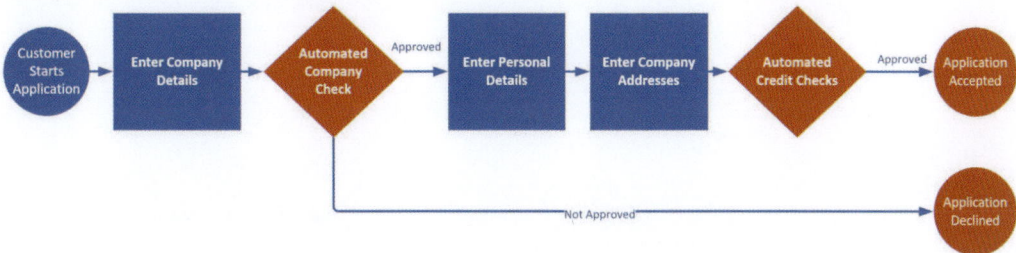

Figure 4.6 – Auomated version of onboarding process

The automated version of the onboarding process allows customers to become clients, potentially within minutes or seconds of starting an application. Back-office staff members will then be free to manage exceptions to the process, rather than being part of the main onboarding journey itself. The following case study activity further demonstrates the process for identifying optimization opportunities.

Case study – a high-level model of the existing data structure

The discovery workshops flagged up several processes that would benefit from optimization at Inveriance Corps. Each of these business processes has been assessed, and an optimized solution is proposed, together with the estimated benefits.

The following table lists the outcome of the business process optimization assessment:

Area	Proposed optimized solution	Estimated optimization benefits
Customer service	Consolidate the various systems into Dynamics 365 Customer Service and the Power Apps portals' customer service module.	20% cost reduction 50% improvement in customer satisfaction Centralized customer database across all business units
Sales	Consolidate the various systems into Dynamics 365 Sales.	20% cost reduction 40% reduction in lost business Consistent sales process across business units
Finance	Consolidate the various systems into Dynamics 365 Finance and Operations.	20% cost reduction
Marketing	Consolidate the various systems into Dynamics 365 Marketing.	30% cost reduction 20% increase in conversion to sales
Field services	Consolidate field service operations using Dynamics 365 Field Service.	20% cost reduction
Partner management	Consolidate partner management operations using Dynamics 365 Sales and the Power Apps portals' customer service module.	20% cost reduction

Table 4.1 – The proposed process optimizations at Inveriance Corps during the discovery phase

The high-level business process optimization is presented to the project stakeholders for planning and prioritization.

Balancing digital transformation risk factors through planning and mitigation

Identifying risks to a project will help guide key decisions early in the project toward a satisfactory conclusion. During the discovery phase, you will want to review the organization and the project for the following risks.

These are the types of potential project and organizational risks:

- Non-tangible risks
- Team capabilities and skillsets
- Project timeline risks
- Budget constraint risks
- The organization's competitors

As part of the discovery phase, you will want to identify the different risks to the project and put in place a mitigation strategy for dealing with those risks during the project's life cycle.

Through an analysis of an organization's business process strengths, weaknesses, opportunities, and threats (**SWOT analysis**), you will gain visibility over areas of concern to be aware of (such as potential risks to the project due to budget constraints or competition). You will also identify areas where the Power Platform can add value (such as an abundance of manual processes that can be optimized using the platform's features).

The case study activities that follow illustrate the risk assessment and mitigation strategy process.

Case study – the SWOT analysis

During the discovery workshops, you have identified the strengths, weaknesses, opportunities, and threats to the digital transformation project at Inveriance Corps through a series of questions and your research. The following diagram illustrates the results of the SWOT analysis:

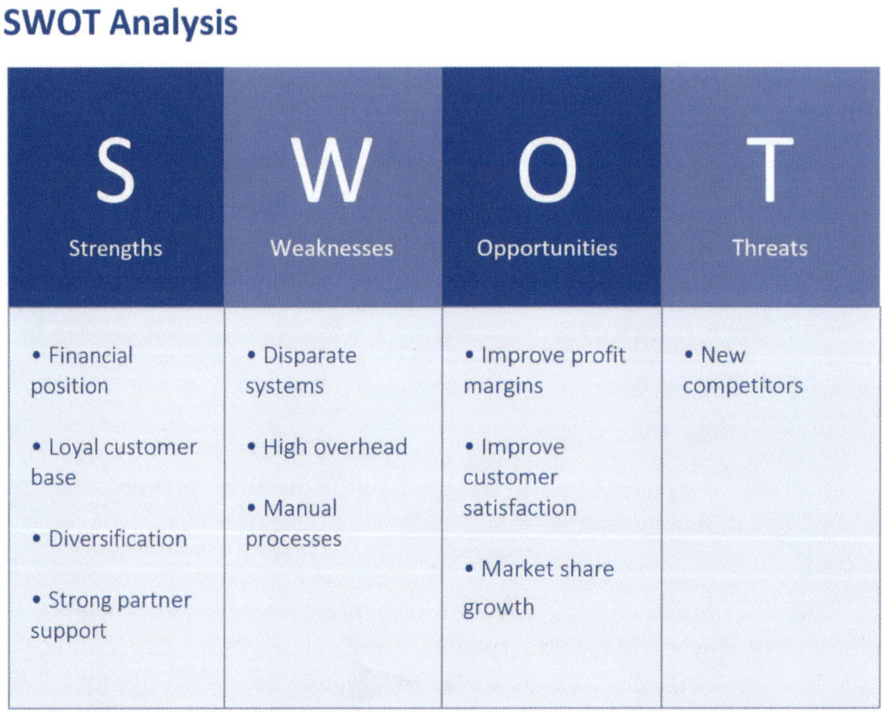

SWOT Analysis

S	W	O	T
Strengths	Weaknesses	Opportunities	Threats
• Financial position • Loyal customer base • Diversification • Strong partner support	• Disparate systems • High overhead • Manual processes	• Improve profit margins • Improve customer satisfaction • Market share growth	• New competitors

Figure 4.7 – Example results of a SWOT analysis at Inveriance Corps

Having identified the project's risks and mitigating factors and an understanding of the customer gained through SWOT analysis, you are now better placed to make the decisions that will drive the project to a successful conclusion. The following section discusses mitigation strategies for risks identified during the discovery phase.

Case study – an initial project risk analysis

The information gathered from the pre-discovery and discovery phases of the project identified several risks to the project. These risks are listed in the following table, together with the proposed mitigation strategy:

Risk types	Risks	Mitigation
Non-tangible risks	Fear of restructuring from key stakeholders	Involve stakeholders in the direction of the consolidation.
Team capabilities and skillsets	A lack of Dynamics 365 Finance and Operations knowledge within the team and a shortage of Power Platform developers	Onboard a partner to support the finance and operations implementation. Engage an outsourcing development partner.
Project timeline risks	An aggressive timeline may be difficult to adhere to.	Propose a phased approach for realistic early wins.
Budget constraint risks	A yearly budget means finance processes would not be possible to implement in the first 2 years.	Propose a phased approach to fit within yearly budget constraints.
Organization's competitors	Competitors have a superior onboarding portal for new customers already in place, reducing a potential new customer stream.	Propose the prioritization of an updated onboarding portal.

Table 4.2 – Risks identified during the discovery phase and proposed mitigation strategy

Identifying project risks early on means stakeholders and the project team are better placed to make the necessary decisions and adjust the project scope and timelines to reach a satisfactory conclusion. You may be involved in the analysis of an organization's strengths, weaknesses, opportunities, and threats (the SWOT analysis).

Summary

In this chapter, you have learned how to create a high-level model for business processes and data stores, identified automation opportunities within these business processes, and mitigated risk factors that could affect the outcome of a project. You now also understand the benefits of clearly defined success criteria. These discovery phase activities will prepare the foundation for the Power Platform implementation project, guiding it through challenges that may arise by preempting issues and providing predefined strategies for dealing with them.

In the next chapter, you will delve deeper into the existing architectural landscape, identify the location and quality of existing data sources, and create a detailed business process model that reflects the organization's day-to-day activities.

5
Understanding the Existing Architectural Landscape

In this chapter, you will assess the data sources and architectural landscape at Inveriance Corps, gaining a deep understanding of the starting point for the digital transformation project. You will learn to evaluate the overall enterprise architecture, the current sources of data, and their locations and use cases. You will then document the current architecture and data models to cement that understanding and facilitate the requirement-capture conversation.

In this chapter, we are going to cover the following main topics:

- Assessing the existing enterprise architecture
- Identifying existing sources of data, their usage, and quality standards
- Documenting the organization's architecture and detailed business processes

Understanding the existing architectural landscape and business processes is an important first step on the way to defining the target architecture. Decisions made during the design process will consider the current architecture.

Assessing the existing enterprise architecture

Enterprise architecture models represent a business's structure and the relationships between its various domains. The domains include physical, organizational, and technical components. A full enterprise architecture discussion is beyond the scope of this book. We can, however, draw value from a baseline analysis.

An evaluation of the current enterprise architecture provides perspective, which you can use to decide where Power Platform best fits within an organization. Solution architects assess the baseline architecture and draft the proposed model that considers the enterprise architecture roadmap for the organization. With the plan in hand, you have an effective high-level directive, allowing you to focus project activities on getting from the as-is situation to the to-be end state.

Understanding the current enterprise architecture

To start the evaluation of the current enterprise architecture, you would ask the following questions:

- What are the current pain points and known open issues within the enterprise?
- What inconsistencies exist in the way the enterprise performs its functions?
- What quality issues have been identified within the organization?

The answers to these questions will help you gain an understanding of where the business is seeking to find solutions to long-standing problems or pain points, and where Power Platform can solve those problems.

Understanding the upcoming changes that may have an impact on the enterprise architecture

Organizations are ever-evolving and changing. While evaluating the as-is state of an enterprise, having visibility of what change is around the corner will help you strategically place Power Platform to provide long-term solutions to upcoming challenges brought about by change.

The following types of questions will help you gain an understanding of the potential changes that may impact the enterprise architecture:

- Is any new business or technical infrastructure being introduced in the future that will have a material impact on the enterprise architecture?

- What new business processes or significant technical functionality do you plan to bring into the organization, both short- and long-term?

- What operational changes can take place that will impact the enterprise architecture?

The answers to these questions will help make architectural decisions that will guide the Power Platform implementation to continue providing value to an organization, if and when these potential changes occur.

Understanding the desired enterprise architecture

Once you understand the current environment and potential impacting changes, you can start drafting a model for the desired enterprise architecture, typically involving the following activities.

- Drawing an enterprise architecture roadmap for the areas that relate to Power Platform and the Microsoft stack

- Proposing options for desired architecture together with a trade-off analysis, comparing each option to identify the best fit for the organization

Understanding the current enterprise architecture, potential changes, and the desired state, you have an achievable roadmap that will help you select the right Power Platform blueprint and implementation strategy to meet an organization's needs head-on.

Identifying Power Platform data sources, their usage, and quality standards

Power Platform applications can consume data from a wide range of sources. Identifying these data sources provides an early view of how data will be fed in and out of Power Platform and how it will be consumed. We can also find out about any data cleansing or normalization that may be required. This exercise will be illustrated using our case study at Inveriance Corps.

Case study – current data sources at Inveriance Corps

Having reviewed the high-level architecture diagram drafted during the discovery phase, several key data sources have been identified and are highlighted in the following diagram:

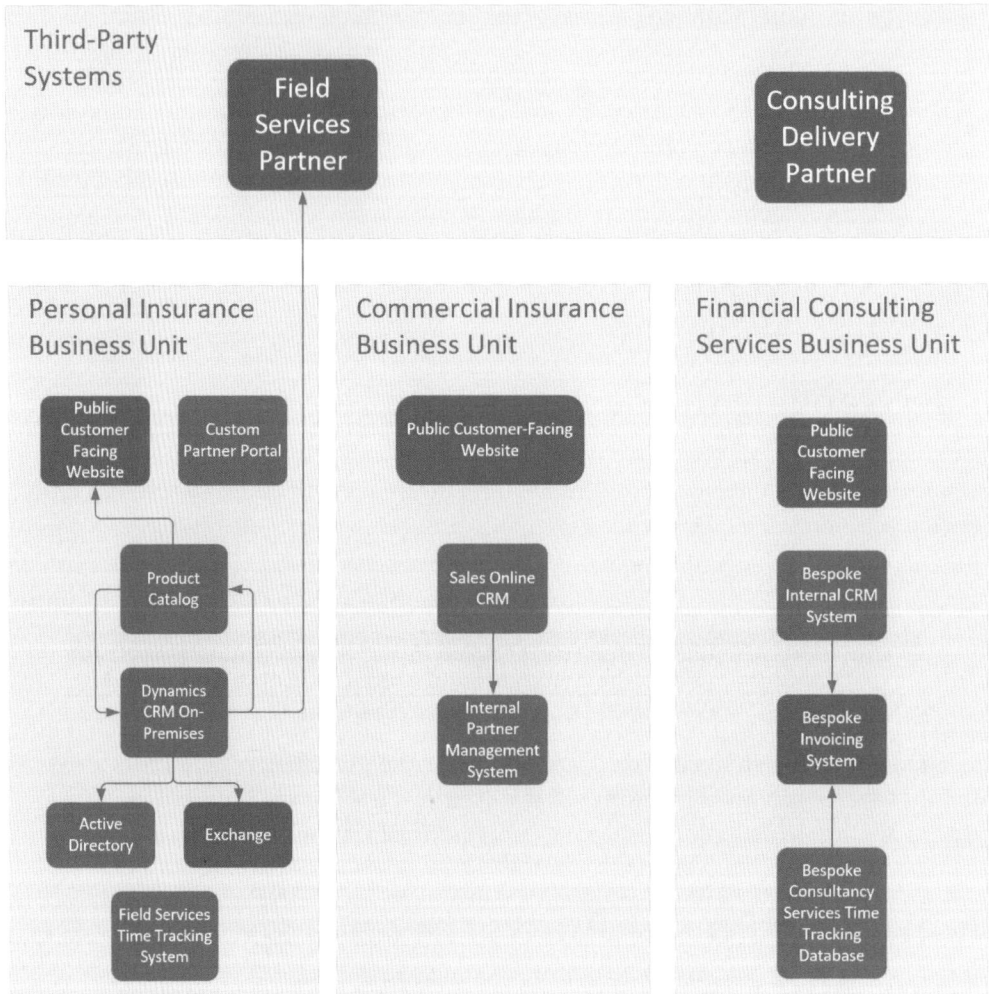

Figure 5.1 – Key data sources at Inveriance Corps

Having identified the key data sources to be used as part of the Power Platform implementation, you can now define their usage. Data sources may be imported into Power Platform as a one-off migration process, integrated in real time, or scheduled for synchronization. The initial data usage analysis provides insights into how data is currently used.

A rough benchmark for data quality is also set based on discussions and a review of data samples where appropriate. The estimated number of duplicate records, the referential integrity of the data, and the overall data hygiene are identified for each data source. The following table lists a few of the key data sources, their usage, and quality standards:

Data source	Type	Usage	Quality standards
Product catalog	Master product catalog for personal insurance	Automated integration for consumption by all personal insurance systems	Duplicates – **low** Integrity – **high** Overall quality – **high**
Dynamics CRM customer data	Customer data	To be migrated into Power Platform solutions	Duplicates – **high** Integrity – **medium** Overall quality – **medium**

Table 5.1 – Key data sources, their usage, and quality standards at Inveriance Corps

The complete data source assessment provides a base for the requirement-capture discussions that are to follow.

Documenting the organization's architecture and detailed business processes

The output from the activities in the enterprise architecture assessment section in this chapter provides a baseline understanding of the systems in place at an organization. You can then extend this understanding into architectural diagrams and documentation that will facilitate the upcoming design process.

The answers to the following questions will help you to gain an understanding of systems architecture within an organization.

1. What systems or services do you currently use to do the following?

    I. Manage customer data

    II. Manage staff members and their access to systems

    III. Send and receive emails

    IV. Message and collaborate between staff, vendors, and other third parties

2. Where are these systems or services hosted?

3. How do staff members access these systems or services?

4. What systems or services do your customers use to interact with your organization?

5. What systems do partners and third-party organizations use to interact with your organization?

6. What infrastructure do you have in place for managing integrations or messaging between systems?

The preceding sample questions are a conversation starter that will lead to more detailed discussions on each topic and result in a greater understanding of the existing architecture. The next step is to translate these discussions into diagrams and supporting documentation that illustrates the architecture and facilitates the upcoming dialogue design and implementation activities.

Using our case study at Inveriance Corps, you will learn to translate the results of these questions into an architectural blueprint.

Case study – assessing the existing architecture at Inveriance Corps

Through several workshops and analysis sessions with the owners of the relevant systems and SMEs at Inveriance Corps, you have gained an understanding of the organization's existing architecture through the following Q&A session:

Architecture assessment session results	
Question 1	**What systems or services do you currently use to manage customer data?**
Answer	Each business unit uses a different system, as follows: • **Personal insurance business unit:** Dynamics CRM 2016 on-premises is in use by the personal insurance unit for general CRM and sales. A custom customer-facing website backed by a MySQL database, hosted in data centers where customers can access their account details and policy documentation. This customer data is synchronized with Dynamics CRM online via a scheduled download to SQL. Then via a scheduled command-line windows application that queries the MySQL database. After that via a VPN connection to the servers hosting the MySQL database. • **Commercial insurance business unit:** Customer data is managed within Salesforce SaaS. • **Financial consulting services business unit:** A bespoke internal CRM system that manages all customer data. The system is hosted within collocated data centers with a SQL server backend. Office networks across the globe connect to the data center via a VPN. • **Headquarters:** Customer records are stored within a central legacy CRM database.

Architecture assessment session results	
Question 2	**What systems or services do you currently use to manage staff members and their access to systems?**
Answer	All business units and headquarters use an on-premises instance of AD connected across WANs via VPN connections.
Question 3	**What systems or services do you currently use to send and receive emails?**
Answer	Exchange on-premises is used across the business.
Question 4	**What systems or services do you currently use to message and collaborate between staff, vendors, and other third parties?**
Answer	SharePoint is used to manage documentation by a small number of teams. Instant messaging services are not currently widely used within the organization.
Question 5	**Where are these systems or services hosted?**
Answer	All systems are hosted on-premises except for the commercial insurance business unit, which uses Sales Online hosted as a SaaS.
Question 6	**How do staff members access these systems or services?**
Answer	Staff members log on to their workstation or laptop using their on-premises AD credentials while connected to the internal corporate network, or via a VPN connection if remote.
Question 7	**What systems or services do your customers use to interact with your organization?**
Answer	All business units use a public-facing website hosted in collocated data centers. Email communications use Exchange hosted on-premises.
Question 8	**What systems do partners and third-party organizations use to interact with your organization?**
Answer	• **Personal insurance business unit:** A custom-built partner portal hosted in collocated data centers. • **Investments business unit:** An internal partner management system that interacts with partner organizations.
Question 9	**What infrastructure do you have in place for managing integrations or messaging between systems?**
Answer	Integrations have been implemented as required. The organization does not currently have any messaging queueing or API management solutions in place.

Table 5.2 – Architecture assessment session results

Based on these answers and further detailed dialogue into each of the architectural areas, we can draw a model of the current solution architecture at Inveriance Corps:

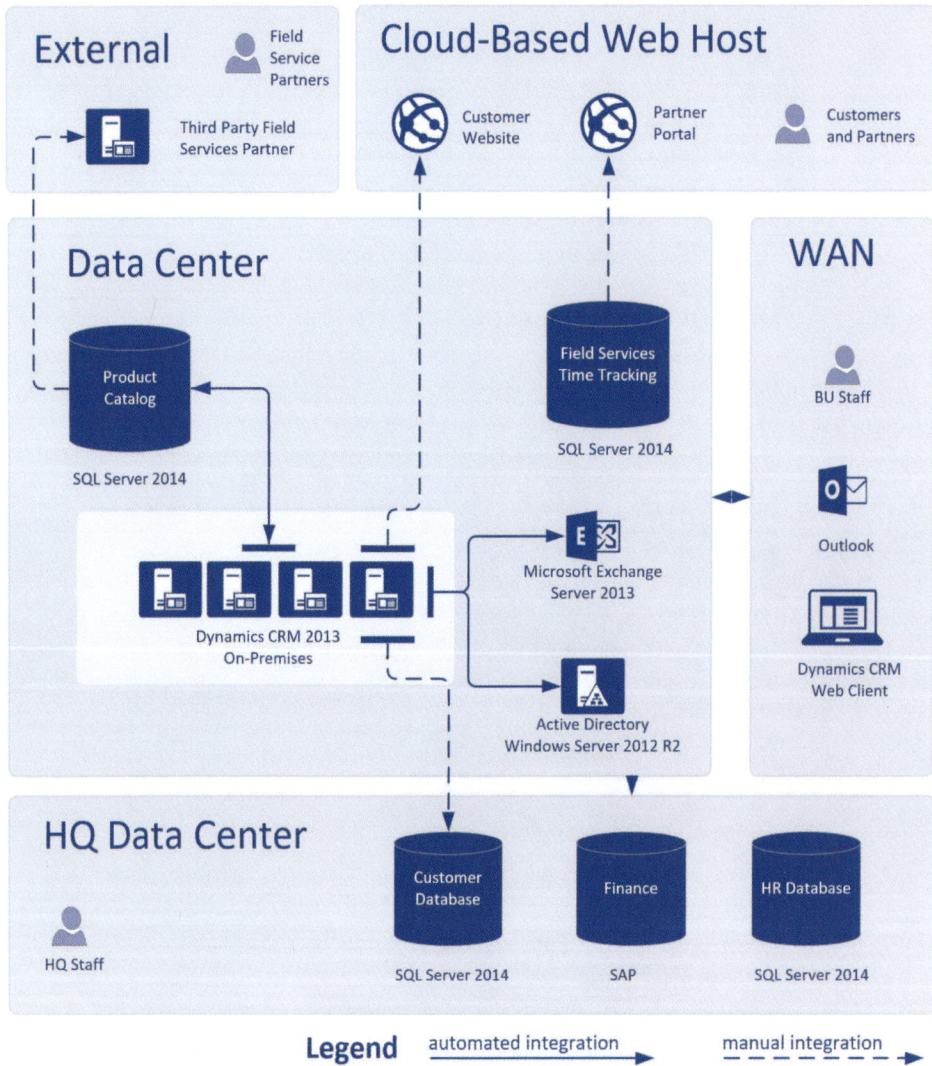

Figure 5.2 – The systems architecture overview at Inveriance Corps

A systems architecture diagram is a key document that provides a clear understanding of the systems in place and their interactions. The diagram will be refined during the design phase to illustrate how the current architecture will change once the Power Platform project is underway.

An architecture assessment summary

The architecture is primarily hosted within on-premises systems and collocated data centers. A substantial portion of systems are custom-built and require considerable ongoing maintenance. Multiple separate customer databases have resulted in data silos that are integrated manually with the central headquarters' customer database.

Assessing the current organization's architecture provides a window through which we can look at multiple possible routes for implementing and integrating Power Platform components and related Microsoft services.

Summary

In this chapter, you have learned how to assess the current architectural landscape, identify the key data sources and quality standards, and draw up documentation for the current system's architecture. These key data points provide the basis for a fruitful discussion during requirement-capture sessions that will follow.

In the next chapter, you will start the requirements analysis and engineering stages by refining the digital transformation goals and identifying functional and non-functional requirements.

6

Requirements Analysis and Engineering for Solution Architecture

In this chapter, you will learn how to capture an organization's digital transformation goals through a systematic approach to requirements analysis. You will review the organization's high-level requirements, laying an outline template to capture detailed functional and non-functional requirements. These requirements will be documented and consolidated against the organization's vision for a digital future, steering the project to meet its digital transformation goals.

In this chapter, we are going to cover the following main topics:

- Overview of effective requirements analysis and engineering

- Preparing the requirements gathering sessions

- Delivering the requirements gathering sessions

- Post-requirements capture review and sign-off

Effective requirements capture is crucial for a successful Power Platform implementation. It can mean the difference between a solution that solves an organization's problems and an implementation that never sees the light of day. The requirements identified and refined at this project stage will direct your design and build activities. In this chapter, you will learn how to answer this fundamental question: *what are the organization's needs, and how can they be addressed in the most effective way possible?*

Overview of effective requirements analysis and engineering

The success of Power Platform projects, much like any other software implementation, is predicated on having clearly defined requirements that address an organization's business needs. Solution architects plan and conduct requirements capture workshops and collaborate with individuals at all levels. They ask guiding questions to crystalize the organization's vision into a set of requirements that can then be realized as implementation tasks. The following diagram illustrates the three stages of the requirements capture phase:

1 Workshop preparation	2 Workshop delivery	3 Post workshop
• Define the desired outcome • Review previously defined requirements • Define the agendas for each workshop • Identify attendees for each workshop • Schedule the workshops • Share the pre-requisites • Prepare the equipment/demo • Prepare the baseline documentation • Arrange any support that is required	• Start with the desired outcome • Drive the agenda • Ask guiding questions • Identify functional and non-functional requirements • Assess feasibility • Manage exceptions • Manage conflicting requirements • Make use of templates to record the requirements • Help stakeholders share your vision of the solution	• Distribute workshop minutes and actions • Formalize the sign-off (if required) • Review and consolidate the notes

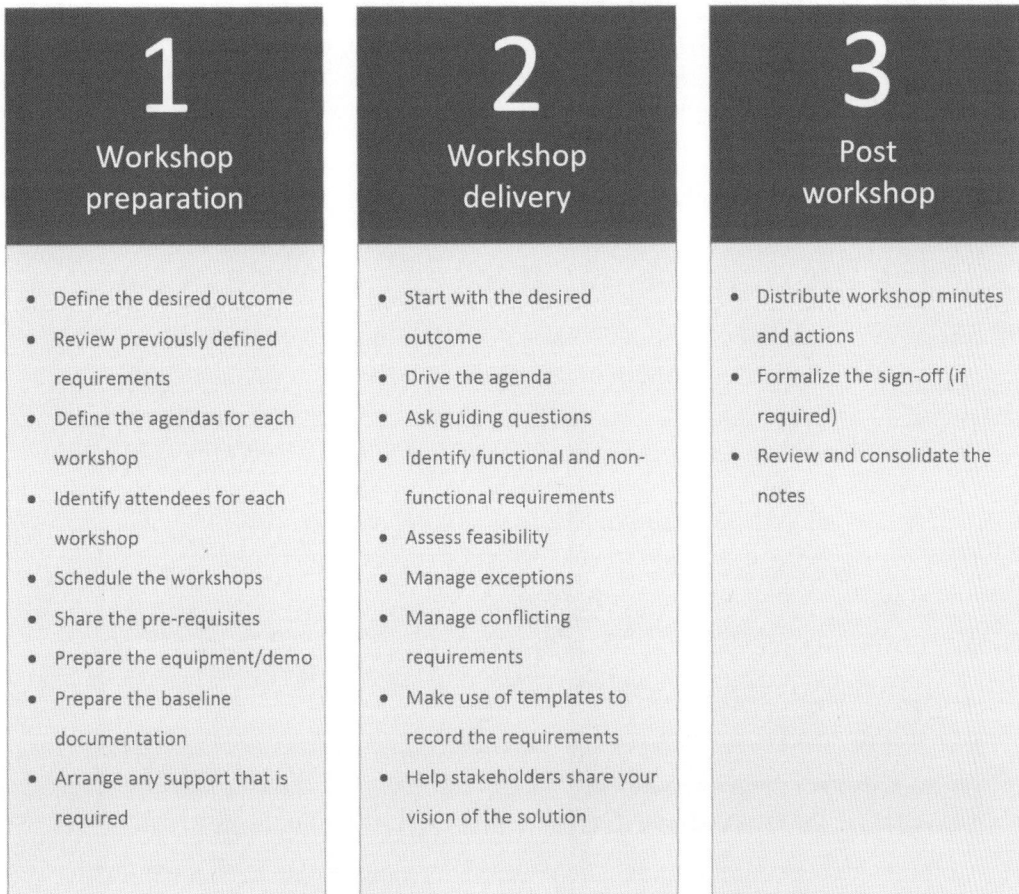

Figure 6.1 – The three stages of the requirements capture phase

In this chapter, you will learn how to navigate through the three stages of the requirements capture process. The first step to a successful requirement gathering exercise is planning, which is the subject of the following section.

Planning the requirements gathering sessions

The saying *"fail to prepare, prepare to fail"* certainly applies to requirements analysis. As a solution architect, you will work with stakeholders, project managers, and other interested parties to plan the requirements gathering sessions.

Planning activities can be broken down in the following way.

Defining the purpose and desired outcome of the sessions

You will define a high-level goal and desired outcome for the requirements gathering exercise, along with each workshop or session. Special consideration must be made to ensure the desired outcomes for the sessions align with the high-level project goals and key success criteria that were previously defined. This will serve as a compass for the duration of the requirements gathering exercise, guiding your train of thought toward achieving the organization's vision. An example of a requirements capture workshop purpose and desired outcome is as follows.

Workshop purpose and desired outcome example

This workshop aims to understand the use-cases for the new customer onboarding portal. The desired outcome is to capture a clear set of requirements for implementation.

Reviewing previously defined requirements

The customer and organization might have already communicated a set of requirements, which can serve as a starting point for conversations during the formal requirements capture sessions. Additionally, this information can be used to pre-assess the feasibility of the business needs even before the full requirements sessions are underway. As a result, the customer does not have to repeat themselves, and the requirements sessions are expedited thanks to prior knowledge and pre-assessments.

Defining a clear agenda

A clear agenda provides direction to the proceedings of the requirements capture. Depending on the implementation, more than one workshop session might be required, with sessions split across different areas of concern. For example, you might decide to have one workshop focusing on the business processes requirements and a second targeted toward defining the security and architectural needs, each with its own set of attendees and agendas to match.

Identifying attendees and stakeholders

Having defined an agenda for each workshop session, you will identify the individuals (or roles within the organization) whose input will be required during the session. Certain workshops, such as architectural and security review sessions, will be more technical in nature. These technical workshops will ideally include the relevant SMEs and infrastructure owners. Business process workshop sessions will include users, their managers, and other stakeholders with a vested interest in the workshop's area of concern.

Also, consider that staff might feel less inclined to voice their opinions and concerns if the management is present, and they might prefer to stay silent, deferring to their superiors. Under those circumstances, you might contemplate including management in final decision-making sessions only, freeing up the general requirement capture sessions for users and SMEs to speak freely.

Scheduling the workshops

Having identified the agenda and attendees, it is time to schedule the requirements capture sessions. The duration of these sessions will vary depending on the agenda, the amount of ground to cover, and the complexity of the processes or systems being discussed. You will work with the company project owners to find a suitable place and time for the workshops.

Sharing the session prerequisites with the attendees

Some workshop sessions could benefit from the use of interactive documents such as editable word documents and whiteboarding tools. Providing links to these tools before the workshop will allow attendees to test access and facilitate the workshop session.

Additionally, you can look to furnish attendees with any documentation or templates that they should fill in before the start of the session, as this prework will expedite the requirements capture process. For example, distributing a set of Excel spreadsheets with tables to be filled in by the applicants containing a list of team names and their members will mean this information will be readily available to you during the requirements capture session.

Preparing facilities, equipment, and demonstration platforms

Depending on the nature of the workshop session, you might need to use equipment such as projectors and other facilities. It is important to prepare these before the start of the workshop to ensure a smooth-running session. While having conversations during the workshop, the use of a demonstration system to illustrate the features and capabilities of Power Platform will be beneficial to attendees. They will be able to understand the standard capabilities of the product and guide their opinions toward processes that work with the product.

It is also a good idea to set up demonstration systems in advance with limited customer branding and configuration to make the solution relevant to the workshop's area of interest:

The typical facilities used in a requirements gathering workshop

Online meeting for remote attendees	Workshop	Meeting room
Whiteboarding facilities		Projector screen
Baseline demo system		Requirements gathering templates

Figure 6.2 – Preparing the requirements gathering workshop's resources and facilities

Preparing the baseline documentation

Often, it is useful to have a set of requirements capture templates and baseline documentation that can be used during the workshops. You can then use these templates throughout the sessions, guiding questions in such a way that you can get to the core needs of the organization.

In this chapter, we will work through a set of templates that can be reused as part of your future requirements capture workshops.

Arranging for any support required during the workshop sessions

Depending on the size of the workshop sessions, it might be useful to enroll the assistance of a scribe to help note down the requirements while the discussions are ongoing.

Power Platform's functional and technical consultants make great teammates during the requirements sessions, complementing your knowledge and assisting in recording the requirements and taking notes. As a solution architect, you can decide whether the project's size and complexity would benefit from additional help during the requirements capture sessions. You can then arrange for those other resources to be present during the workshop.

Delivering the requirements gathering sessions

Having prepared the requirements capture sessions in advance, you are now ready to start delivering the workshops. One of the first things you want to do is set the scene by setting out the desired outcome of the workshops and reviewing the agenda.

Starting with the desired outcome

At the start of the workshop, you will want to clearly set out the desired outcome of the workshops so that everybody in attendance is on the same page. Understanding the overall aim of the workshop with a clear mission statement will guide the conversation to achieve the desired goal.

Driving the agenda

The requirements gathering workshops will follow a predefined agenda. This might be in the form of allocated sets of time for specific business processes or areas of the project. As a solution architect, it is important to ensure the items on the agenda are covered. Additionally, you should guide the discussions to ensure that the requirements for each item on the agenda are recorded.

It is often the case that discussions go off on a tangent, and it is the role of the solution architect to acknowledge those additional topics for future discussion and bring the items on the agenda back to the conversation. This will help prevent them from reaching the end of the workshop without having gathered the necessary requirements, having to fill in the gaps through less efficient means such as questions and answers via email, or having to schedule subsequent workshops to cover the remaining items.

Refining the high-level requirements

During the discovery sessions carried out in *Chapter 3, Discovery and Initial Solution Planning, and Chapter 4, Identifying the Desired Business Process, Risk Factors, and Success Criteria*, you will have identified high-level business processes, baseline data models, and the success criteria for the digital transformation project.

The key success criteria will provide a rudder for the requirements capture sessions, guiding the discussions toward answering the question *"How can we achieve the outcome for success criteria X?"*

An example of key success criteria could be to *"reduce system maintenance and support costs."* You can then ask the questions that will lead to the real underlying requirements behind that success criteria. The question of *"how could be reduced system maintenance support costs?"* is an open-ended one that might lead down multiple routes, and you would then investigate each of those routes to find the core business requirements.

Continuing with this line of questioning will unravel the requirements behind each success criteria.

Identifying functional requirements

Functional requirements describe how the solution should behave. As the workshop progresses, you will be responsible for asking questions that will guide the conversation, allowing the organization's core needs to surface so that they can be understood and recorded.

Asking guiding questions

Typically, you will ask a set of questions during the requirements work session to understand and delve deeper into the requirements. Those questions could include the following:

- What are the activities and actions required from a process on a regular basis?

- Who is involved in these regular activities?

- Does this process require any data? And where does this data come from?

- Why do you need this process or action?

Asking these types of open-ended questions will open the discussion, leading to a more detailed explanation of the actual business needs. You can then ask yes and no questions to confirm your understanding of the requirements.

You will listen to stakeholders at all levels of the organization, from users to managers and C-level executives. These questions will clarify and crystallize the real organizational need behind each requirement.

You will want to ask the following questions to get to the requirements:

- **Who** needs the process/action/feature?
- **What** does that person need from the process/action/feature?
- **Why** does that person need this process/action/feature?

Here is a sample requirement capture interaction that follows the proposed sequence of questions:

A manager expresses a need to export an Excel document containing customer invoices every month.	
Q	**Who** needs this monthly invoice exported to Excel?
A	The customer service team members. They are responsible for the invoices.
Q	**What** do they need from the export?
A	A list of all invoices for the last calendar month, including the invoice total, customer name, customer type, product type, and invoice date.
Q	**Why** do the customer service team members need this data to be exported?
A	So that the customer service team can then process the exported Excel invoice data, filtering out invoices where the customer type is "*Commercial Insurance*." The customer service team can then import the filtered invoice list into the finance system.
Q	**Why** does the customer service team need to import this information into the finance system?
A	So that the finance team can send reminders to the commercial insurance customers with invoices over $1,000 to ensure payment is received. Also, the finance team uses this data to present a report to the board of directors. The report shows a chart of the total commercial insurance invoiced per month and per product type for the last year so that the board can project the cash flow for the organization.

Table 6.1 – An example Q&A session to gather functional requirements

Note that you would need to keep asking **why**-type questions until the actual business needs have been identified. Having guided the workshop, you now understand the requirements to be as follows:

Invoicing requirements		
Who	**What**	**Why**
The finance team	need a list of commercial insurance invoices totaling over $1,000 for the last calendar month	to send reminders to these customers to ensure payment is received.
The board of directors	need a report showing a chart with the total commercial insurance invoiced per month, per product type for the last year	so that they can project cash flow for the organization.

Table 6.2 – An example of the functional requirements

As it turns out, the actual business needs were quite different from the initial requirement expressed by the manager. Having delved deeper, we find the essence of the organization's requirement, which can then be used to design a solution that best addresses the business need. You should aim to understand and define the processes that drive the business rather than focus on the features and functionality. Therefore, the exercise aims to answer the following underlying question: *"How will someone successfully use the Power Platform solution to solve a business problem?"*

Requirements Capture Tip

When requesting information and asking the question *"why do you need this process/requirement?"*, it is important to do so with tact to avoid causing a defensive attitude from the workshop attendees. Explain that the answers to these questions will help refine their requirements, thus resulting in the best solution for their needs. It will help reconcile in the audience's mind that the reason for the questions is not to query their understanding or level and knowledge of a subject area. Instead, it is to help understand their need so that you can provide an optimal solution, which might be something other than what the audience anticipates.

Making use of whiteboards and other visualization tools

Using visual aid tools such as whiteboards, diagram creation tools, and other means of planning systems will facilitate the requirements capture sessions. Workshop attendees will be able to follow the more complex nuances of business processes through visual cues presented to them either on screen or in a physical workshop session. Depending on the audience, you might encourage the interactive collaboration on a whiteboard or diagram to "*drag and drop*" into place the components that make up a business process.

The following diagram illustrates a typical process diagram that could be used during a whiteboarding exercise to gain an understanding of an approval process:

Example process whiteboarding exercise diagram
Sample project setup and sign-off whiteboard

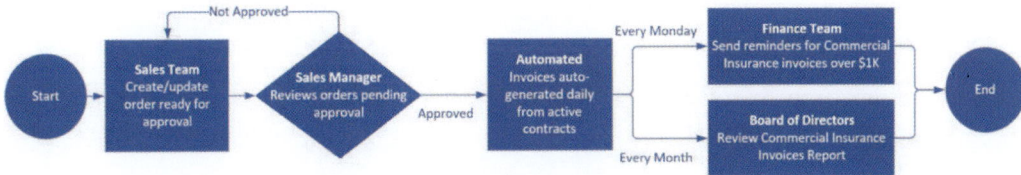

Figure 6.3 – An example process whiteboard diagram

Taking advantage of illustrations and diagrams during the requirements conversation will lead to a deeper understanding of the requirements. Additionally, it will bring everyone who is in attendance up to speed more quickly while keeping everyone on the same page during the requirements capture exercise.

Identifying non-functional requirements

Non-functional requirements concern areas of the solution that do not directly relate to behaviors in the system. The performance of a system is a typical example of non-functional requirements (for example, a portal needs to be able to handle up to 100 concurrent users). These might not be at the forefront of the workshop attendee's minds, who might be focused on the functional aspects of the business processes. However, they do need to be identified and recorded to ensure the system functions as expected.

Recording non-functional requirements

You will want to identify whether any of the following considerations apply to the Power Platform solution:

- **Availability** refers to the uptime expected from the system and any systems redundancy considerations (for example, 99.9% uptime and a maximum of 10 minutes of outage during deployment)

- **Compliance**: refers to the regulatory requirements (for example, GDPR compliance and the data retention requirements)

- **Performance** refers to the metrics for the system's minimum and maximum capacity and throughput (for example, the ability to handle up to 1,000 applications per day and up to 100 concurrent portal users creating new product applications)

- **Privacy**: refers to data privacy considerations (for example, how personal data will be stored, who will have access to personal data, and how long it will be stored for)

- **Recovery time**: refers to how long the system would take to recover in the event of a failure (for example, the system should recover within 30 minutes in the event of an API failure)

- **Security**: is a definition of who will have access to specific data and/or systems along with the level of access (for example, the level of access to customer data for different roles in the organization and access to specific application types).

- **Scalability**: specifies the current and future capacity requirements (for example, the application can handle 100 concurrent staff members, which will increase by an additional 100 staff per year

Non-functional requirements should be recorded as a clear mandate, typically with a measurable metric. An example of a poorly worded requirement is *"Portal users should be able to complete an application quickly."* The statement is ambiguous, and it is impossible to measure compliance accurately. The requirement could be refined in consultation with the customer for a more concrete statement: *"Portal users should be able to complete an application within 2 minutes."* Therefore, this clear requirement can be considered during the design and build stages, setting a clear goal in mind.

Qualifying non-functional requirements

Some non-functional requirements might be out of your control, and you will need to be aware of the constraints and risks they could pose to the solution. System performance is a typical non-functional requirement that might not be fully within your control. A typical example of a demanding requirement is that *"Portal pages must have an average load time under 1 second."* Depending on the use case, delivering a Power Apps portal that offers an average 1-second page load time might not be feasible. You will need to assess whether it is possible to comply with non-functional requirements, analyzing the solution's ability to address dependencies.

Any risks to the project delivery schedule should be raised during the early stages of the project. Early assessment, mitigation, and resolution of the risks associated with non-functional requirements are essential for a smooth Power Platform implementation, and they will prevent the customer from perceiving the solution as defective due to non-compliance with the recorded and implied requirements.

Measuring the compliance of non-functional requirements

Certain non-functional requirements can be measured for compliance. When that is the case, the measurement method should be specified in the requirement itself. A performance-related requirement could be found to be non-compliant if measured from an unexpected source or client type.

An example of a measurable requirement is that *"The average page load time for the Power Apps portal should not exceed 5 seconds when tested on the top 3 browsers (by market share) from load-testing servers located in the organization's corporate datacenter"*.

The requirement is measurable and specifies the way it can be measured. However, you might want to delve deeper into the network routes used by the load-test servers to reconfirm that there are no atypical bottlenecks that would make it difficult or impossible to comply with the requirement (for example, the servers only connect to the internet via a proxy or VPN network that degrades bandwidth or increases latency).

Assessing requirement feasibility

As the sessions progress, you will start to gain an idea of whether the requirements can be implemented using out-of-the-box functionality, or whether customization and additional third-party components will be needed. Some of the requirements might be beyond the bounds of feasibility given the timescales for implementation. You will want to ensure that the requirements are feasible by checking the following:

- You have access to the data that is required by a specific process.

- The implementation of a requirement is within the timescale of the project.

- The requirement falls within the functional scope of Power Platform and its related product capabilities.

Having assessed the requirements and their feasibility, you will want to check whether there is anything that will prevent them from being implemented in a production environment. At the point of requirement capture, you should flag where you see a clear feasibility shortfall or risk to the implementation, opening the discussion to alternative processes that could address the needs of the organization.

Managing conflicting requirements

Throughout the requirements capture sessions, often, you will all find conflicting or overlapping requirements between individual teams and business units within an organization. Your role as a solution architect will be to guide the discussion toward understanding those requirements and helping to define processes that could form a compromise between those conflicting requirements.

You should look to stay away from internal company politics to focus on understanding the requirements and provide solutions that will address most of the organizations' needs. When requirements are conflicting, it is important to identify individuals within the organization with the decision-making power and capacity to choose the best solution for the organization.

Managing exceptions

Typically, organizational processes have a happy or successful path through which normal day-to-day actions occur. While many processes have exceptions, you would not want to focus the requirements capture and resulting design on these exception paths. It is important to be aware of process exceptions early in the design process, as failing to recognize these exception paths will result in additional charges and potential refactoring to the system at a later stage.

An example of one such exception would be the implementation of an identity check in a Power Apps portal. Customers enter personal information into a form and press the submit button to initiate an identity verification integration. Most of the time, customers will either get a pass or fail response from the integration. However, there is the possibility that a technical error such as a network disconnection, transient failure on the integration, or other technical issues will result in an exception (the result is neither pass nor fail).

The following diagram illustrates how a solution architect could perform a cost-benefit analysis for system outage exception management. Two options are presented, as follows:

- The first option relies on the manual processing of the exception.

- The second option automatically falls back to a secondary supplier if an outage occurs.

Having analyzed the benefits of the second option, the impact and frequency of the potential outage, the build costs, and the operational costs, you would then work with the product owners to decide on the solution that is best suited for the organization:

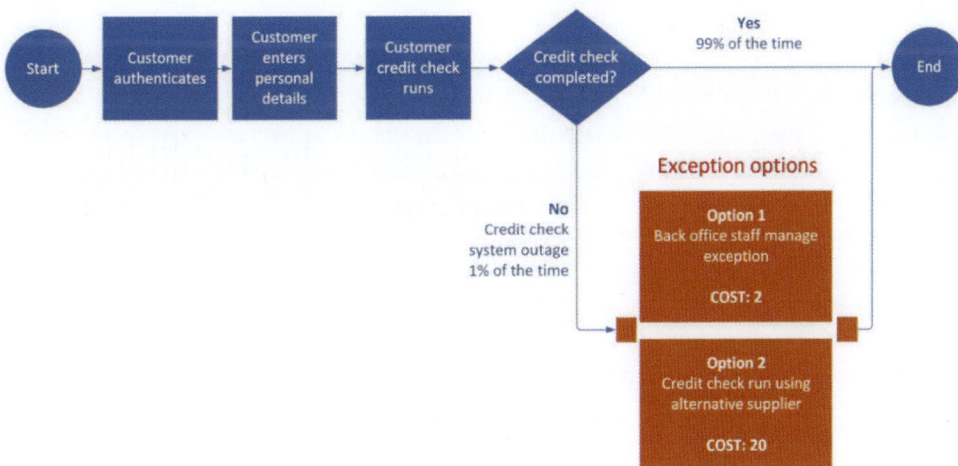

Figure 6.4 – Diagram presenting two options for managing exceptions within a customer onboarding process

Defining a requirement for what should happen in those exception conditions is important so that the user can be alerted accordingly. Additionally, back-office staff members will know what they should do when a technical error occurs. If this scenario is deemed to happen very infrequently, you should guide the requirements to use a training route. The back-office staff could look at these verification errors and perform manual actions to remedy the process. However, suppose the exception is deemed to happen frequently. In that case, a requirement could be defined to perform an automated action in such an event (for example, automatically processing the exception or guiding the user to an alternative route).

Managing exceptions during the requirements capture phase will be a balancing exercise between implementing an airtight solution that covers all eventualities versus the implementation time and cost.

> **Applying the Pillars for Great Architecture – Balancing Decisions**
>
> It is in the exceptions where you can add the most value as a Power Platform solution architect, guiding the requirements to implement a robust system that can recover past transient failures. In the upcoming chapters, we will discuss retry strategies and the orchestration of integration requests to ensure the most resilient process and best possible outcome for the users.

Managing scope creep

Scope creep will happen to any project if left unchecked. The overarching scope of a Power Platform project will be defined during the workshop preparations. You will want to guide the requirements to ensure they are aligned with the overall goals of the project and the workshop agenda. Requirements that deviate from these goals and agendas should be assessed and reviewed with the product owners or project managers to decide whether they should be brought into scope. Additionally, considerations should be made for any increased implementation timescales and project risks.

The requirements capture stage will also show how the project scope will be governed. Depending on the commercial arrangements for the project, a change request process might be applied to bring in a requirement beyond the project's overarching scope. Projects that ignore project governance and allow scope creep to take hold of a project have a low chance of success. You can help define the project governance for the Power Platform implementation by clearly defining and documenting the change request process to be followed, along with a mechanism for enforcing it.

Leveraging requirements capture methodologies and templates

A requirements capture can be carried out through various methodologies. Agile is one of the more popular ones, where requirements are captured using epics and user stories that break the requirements down into manageable chunks. Agile development focuses on the incremental delivery of features and requirements, aimed at providing value earlier in the implementation. The following diagram illustrates how the requirements for a typical Power Platform implementation could be broken down into Agile epics, features, user stories, and tasks:

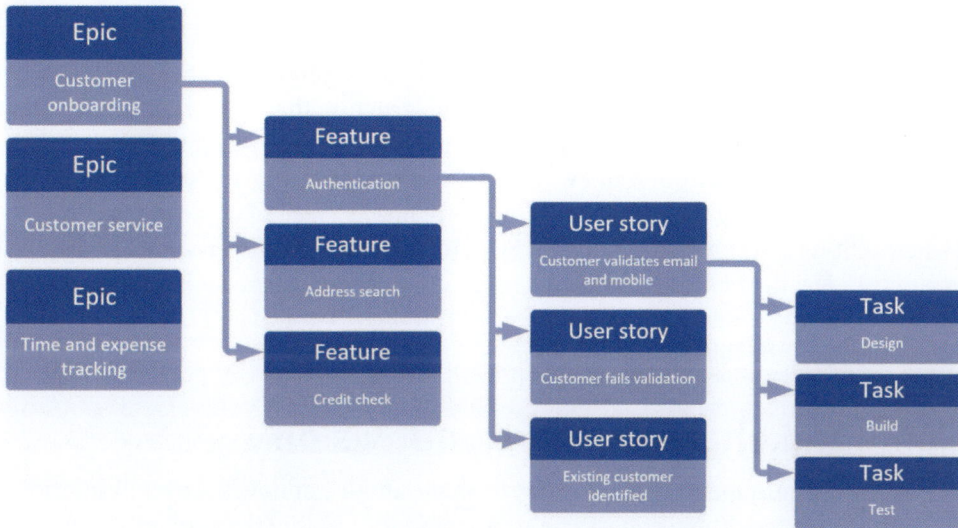

Figure 6.5 – A typical Power Platform implementation using an Agile task management structure

Agile development is a broad and wide topic, worthy of a book on its own, and beyond the scope of this publication. Azure DevOps has embraced Agile development practices (among others), and it is often an essential tool for a Power Platform implementation. Please review the following documentation for additional information on Agile development and Azure DevOps.

Agile Development Reference Documentation

For additional details on Agile development, please refer to the following documentation.

What is Agile?:

```
https://docs.microsoft.com/en-us/devops/plan/what-
is-agile
```

Azure DevOps and Agile:

```
https://docs.microsoft.com/en-us/azure/devops/
boards/work-items/guidance/agile-process-
workflow?view=azure-devops
```

A template will facilitate the consistent recording of the requirements across multiple workshop teams and projects. They provide a solid structure through which requirements can be recorded. However, you will want to foster creativity and open discussions by not enforcing a rigid structural framework for requirements capture. Use templates on a case-by-case basis during the requirements capture phase. Decide on the best method to use, whether it is requirements capture entry onto templated documents, or a freestyle approach using whiteboarding design diagrams and **user experience** (**UX**) mockups. These notes, diagrams, and whiteboard sessions can then be translated into formal requirements once the discussion has taken place.

Helping stakeholders share your vision

As you capture requirements, you will start to shape an idea of how the overall solution could be implemented. Then, you will be responsible for guiding those requirements to make the best use of the Power Platform implementation and its related components. You can then communicate this vision of how the Power Platform implementation addresses business needs and how the organizational business process could be shaped and modeled to leverage the product's capabilities. Following this, you will be ready to stand up for your proposed solution and perspective, communicate this vision to stakeholders and decision-makers, and help them understand how it will enable them to achieve their goals.

Take care to present your vision without appearing condescending or dismissive of their opinions. That is one area where less experienced solution architects may find themselves at odds with their audience, upsetting the status quo, and conveying an attitude that might appear dismissive of the customer's preferences and opinions. Navigate that fine line between listening and conveying your intention to help the business make the most out of the Power Platform capabilities and achieve the best possible outcome for the organization.

Post-requirements capture review and sign-off

Several activities follow the completion of the requirements capture sessions. These are described in the sections that follow.

Reviewing the requirements capture workshop sessions

You will want to review any notes, diagrams, whiteboarding sessions, and collateral information you have gathered during the requirements sessions shortly after their completion, while they are still fresh in your mind. These can then be translated and refined into formal items that are recorded within the requirements document.

At this point, you will also want to distribute any meeting minutes or actions captured during the requirements workshop sessions.

Confirming/re-aligning the requirements to your digital transformation goals

Having collated a requirements document, you will look to review the items recorded to confirm they align with the overall digital transformation goals of the project. Some of the requirements might require adjustment, while others might require further dialogue and clarification if found to be at odds with the aims of the project (see the *Managing conflicting requirements* section for more details). Solution architects review and cross-check the requirements as follows:

1. Check whether the requirement is complete, ensuring that who needs the functionality, what is needed, and why it is needed is understood.

2. If estimates have been offered, review whether they are accurate and feasible, and check whether any revisions are required.

3. Ensure the priorities for the requirements align with the overall organizational goals and needs of the project owners.

4. Check the scope and confirm there are no missing requirements or gaps in the implementation.

5. Check the requirements are aligned to overall business objectives. Make provisions for any identified exceptions.

6. Verify the stakeholders agree with the captured requirements.

7. Check that the roadmap for the next iteration exists and that there is a roadmap for the entire project.

Having confirmed the project goals, you can start planning high-level estimates for the project. This early envisioning of the solution and build estimates could lead to a discussion, a potential replanning exercise, and the proposal to work on a phased approach to benefit from Power Platform capabilities as soon as possible.

Summary

In this chapter, you learned how to prepare requirements gathering sessions, deliver effective workshops, and conclude the phase with a thorough review of the project scope. Effective requirements capture is the key to ensuring the project scope is understood by all, the design is built on a solid foundation, and the Power Platform solution solves the customer's problems.

The next chapter will teach you how to map the customer's requirements to Power Platform and Microsoft cloud-based solution capabilities through fit-gap analysis.

7
Power Platform Fit Gap Analysis

Fit gap analysis is a process that identifies where gaps exist between business or operational requirements and the system capabilities. In this chapter, you will learn how to perform a practical fit gap analysis for our case study at **Inveriance Corps**. You will learn how to align Power Platform capabilities, Dynamics 365, Microsoft 365, and Azure components to organizational requirements. We will also consider AppSource apps and third-party solutions for inclusion.

Power Platform licensing and API limits will be considered during the assessment process. The usage of **Proof of Concepts (POCs)** will be discussed as a means of validating a solution's ability to solve specific requirements. Having identified the optimal solution, you will then learn how to determine the overall scope for the solution, setting the right expectations upfront.

In this chapter, we're going to cover the following main topics:

- Introduction to Power Platform fit gap analysis
- Deep-diving into feasibility analysis
- Best fit analysis deep-dive – aligning Microsoft product capabilities

- Evaluating AppSource, third-party, and custom solutions to meet functional gaps
- Validating solutions through POC implementations
- Determining the overall scope for the solution and setting the right expectations

Fit gap analysis is an integral part of the application life cycle as it provides clarity on the areas of the implementation that will require additional effort to complete. It also highlights the processes that require support from components outside the core Power Platform capabilities.

Introduction to Power Platform fit gap analysis

One key benefit of fit gap analysis is that it is easy to implement, and the results help identify actions needed to address gaps in product capabilities. You will have a better understanding of the effort required to fulfill the business requirements and make informed decisions on the solution that best fits the organizational needs. Based on your findings, you may also propose changes to these requirements. The net result from the fit gap analysis is to maximize the organization's Power Platform investment by aligning the implementation with the native product capabilities.

While performing fit gap analysis on a Power Platform implementation, you will balance the need to fulfill a requirement with the implementation cost and the impact on delivery timescales. The decision triangle in *Figure 7.1* illustrates the decision process. As the scope increases, the costs to implement a requirement and project schedule change accordingly:

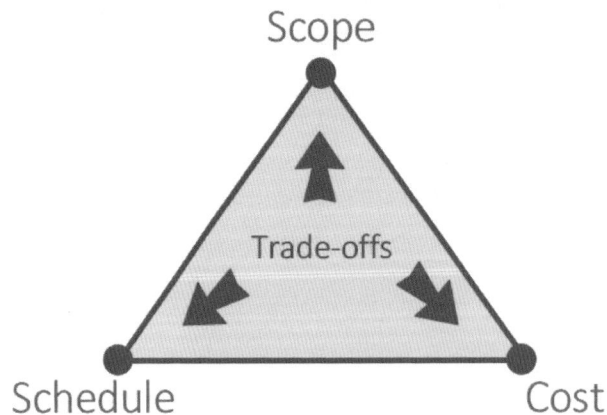

Figure 7.1 – Fit gap analysis decision triangle

You will learn how to match requirements against Microsoft product capabilities, assess whether they are technically feasible, and identify compliance considerations that may impact implementation.

> **Applying the Pillars for Great Architecture – Balancing Decisions**
>
> Running a fit gap analysis on an organization's requirements will provide you with the knowledge to make an informed decision during product selection, configuration, and development cost estimates. You will then be in the unique position of being able to propose a solution that balances all these factors to achieve the best outcome for the organization.

Power Platform fit gap analysis essentials

Fit gap analysis can be carried out with a simple **Excel document** and within **Azure DevOps user stories** or tasks. Whichever tool you use to perform your analysis, you will want to use a consistent set of **fit gap qualification criteria**.

Power Platform implementations have their own considerations when performing a fit gap analysis. As a minimum, you will want to identify the following for each requirement.

Severity of gap

Identifying severity gaps is a crucial part of the fit gap analysis. The severity gap recognizes whether a requirement can be fulfilled using **standard product capabilities** (**Fit**) or whether there is a gap in the Power Platform product capabilities that will require some level of effort to deliver the requirement.

Some projects use the *Partial Gap, Full Gap,* and *No Gap* categories. Solution architects adjust the terminology used depending on specific project needs. Consistency in the gap categories is key. The following screenshot shows a requirement being categorized with gap severities tailored to a typical Power Platform implementation.

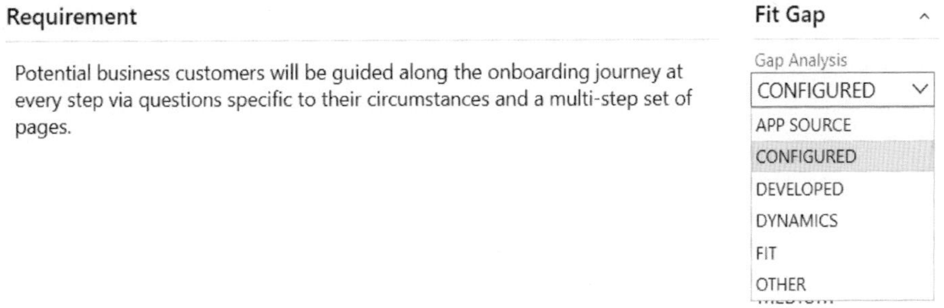

Figure 7.2 – Categorizing the severity of a gap in a Power Platform requirement

The proposed gap categories indicate the level of effort and the implementation route required to fill that gap. A description for each of the proposed gap categories follows:

- **FIT** – The requirement can be fully implemented with the Power Platform components using little or no configuration.

- **CONFIGURED** – The requirement can be implemented by configuring Power Platform components (for example, the creation of tables, forms, and flows for business process automation). The gap can therefore easily be fulfilled without the need for custom development or components outside the Power Platform framework.

- **DEVELOPED** – The requirement is beyond the capabilities available through standard Power Platform configuration and would require the development of a custom component. This will typically involve the development of a Dataverse plugin or workflow using .NET code, **PCF** controls, or Power Apps Portal custom JavaScript code.

- **DYNAMICS** – The requirement is recognized as being a general feature of a Dynamics 365 application. Implementing the functionality using base Power Platform components is not considered a cost-effective endeavor. Once there are enough requirements that match the capabilities provided by Dynamics 365 applications, it is a good indication the project would benefit from using Dynamics 365 as a base platform for the solution.

  Matching requirements to Dynamics 365 applications and industry accelerators is discussed in more detail in the following sections.

- **APP SOURCE** – The requirement does not match the functionality available in Power Platform or Dynamics 365, and custom development is not considered the best option due to the complexity of the functionality, a development skills gap in the team, or ongoing support considerations for a custom solution. Matching requirements to third-party solutions is discussed in more detail in the sections that follow.

The effort required to close the gap

Having identified a gap in the standard product capabilities, you can then proceed to quantify the effort required to fill that gap. Depending on the ways of working used by the project, you may carry out these high-level estimates using t-shirt sizes, agile story points, or other means of estimating effort.

All these approaches will give you an indication of the effort required. Using the same approach consistently within a project makes sure that the estimation method provides a real indication of the effort required, which can then in turn be used during decision making and planning.

The following screenshot illustrates the use of this book's fit gap analysis template to estimate the implementation effort for a requirement using t-shirt sizes.

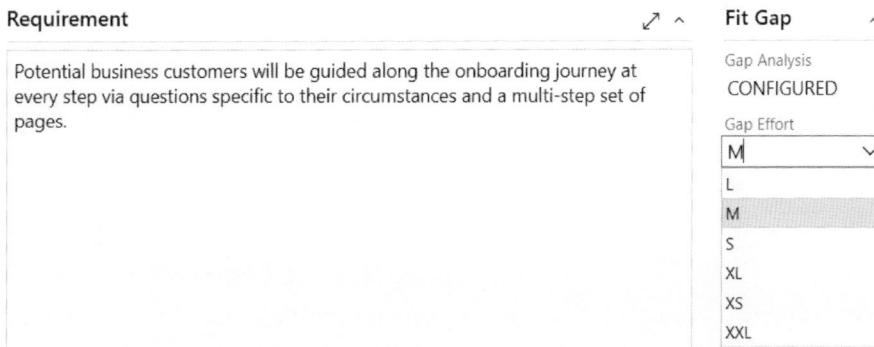

Figure 7.3 – Sizing effort during fit gap analysis

Sizing requirements may be part of a team exercise with functional consultants and developers. It is often beneficial to include team members involved in implementing a requirement during the sizing exercise. It will give you insights into technical areas that may have otherwise been overlooked. You can then make necessary adjustments and size the requirements according to the implementing team's level of expertise and skillsets.

Priority

During the requirement capture sessions, you may have identified priorities for the various requirements. A fit gap analysis session is an opportunity to review or complete the prioritization of requirements. Requirements may be prioritized in several ways, including using *low/medium/high* priorities and numeric priorities ranging from *1 to 10*.

The following screenshot shows how this book's fit gap analysis template is used to prioritize a requirement:

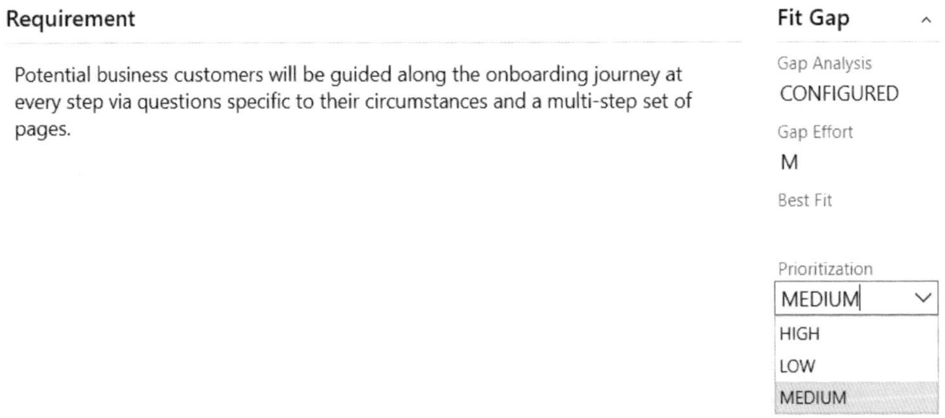

Figure 7.4 – Requirement prioritization during fit gap analysis

Requirement prioritization helps guide the decision-making process. You might consider descoping low-priority requirements with a high implementation effort, requiring custom development, or requiring third-party solutions. In this scenario, the implementation effort and ongoing support overheads may outweigh the benefit a requirement brings to the organization.

Feasibility

During the requirement capture sessions, you will have gained an understanding of whether it is feasible to implement a requirement. During the fit gap analysis, you will re-assess the feasibility of the requirement to identify technical or compliance risks to the implementation.

Requirement feasibility may be recorded in several ways. The following screenshot shows a requirement's feasibility being recorded using this book's fit gap analysis template.

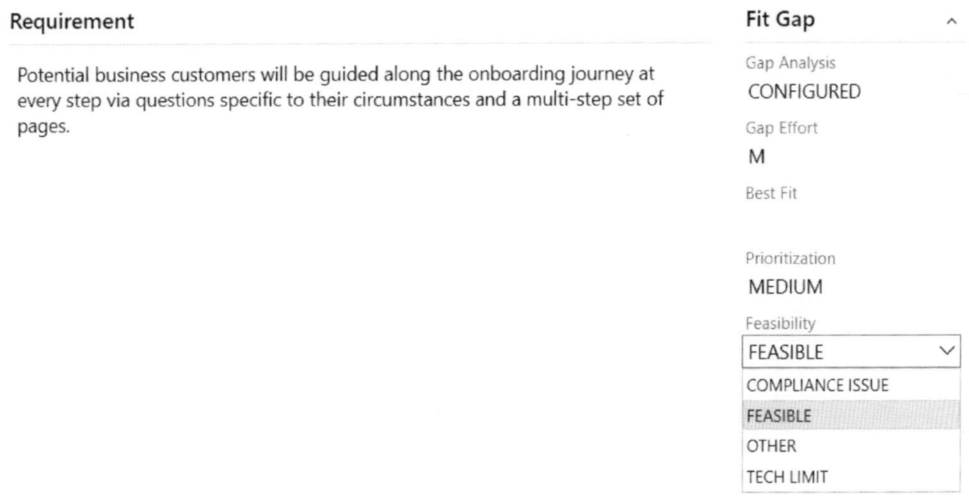

Requirement	Fit Gap	^
Potential business customers will be guided along the onboarding journey at every step via questions specific to their circumstances and a multi-step set of pages.	Gap Analysis CONFIGURED Gap Effort M Best Fit Prioritization MEDIUM Feasibility FEASIBLE ⌄ COMPLIANCE ISSUE FEASIBLE OTHER TECH LIMIT	

Figure 7.5 – Feasibility assessment as part of the fit gap analysis

Feasibility assessments are discussed in more detail in the upcoming fit gap analysis deep-dive sections.

Best fit

This optional step allows you to record the Power Platform component that is best suited to implement a specific requirement. While not necessary, this categorization will provide you and the reader of the fit gap analysis report with an indication of how the requirement could be implemented. This categorization also provides some context as to the sizing and feasibility assessments for the requirement.

It is useful to provide a list of the most used components within Power Platform and any related applications. You would look to adjust the component list to suit your practice's areas of interest if necessary. The following screenshot shows a requirement being categorized as well suited to be implemented as Power Apps Portals using this book's fit gap analysis template.

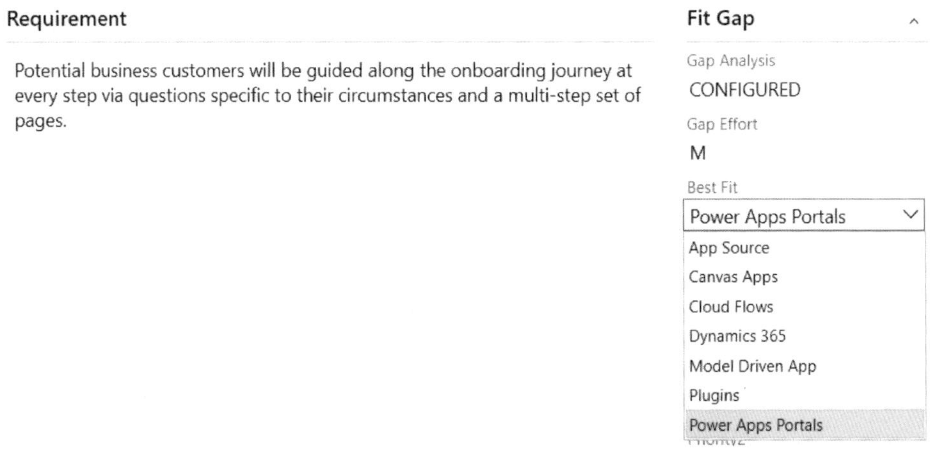

Figure 7.6 – Identifying components that best fit a requirement during fit gap analysis

Some features may require multiple components to be fully implemented. In such scenarios, you would consider identifying the main component to be used and include the additional details in a notes section.

Identifying the components that are best suited to fulfill a requirement will provide the build team members and stakeholders with a concise list of components. This list can then be used for licensing considerations and as an architectural stocktake of the proposed solution.

Notes

A general notes section for each requirement allows you to record additional details or context that may not be otherwise obvious. **Notes** allow you to record recommended implementation strategies, feasibility considerations, reasons why a requirement cannot be implemented, and references to alternative components that could be used to fulfill a requirement gap.

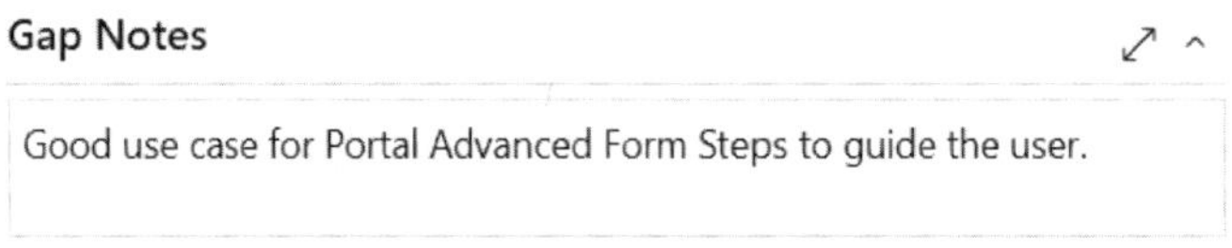

Figure 7.7 – Fit gap analysis notes

Notes become an invaluable resource for context, allowing the reader to *catch up* on the train of thought and constraints that were considered when the fit gap analysis took place.

Fit gap analysis outcome

The completion of a fit gap analysis will result in a report listing the gaps identified for each requirement in the solution and will flag up any feasibility concerns that may have otherwise put a spanner in the works of an otherwise successful implementation. The following screenshot illustrates an example section for a Power Platform fit gap analysis report that uses the templates used in this book.

Title		Gap Analysis	Effort 2	Best Fit	Prioritization	Feasibility	Gap Notes
Agent co-browsing	···	CONFIGURED	M	Model Driven App	LOW	COMPLIANCE ISSUE	Local regulations ...
Customer self servic...	···	FIT	S	Model Driven App	MEDIUM	FEASIBLE	
Portal users will be ...	···	CONFIGURED	M	Power Apps Portals	MEDIUM	FEASIBLE	Good use case for...

Figure 7.8 – Example fit gap analysis output in Azure DevOps

Excel is also an excellent tool for fit gap analysis, and the resulting worksheet may also be imported into Azure DevOps at a later stage.

Requirement	Gap Analysis	Effort	Priority	Feasibility	Best Fit	Notes
Potential business customers will be guided along the onboarding journey at every step, via questions specific to their circusmstances, and a multi-step set of pages.	CONFIGURED	M	MEDIUM	FEASIBLE	Power Apps Portals	Good use case for Portal Web Form Steps.
Customer service staff need to have access to all the data entered by the prospective customers during their onboarding journey.	FIT	S	HIGH	FEASIBLE	Model Driven Apps	
Agents need to be able to support customers throughout the onboarding journey through a co-browsing facility, allowing the agent to view the customer's screen.	APP SOURCE	L	LOW	COMPLIANCE ISSUE	App Source	Local regulations prevent co-browsing in certain countries. Two App Source solutions found.

Figure 7.9 – Example fit gap analysis output in Excel

The following sections deep-dive into the considerations you will need to go through to perform an effective Power Platform fit gap analysis.

Deep-diving into feasibility analysis

One of the key benefits of Power Platform fit gap analysis is being able to identify whether it is feasible to implement the requested features and requirements. As part of the feasibility analysis, you will identify technical limitations or regulatory restrictions. At the same time, you will assess the requirements to identify superfluous or outdated processes that may result in that part of the solution not being used when in production.

We will now work through each of the feasibility considerations one by one.

Will a feature be used?

When reviewing requirements, you will seek to understand whether features will be used when the Power Platform solution is in production. By understanding the need behind a requirement and having oversight of the Power Platform product roadmap and also the organization's plans for the system, you will be in a position to flag up features that may not be required in the long term.

An example could be a requirement that relies solely on a feature soon to be deprecated or a feature that supports a business process that is due to be changed before or shortly after the requirement is put into production.

Identifying features that could potentially fall into the unused pile means you can propose an alternative or simply propose to descope the requirement, thus freeing up resources for other areas of the implementation. Flagging these potentially used features in your fit gap analysis report accordingly will facilitate such discussions with stakeholders.

Is it technically possible to implement a feature?

It is vitally important to identify and flag up requirements and features that may pose technical challenges or implementation hurdles. The earlier these roadblocks are found, the sooner you will be able to mitigate their impact on the project. Furthermore, there will be times when some requirements will simply not be technically feasible with the available product capabilities or time/resource constraints.

During the fit gap analysis, you will use a wide range of technical expertise, combining the following:

- Your knowledge of Power Platform capabilities
- Your implementation team's experience
- The wider Power Platform community
- Microsoft's support framework

Utilizing this pool of knowledge, you will be in a position to categorize a requirement or feature as feasible or otherwise.

At times when an answer is not readily available, you would look to carry out a *spike* into the feature in question. Performing a limited internal POC or testing the product capabilities to gain confidence that a particular component or implementation strategy will fulfill the requirement.

Having completed this exercise, you will then be in a position to categorize the technical feasibility of a requirement.

Are there any processes that have been overlooked?

It is sometimes possible to overlook a business process during the requirement capture and engineering stages. It may not be a process that has been previously identified by the organization but may nonetheless play a part in the Power Platform solution.

While reviewing multiple requirements for feasibility, you may find that, when combined, the individual requirements make up a distinct business process. At that point, you can flag this up and update the business process models accordingly.

Are there any regulatory compliance issues?

Business applications are often subject to regulatory and compliance requirements. Organizations themselves may have internal policies for the processing of personal data. Your role as a solution architect is to work with the organization's teams, with compliance and law experts within the organization, and liaise with external compliance advisors and regulatory bodies where necessary.

The following are some examples of regulatory and compliance constraints that may be imposed on a Power Platform implementation.

- **Data retention policies**: How long should data of different types be stored and/or processed?

- **Privacy policies**: Dictating who can see certain types of data (for example, personal data), and how the data can be accessed.

- **Regulatory requirements**: This may be in the form of industry-specific laws or regulatory requirements (for example, the organization may be required to store customer records for *x* number of years, except when the prospect does not become a customer, requiring the deletion of their data within *x* days).

Working with business analysts and compliance experts within the organization, you will seek to identify these mandated requirements and work with the team to retrospectively incorporate these compliance features if necessary. Finally, you will flag up in the fit gap analysis report the feature that cannot be implemented due to regulatory restrictions and propose alternatives that comply, or arrange to descope the requirement altogether.

Feasibility analysis outcome

The following screenshot illustrates a requirement being classified as having a compliance issue using this book's fit gap analysis template.

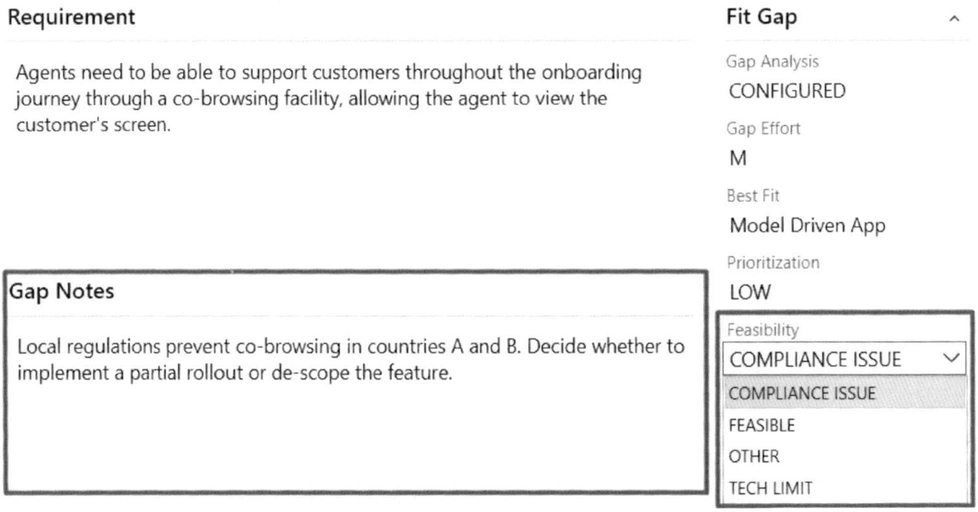

Figure 7.10 – Example feasibility analysis

Having completed a feasibility analysis, you will have a clear picture of the requirements that can be implemented, the ones that are constrained by technical or regulatory limitations, and the ones that should not be implemented as they will not be used in a production environment. You are now in a position to make the necessary recommendations to address any feasibility gaps.

Deep-diving into best fit analysis – matching Microsoft product capabilities

The earlier sections in this chapter discussed the basics of matching up requirements to Power Platform capabilities and the wider Microsoft ecosystem. As a solution architect, you will look to have an understanding of the Power Platform feature sets and the applications and extensions that co-exist within the Dataverse framework.

When matching up a requirement to a product, you will also have a view of the components product roadmap and the organization's long-term plans for the use of the system. You can then select the Power Platform component that best suits the technical requirement and these long-term considerations.

Matching requirements to Power Platform components

As a Power Platform solution architect, you will seek to identify the Power Platform components that are best suited to fulfill a requirement. Through your knowledge of the platform's capabilities, you would look at mapping requirements to the following components:

- Model-driven apps
- Power Apps Portals
- Canvas apps
- Power Automate
- AI Builder
- Power Virtual Agents
- Power BI
- Dataverse

Power Platform provides a highly flexible framework for creating business applications and lends itself to being tailored to particular users' needs. A Power Platform solution is not fixed in scope once applied and can evolve.

Matching requirements to Dynamics 365

Organizational requirements may sometimes steer the implementation toward the realm of Dynamics 365 applications. Knowing the capabilities of each application will help you identify opportunities for expediting the implementation of a business application by leveraging Dynamics 365.

The following applications either share or leverage the same Dataverse framework as standard Power Apps and should be considered for inclusion during your fit gap analysis.

Dynamics 365 application	Best fit when an organization requires the following features and processes
Sales	• Sales-focused processes. • Lead and opportunity management. • Contract and invoice processing.
Customer Service	• Case-management-focused solution. • Agent-leveraged knowledge management. • Manage service management agreements. • Customer self-service portals.
Marketing	• Marketing campaigns and email mailshots. • Organize and publicize events. • Customer surveys. • Marketing event portals.
Field Service	• Service-delivery-focused, typically across geographical locations. • Lead and opportunity management. • Contract and invoice processing. • Scheduling of resources. • Time and expenses tracking and billing.
Project Operations	• Project-delivery-focused. • Lead and opportunity management. • Contract and invoice processing. • Scheduling of resources. • Time and expenses tracking and billing.
Commerce	• Merchandizing products and services. • Manage orders. • Create digital storefronts. • Customer profile and engagement management. • Omnichannel experience.
Customer Insights	• Gain customer insights across multiple sources. • Enrich customer data with third-party sources. • Derive insights from custom or prebuilt AI models. • Unify customer data with operational and IoT data in real time.

Table 7.1 – Third-party solution review checklist

It is important to note that moving from a Power Apps application to Dynamics 365 would require a migration, as there is currently no standard method of converting a Power Platform application into a Dynamics 365 instance. Therefore, the decision to use or not use Dynamics 365 applications as a starting point should carefully consider the current and future organizational requirements. Conversely, if the organization's requirements leverage a small percentage of the features provided by a Dynamics 365 application, you could then consider using Power Platform applications to build the customer's requirements.

> **Further Reading**
>
> Please go to `https://docs.microsoft.com/dynamics365/` for full product documentation on all Dynamics 365 applications.

Matching requirements to industry accelerators

Microsoft, Adobe, and SAP have worked together to create what is known as a Common Data Model, a common language used by industries across the globe to structure data and processes, providing solution providers with pre-built Power Platform and Dynamics 365 applications tailored for specific industry verticals.

Microsoft's offering currently focuses on the following industries:

- Automotive
- Education, including higher education and K–12
- Healthcare
- Media and entertainment
- Nonprofit
- Telecommunications

As you perform your fit gap analysis, you will assess the organization's requirements industry sectors. You may identify opportunities to leverage the industry accelerators to expedite the Power Platform implementation.

> **Further Reading**
>
> Please go to `https://docs.microsoft.com/dynamics365/industry/accelerators/overview/` for detailed information on Microsoft's industry accelerators for Power Platform and Dynamics 365.

Best fit analysis deep-dive – matching AppSource, third-party product capabilities

Microsoft AppSource provides extensions to the standard Power Platform and Dynamics 365 product capabilities. As part of the discovery phase, you will make use of this resource to fill any gaps in Microsoft solution's feature sets.

AppSource components are available for review at `https://appsource.microsoft.com/`.

The proposed rationale behind using an AppSource and third-party component to fulfill organizational requirements is as follows:

- The standard Power Platform functionality does not fulfill a requirement.
- It is not possible to adapt the requirement to match the Power Platform feature set.
- One or more AppSource components exist that fulfill the requirement.
- The AppSource components have been trialed in a POC, demonstrated, and rated internally to confirm their fitness for purpose.
- The vendor has been identified as a company of sufficient repute to satisfy organizational procurement requirements.
- The vendor has confirmed support for future updates of Power Platform.
- The licensing and maintenance costs are aligned with the project's budget.
- The cost/timescales for developing a custom solution to fulfill the requirement are too large, making the AppSource solution a better option.

Following the preceding assessment steps, you will then be in a position to make the most informed decision, selecting the component that best fulfills the project's needs, even if it means developing a custom solution in-house when suitable AppSource or third-party components are not available.

> **A Pillar for Great Architecture – Build and Operation Efficiency**
>
> The decision to use an AppSource component will often have an impact on the overall project implementation time and the ongoing operational efficiency of the production environment. To that end, you will review AppSource solutions to ensure they deliver these benefits. You will quantify the expected build time gains, ongoing costs, and support prospects for AppSource solutions by trialing these components, communicating with the vendor's sales and support channels to ensure the component meets the overall needs of the organization.

You will now work through a typical AppSource component use case scenario.

Case study – matching Inveriance Corp's requirements to AppSource components

Inveriance Corps has stated a requirement for their customer onboarding portal. The requirement is as follows:

> *Back-office agents will be able to offer customers currently browsing on the onboarding portal a co-browsing experience, where the agent can see the customer's browser window contents, allowing them to guide the user through the onboarding application process. The customer may also be able to communicate with the agent via webchat and accept the co-browsing invitation from the agent.*

As part of the third-party assessment process, we proceed to review the solution. The following table lists each of the review steps and the outcome of the review for this particular requirement.

AppSource component assessment		Notes	Result
1	The standard Power Platform functionality does not fulfill a requirement.	No co-browsing is available in the Power Apps portal or related components.	✓
2	It is not possible to adapt the requirement to match the Power Platform feature set.	The requirement is fixed and mandatory.	✓
3	One or more AppSource components exist that fulfill the requirement.	Co-browsing AppSource component "Power Co-browse" identified.	✓
4	The AppSource components have been trialed in a POC, demonstrated, and rated internally to confirm their fitness for purpose.	A vendor demo and a trial solution have been installed, demonstrated, and proven to work as required.	✓
5	The vendor has been identified as a company of sufficient repute to satisfy organizational procurement requirements.	Confirmed with the customer.	✓
6	The vendor has confirmed support for future updates of Power Platform.	Confirmed by the vendor via their online literature.	✓
7	The licensing and maintenance costs are aligned with the project's budget.	Confirmed licensing costs with vendor and customer.	✓
8	The cost/timescales for developing a custom solution to fulfill the requirement are too large, making the AppSource solution a better option.	Developing a co-browsing solution would not be feasible within project timescales.	✓
Outcome: AppSource component is the best option to fulfill the requirement.			

Table 7.2 – Third-party solution review checklist

The outcome of the review process identifies a component titled "Power Co-browse" as the best solution for fulfilling the customer's requirement. The procurement process for the AppSource solution is initiated for inclusion in the build.

Validating solutions through POCs

As you are working through a fit gap analysis, you may find instances where it would be beneficial to implement a POC for a specific area of the solution. You would look to create a POC to achieve one of the following:

- Provide early hands-on access to users, allowing them to try out potential solutions for themselves and confirm a requirement is met.

- Present Power Platform's out-of-the-box capabilities to users to validate that their features solve a specific problem.

- Test whether an implementation strategy is a viable solution for fulfilling a requirement.

- Validate that a third-party component is suitable for incorporation as part of a Power Platform implementation.

- Validate whether integrations or complex feature sets are required, or whether they could be simplified.

POCs provide early glimpses of what the final system might look like, allowing you to validate solutions as a low-risk exercise.

Summary

In this chapter, you have learned how to perform effective Power Platform fit gap analysis. With this knowledge, you can now assess an organization's requirements and make the most informed implementation decisions and recommendations to steer the project to a successful outcome.

In the next chapter, you will deep-dive into the Power Platform design process and explore detailed solution architecture blueprints, component re-use patterns, data migration, and test strategies.

Part 3: Architecting the Power Platform Solution

In this section, you will lead the full design process for our theoretical digital transformation scenario at Invexxa Corps. By the end of the section, you will have completed designs for the solution topology and defined the data model, integrations, and overall security concept. This section contains the following chapters:

- *Chapter 8, Leading the Power Platform Design Process*
- *Chapter 9, Effective Power Platform Data Modeling*
- *Chapter 10, Power Platform Integration Strategies*
- *Chapter 11, Defining Power Platform Security Concepts*

8
Designing the Power Platform Solution

In this chapter, you will learn how to lead the design process using our fictional case study at **Inveriance Corps** and communicate decisions through effective design visualizations. You will create a blueprint that defines the **Solution Architecture**, PowerApps Portals user prototypes, **application life cycle management** (**ALM**) processes, and an automation strategy that leverages Power Automate capabilities. You will learn how to design supportable customizations, component reuse patterns, and data migration strategies. By the end of this chapter, you will be able to group requirements based on user roles or tasks, and design data visualization strategies.

In this chapter, we are going to cover the following topics:

- Defining the Power Platform Solution Architecture topology
- Power Platform detailed design
- Facilitating understanding through descriptive visual designs
- Defining user experience prototypes for customer-facing and internal applications
- Designing data migration strategies
- Defining the application life cycle management process

This chapter emphasizes descriptive and compelling design visualizations for Model-Driven Apps, PowerApps Portals, and Canvas Apps, all of which are a vital part of the implementation as they facilitate understanding of the task at hand for all team members and project stakeholders.

Defining the Power Platform Solution Architecture topology

A **Solution Architecture topology** describes the logical and physical components that make up a Power Platform implementation. During the design process, you will likely ask yourself the question, what is the best software architecture pattern? You would then look at the wide variety of tools and services and options available within the Microsoft ecosystem and find the answer to your initial question. The answer is that there is *no best architectural pattern*. When designing a Power Platform implementation, Solution Architects review the platform as-is, the desired short and long-term goals, and design the architecture that is best suited to fulfill these goals. The design decision process considers technical, commercial, and business constraints, guiding the implementation toward solutions that can be achieved within budget and desired timescales.

The product roadmap and future Power Platform feature upgrades and deprecations are also considered during the design stages. The Solution Architect creates a long-term roadmap for the Power Platform implementation itself.

In this section, you will work through the various considerations and decisions when designing a Power Platform solution, to come up with the best possible design for an organization's specific situation.

Understand the current state

Power Platform solutions are often implemented to complement or replace existing business application architecture and business processes. During the discovery and analysis phases, which were discussed in previous chapters, you will understand the extant systems and processes and how a Power Platform solution is best positioned to add value to the organization. Armed with the information gathered, you would create an architecture topology diagram with just enough detail to facilitate design discussions and draft the proposed Solution Architecture.

As a Solution Architect, you will decide the level of detail to be included in the **topology diagrams** for the as-is architecture, depending on the complexity and the required level of integration of existing systems. The following diagram illustrates a typical as-is architecture topology diagram for an organization looking to transform its bespoke time tracking, customer portal website, and Excel/SQL-based CRM systems:

Current Architecture Topology

CRM, Time Tracking, Invoicing and Customer Portal

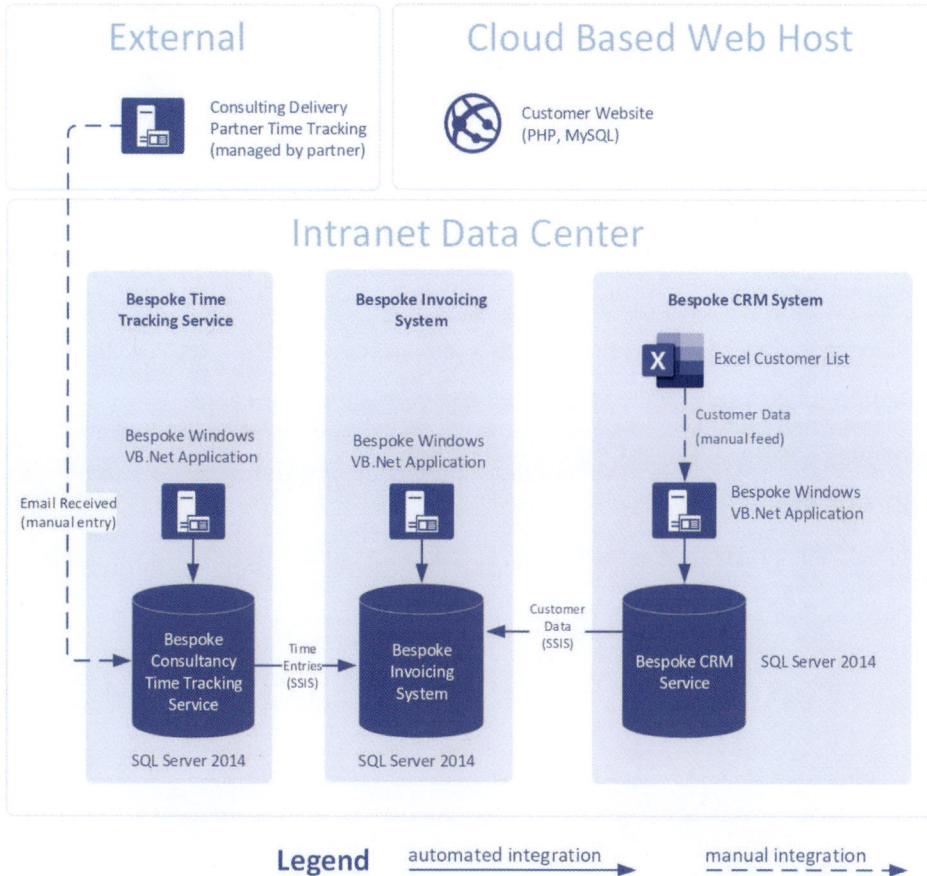

Figure 8.1 – Example as-is architecture topology diagram

The preceding diagram describes the existing CRM, time tracking, and customer portal systems within an organization, illustrating the type of integrations between systems at a high level.

Additional details (for example, network layers and protocols, security, and authentication processes) may be added to the diagram if it would help team members visualize the to-be Solution Architecture. Conversely, a simpler solution diagram (or no diagram at all) would also suffice, depending on the complexity of the implementation.

Considering existing systems, databases, and locations, the as-is architecture diagram helps guide the design decisions for the Power Platform solution.

Understand the to-be state

The discovery, requirements capture, and fit-gap analysis exercises discussed in the previous chapters describe activities that result in a deep understanding of the organization's goals and expectations from a Power Platform solution. These are some of the typical documents and artifacts that will help create a Power Platform Solution Architecture topology:

- Discovery phase documentation, notes, and architectural overview diagrams
- Requirements capture documentation and workshop notes
- Business process models
- Data models
- Fit-gap analysis results

Having reviewed the preceding documentation and collaborated with the organization's stakeholders, SMEs, and system owners, Solution Architects are ideally positioned to design a Power Platform architecture topology that addresses the organization's short and long-term goals.

Considering the project's constraints

Most projects will have explicit or implied constraints, be they financial, technical, or operational. When designing the Solution Architecture topology for an organization, these constraints play a part in the decision process. The project will have specific budgetary and financial constraints that the implementation must adhere to to be accepted by the organization. When defining the Solution Architecture, you would typically take into account the following costs:

- Power Platform licensing
- Dynamics 365 application user licenses
- Power Platform and Azure storage
- Third-party or external component licenses
- Implementation build
- Ongoing support and maintenance
- Other one-off or running costs that may apply

As a Solution Architect, you will prepare a cost calculator that allows the business to make an informed decision regarding any proposed solution's ongoing costs and maintenance overheads. The following figure illustrates a solution cost calculator that's presented to the customer when implementing a Power Platform and Dynamics 365 Sales implementation:

Microsoft Power Platform - Licensing Options Selector

Summary

Model-Driven App users	120	The number of users with full access.
Self Service Portal Users	2,000	The number of users with time-entry access only.
Build costs	€ 48,360 and € 62,868	Estimated costs. Calculated from the build hourly estimates as 8 hour days.
Instances	1 x Production 2 x Sandbox	
Monthly license cost	€ 29,200	Cost of all licenses and Azure components where applicable.

Details

Options for staffing managers, contract managers and general back-office users

Option	Selected?	License	Number of Users	Number of Logins p/m	Cost per License	Monthly License Cost	Est. Design and Build Days	Description
1	Selected	D365 Project Operations Per User	120	-	€ 110.00	###########	60	Full access to Model Driven App capabilities. User can create pitches, perform staffing, project management, and contract management. 250Mb per User.
2		D365 Sales Attach D365 Base SKU Per User	120	-	€ 6.97	€ 836.40	20	This license provides additional storage within Dynamics instances. 250Mb per User.

Options for consultants logging time off requests, and profile self management

Option	Selected?	License	Number of Users	Number of Logins p/m	Cost per License	Monthly License Cost	Est. Design and Build Days	Description
1		Consultants (Limited Team member access)	2000	-	€ 8.00	###########	8	Team Member access to Model Driven app.
2		External Consultants (Power Apps Portal Users)	2000	8000	€ 70.00	€ 5,600.00	18	
3	Selected	Power Apps Per-App Subscription	2000	-	€ 8.00	###########	18	Power Apps Portal access. Users able to log time off requests, manage their own resource profile skills, certifications and skill ratings. Includes mobile access.
4		Internal Consultants (Power Apps Portal Pay as You Go)	2000	-	€ 10.00	###########	18	
5		Consultants (Bespoke Azure Web App)	2000	DEV € 9.49 / TEST € 54.75 / PROD € 73.00 / DEV € 250.00 / TEST € 250.00 / PROD € 250.00 / DEV € 300.00 / TEST € 300.00 / PROD € 300.00		€ 1,787.24	25	Custom Azure web application using Microsoft 365 AD user authentication, allowing the user with the ability to log time entries against projects, and request time off. Hosting pricing is for up to 4000 consultants. Requires ongoing maintenance and support of custom solution.

Figure 8.2 – Example Power Platform solutions options selector spreadsheet

The preceding example worksheet presented the customer with two options for back-office users and five for field resources, allowing the project owners and stakeholders to make an informed decision.

Presenting the customer with several architecture options and the associated licensing and build costs allows the business to select the best solution to fulfill their needs within the project's financial constraints. It also provides transparency and a platform for collaboration with the customer.

While consulting with the organization, you can present the pros and cons of each Solution Architecture option, and help product owners select the best option for their needs. Once an option has been selected, a more detailed architectural blueprint can be created for the Power Platform solution.

Architecture that fits short and long-term objectives

When designing the Solution Architecture topology for a Power Platform project, the Solution Architects take into account the short-term project goals (replacing legacy systems may be a typical example) and the long-term goals (which may include all systems and business processes or a complete overhaul and digital transformation of the organization). The Solution Architecture topology will take two objectives into account, and propose a solution that fulfills both these goals. Let's take a look at these.

> **Pillar for Great Solution Architecture – Balancing Decisions**
>
> The Solution Architected topology you propose will take future goals into account. For example, you may find that short-term goals could be fulfilled with a simple Power Platform model-driven app. However, the long-term goals may be more closely aligned with the Dynamics 365 Sales application.
>
> During the design process, you will delve deeper into the long-term goals to decide whether a Power App, a Dynamics 365 application, or a combination of both, would be the best solution for the business in terms of build complexity, licensing, and maintenance costs. Note that a move from Power Apps to a Dynamics 365 application would typically require a substantial migration effort.

Linking the architectural building blocks

When designing the Solution Architecture topology for a Power Platform implementation, you will consider how components interact with each other and external systems. The discovery and analysis phases of the project will have yielded several useful documents, and the requirements capture phase will have identified systems to be integrated. The Solution Architecture topology will take those systems and integrations into account, and illustrate the connections between the Power Platform and external systems. The following diagram illustrates the interaction between Power Platform components and an external timesheet tracking system:

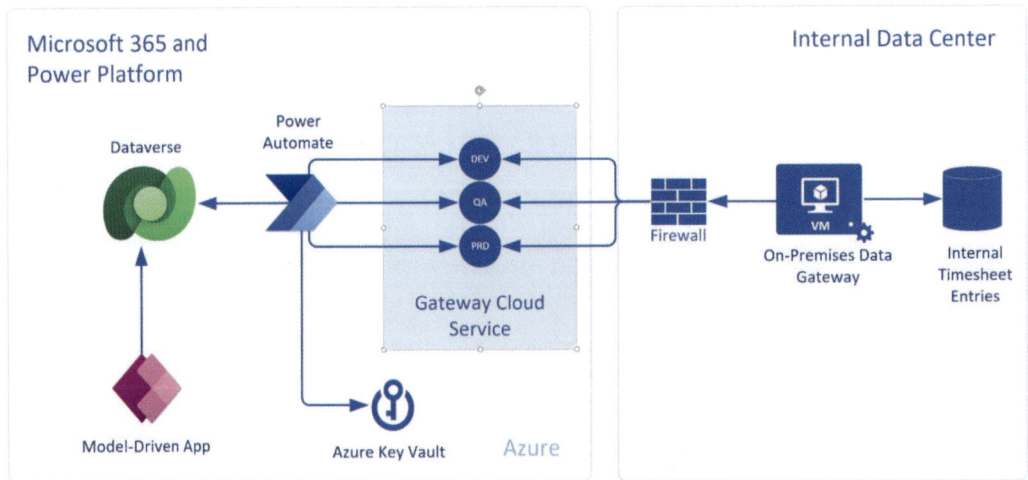

Figure 8.3 – Example Power Platform solutions architecture topology showing interactions

The level of detail in the Solution Architecture topology diagrams will vary, depending on the requirements and complexity of the project. Some projects will also have stringent security directives, which the architecture topology will need to address. As the Power Platform Solution Architect, you will decide on the level of complexity required to illustrate the Solution Architecture topology, including enough detail for the design to be useful as a discussion point with product owners and as a design guide for the implementation team.

Presenting multiple architecture options to facilitate selection

It is often useful to provide an organization with more than one implementation option, allowing product owners to review the pros and cons of each option. An **options selector** listing the various pros and cons is a useful tool for you as the Solution Architect and the customer as the reviewer.

The following diagrams present two options for implementing a Power Platform solution. The first option includes a Model-Driven app as the main component:

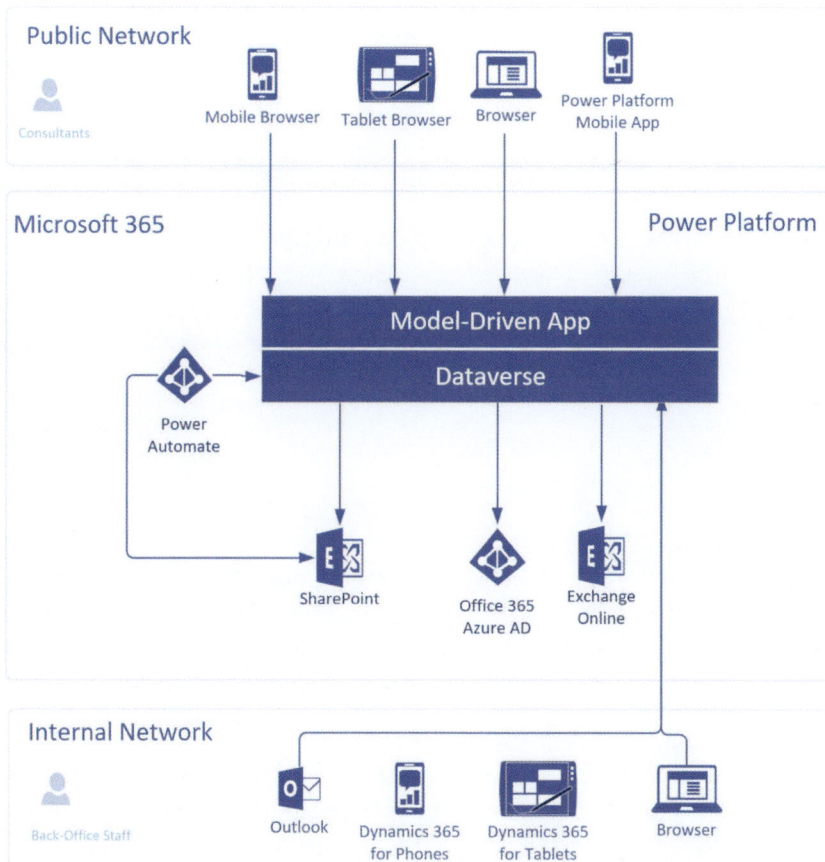

Figure 8.4 – Example solution topology diagram presenting a Model-Driven app-only option

The second diagram presents a solution that includes a Model-Driven App and Power Pages:

Option 2
Model-Driven App + Power Pages

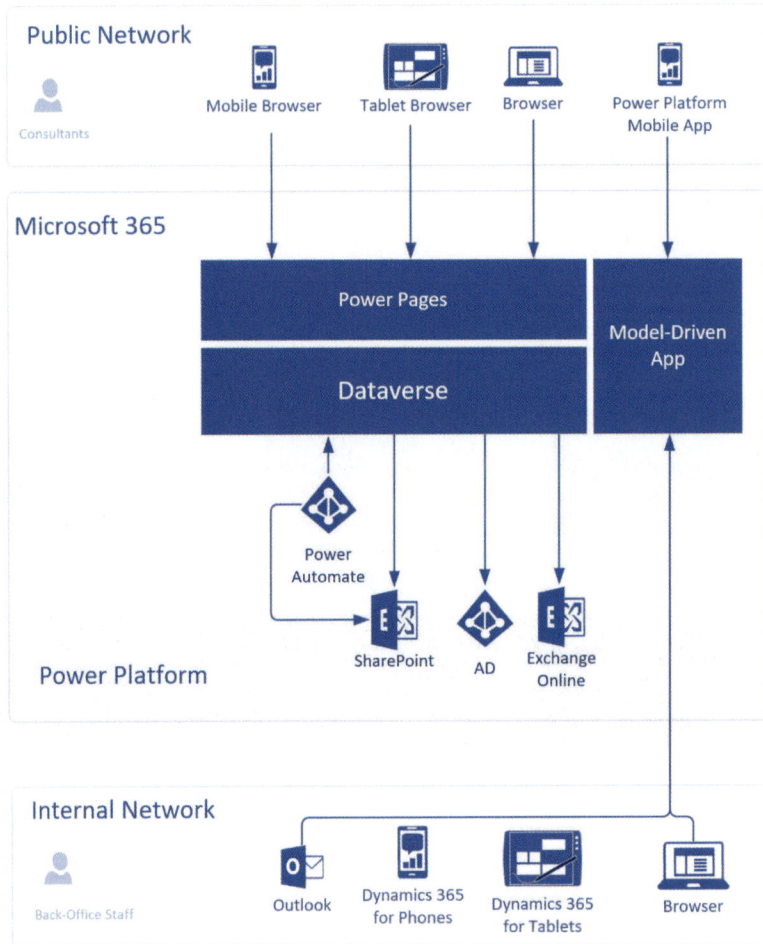

Figure 8.5 – Example solution topology diagram presenting a second option, including a Model-Driven app and Power Pages

Having presented various options and the pros and cons of each, you will be in a position to decide, together with the product owners, on the best option to fulfill the organization's short and long-term goals. The selected option can then be expanded on, and the Solution Architecture topology diagram can be enhanced to include enough detail for the implementation team to use as a blueprint.

Review iterations

While creating the Solution Architecture topology, you will go through several review iterations with the product owners, stakeholders, and other individuals with a vested interest in the Power Platform implementation. These review sessions aim to further refine the Solution Architecture, with each session bringing the design closer to the organization's needs.

Product roadmap

While creating the Solution Architecture topology, you will take into account the product roadmap for Power Platform components, the business applications, and any third-party components being considered. New features are constantly being added to Power Platform, and these are announced in advance for preview before they are available for general availability. As new functionality is introduced, certain features are, at times, deprecated. These deprecations or application end-of-life are also announced. Solution Architects review upcoming features and new applications so that the architecture being created is viable throughout the lifetime of the solution.

> **Reference Documentation**
>
> The following link provides details of upcoming Power Platform releases, Dynamics 365 updates, and product applications:
>
> `https://powerapps.microsoft.com/roadmap/`

Power Platform detailed design

The Solution Architecture topology provides the structure for the Power Platform solution. Once this foundation is in place, you can create a detailed design for the implementation. This section discusses the various patterns, considerations, and ideas for creating detailed Power Platform designs.

Power Apps design patterns

Having decided that you will be using Power Apps for your project, you are presented with several choices. Typically, you will select from one of these three main options:

- **Custom App**: Power Apps can be built from the ground up, using the Dataverse as a base, and extending it to complete the project. Tables, columns, and forms are built to match a wide range of requirements. While Power Apps provide flexibility through a blank canvas approach, the trade-off may be in the implementation time. Building a sales-related Model-Driven application from scratch may take longer than using a base Dynamics 365 application or a partner starter app.

- **Dynamics 365**: Dynamics 365 is, in essence, a Power Apps application that has been built to fulfill specific business needs (for example, customer service, sales, marketing, and more). As a Solution Architect, you will, at times, find using Dynamics 365 applications to be the best solution for the organization in terms of implementation time and technical capabilities.

- **Partner App**: Microsoft partners have created a wide range of Power Platform and Dynamics 365 applications that can be leveraged, expediting the implementation of Power Platform solutions, and providing enhanced capabilities not available with the base Microsoft product. As a Solution Architect, you will know these partner applications or research them during the design process, to identify whether a partner application is the best solution to fulfill a requirement.

Having reviewed your options and selected the one that best suits the project, you can drill down into the implementation details and select the types of Power Apps to be used. The next section discusses the design process for the various Power Platform components.

Dataverse design

Most Power Apps rely on Dataverse for storing and processing configuration and operational data. Canvas Apps often use Dataverse, though not exclusively as they may work off alternative data sources such as SharePoint, Excel, and many more.

When building a Power Apps application, Solution Architects define the tables that hold operational data. An entity-relationship diagram allows all members of the implementation team to work off the same page, and the resulting data structure is more likely to be coherent and maintainable.

When using Dynamics 365, several Dataverse tables are included to support the functionality of the application. When opting for a custom Dataverse model-driven app, the majority of the tables will be created during the implementation phase, as the number of tables included as standard is limited to basic entities such as contacts, accounts, and tasks.

> **Note on Restricted Tables**
>
> Specific tables are restricted, depending on the available product licenses. For example, the Case table requires one of these licenses:
>
> **Dynamics 365 for Customer Service Professional edition**
>
> **Dynamics 365 for Customer Service Enterprise edition**
>
> **Dynamics 365 Customer Engagement plan**
>
> **Dynamics 365 plan**
>
> For further details, please reference `https://docs.microsoft.com/power-apps/maker/data-platform/data-platform-restricted-entities`.

Model-Driven Apps design

Designing **Model-Driven Apps** tends to be a visual exercise. Alongside entity-relationship diagrams, you will be responsible for designing application forms, views, business process flows, and the business process that underpins the application.

Functional consultants and Power Platform developers will rely on your designs to build the solution. Therefore, the designs will become a guiding map through which the implementation team will draw its inspiration and guidance. With a design in place, the project has a higher chance of resulting in a coherent Model-Driven App that is easy to build, use, and maintain.

During the design phase, it may be useful to carry out design workshops, which are an extension of the requirements capture sessions performed earlier in the implementation. These may be informal sessions where stakeholders, product owners, and quite possibly the implementation team are present, collaborating to draft a wireframe for the forms and content users will be presented with.

Interactive design sessions where the Solution Architect or designer collaborates with participants to *drag and drop* forms, sections, and fields are often an expedient way to reach the desired result, which is to create a design that solves the business problems in the best possible way.

Form designs

The following diagram illustrates a typical whiteboard exercise for a Model-Driven App's form design session:

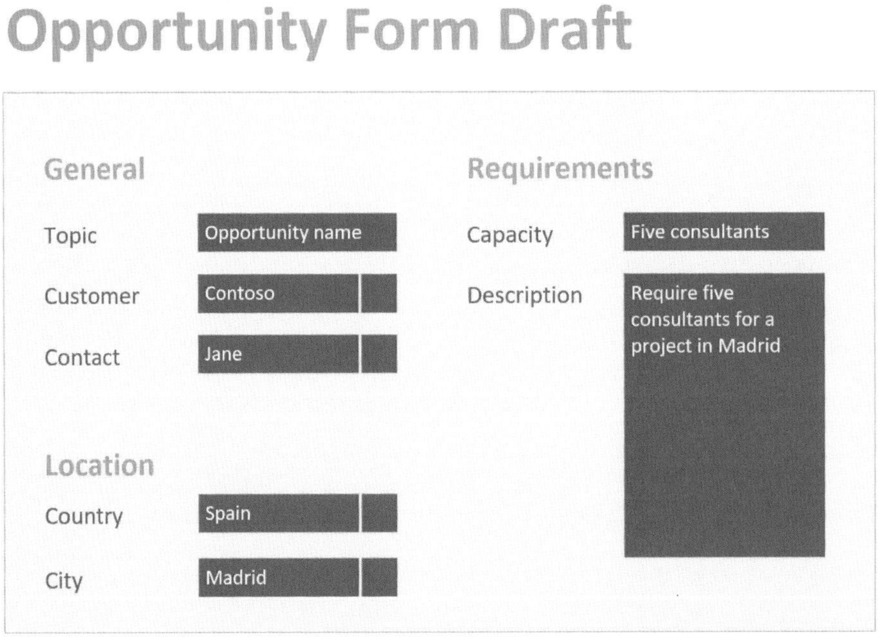

Opportunity Form Draft

General		Requirements	
Topic	Opportunity name	Capacity	Five consultants
Customer	Contoso	Description	Require five consultants for a project in Madrid
Contact	Jane		

Location

Country	Spain
City	Madrid

Figure 8.6 – Example Model-Driven App form design

Form designs go through multiple iterations of change, making simple wireframe diagrams ideal for quick live updates during workshops. Their purpose is to illustrate the form's structure, the fields that will be presented to users, and the type of data that would be entered during the normal use of the form, including sample data so that the viewer can visualize their use of the application.

Dashboard designs

Similar to form design, Model-Driven App dashboards also benefit from simple upfront designs, which may be created during the design workshops. Solution Architects help stakeholders and product owners craft dashboard layouts that contain just enough information for the viewers to understand what the result will allow them to see on those dashboards.

The Solution Architect, in collaboration with the stakeholders and product owners, can quickly adjust the contents, layout, and structure of these dashboards using a graphical design tool.

The implementation team can then use these dashboard designs to build the solution. The following diagram illustrates a simple dashboard design that might be used during an interactive session with the project stakeholders:

Model-Driven App
Dashboard Whiteboarding Diagram

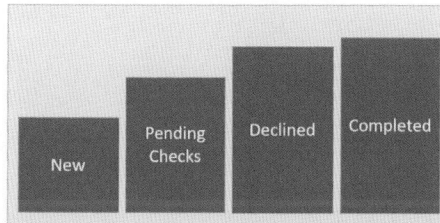

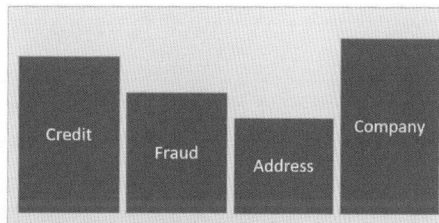

Figure 8.7 – Example Model-Driven App dashboard design

Now let us understand the business process flow designs.

Business process flow designs

Business processes form a key part of Model-Driven Apps. As a Solution Architect, you will review the requirements and process models captured in the earlier sessions and create designs for how these will be implemented within a Power Platform application.

Depending on the implementation, this may take shape in the form of business process flow designs or general process automation processes. The decision to use business process flows will often be driven by the need for users to visualize a multi-stage journey. If the user could benefit from such a view, business process flows are an ideal solution as data is relatively easy to configure.

The following diagram illustrates how a process can be broken down into stages and can be then built into a business process flow:

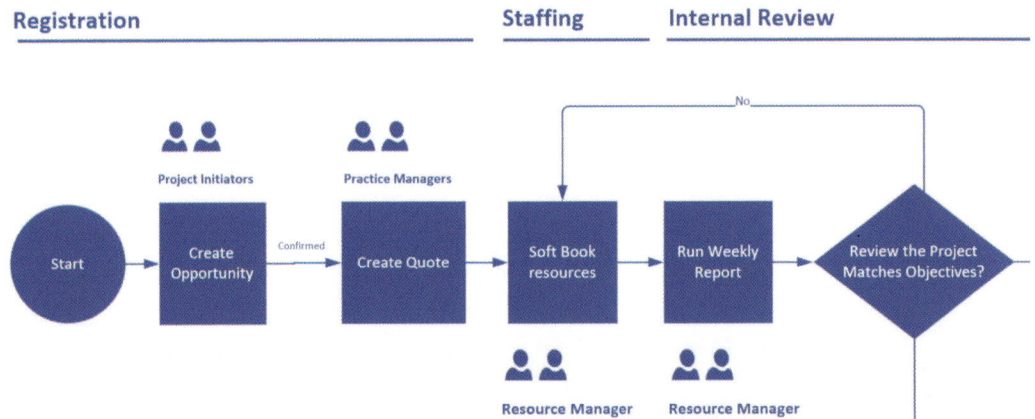

Figure 8.8 – Model-Driven App business process flow design breakdown

Solution Architects work with stakeholders during the design phase to develop the ideal process flows, moving the various tasks, personas, and data points into place. During an interactive session with stakeholders, everyone can agree on the flow of the process and the sequence of events that the system users will follow.

Once agreed, the implementation team can use these design diagrams to build the various processes within the Model-Driven App.

State machine designs

Specific Model-Driven App processes benefit from status management. Depending on the complexity of the process, and the status transitions involved, it may be helpful to create a state model diagram or a state machine design.

Let's see some advantages:

- **State machine diagrams** define the transitions between the statuses of record or overall process, allowing the Solution Architect to visualize the various paths a process may go through.

- Any exceptions that need to be handled as part of the implementation become apparent when visualizing the status flow.

- The state machine diagrams also provide stakeholders with a visual cue for how their data will transition throughout the lifetime of a business process journey.

- State machine diagrams are vital components of any state-driven application. They should be drafted early in the process, feeding into all other Model-Driven App designs as a base status structure.

The following diagram illustrates a state machine diagram for a customer onboarding process:

State Machine Diagram

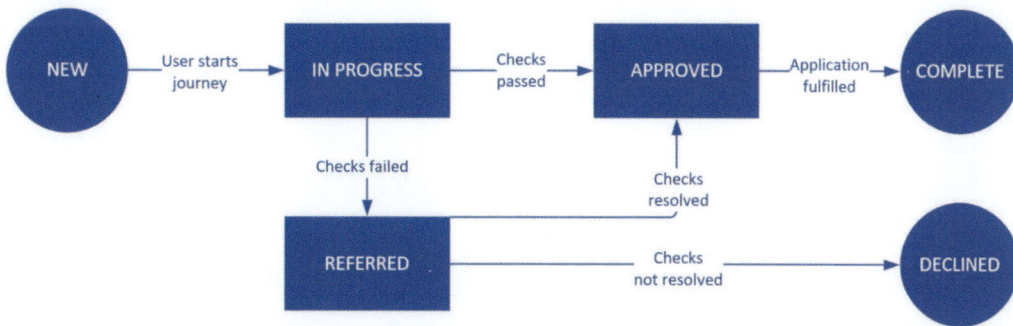

Figure 8.9 – State machine diagram for a customer onboarding journey

The implementation team can then work off the state machine diagrams and build the necessary state transitions, triggers, and automation logic to fulfill the design.

Designing Model-Driven Apps using additional components

When designing Model-Driven Apps, Solution Architects consider additional components that can be leveraged within forms and dashboards.

Canvas Apps may be embedded within Model-Driven App forms to present a rich user interface that would not usually be possible using the standard form components. Therefore, your design will include Canvas Apps where a requirement demands it.

The various designs, artifacts, and documents that are created as part of the Model-Driven App design process can then be used within the implementation tasks. It is often useful to include the designs (or a reference to them) in the implementation team's task management tool. This means that team members can work directly off these designs and create a solution that matches the vision created by the Solution Architect.

Canvas Apps design

During the Canvas App design phase, it is often helpful to create mockups or wireframes of what the users would see and the components they will interact with, so that a non-functional UI prototype can be rapidly developed without opening the editor.

Canvas Apps rely on connectors to interact with data sources and APIs to perform the various tasks a user may carry out on the user interface. As a Solution Architect, you will identify the data sources and connectors that will be used within the application. Power Platform implementations tend to use Dataverse as their primary data source. Therefore, the Canvas App design would include the tables the user would access.

Canvas Apps provide a rich set of logic building blocks that can be used to present users with a user interface that fulfills complex tasks on their behalf. A Solution Architect needs to identify the best location for business logic. Complex business processes are often best kept within the Dataverse and Power Automate layers rather than being built within Canvas Apps. This allows business logic to be reused within other Power Platform applications.

The following diagram illustrates an example UI design where the user interface transitions through three steps, allowing the user to enter information at each stage within a Canvas App:

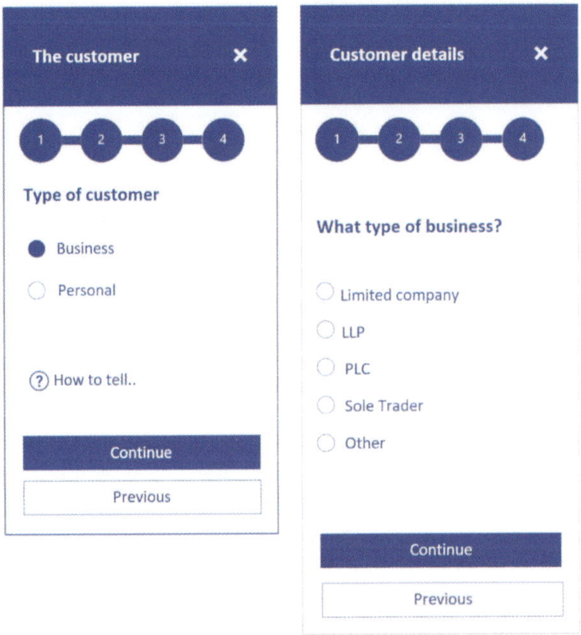

Figure 8.10 – Example Canvas App UI design

Canvas Apps can also be included within Teams channels to provide a rich UI through which users can interact with an application and the data sources that are attached to it. When designing Canvas Apps, you can identify use cases where they may be embedded into the Teams application and create a design for a Canvas App that lends itself to be placed within a messaging tool.

The visual nature of Canvas Apps lends itself to graphical UI and UX design. The diagrams you create during the design sessions with stakeholders can then be used by the implementation team and become the blueprint for the application user interface.

Designing Power Pages (previously known as Power Apps Portals)

When designing **Power Pages** solutions, you will be building design documentation that the implementation team will use. The design documentation needs to be of sufficient detail so that the consultants and developers can proceed with the configuration and development tasks.

Power Pages have multiple implementation paths. From wizard-driven journeys using Advanced Form steps to **single-page applications** (**SPAs**), they provide a base framework for public-facing websites.

Key Portal design considerations

There are three key areas that Solution Architects should consider when designing a Power Pages application:

- **User authentication and security**:

  Users may access Power Pages either in an authenticated or anonymous state. One of the key decisions of a Portal design will be to define whether users will require authentication to access certain application features and the type of authentication that will be used. The authentication method selected will impact the overall design solution and will be carefully chosen at the design stage.

  The authentication options that are available for Power Pages at the time of writing are as follows:
  - **Azure AD (OpenID Connect)**
  - **Azure AD (SAML 2.0)**
  - **Azure AD (WS-Federation)**
  - **Azure AD B2C (OpenID Connect)**
  - **AD FS (SAML 2.0)**

- **AD FS (WS-Federation)**

- **Microsoft (OAuth 2.0)**

- **LinkedIn (OAuth 2.0)**

- **Facebook (OAuth 2.0)**

- **Google(OAuth 2.0)**

- **Twitter(OAuth 2.0)**

- **Local authentication (deprecated)**

> **Reference Documentation**
>
> Please refer to the Power Apps Portal/Power Pages authentication documentation at `https://docs.microsoft.com/en-us/ powerapps/maker/portals/configure/configure- portal-authentication` for more information.

- **User interface:**

Power Pages are graphically driven websites that are configured via their corresponding administration app. Portals may be SPAs or multi-page applications with drill-down lists, multi-step journeys, and more. Whichever option you select, you will want to create a UX wireframe that illustrates the components to be built.

The wireframe designs will also be useful artifacts during stakeholder discussions and uses. Non-technical individuals will be able to understand how the Portal will be built thanks to visual cues in your user experience designs.

The following diagram illustrates an example Portal UX journey:

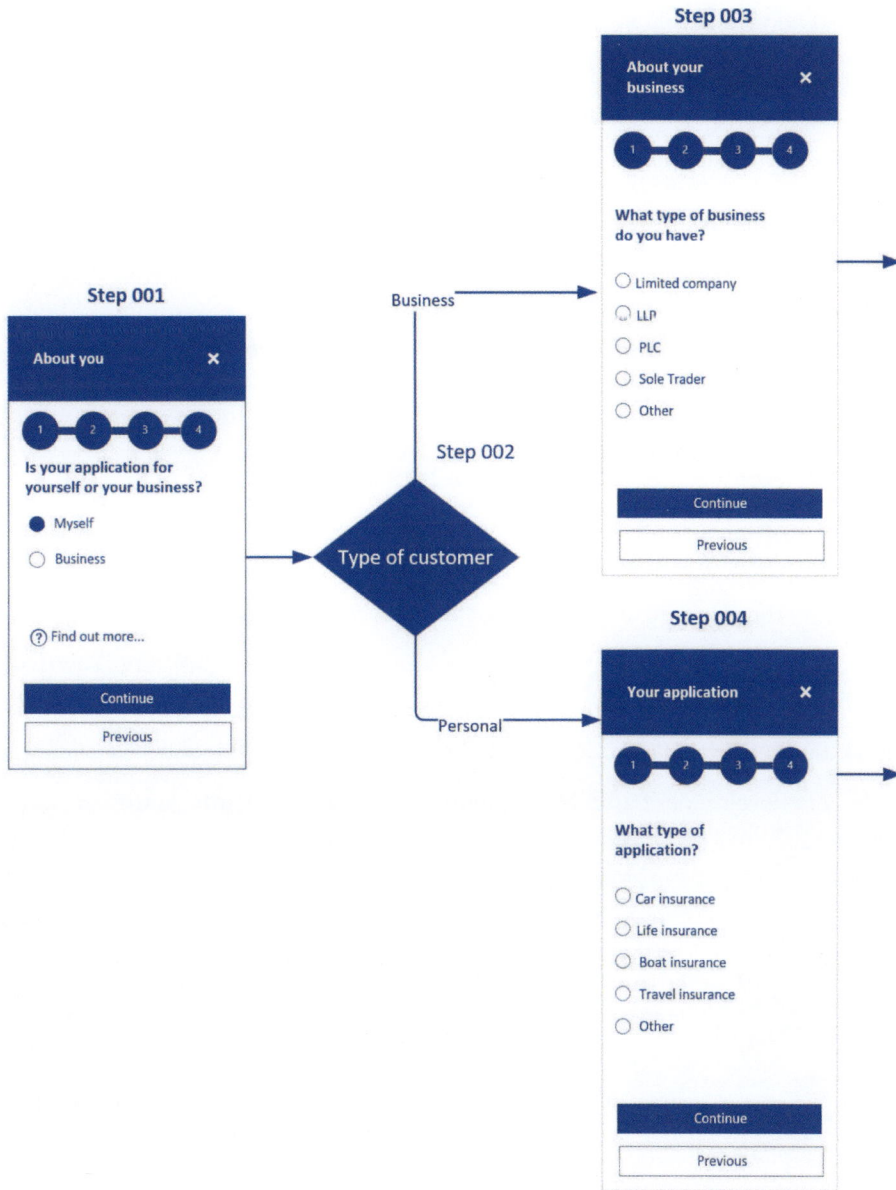

Figure 8.11 – Example Power Pages journey design

- **Portal configuration versus development**:

  Power Pages provide extensive configuration capabilities thanks to their various UI-building tools. Forms are usually built using the same editor as Model-Driven Apps. During the design phase, you will review the requirements and use case scenarios to identify areas that may require custom development. Favoring configured solutions versus custom development expedites implementation and keeps maintenance costs low.

  There are instances where creating coded solutions is the best option. When a portal requires custom development, you will aim to create design and coding guidelines for developers to follow. Portal custom development may be carried out using one or more of the following options.

- **Power Pages custom development options**:

  - **JavaScript**: Client-side code that extends the functionality of forms or pages.
  - **Liquid Templates**: Server-side logic is used to retrieve data from DataVerse and extend the standard Portal page's rendering capabilities.
  - **Power Control Framework**: These are now available within Power Page forms and extend the standard field capabilities.
  - **Dataverse Plugins**: These use the .NET development language.

  Custom development and .NET plugins and **Workflow Code Activities**, in particular, may be considered as options when the standard Portal functionality does not fulfill the project requirements, and the requirements may not be adjusted to work with the out-of-the-box feature set:

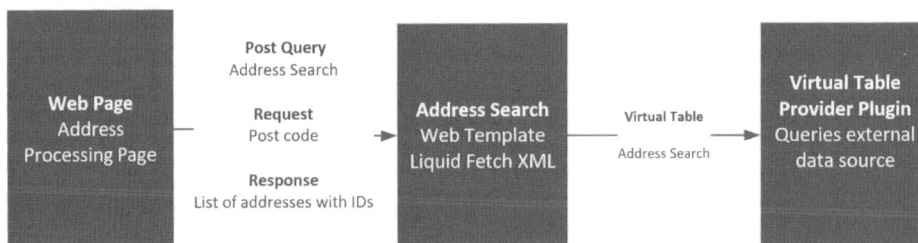

Figure 8.12 – Example Power Pages custom development design – browser to server interaction

The preceding diagram illustrates an example design that includes interaction between the browser, the Portal application servers, and custom plugin components for an address search page.

Roadmap for Canvas and Model-Driven Apps

Canvas Apps, Model-Driven Apps, and Portals have a roadmap of features published regularly. Solution Architects reference the application's roadmap, including features that are coming soon and would be beneficial to the project. Similarly, any capabilities that are due to be deprecated would also be taken into account so that they can be excluded from the design to prevent refactoring and expensive reimplementation in the future.

Reference Documentation

The Power Platform and Dynamics 365 roadmap can be found at `https://powerapps.microsoft.com/roadmap/`.

Power Automate design

Power Automate provides a rich business process automation framework through which consultants create complex business processes via a drag-and-drop user interface. It provides a no-code alternative to custom development.

During the design phase, Solution Architects will concern themselves with the following areas.

Triggers

Cloud Flows use various types of triggers to initiate the execution of business processes. Solution Architects review the requirements and create automation designs that specify the types of triggers that will be used by the implementation team.

The three types of Cloud Flows triggers are as follows:

- **Automated Flows**: The process is triggered by an event such as a Dataverse row being added or an email being received.

- **Instant Flows**: The process is triggered by the user pressing a button on a form.

- **Scheduled Flows**: The process is triggered at a specified frequency (for example, every day at 00:00 hours)

Typical Power Platform Cloud Flows tend to use Dataverse table actions as a trigger, initiating an automation process when a record is created, updated, or deleted, or when a custom action is executed. It is important to define project best practices when Flows are created using trigger settings that are appropriate for the project's needs.

Defining retry strategies and concurrency requirements for Cloud Flow triggers will help result in a consistent implementation across the project's business processes, improve resilience, and reduce unexpected behaviors caused by race conditions.

The Dataverse triggers that are available within Cloud Flows are as follows:

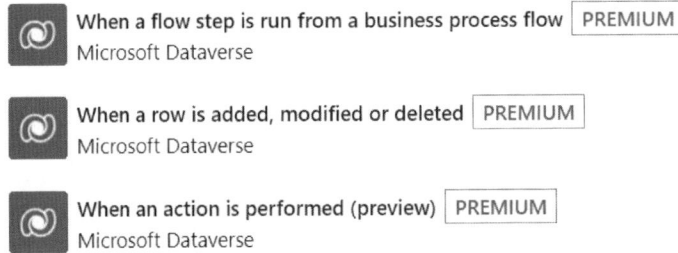

When a flow step is run from a business process flow PREMIUM
Microsoft Dataverse

When a row is added, modified or deleted PREMIUM
Microsoft Dataverse

When an action is performed (preview) PREMIUM
Microsoft Dataverse

Figure 8.13 – Dataverse Cloud Flow triggers

Dataverse triggers default to retrying the execution of a Cloud Flow four times. While this may be sufficient for many applications, there are instances where the execution of a process is critical to the business. In those instances, the retry policy will need to be changed from its default settings, as shown in the following screenshot:

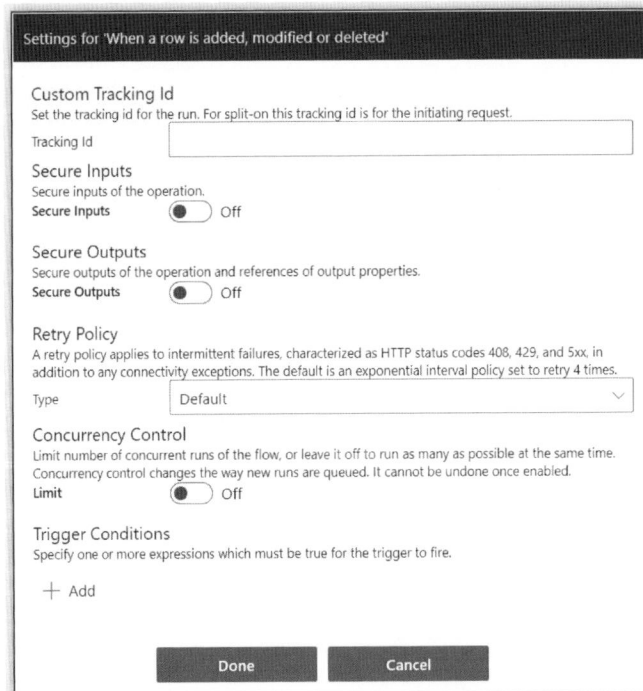

Settings for 'When a row is added, modified or deleted'

Custom Tracking Id
Set the tracking id for the run. For split-on this tracking id is for the initiating request.
Tracking Id

Secure Inputs
Secure inputs of the operation.
Secure Inputs   ● Off

Secure Outputs
Secure outputs of the operation and references of output properties.
Secure Outputs   ● Off

Retry Policy
A retry policy applies to intermittent failures, characterized as HTTP status codes 408, 429, and 5xx, in addition to any connectivity exceptions. The default is an exponential interval policy set to retry 4 times.
Type   Default

Concurrency Control
Limit number of concurrent runs of the flow, or leave it off to run as many as possible at the same time. Concurrency control changes the way new runs are queued. It cannot be undone once enabled.
Limit   ● Off

Trigger Conditions
Specify one or more expressions which must be true for the trigger to fire.
+ Add

Done   Cancel

Figure 8.14 – Default Cloud Flow configuration for Dataverse triggers

Upgrading the **Trigger retry policy** settings for critical processes will help ensure the Cloud Flow is executed when the system is under load (for example, during peak periods of Dataverse API usage).

The following screenshot illustrates a Cloud Flow trigger that's been configured to retry every 30 seconds up to 90 times:

Retry Policy

A retry policy applies to intermittent failures, characterized as HTTP status codes 408, 429, and 5xx, in addition to any connectivity exceptions. The default is an exponential interval policy set to retry 4 times.

Type	Fixed Interval ∨
* Count	90
* Interval ⓘ	PT30S

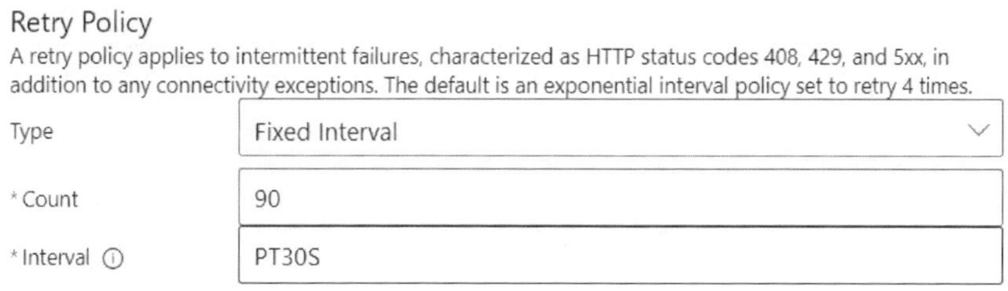

Figure 8.15 – Cloud Flow trigger set to retry every 30 seconds up to 90 times

Under certain circumstances, an exponential trigger retry policy will provide an even more robust Cloud Flow implementation strategy. The policy illustrated in the following screenshot will retry the trigger up to 30 times every 30 seconds, and the retry frequency increases exponentially up to 1 hour:

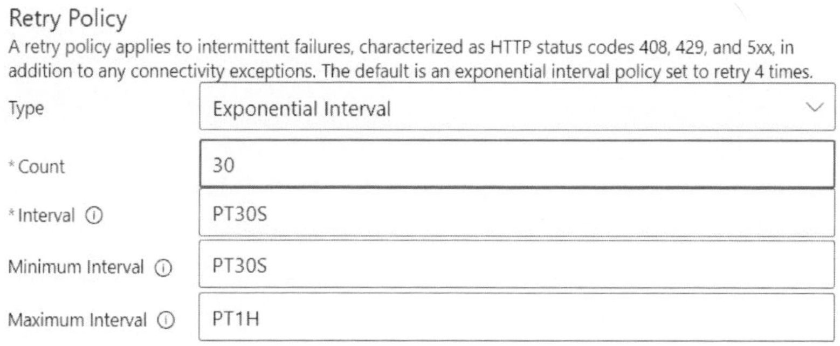

Retry Policy

A retry policy applies to intermittent failures, characterized as HTTP status codes 408, 429, and 5xx, in addition to any connectivity exceptions. The default is an exponential interval policy set to retry 4 times.

Type	Exponential Interval ∨
* Count	30
* Interval ⓘ	PT30S
Minimum Interval ⓘ	PT30S
Maximum Interval ⓘ	PT1H

Figure 8.16 – Cloud Flow trigger set to use an exponential retry policy

In addition to the retry policies, the level of parallelism that's used by Cloud Flows executions may be controlled via the trigger settings. Multiple instances of a Cloud Flow may be triggered in parallel by default. The default setting benefits general automated processes, as parallel processing results in higher execution performance. There are instances where having a Cloud Flow being triggered multiple times in parallel may cause unexpected results.

During the design phase, Solution Architects identify processes that may not be executed multiple times in parallel. A typical example is a potentially long-running process that executes on schedule every 30 minutes. If having multiple instances of the process running at the same time is likely to cause unexpected results due to two processes reading and writing to the same data, the concurrency of the Cloud Flow should be set to 1.

Equally, if there is no benefit to multiple instances of a process running in parallel, changing the Cloud Flow's degree of parallelism to 1 would ensure only one instance may run at any one time. The following screenshot shows the trigger's concurrency control parameter set to run only one instance of a Cloud Flow at a time:

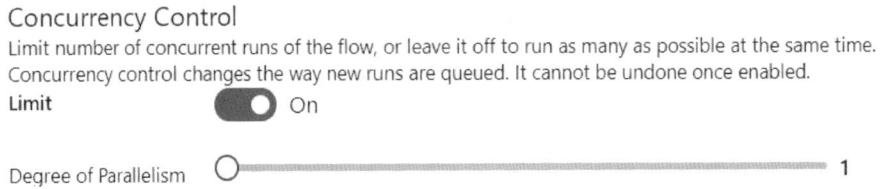

Concurrency Control
Limit number of concurrent runs of the flow, or leave it off to run as many as possible at the same time.
Concurrency control changes the way new runs are queued. It cannot be undone once enabled.

Limit   On

Degree of Parallelism   1

Figure 8.17 – Cloud Flow trigger will run only one instance at a time

Cloud Flows may be triggered by a wide range of events, such as HTTP requests, SharePoint actions, and more. As a Solution Architect, you will identify the best trigger to fulfill a business requirement and create a blueprint for the flows that will be built by the implementation team.

Common actions

Power Automate Cloud Flows have a wide range of actions available. Power Platform Solution Architects are aware of the Dataverse actions available to understand the framework's automation capabilities within the context of Model-Driven Apps, Canvas Apps, and Portals. The Dataverse actions that are available within Cloud Flows at the time of writing are as follows:

Add a new row PREMIUM
Microsoft Dataverse

Relate rows PREMIUM
Microsoft Dataverse

Delete a row PREMIUM
Microsoft Dataverse

Search rows (preview) PREMIUM
Microsoft Dataverse

Download a file or an image PREMIUM
Microsoft Dataverse

Unrelate rows PREMIUM
Microsoft Dataverse

Get a row by ID PREMIUM
Microsoft Dataverse

Update a row PREMIUM
Microsoft Dataverse

List rows PREMIUM
Microsoft Dataverse

Upload a file or an image PREMIUM
Microsoft Dataverse

Perform a bound action PREMIUM
Microsoft Dataverse

Perform a changeset request PREMIUM
Microsoft Dataverse

Perform an unbound action PREMIUM
Microsoft Dataverse

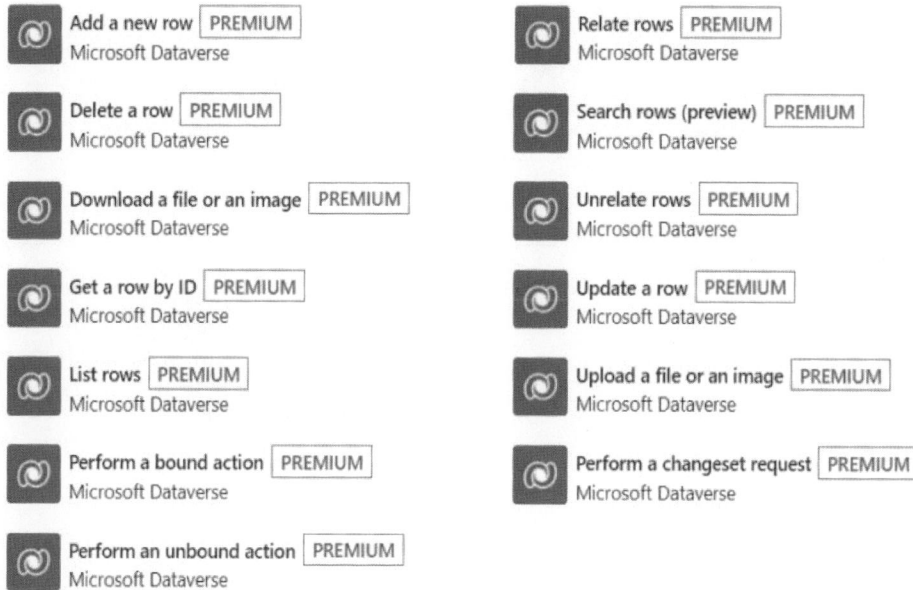

Figure 8.18 – Dataverse actions available within Cloud Flows

Power Platform Solution Architects also consider actions relating to Outlook email notifications and SharePoint document management events in the Power Automate designs.

> **Power Automate Reference Documentation**
>
> For more details on Power Automate's triggers, actions, and capabilities, please go to `https://docs.microsoft.com/power-automate/dataverse/overview`.

Power Automate limits

Power Automate Cloud Flows are bound by API limits. Solution Architects take these limits into account so that the normal function of this solution is unaffected by their enforcement and compliance with purchased capacity.

Power Automate designers are also conscious of the Dataverse API limits when creating Cloud Flows, especially those expected to transact a high number of Dataverse API requests. The Dataverse API has a 5-minute sliding window, within which a user may perform a maximum number of API requests before the calling client is throttled. Power Automate handles throttling responses to a certain extent. However, the Cloud Flow design will need to consider the retry policy on Dataverse actions to ensure the process does not fail under load.

Cloud Flows are subject to three key types of limits:

- **Limits for automated, scheduled, and instant flows**:

  Cloud Flows are subject to several design limits (for example, the maximum number of action steps, variables, and parallel concurrent executions) and operational limits (for example, actions per 5-minute sliding window, content throughput per 5 minutes, and 24 hours).

  Solution Architects are aware of these Power Automate limits and must consider whether Cloud Flows is a suitable solution, depending on whether the projected usage and throughput required from the process falls safely within the limits of the Power Platform framework.

  > **Reference Documentation**
  >
  > For more details on limits for automated, scheduled, and instant flows, please go to `https://docs.microsoft.com/power-automate/limits-and-config`.

- **Request limits and allocations**:

  Cloud Flows consume Power Platform requests on every action they perform, including conditional statements, variable initialization and updates, and other action steps within the Cloud Flow designer, except for the Scope action step. The user request limits vary, depending on the license being used to execute the Cloud Flow. Power Automate's per-flow plan has a much greater number of Power Platform requests allocated per 24-hour period than the Power Platform and Dynamics 365 user licenses.

  During the design phase, Solution Architects will consider how the Cloud Flows will be executed and the most optimal licensing strategy for the processes, and then design accordingly. A Power Automate per-flow license would be suitable for use when a specific Cloud Flow is expected to use a large number of Power Platform requests on a given day.

  Note that Power Platform request consumption is measured at its peaks. For example, if a process uses 10K requests per day, except for the first day of the month, where it uses 100K Power Platform requests, the licensing strategy will have to cater to the peak. In this scenario, the Cloud Flow will require sufficient capacity to consume 100K Power Platform requests per day.

Solution Architects carefully consider the projected Power Platform API request consumption for specific processes and the solution as a whole to preempt high-cost licensing situations. The design will consider the license limits and guide the decision to use the Cloud Flows or an alternative component that, while less configurable, is not bound by the same Power Platform request limits.

> **Reference Documentation**
>
> Please refer to the following documentation for the latest Power Platform license user request limits: `https://docs.microsoft.com/power platform/admin/api-request-limits-allocations`.

- **Service protection API limits**:

  Like any other client communicating with the Dataverse API, Cloud Flows are bound by service protection API limits put in place to safeguard the availability and performance of the platform for all users.

  Of particular interest is the 5-minute sliding window API request limit. Cloud Flows that exceed these limits when communicating with Dataverse will receive a throttling response, and their function will be impacted.

  Solution Architects take care to design a Cloud Flow implementation strategy that considers the projected Dataverse throughput that's expected from normal and peak processing times. The most appropriate solution for a particular task is selected on that basis. For example, suppose a process requires two million records to be imported into Dataverse within 1 hour. In that case, a Cloud Flow will likely be flagged for throttling due to the high volume of API requests and the consumption of Power Platform requests. An alternative solution, such as a bulk data import, may be better suited for the large volume of data to be imported.

  > **Reference Documentation**
  >
  > For more details on service protection API limits, please go to `https://docs.microsoft.com/powerapps/developer/data-platform/api-limits`.

In short, Solution Architects create Cloud Flow designs that carefully consider their usage, the consumption of Power Platform requests, and limit consumption to ensure the normal production usage by Cloud Flows is within the purchased limits.

Monitoring

Power Automate and Cloud Flows include monitoring tools where administrators review failed processes and usage statistics. The Power Platform **Admin Centre** provides an overview of Power Platform usage, as shown in the following screenshot:

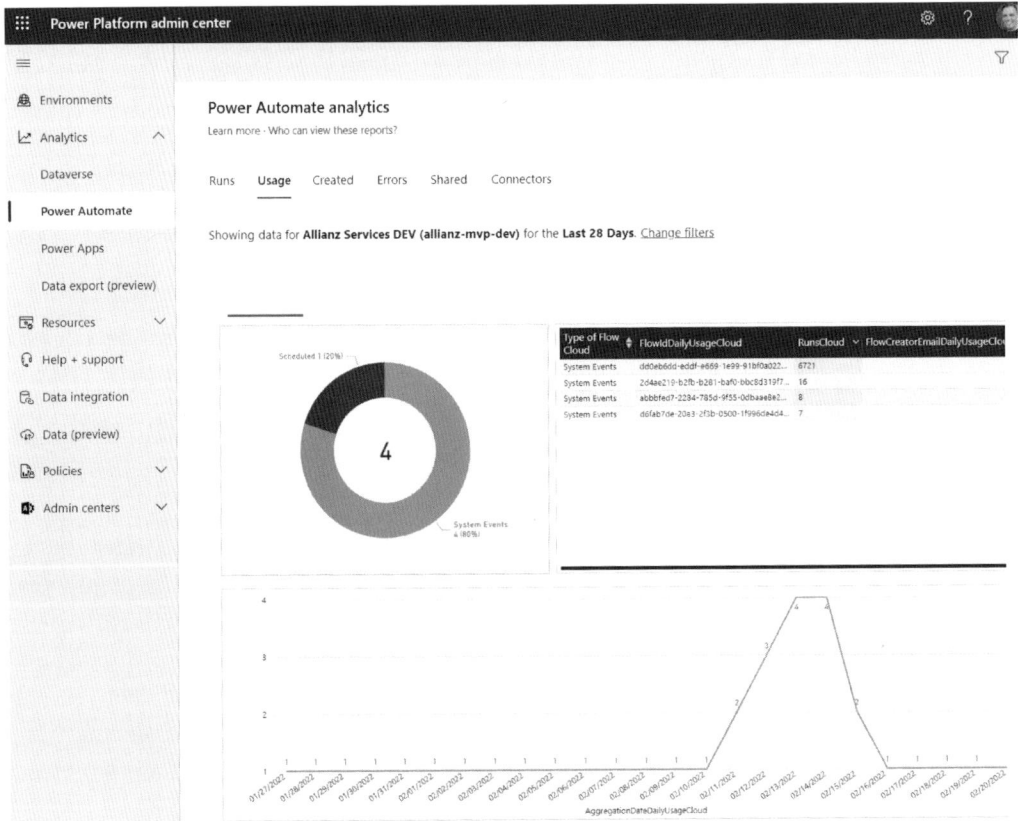

Figure 8.19 – Power Platform analytics overview page

The Power Platform request consumption may be viewed on a per-flow basis via the Cloud Flow analytics page. Solution Architects use this page to review the consumption of requests and make projections on the expected capacity and licensing required for the system to perform in a production environment (and other development and test environments):

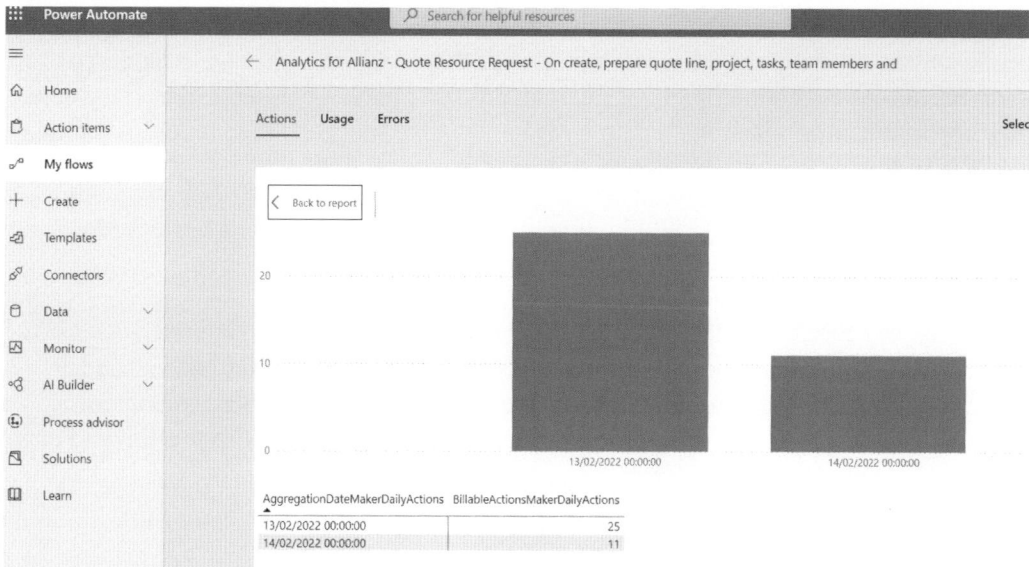

Figure 8.20 – Cloud Flow analytics page

In addition to the built-in Power Platform monitoring tools, day-to-day operations may be facilitated by implementing an error logging strategy. Exceptions during Cloud Flow execution may be caught, recorded, and surfaced within a Model-Driven App dashboard. This kind of logging and monitoring strategy tends to be easier to use than the built-in Power Platform tools and makes the system easier to use and maintain.

Resilience

An optimal Cloud Flow implementation carries out its functions with minimal administration overhead. Solution Architects create designs that include retry strategies that prevent processes from failing unnecessarily when transient exceptions occur. Power Automate includes a built-in retry strategy within many of its actions, specifying the number of retries to carry out when an error occurs and the delay between each retry.

By default, similar to the trigger retry policy mentioned in the earlier sections of this chapter, the default Cloud Flows configuration retries actions up to four times. As a Solution Architect, you will set out the retry strategy for critical actions (for example, if you're attempting to communicate with a critical API, the default policy will be changed to 30 retries every 10 seconds).

Solution Architects design the blueprints for Cloud Flows with exception handling in mind, which may be in the form of a logical path that's followed when an exception or error occurs. An exception handling catch-all process can create log entries in Dataverse, alerting system administrators that an error has occurred and that the process may require remedial action.

Solution Architects aim to design Power Automate processes that are as resilient as possible within the project's technical and commercial constraints.

Business process flow management

Cloud Flows can interact with business process flows that are presented within Model-Driven Apps forms.Auto-progressing to the next stage of a business process is a typical automation task that makes the user's life easier, reduces the scope for user error, and may be implemented using Power Automate.

Conclusion

In this section, you learned about the various items you will need to consider when designing Power Platform applications. You will use these techniques and tools to design solutions that add real value to an organization, are easy to build, and are cost-effective to maintain.

Facilitating understanding through descriptive visual designs

Power Platform solutions are often visual, presenting rich graphical user interfaces to back-office staff and clients. The tools that are used to configure and build Power Platform applications are also often visual. Solution Architects often benefit from using visually descriptive designs to represent a Power Platform solution.

These are some of the benefits of a visual solution design strategy:

- **Brings non-technical users on board**:

   A picture speaks a thousand words. Visual designs give stakeholders and project owners a clear view of how the system will be built, in a format they can understand. Due to this, they are more readily brought on board and are more likely to accept your vision of a Power Platform future.

- **Facilitates presentations and workshops**:

  Visual designs are powerful tools during sessions with stakeholders and users, allowing you to quickly adjust system areas in front of their eyes, which would otherwise take hours or days to change. The visuals facilitate a discussion with the audience and allow you to reach the desired result, capturing a solution that best solves a customer's problem with the fewest iterations.

- **Easy to onboard new team members**:

  Visual designs allow new team members to get up to speed much quicker than having to read lengthy textual documentation. They can also follow your instructions faster, resulting in shorter implementation times.

As a Solution Architect, you will seek to use the visual design diagrams illustrated in the earlier sections of this chapter to boost the design sessions and implementation phase's productivity.

Defining user experience prototypes for customer-facing and internal applications

Power Platform implementations with substantial customer-facing user interfaces benefit significantly from early **user experience (UX)** prototypes, allowing stakeholders and potential users to try out an application before it is built. This activity has various benefits.

Benefits of UX prototypes

Let's look at some of the benefits of the UX prototypes:

- **An early trial of the application's UX**:

  Creating a UX prototype takes much less time than building a Power Platform application. Users that try out a mocked-up application version using a UX prototype can provide crucial feedback early on in the project that may change the course of the implementation for the better.

- **Reduces implementation costs**:

  The ability to review an application with user feedback reduces overall implementation costs, as the solution is steered toward a successful outcome early on. The number of build interactions and releases is reduced.

Leveraging the design strategies and visualizations presented in the earlier sections of this chapter will help an organization and implementation teams by providing a set of *living documents* that are easy to understand and update. They, in turn, will be able to implement the solutions described in the design documentation more effectively and yield a better solution in a shorter time.

Designing data migration strategies

A migration strategy provides a clear understanding of the activities, steps, and impact of moving from one system to another. Solution Architects design migration strategies by considering the following factors:

- The volume of data to be migrated

- The structure and format of the data to be migrated

- The route to access the source data

- The destination for the data

- The level of data processing required by the data

- The impact of potential API throttling

- The production downtime required

In *Chapter 3, Discovery and Initial Solution Planning*, high-level migration estimates and efforts were discussed. This section expands on this preliminary analysis to flesh out the complete migration strategy for a Power Platform implementation.

When designing a migration strategy, Solution Architects consider the capabilities that are available within the Power Platform feature set, which include the following:

- Data Flows

- Power Automate

- Excel imports

Each of these tools provides varying throughput capabilities and lends itself to different use cases. As a Solution Architect, you will select the most appropriate data migration route.

> **Note**
>
> While several third-party tools are available that import data into Dataverse, for conciseness, we will consider the toolset that's available within the Power Platform framework within this book.

Having reviewed the factors in migrating a solution, the resulting analysis may be consolidated in a migration strategy summary. The following table provides an example migration strategy analysis that's designed to move case management data from legacy systems onto Dataverse for use within a Model-Driven App:

Migrate From	Migrate To	Strategy
Dynamics CRM 2013 on-premise, Access database, Excel	Dataverse and Model-Driven App	A phased migration, one business unit at a time, using Data Flows and/or Power Automate, and manual imports into Dataverse
Sizing		
Volume	1,000 records	M
Structure and format	In hierarchical data, each business unit has a different format and source type	L
Access to source	Accessible offline	S
Processing required	Normalization into a consolidated product catalog	L
Throttling considerations	Low volume	S
Production downtime considerations	No downtime expected	S
Overall Sizing		
A low-risk migration that can be carried out using offline data		L

Table 8.1 – Example data migration strategy for case management data

Once the data migration factors are understood, you can design a detailed data migration strategy.

Defining the application life cycle management process

Application life cycle management (**ALM**), which was introduced earlier in this book, is a set of disciplines through which Power Platform projects can be defined, implemented, deployed, and operated through a controlled framework. Solution Architects define ALM processes for a Power Platform implementation, enabling the orchestration of project tasks, build activities, testing, deployment, and implementation review.

The following diagram illustrates the activities and areas that are covered by Power Platform ALM:

Figure 8.21 – Power Platform ALM

An effective Power Platform ALM strategy can be created by following these steps:

1. **Plan an environment strategy:**

    Typical Power Platform implementations benefit from having a minimum of three environments: a development environment, a test or QA environment, and a production environment. The use of a pre-production environment should be considered for mission-critical services.

2. **Set up an Azure DevOps project:**

    This will be the base of operations for your Power Platform implementation. It is where the requirements, tasks, and issues will be managed and distributed across the team members.

    This will also be the home of the source control repositories. As part of the initial source control setup, Solution Architects define the branching strategy and pull request process (for Git-based source control) for the team members to use.

3. **Create a Power Platform solution and publisher:**

    As a Solution Architect, you will be well-positioned to define the Power Platform solution strategy that the team members will use. As a minimum, the project will use a base solution, where the configurations and customizations will be placed. Additional apps and flows may be stored within the solution for later deployment to the test and production environments.

4. **Create a development export pipeline:**

    This will be the Azure DevOps pipeline that will extract the Power Platform solution from the development environment and place it in source control for later deployment. Automated tests may also be included in the pipeline tasks to ensure the health of the solution before its release.

5. **Build the Power Platform solution:**

    This is where the actual project implementation takes place – that is, the configuration of Dataverse, Model-Driven Apps, Canvas Apps, Flows, and plugins. All these activities result in components that are added to the Power Platform solution.

6. **Create a deployment pipeline**:

   The deployment pipeline takes the solutions and data that have been exported from the development environment and imports them into the target environments. This may be either an automated process or manually triggered on-demand, depending on the release strategy you decide for the project.

7. **Grant access to users**:

   Once the solution has been deployed, the final step is to assign licenses and security roles to the users.

With the Power Platform ALM process in place and in full swing, the project is in a good position to deliver the solution.

Summary

In this chapter, you learned how to create a Power Platform Solution Architecture topology that reflects the organization's business needs. You have gained a thorough understanding of the various items you should consider when designing Power Platform components and the benefits of visual design.

In the next chapter, you will learn how to translate complex business requirements to visual data models, design extensible Power Platform ERD diagrams, and define core reference data models. You will also learn about factors to consider when integrating with or exporting external data.

9

Effective Power Platform Data Modeling

A solid data model is critical for successfully implementing a Power Platform solution. Data models are the foundation for the business logic and the user interface through which staff and clients interact with the system.

In this chapter, you will learn how to create highly visual designs that translate complex business requirements into a model that helps the organization build a solid foundation for the implementation of Power Platform applications. You will learn how to decide when to integrate with external data and when to import it into Dataverse. By the end of this chapter, you will understand the decision-making process behind creating custom tables, selecting data types, and creating reference data used by Power Platform applications.

In this chapter, we are going to cover the following topics:

- Translating complex business requirements into visual data models
- Deciding factors for integrating or importing external data sources
- Defining extensible Power Platform data models
- Optimal reference and configuration data modeling strategies

- Establishing table relationships and cascade behaviors
- Power Platform data modeling best practices

Data modeling designs provide a view of the Dataverse table structures, **Data Lake Storage**, and other external data sources. Effective data modeling is a crucial step in a Power Platform project, as it defines the flow and storage of data that guides the overall application design.

Translating complex business requirements into visual data models

Multiple modeling strategies and methods can be used in data models. Typical modeling notations include **Crow's Foot, UML, Chen's**, and **IDEF1X**. This book will focus on general considerations when creating data models rather than on specific notation characteristics.

When creating data models for Power Platform implementations, solution architects aim to create a view of the data from different perspectives. The readers understand how the components work together and help consultants build cohesive Power Platform implementations.

In this section, we will focus on the following types of data models and diagrams:

- Logical data models
- Object diagrams
- Physical data models

Creating logical data models

Logical data models are often drafted during the discovery phase. They are high-level visual representations of the data that are used by the Power Platform implementation. Logical models may not necessarily correspond to physical tables within the system. They represent a high-level view of how the data items are stored and interact with each other.

When creating logical data models, solution architects typically use business names and terms relatable to stakeholders. These logical data models are useful discussion tools in workshops and other interactive sessions.

The following diagram illustrates a sample logical data model for a customer onboarding application:

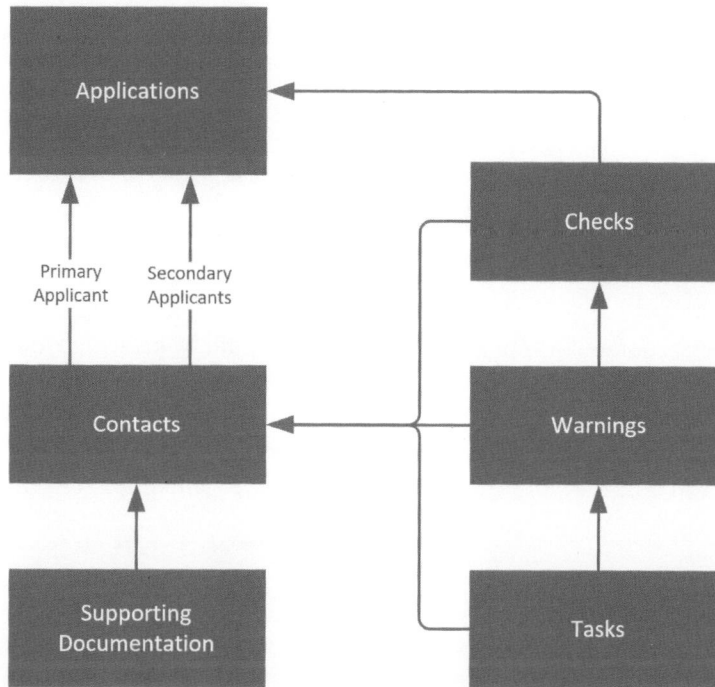

Figure 9.1 – Logical data model of an onboarding application

The preceding diagram describes a system whose primary purpose is to record application records for new customers (contacts). The customers will be required to submit supporting documentation and undergo several checks. These checks may result in warnings being flagged up that generate tasks for the back-office staff to review.

The purpose of logical data models is to include just enough information to illustrate the data structure and its usage using business terms, without burdening the reader with technical details. Depending on the size and complexity of the implementation, solution architects may create multiple logical models that focus on different areas of the implementation. As a solution architect, you will choose between creating individual diagrams that focus on specific business areas, versus a single diagram encompassing the entire solution.

Logical data models are often complemented by object diagrams, which are the subject of the next section.

Creating object diagrams to facilitate understanding and discussions

Object diagrams present an additional view of the data of the Power Platform data model. These diagrams are often easier to read and understand than physical and logical data models, as they illustrate complex subjects using relatable examples.

Solution architects create object diagrams to validate assumptions and theories regarding the required data structures. These object diagrams are often drafted during whiteboarding sessions together with domain experts. Objects and the relationships between them are adjusted to find the most optimal solution for the application data.

Data illustrations

Data illustrations containing actual sample data, as it would be presented to the users, are often useful during discussions with stakeholders and product owners. The following diagram illustrates a data structure for a customer onboarding application made up of sample records and their relationships. The diagram aims to provide a visual aid to help the viewer understand how the various data points would tie together in a real-life scenario:

Sample Data Structure

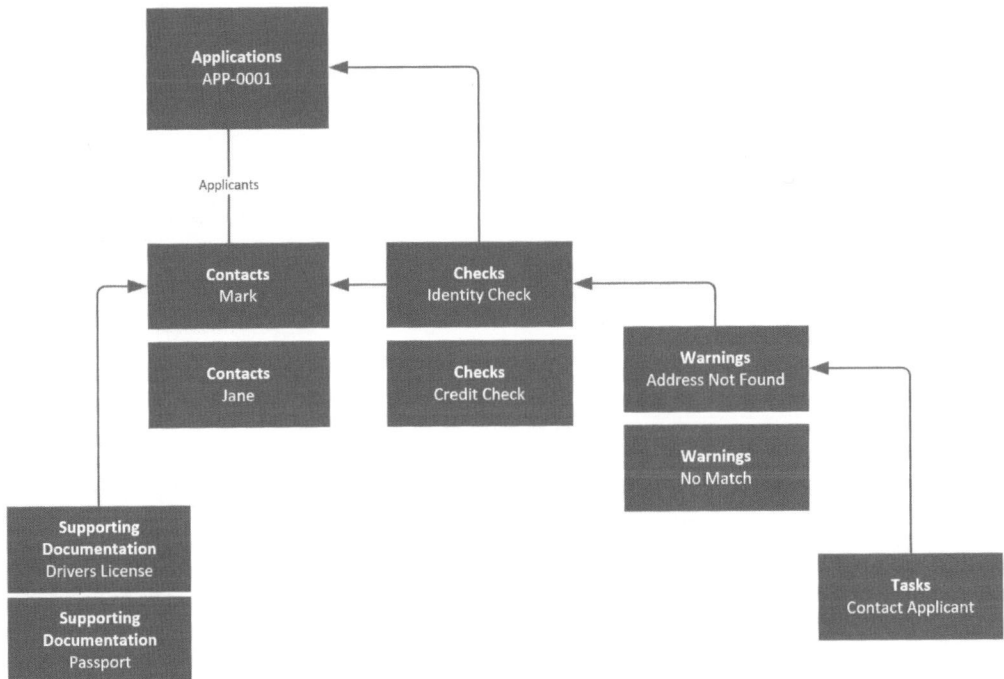

Figure 9.2 – Object diagram for onboarding an application

The preceding diagram shows how a customer (contact), having submitted an application, has triggered a set of validation checks, and several warnings and work items being raised for the back-office staff to address. The object diagram presents a real-life scenario for how the data is made up, leading to a better understanding and improved design decisions. Using object data models helps identify missing data items and exceptions early in the design process.

Timeline-based data models

Timeline-based data models illustrate the way data transforms at specific points in the business process. The following diagram presents the timeline for a customer onboarding process, with tables populated with additional data as the journey progresses:

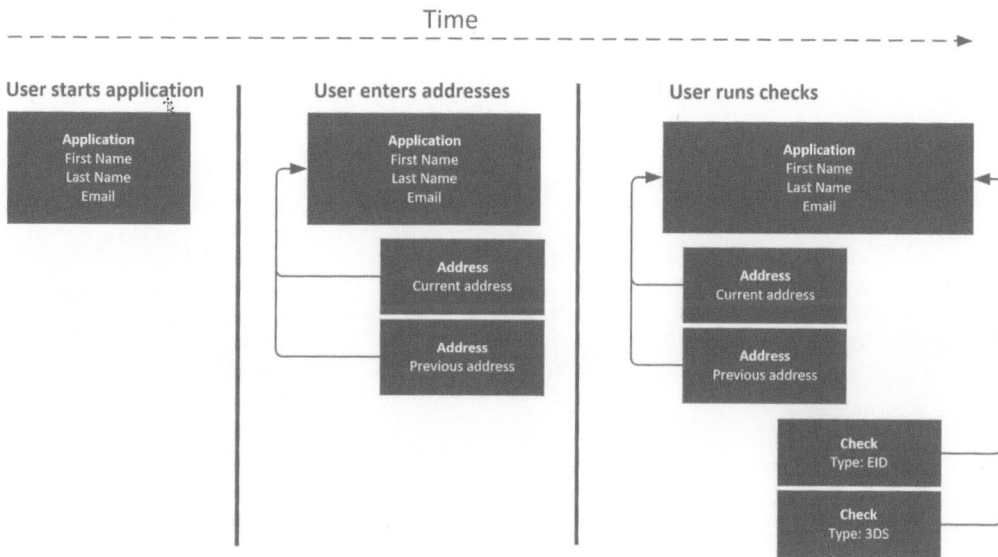

Figure 9.3 – Timeline-based object diagram

Power Platform implementations sometimes require existing data models or table structures from a previous implementation to be updated. It is often helpful to visualize the changes that will be required in the data structure. Diagrams highlighting the delta or changes in the data structure often provide a clear understanding of the work required to achieve the desired result.

Diagrams highlighting changes

Diagrams highlighting the delta in data structures can help clarify understanding of the work required to achieve a certain change. The following diagram illustrates a Dataverse structure that has changes highlighted:

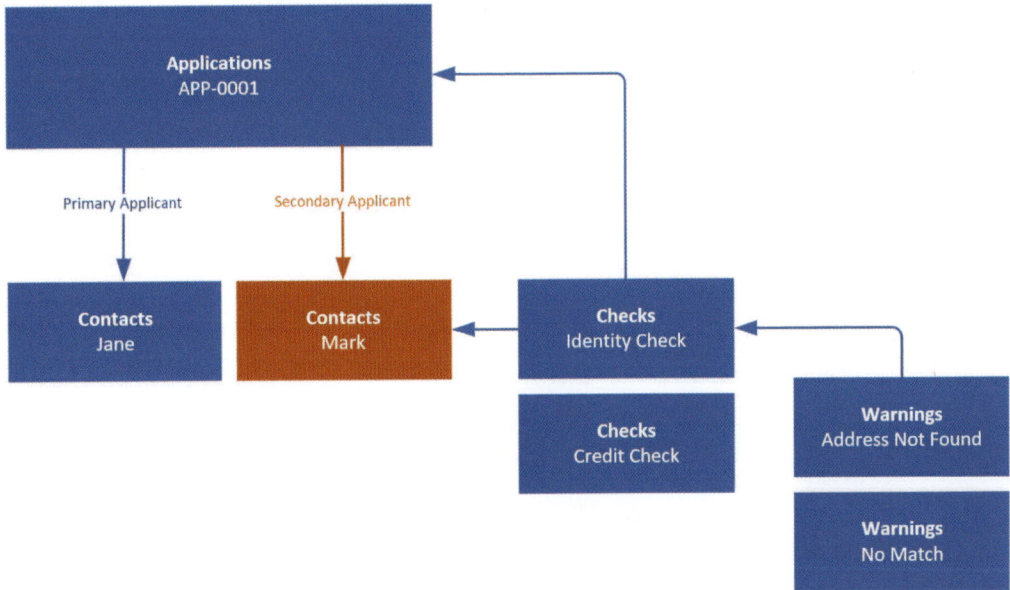

Figure 9.4 – Delta object diagram highlighting changes required to implement a feature

When updating an existing implementation, it is often helpful to highlight the changing areas. Viewers can visualize the components that will require modification and any risks associated with the planned update.

Since object diagrams are easy to draw and understand, they often precede the lower-level physical data models, which is the topic of the next section.

Creating physical data models that support the implementation

Physical data models are lower-level representations of the way data is stored and linked. Software architects create physical models to facilitate technical understanding of Power Platform data structures. Developers and consultants benefit from these entity diagrams as it gives them a visual of the tables and columns to be built. Business analysts, stakeholders, and subject matter experts also refer to physical data models to gain a deeper understanding of how their system's underlying data structure behaves, and how it could potentially be extended.

While usually based on a Dataverse foundation, Power Platform implementations may use external data sources such as **Azure Data Lake Storage** and connect to other data storage systems such as SQL database and SharePoint. Physical data models include external data storage components, presenting the viewer with a complete diagram overview containing enough technical detail for the in-depth analysis of the data structures to be built.

Entity-relationship diagrams

Physical data models may be drawn using various notations. Solution architects review the requirements, analyze business needs, and define a data structure that takes into account future iterations of the solution and the long-term roadmap for the organization. The following entity-relationship diagram illustrates a high-level data model for a Power Pages solution:

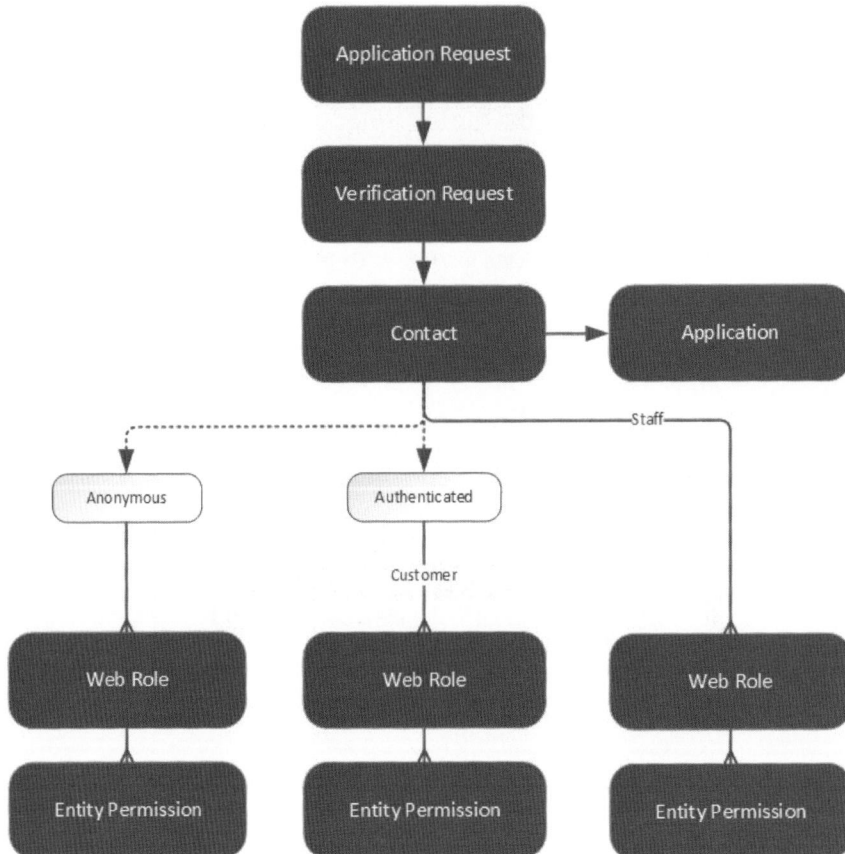

Figure 9.5 – High-level Dataverse entity-relationship diagram

Entity-relationship diagrams may be as simple or as complex as the implementation requires. More advanced ERD diagrams may also contain table columns and relationships between them. The following diagram illustrates a **Crow's Foot** entity-relationship diagram representing the physical structure of a new customer onboarding application:

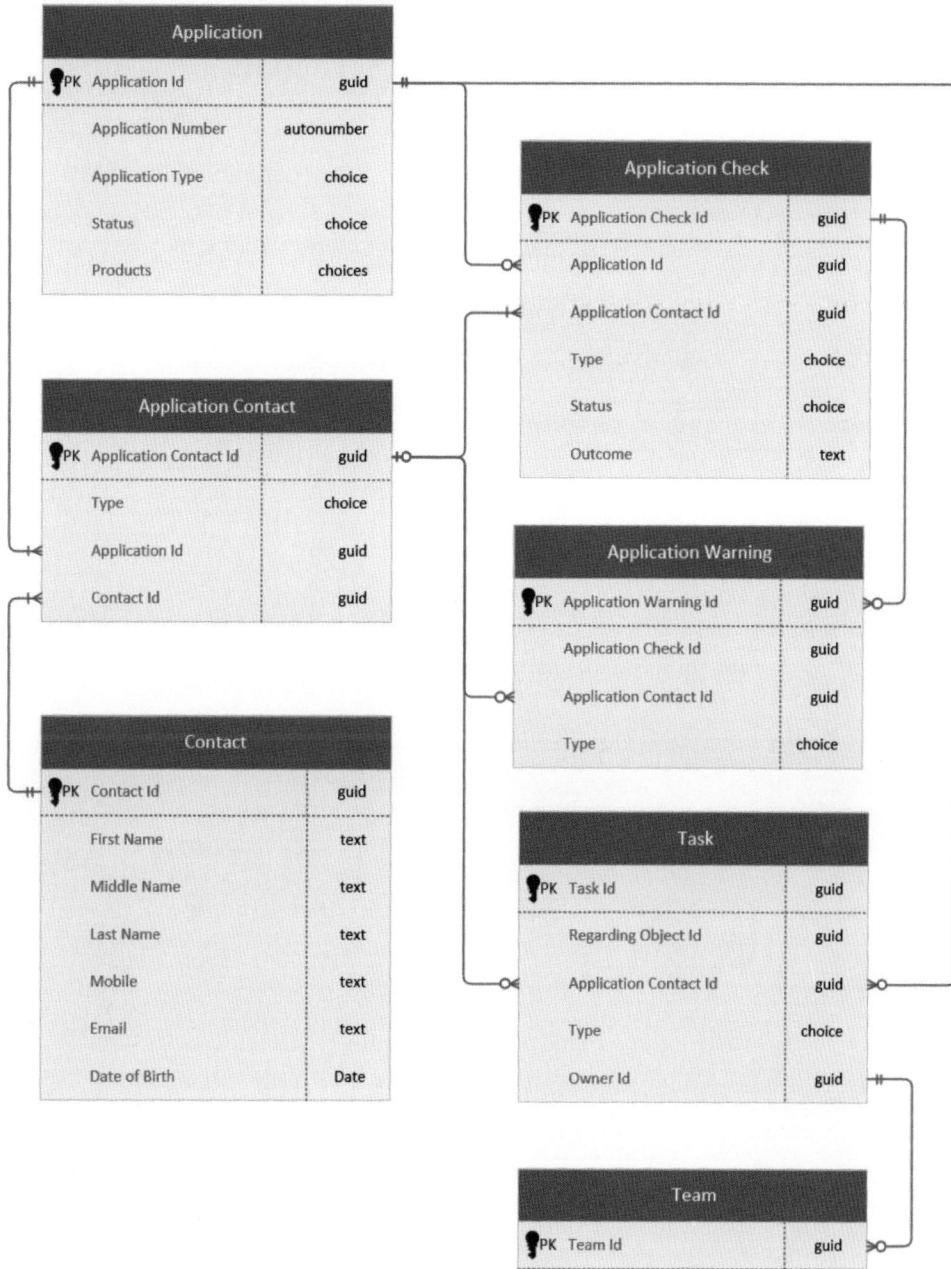

Figure 9.6 – Physical data model of an onboarding application

The connectors between the entities indicate the type of relationship. ERD editors typically provide a means of configuring the connectors to specify one-to-many, many-to-many, and whether records are optional or mandatory.

The following screenshots show how a one-to-many relationship between two tables is configured using Visio. The "many" side of the relationship is configured as follows:

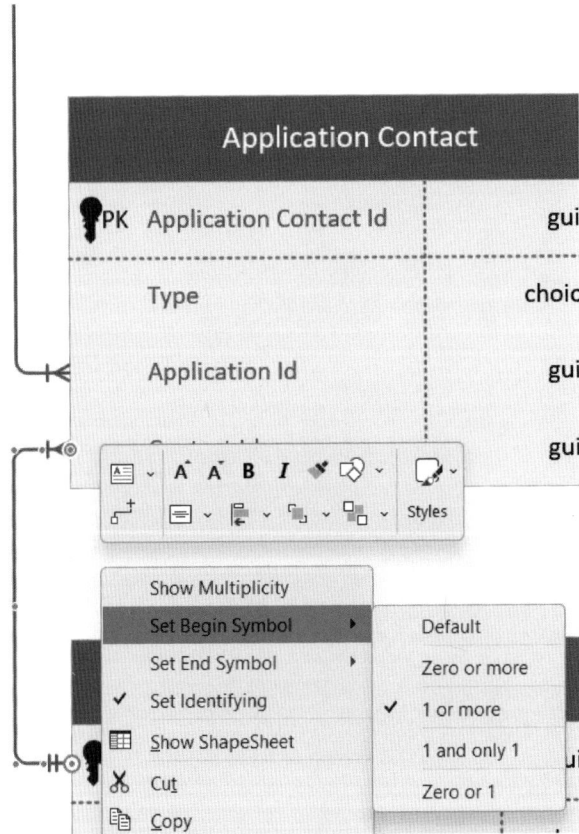

Figure 9.7 – Configuring the "many" side of a one-to-many relationship

Next, we will see the "one" side of the relationship is configured as follows:

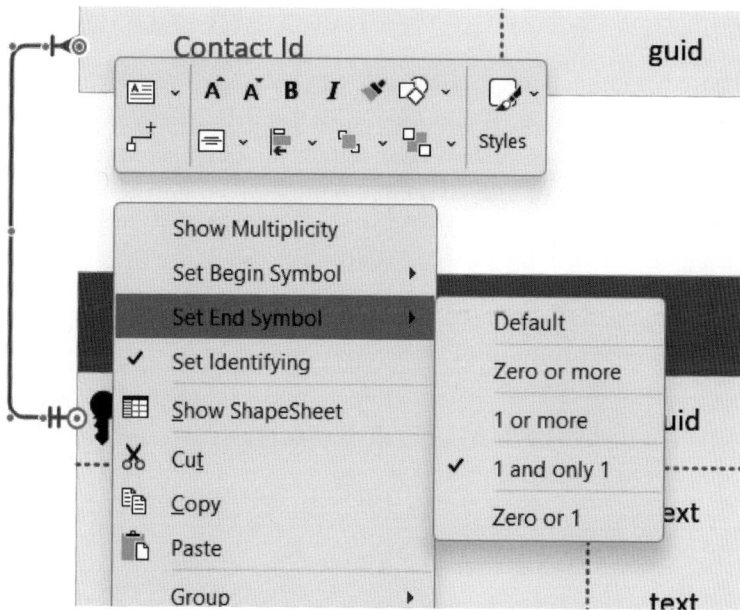

Figure 9.8 – Configuring the "one" side of a one-to-many relationship

The relationship in the previous example defines as one-to-many, with the "many" portion of the relationship requiring at least one record. Please refer to the documentation provided by your ERD editor of choice for further details on the notation and options available.

Physical data models include as much detail as required to support implementation activities and documentation. The columns that are displayed in these entity-relationship diagrams are carefully chosen to support build tasks. While useful to the internal workings of Power Apps, system fields are often excluded from these diagrams to avoid obfuscating the solution.

Solution architects leverage physical data models to help them make pivotal decisions that will direct the course of a Power Platform implementation. While drawing these diagrams, you will have the unique opportunity to rapidly try out various options and quickly make adjustments that cater to long- and short-term project goals.

A solid Dataverse data model design provides a foundation for its Power Apps applications. Entity-relationship diagrams are living documents that will change as new features and components are added to the implementation. As a solution architect, you will aim to capture sufficient detail in your designs and anticipate future requirements so that refactoring and retrofitting new data models and structures is limited to a minimum (or none at all).

Strategies for creating effective data models and diagrams

While a great-looking data model is certainly inspiring, a model that has been carefully designed to be expandable, easy to build, and cost-effective to maintain will help steer a Power Platform solution toward a successful outcome.

The following are a set of strategies and considerations solution architects use to create effective data models:

- **Focus on core tables first:**

   All implementations center around a key set of core data points. Domain experts and stakeholders will be able to relate to these core tables more than the various other lesser-known data points and system records. This makes conversations and design sessions more productive. Focusing the initial design activities around these central tables rather than less relevant data points will help you achieve an optimal design quicker.

- **Validate open questions via prototyping:**

   Power Platform lends itself well to rapid prototyping. New environments can be spun up or copied quickly and with ease. Solution architects leverage Power Platform's fast prototyping capabilities to validate theories, assumptions, and open technical questions. Having more than one team attempt to prototype a solution will also provide additional insights and alternative solutions that you may not have otherwise gained. These insights are particularly useful for critical areas of the implementation, where a high degree of confidence is required before embarking on implementation activities.

   POCs are usually internal technical exercises that do not require the polish that's reserved for implementations intended for production. Once open questions have been answered, POCs should always be discarded to make space for the next implementation task and ensure non-production-ready solutions make their way to a live system.

- **Balance short and long-term goals**:

  When designing data models, a Power Platform solution architect's most pressing need is to design a system that fulfills the project's short-term goals. Long-term goals, however, are also considered during the implementation. Solution architects cater to these long-term goals by designing a data structure that can be extended. Power Platform solution architects ask themselves how the design could be adjusted to suit long-term goals when deciding whether to use a specific table or data structure.

  Conversely, you will look to balance these design decisions so as not to burden the system (and the build team) with a large number of future requirements, or features that may never be used.

- **Design data models with user experience constraints in mind**:

  UI-centered Power Platform applications have specific requirements and constraints when using Dataverse as a backend. Hierarchically navigating data is one such area that requires careful thought when modeling Dataverse tables. Model-driven apps and Power Apps have standard ways of traversing data structures. Excessively normalizing data models may result in complex table hierarchies, resulting in applications requiring costly custom development to present the data to users.

  Solution architects are aware of these constraints and design data models that lend themselves to be used by Model-Driven Apps and Power Apps portals.

- **Make data accessible to citizen developers**:

  Similar to user experience constraints, self-service access to data such as via Power BI reporting and Excel exports is considered by solution architects when creating data models. These self-service reporting applications tend to allow one navigation level in a data hierarchy.

- **Comply with data retention policies and regulatory requirements**:

  Taking data retention policies into account when the data model is defined helps solution architects preempt any compliance hurdles. Power Platform solution architects work with business analysts and members of the organization's legal team to identify applicable policies and regulatory requirements. These requirements are then taken into account during the design phase.

For example, if the organization has a mandatory 7-year data retention policy on all documents stored in SharePoint, the data model's design would consider this. Given the data retention policies in force, the design would most likely use SharePoint for storing documents for the long term. Temporary files would be stored in an alternative location, such as Dataverse file attachments or Azure storage.

- **Make external data accessible**:

  Data external to the Power Platform solution poses some challenges and questions for the solution architect to answer. The data may be imported as a one-off task, fed into Dataverse on schedule, accessed in real time from the Power Apps applications, or a combination of all these options.

  Solution architects analyze the external data, current scenarios, and future use cases to decide on the ideal solution while considering the implementation and operational costs. The data model will reflect this decision and make space for the data to be stored within the platform if that is the best implementation route.

- **Cater for international operations**:

  Depending on the target user base, the needs of multi-national clients and staff members may need to be considered during data modeling exercises. Solution architects consider both localization and multi-currency requirements and design a data model that caters to the needs of both.

This section described the various options for translating complex business requirements into data models, representing the desired systems and processes from varying perspectives. In the next section, we will be discussing the pros and cons of data imports versus integrations.

Deciding factors for integrating or importing external data sources

Power Platform applications are capable of accessing data from a wide variety of sources. Solution architects identify the data required for the operation of Power Platform solutions and define the best way for applications to access this data.

Let's look at the locations where external data that's used by Power Platform applications can be found.

Dataverse

Dataverse is the ideal location for data that does not already exist in another system and is the default storage location for most Power Platform implementations. Dataverse is typically considered a good option for new applications and business processes. Data that's managed within Dataverse benefits from its enhanced administration and process automation capabilities.

Copying data to Dataverse

External data that's required by Power Platform applications may be copied into Dataverse, either as a one-off task, a scheduled import, or a real-time push into the Web API. The data is then copied into Dataverse.

Connectors, dataflows, and the Web API are the three fundamental mechanisms through which data may be copied into Dataverse:

- **Connectors**: Cloud Flows have access to connectors that are capable of communicating with various data sources. External data may be retrieved according to a schedule or on demand from external systems using these connectors, copying the data to Dataverse, thus making it available for Power Platform applications to consume.

  Data imports using Cloud Flows tend to be best suited to lower volumes of data imports due to the throughput constraints and API licensing costs associated with Power Automate Cloud Flows.

  > **Reference Documentation**
  >
  > The following document lists the connectors available for use within Cloud Flows: `https://powerautomate.microsoft.com/connectors/`.

- **Dataflows**: Dataflows can be used by Power Platform applications. A separate Dataflow license is not required as its usage is bundled with Power Apps licenses. Data from external sources may be retrieved, transformed, and copied into Dataverse.

  Dataflows are well suited for high-volume data transfers. They are configured via a graphical user interface that uses Power Query to define the data transformations. Dataflows will be discussed in more detail later in this book.

> **Reference Documentation**
>
> The following document provides full details of dataflow capabilities
> `https://docs.microsoft.com/power-query/dataflows/`
> `overview-dataflows-across-power-platform-`
> `dynamics-365.`

- **Web API**: External services can "push" data into Datavarse by connecting to its Web API, and performing CRUD transactions or calling actions that result in data being stored in Dataverse.

    This type of data import mechanism may be used where there is a need for new operational data to be placed in Dataverse in real time.

Copying data to Azure Data Lake

Azure Data Lake can be used to store data of any size and shape to power processing and analytics using tools such as Power BI. Solution architects work with enterprise architects to identify if there is a need for a big data store.

Azure Synapse Link for Dataverse allows you to transfer Dataverse data into Azure Data Lake. In turn, Azure Data Lake analytics tools gain near-real-time insights into Dataverse data.

> **Reference Documentation**
>
> The following document provides an overview of the Azure Synapse Link for Dataverse capabilities: `https://docs.microsoft.com/`
> `powerapps/maker/data-platform/export-to-data-lake.`

Direct access to external data

Power Apps includes several options for external data access directly from an external source in real time (or near-real-time). The following is a list of options for accessing external data from Power Apps:

- **Connectors**: Canvas Apps have access to connectors and, as a result, can interact with external systems and retrieve data in real time. Model-Driven Apps and Power Apps portals do not have access to connectors. However, Canvas Apps can be embedded in a Model-Driven App or Power Apps portal, allowing them to access external data sources using the embedded Canvas Apps' connectors.

Accessing external data via Canvas Apps connectors is typically used where there is a need for the advanced UI and UX capabilities afforded by Canvas Apps. Accessing external data from within the application is a natural next step. Canvas Apps would not typically be considered the first option for implementing integrations with external data sources, as it creates a dependency on the embedding of the Canvas App within other Power Apps to retrieve the data.

- **Virtual Tables**: Dataverse virtual tables provide seamless integration with OData v4 data sources as standard (access to **Azure Cosmos DB data sources** is also available via AppSource).

  Through custom plugin development, Dataverse Virtual Tables may also access additional data sources, further extending their use to many other databases and external systems. Any system that a Dataverse .NET plugin may access can therefore be surfaced as a Virtual Table.

  The *Defining extensible Power Platform data models* section specifies Virtual Table limitations and capabilities.

- **Real-time integration**:

  Real-time integration is usually achieved through one of the following options:

  - **Azure Logic Apps**: Power Apps can leverage the advanced connectivity within Azure Logic Apps to connect with external data sources and retrieve data using its range of connectors. HTTP triggers initiated from Model-Driven apps may query Azure Logic Apps to retrieve external data in real time. The call to Azure Logic Apps may be initiated within a **Dataverse plugin** or code activity.

  - **Azure Functions**: Similarly to Azure Logic Apps, functions may be used by Power Apps to query external data sources using the enhanced capabilities afforded by .NET Azure Functions. Azure functions may be called from Dataverse Plugins and code activities.

  - **Cloud Flows**: Cloud Flows may be used to query external data directly from within Power Apps. Model-driven apps may initiate a call to a Cloud Flow from a button, a business process flow, a Dataverse action, or a standard CRUD table action. These, in turn, trigger the execution of a Cloud Flow that may use connectors to retrieve data from external data sources and either store it within Dataverse or present it to the user.

- **Dataverse Plugins**: Plugins are built using the .NET development language, giving them access to advanced logic and connectivity capabilities. Power Platform applications may call on Dataverse Plugins and code activities to connect with external data sources, retrieve data, and store it within Dataverse or return it to the caller for surfacing directly in the UI.

This section discussed data imports versus data integrations. In the next section, we will dive into extensible Power Platform data models.

Defining extensible Power Platform data models

When creating a model for the data to be stored within Dataverse, solution architects review the business requirements, alongside Dataverse's capabilities, and aim to create a design that fulfills short-term and long-term goals. To make those design decisions, solution architects must have a thorough understanding of Dataverse's table and column capabilities, which are as follows:

Dataverse table types

At a high level, Dataverse tables may be categorized as either standard tables, activity tables, or virtual tables.

An overview of the capabilities and considerations of these three types of tables follows.

Standard tables

Standard tables make up most of the tables that are used within a Power Platform application. They benefit from the full range of security role permissions. They store general business data that resides within Dataverse and do not need to be automatically linked to other activity-enabled tables.

Ownership of standard tables

Standard table data may be configured for ownership at the user/team level or the organization level:

- **User/team table ownership**:

  Rows within tables that have been configured for user/team ownership may be configured with a granular set of permissions, allowing the administrator to create security roles that define the level of access to rows within the table.

You would typically use user/team-owned tables when you need different access levels by users and teams to prevent users from managing data that should not be accessible to their team or user.

- **Organization table ownership**: Organization-owned tables provide fewer security role configuration options. Access is granted to data within the table at the organization level (the rows within the table may not be assigned to a user or team to grant them a higher access level than other users or teams).

Once the table has been created, the ownership level can't be changed, so the table would have to be recreated. For that reason, the ownership level is carefully considered during the data modeling phase.

Activity tables

Activity tables are used to store data items that are typically reserved for user activities (emails or phone calls). When an activity table is created, it is automatically linked to all other activity-enabled tables using the **Regarding** lookup column.

The built-in Dataverse activity tables are as follows:

- Email
- Task
- Fax
- Phone Call
- Letter

Custom activity tables may be created if the built-in activity tables do not fit the business requirements. Activity rows appear in the social pane of activity-enabled tables. Note that it is not possible to convert an activity table into a standard table.

The pros and cons of custom activity tables are as follows:

- **Custom activity table benefits:**

  - Custom activities are displayed alongside other activities, such as emails and phone calls, allowing the system to expand to cover business activities and user interactions beyond the built-in activity tables.

  - Custom activities are rolled up together with other activities.

  - Custom activities may be linked to any table that supports activities.

- **Custom activity drawbacks**:

  - Security for the custom activity tables is configured alongside all other built-in activity records. Security roles can't differentiate between the different activity types. Therefore, granular control over the various custom activity table types is limited compared to standard tables.

  - As custom activities are linked to all tables that support activities, it is not possible to control or pick which tables a custom activity may be linked to.

Virtual tables

As described earlier in this chapter, Virtual Tables provide seamless integration with external data sources and are presented to the Power Apps user as any other table. They can read and write data from OData v4 data sources as standard, Azure Cosmos DB via an AppSource extension, and can be further extended to connect with other external systems through custom plugins.

Once a Virtual table has been configured, Power Platform applications can read and write to the external data source in real time. It behaves mostly the same as a standard Dataverse table.

The key limitations when using Virtual Tables are as follows:

- Security roles for virtual tables may be configured at the organization level only, as user and business unit-level permissions are not available.

- The model for external data must conform to Dataverse columns, and the data source must use GUID-based primary keys.

- Auditing, search functionality, charts, dashboards, queues, and offline caching are not available for Virtual Tables.

- Virtual tables may not be configured as activities.

- It is not possible to switch a Virtual Table to a standard Dataverse table and vice versa.

- Offline caching of Virtual Table data is not supported.

- Virtual tables may not be configured with the **queues** feature.

> **Reference Documentation**
>
> Virtual Tables and their capabilities are described in more detail in the following document: https://docs.microsoft.com/powerapps/developer/data-platform/virtual-entities/get-started-ve.

Selecting column data types

The different types of Dataverse columns provide different capabilities and present users with varying UXs and behaviors. When defining the data model, solution architects consider which column types best fit the business requirements.

This section describes key considerations when selecting Dataverse column types.

Here, we will understand the differences in the Choice, Choices, and Lookup columns. We will also get to understand the similarities that the Lookup, Choice, and Choices columns share. They all present users with a means of selecting from a list of items. Let's dive deeper into this:

Choice columns:

Choice columns provide users with a single-select dropdown, and they are best suited for the following use cases:

- When users need to be able to select a single item from a list.

- When it is certain that future business needs will not require additional data points to be associated with the user's selection. For example, let's say there's a Country choice column listing all countries. If, in the future, it will be required to associate a currency with the country, a Lookup column for the Country table would be better suited.

- When the list contains a small number of items. Choice columns may list a maximum of approximately 200 values.

- When the user does not need to search through the items in the Choice to make a selection. The Model-Driven and Power Apps UIs do not provide search capabilities for Choice columns as standard.

- When the built-in localization capabilities are required. Choice columns provide multi-language localization as standard.

- When the list items do not require a standard means of retiring or deactivating values. Choice list items may not be deactivated, only removed from the Dataverse definition.

- When the list of items does not need to be filtered using standard functionality. Filtering the Choice columns with a Model-Driven app or Power Apps portal form would require custom JavaScript development.

- When the data entered by the user needs to be stored as a whole number in the row.

- When the list of items needs to be stored as part of the Dataverse solution. Dataverse manages Choice value merge resolution by appending the publisher prefix to the value of Choice items.

- When the administration of the Choice list's content does not need to be managed by non-administrators. Adding/removing Choice list values requires administrator/customizer permissions, and is best handled through a formal deployment process.

Choices columns:

Columns of the Choices type are similar to Choice columns but with two key differences:

- They behave the same as Choice columns, except that the user can select multiple items from a list.

- They may be used to aggregate multiple Choice column selections into a single Choices column.

- Business process flows do not support Choices at the time of writing.

- Classic/real-time workflows cannot set the values of Choices columns. A Net code activity would be required.

Lookup columns:

Lookup columns allow users to select from a reference table. You can use Lookup columns instead of Choice/Choices in the following use cases:

- When the business requires a more extensible use of reference data. Using the Country table example, a lookup to a country table would allow the application to identify the currency for the selected country using a Currency column.

- When a means of retiring values by using validity dates and deactivating records is required.

- When the column will be used by Model-Driven Apps or Canvas Apps that require a user interface that scales to a large number of items.

- When the user needs to be able to search through the list of items.

- When the data that can be selected by the user needs to be filtered by views or security role permissions, and when filtering the list may be dependent on other columns on the form.

- When the reference or master data for the list is to be migrated/imported into the target production environment.

- When data is to be maintained by designated business users that do not require administrator/customizer permissions.

- When the selected item should be stored in the row as an entity reference.

- **Date/Date Time columns**:

  Data and Date Time columns are used interchangeably. They may be configured to be user timezone-aware.

- **Numeric columns**:

  These are used when the data is to be stored as whole numbers, decimals, or floating-point numbers.

- **Customer columns**:

  This is a special type of lookup that allows users to select from either the Contact table or the Account table and is used accordingly.

- **File/Image columns versus Notes versus SharePoint versus Azure Storage**:

  Let's look at the different storage types:

  - **Dataverse file storage**: File and image columns may be used to upload reference data. They follow the row's permissions. They are limited in size and are best used for smaller documents.

  - **SharePoint file storage**: SharePoint follows its own set of permissions, which are not synchronized with Dataverse row permissions or security roles.

  - **Azure Storage**: This uses a separate standalone security model. Access to files in Azure Storage may be granted for specific periods using a link. Azure Storage may be used to store larger files.

- **Yes/No columns**:

  Yes/No columns are simple binary fields. They are set to either yes or no by default, as configured in the column editor. For that reason, they are best used in scenarios where it is acceptable for a default value to be set.

  If having a default value will result in undesirable behavior from the application, a Choice column may be used. A Choice column with Yes and No options allows for a null as a default value, which can then be used to prompt users for data entry.

- **Calculated columns**:

  Calculated columns are read-only fields, where the value is recalculated at the time the record is retrieved.

  They can process data from the current record and related records in many-to-one relationships. The calculations may include other rollup columns.

  Plugins, workflows, and Cloud Flows can't be triggered based on calculated column events. They can, however, read their values.

- **Rollup**:

  Rollup columns are used to aggregate values and may include data from related rows:

  - They are recalculated once an hour, or on-demand via the Dataverse API. Cloud Flows and code may call the Recalculate Rollup action on a row to update a rollup column's value.

  - Rollup columns may also include other calculated columns.

  - When aggregating data from related records, rollup columns may be configured to apply filters to select rows that match specific criteria. While plugins, workflows, and Cloud Flows may not be triggered on Rollup column events, they can read their values during execution.

- **Alternate Key columns**:

  Alternate Key columns provide a means of uniquely identifying a row. Once a record's alternative key value has been set, that row may be read/updated/deleted without knowing its built-in primary key or GUIT. Deleting rows using alternate keys as an identifier is restricted to transactions carried out via the Dataverse Web API.

Alternate keys may be created using the following data types:

- Text fields
- Whole numbers
- Lookup fields
- Dates
- Decimals

The solution editor will prevent attempts to create an alternate key column with any other column types. The maximum number of alternate keys that may be created is five per table.

This section listed the key considerations when designing extensible data models. The next section will discuss the configuration options that are available for reference and master data.

Optimal reference and configuration data modeling strategies

Power Platform applications often use lists of reference data. A list of countries or a lookup table listing all the functions within an organization are typical examples. Users select from these lists of reference data to categorize and process records.

Modeling reference data

When planning the structure of reference data within Power Platform applications, solution architects consider the benefits versus the additional complexity adding new tables brings to the solution:

- Create a table instead of a Choice or Choices column if there is a chance the list may need to be enhanced with related information (for example, currencies related to a list of countries).
- Use standard built-in tables if the use case closely matches the table's function.
- Use Azure DevOps Build Tools where possible to promote reference data.
- Maintain the unique IDs of reference data to keep referential integrity and help avoid data duplication. Using Build Tools or the Configuration Data Migration Tools will help maintain the unique identifiers (GUIDs) across all environments.

Modeling configuration data

In addition to reference data, Power Platform applications often require parameterizing logic, allowing non-technical administrators to change the behavior or the links to external systems by changing a setting or a parameter. The key locations for configuration data are as follows:

- **Environment variables**:

  Power Platform provides a convenient means of defining configuration parameters that apply to each environment. These variables may be promoted within Dataverse solutions, making them a good candidate for storing integration URLs and other similar parameters.

- **Custom settings table**:

  A custom table is often used to store parameters and settings used by Dataverse processes and applications. The table may be secured to a certain extent using Dataverse security roles, allowing non-technical administrators to edit these settings.

> **Security Note**
>
> Storing credentials and secrets within custom Dataverse tables is not generally considered a good practice. These are better placed within *Azure Key Vault* or *Plugin secure* configuration strings where appropriate and are the topic of discussion in upcoming chapters.
>
> Please review the Key Vault documentation at `https://docs.microsoft.com/connectors/keyvault/` and the Dataverse plugin configuration documentation at `https://docs.microsoft.com/en-us/power-apps/developer/data-platform/register-plug-in` for further details.

Establishing table relationships and cascade behaviors

Relationships between tables provide referential integrity. Dataverse further enhances these relationships with cascade behaviors, controlling what happens when a parent or child record is deleted. This section describes the different types of relationships, cascade behaviors, and the decision process for their selection.

Types of Dataverse relationships

There are two types of table relationships in Dataverse: one-to-many and many-to-many relationships. Let's take a look:

- **One-to-many relationships**:

  When a Lookup column is added to a table, it automatically creates a one-to-many relationship (also known as a 1-N relationship). One-to-many relationships are used by Power Platform applications to traverse data hierarchies. As well as maintaining referential integrity, creating one-to-many relationships between tables enables the following capabilities:

  - Users can navigate to a related record within a Power Apps form.

  - Multiple tables may be linked together using an `OData` or `FetchXml` query from Cloud Flows and other clients that communicate with the Dataverse API.

  - The ability to add a Quickview from a child record form, displaying the contents of the parent record Quickview.

- **Many-to-many relationships**:

  Many-to-many relationships (or N-N relationships) allow records between two tables to be linked without the restrictions of one-to-many relationships. Use cases for many-to-many relationships vary from associating users with multiple groups to connecting opportunities with competitors.

  The flexibility of many-to-many relationships comes at a cost. Quickviews may not be used, and navigating through a many-to-many hierarchy is somewhat more convoluted when querying data using Cloud Flows and the DataVerse API. As a result, many-to-many relationships are only used when the application has a clear benefit.

- **Custom many-to-many relationships**:

  Custom many-to-many relationships consist of a custom linking table with two one-to-many relationships to two other tables. This creates an effective many-to-many relationship between the two tables. It has the multi-linking abilities of N-N relationships and some of the benefits of 1-N relationships. Quickviews may be used to a certain extent, and querying data is also facilitated.

- **Dataverse connections**:

  Strictly speaking, connections are not Dataverse relationships. However, they provide a means of linking records between connection-enabled tables. The connections may be categorized using roles.

  > **Further Reading on Dataverse Connections**
  >
  > Please refer to the following document for more details on Dataverse connections: `https://docs.microsoft.com/power-apps/developer/data-platform/connection-entities`.

Relationship behaviors

Relationship behaviors control referential integrity by enforcing the links between records based on how the relationship has been configured. They decide whether a user is allowed to delete a record that has child rows associated with it, whether the assignment of a parent cascades to its child rows, and several other options.

The three types of Dataverse relationship behaviors are as follows:

- **Parental**:

  The parental behavior cascades all actions the parent performs onto its child's table rows.

- **Referential**:

  The referential behavior presents two additional options:

  - **Remove link**: The referential remove link option does not restrict the deletion of a parent record and clears the lookup on the child rows that referenced the deleted parent row.

  - **Restrict delete**: The referential restrict delete option prevents a parent record from being deleted if any child rows have a reference to it.

- **Custom**:

  The custom relationship behavior type allows you to granularly configure cascade behaviors for each of the actions that may be carried out on a record.

The cascade behavior may be configured for the following five actions:

- **Delete:**

  When a parent record is deleted, the following cascade options are available:

  - **Cascade all:** Delete all the child rows.

  - **Remove link:** Clear to lookup for child rows that are linked to the deleted parent.

  - **Restrict:** Prevent the parent record from being deleted if child rows exist.

- **Assign:**

  When a parent record's ownership changes, the following cascade options may be configured:

  - **Cascade all:** Assign all child rows so that they match the new owner of the parent.

  - **Cascade active:** Only assign active child rows to the new owner.

  - **Cascade user-owned:** Only assign child rows that are owned by the same user the parent used to have before re-assignment.

  - **Cascade none:** No action is taken on the child rows.

- **Share:**

  When a parent record is shared, the following actions may be configured for its child rows:

  - **Cascade all:** Share all child rows with the same users or teams as the parent.

  - **Cascade active:** Only share active child rows.

  - **Cascade user-owned:** Only share child rows that are owned by the same user as the parent.

  - **Cascade none:** No action is taken on the child rows.

- **Unshare:**

  When a parent record is unshared, the following actions may be configured for its child rows:

  - **Cascade all:** Unshare all child rows with the same users or teams as the parent.

  - **Cascade active:** Only unshare active child rows.

- **Cascade user-owned**: Only unshare child rows that are owned by the same user as the parent.

- **Cascade none**: No action is taken on the child rows.

- **Reparent**:

  When the lookup column for a child record is changed, resulting in the child row pointing to a new parent record, or when a new child record is created that points to a parent record, the following cascade behaviors can be applied:

  - **Cascade all**: The child row will inherit the parent's owner.

  - **Cascade active**: Only active child rows will inherit the parent's owner.

  - **Cascade user-owned**: The child rows will inherit the parent's owner if the owner of the reparented record matches the new parent's owner.

  - **Cascade none**: No action is taken on the child rows.

Configuring cascade behaviors via the options mentioned here controls how the system behaves and the access the user will have to date, depending on the actions they take on records.

This section discussed the features to consider when creating Dataverse relationships. In the next section, we will review data modeling best practices.

Power Platform data modeling best practices

When designing Dataverse models, several general best practices will help drive the implementation toward a successful outcome. The following list outlines the main best practices and considerations solution architects follow when creating data models:

- **Reduce data duplication to a minimum**:

  Storing the same data in multiple locations or tables creates redundant data that can become out of sync. Duplicated data also requires additional maintenance (the data point will have to be updated in more than one location). An optimal design will have little or no data duplication.

- **Identify relationship behaviors early**:

  An area that is often overlooked during data modeling is the definition of relationship behaviors. Working with business analysts to understand and define cascade behaviors for ownership and record deletion constraints will result in a data model that behaves as expected by the users and the business and reduce administration overheads.

- **Update the data model frequently**:

  Data model designs are living documents that can quickly become out of date and obsolete if they're not updated regularly. Customers can be involved in the upkeep of the data model, helping to ensure it is kept up to date with any changes.

- **Leverage data modeling tools**:

  Design applications such as Microsoft Visio are helpful tools for defining data models that are easy to read and maintain. XRM Toolbox contains a range of plugins that help solution architects create and maintain data models. From table and column metadata documentation facilities to the automatic generation of Visio data models, leveraging these modeling tools will help you create and maintain a coherent Dataverse data structure.

- **Focus on the data model design's relevant components**:

  Data models can quickly become overburdened by the sheer breadth of detail that can be included within them. Solution architects target the design documentation to include helpful information for the target audience, excluding tables or columns that are irrelevant to the task.

- **Include external tables in the data model designs**:

  Including data points hosted outside Dataverse in the data model designs will help business analysts, product owners, and the implementation team understand the relationships and links between the Power Platform data and external systems. By including external data in the data, models provide a holistic view of how Power Platform applications interact with the wider domain, which can help build a coherent system.

- **Keep data normalization in check:**

  It is often tempting to create as many tables as required to model the data structure presented by a customer or organization. Solution architects balance the benefits of data normalization into a set of tables with the usability overheads brought on by having a complex data structure. An overly large Dataverse model may become cumbersome, with users having to jump through several hoops to view the data of interest.

  Solution architects aim to keep the data model as simple as possible, challenging calls that add complexity to the design to ensure that if a table is added, it will yield sufficient benefit to warrant the additional complexity to the user interface and data management.

- **Plan ahead:**

  It is easy to fall into design dead-ends when designing a data model. Anticipating future requirements as much as possible helps solution architects design data models that can be extended and adapted to upcoming changes and features.

- **Leverage standard tables:**

  Solution architects try to leverage built-in tables and columns wherever possible. Custom tables are created when the built-in tables do not suit the long- and short-term requirements. This topic will be discussed in more detail in the next section.

Deciding whether to use built-in or custom tables

When deciding on the best place to store information, solution architects review the existing built-in Dataverse tables (and Dynamics 365 application tables, if appropriate) and consider creating a custom table.

The following table includes a set of guidelines and considerations that will help you make this decision:

Consideration		Standard Table		Custom Table
Reduce the risk of configuration overload	✓	Using standard tables usually means reduced data structure complexity and a lower risk of overloading the configuration.	✗	Creating a large number of custom tables may make the application more difficult to use, and often results in redundant tables, increasing the risk of overloading the Dataverse configuration.
Performance	✓	A streamlined application that uses built-in tables and a simpler data structure is more likely to be more performant.	✗	A complex custom data structure may result in lower performance due to the number of relationships to be traversed by processes and the UI.
Closer alignment with Power Platform features	✓	Using the built-in tables is more likely to result in an application that works with Power Platform features (for example, email messaging, and document management).	✗	While Dataverse lends itself to being configured to meet a wide array of requirements, creating a complex custom data structure in favor of using standard tables is less likely to leverage the best Power Platform features.
Benefit from new features	✓	When a new Power Platform feature is released, applications that leverage the built-in tables are more likely to benefit.	✗	Custom tables may not always benefit from new features that are released for the built-in Dataverse or Dynamics 365 tables.
When the business need matches the standard table functionality less than 50%	✗	Attempting to wedge a built-in table to perform a function that it is not designed for is likely to result in a solution that is difficult to build and maintain. There is also a risk of extensively customizing standard tables conflicting with future releases.	✓	When the business need is different enough from the standard table functionality, a custom table would provide a better foundation for the data.

Consideration		Standard Table		Custom Table
When the UX would make use of less than 50% of standard table functionality	✕	Scaling down a complex standard table so that it matches a simple requirement will likely result in a system that is difficult to maintain.	✓	A custom table may provide a simpler user experience than a simplified standard table. The user experience within custom tables may still be further enhanced using business process flows.
When a standard table is seldom used (at risk of deprecation)	✕	Using standard tables that are not often used, and are at risk of deprecation, may result in a system that will require refactoring in the future.	✓	In this instance, the risk of deprecation may be reduced by using a custom table.
When there is a high configuration overhead when using a standard table	✕	Certain built-in tables such as the Opportunity, Case, and Campaign tables have high configuration overheads. Certain components may not be fully removed and some features cannot be deactivated. This may result in over-burdened application and implementation overheads.	✓	If the application does not sufficiently benefit from the standard table features, a custom table would result in a system that is easier to build and maintain.

Table 9.1 – Standard versus custom table decision matrix

Deciding whether to use the Account and Contact tables

The Account and Contact tables that are built into Dataverse provide a large number of features. When defining the Power Platform data model, solution architects decide whether to leverage those features or create a custom table to fulfill a requirement. The following table will help with this decision process:

Considerations		Account/Contact Tables		Custom Table
Likely to need Dynamics 365 Finance and Operations integration using dual-write	✓	Account and Contact tables from tightly bound integration with Dynamics 365 F&O.	✕	Custom tables do not have integration as standard with F&O.
Need to support multiple addresses	✓	The Account table has a unique feature that allows multiple addresses to be associated with it.	✕	Dataverse does not provide a means of configuring a similar multi-address feature on a custom table. Such functionality on a custom table would require development effort.
Require activities rollup and visualization from account to child contact records	✓	Activities rollup to the account record from all child contact records is available only using the Account and Contact tables.	✕	Activities rollup is not available on custom tables.
Need to display standard map controls	✓	Available on the Account and Contact tables as standard.	✕	Standard map controls are not available on custom tables.
Require polymorphic "Customer" lookup columns	✓	Customer lookup allows users to select from either a Contact or Account table.	✕	There is no other polymorphic column type available in Dataverse.
Require the use of Dynamics 365 Marketing lists	✓	Dynamics 365 Marketing lists support for Accounts and Contacts only.	✕	Custom tables may not be used for Dynamics 365 marketing lists.
Require company records that use minimal attributes	✕	Storing minimal attributes on an account or contact table will result in a confusing data model.	✓	When you're storing simple company records (for example, department names), using a custom table will result in a simple implementation.
When performing a temporary import of companies	✕	Importing temporary data into the account and contact tables will result in non-operational data being entered into these key tables. This may result in a confusing data model.	✓	Importing temporary data into a custom table will leave the account and contact tables free for day-to-day use.

Table 9.2 – Using the accounts/contact tables versus custom tables

This section covered data modeling best practices and concluded the topics in this chapter.

Summary

In this chapter, you learned how to translate complex business requirements into highly visual data models, helping the organization and the implementation team understand the business needs and how to address them. You also learned when to integrate or import external data. With this knowledge, you can define extensible Power Platform data models and select optimal table structures and data types that make Power Platform solutions easy to build, extend, and maintain. A solid data model is critical for a successful Power Platform implementation as it provides a foundation for the business logic and the UI that users interact with.

In the next chapter, you will learn about advanced integration patterns. Leveraging core Power Platform capabilities together with Azure will help you fulfill complex business requirements.

10
Power Platform Integration Strategies

Power Platform integrations connect two or more systems to improve business activities. In this chapter, you will design the various integrations that will be required by our fictional case study at Inversa Corps. Microsoft 365 collaboration integrations will be defined, alongside connections to the organization's internal systems using various gateway and proxy strategies. You will also plan to integrate with third-party applications and APIs and define a secure authentication strategy for all inbound and outbound connections. Business continuity strategies will be defined.

Then, you will learn how to create advanced PowerApps Portal integration patterns to fulfill complex business requirements. The design process will identify opportunities to leverage Microsoft Azure to extend the Power Platform solution.

In this chapter, we will cover the following topics:

- Introduction to Power Platform integrations
- Designing Power Platform integrations with Microsoft 365
- Designing integrations with on-premises and cloud-based customer systems

- Defining inbound and outbound authentication strategies
- Designing a business continuity strategy for Power Platform integrations

Understanding the benefits, challenges, and strategies that come with integrations is crucial for successfully implementing a Power Platform solution that adds value to an organization.

Introduction to Power Platform integrations

Power Platform integrations connect to external systems to increase ROI, improve user adoption, and solve business problems that would be otherwise either very difficult, costly, or impossible without them. Integrations, when successfully implemented, result in a synergy between two connected components, benefiting the business thanks to the connectedness of the systems, data, and processes. This section will discuss the benefits, challenges, and activities Power Platform solution architects manage during the integration design phase.

Your role during the implementation of Power Platform integrations

Power platform solution architects lead the design of Power Platform integrations. They have a wide understanding of the capabilities provided as standard by the Power Platform framework, the Microsoft 365 suite of services, Azure components, and third-party solutions. They are responsible for the analysis of the integration requirements – that is, the business needs driving them. Solution architects understand not just the technical aspects of the requirements, but also their benefit to the business. They are aware of the bigger picture, allowing them to present the business with the widest set of options, finding the best fit for the Power Platform implementation and the organization.

Benefits of an integrated Power Platform

There is a reason why integrations play a big part in a Power Platform implementation. They bring in additional capabilities to the solution that would be otherwise difficult or impossible to build. When considering integrations, Power Platform solution architects assess the potential benefits they bring to the solution.

These benefits may include one or more of the following.

Improve usability

Imagine users having to access two (or more) applications to complete a task. This is an all-too-common scenario for many businesses. Imagine that those same users have access to a single application that allows them to perform that same task quickly and easily. The benefits add up to a solution that does the following:

- Provides a better user experience, allowing staff to focus on the task at hand using a single application

- Reduces training time and costs by providing users with tools that are designed with their end-to-end process in mind

- Provides increased productivity by reducing manual processes and associated errors

An integrated Power Platform solution has the potential to improve user experience by making technology work for the users.

Optimize data volumes

Power Platform integrations often allow users to access external data directly from the source. Therefore, the external data stays in its original location and does not need to be copied or synchronized into Dataverse. Data transfer and storage volumes are consequently reduced, while users or business processes have access to the data they need when they need it.

In the following sections, you will learn how to identify the best integration strategy, whether it be real-time or asynchronous, or push or pull, potentially reducing the volume of data that needs to be managed by the Power Platform.

Provide real-time access to data

Specific use case scenarios would benefit from a real-time integration with an external system, API, or data source, providing users access to the latest information. Various teams and business areas may be used to access different systems to perform their daily activities. Real-time integration from a Power App pulls the data onto Power Platform when needed, removing the need to access a second system to process the same information.

Reduce implementation costs

It is sometimes more cost-effective to integrate with an external service than attempt to replicate its functionality within Power Platform. Integrating with external systems brings additional business benefits to the application and has the potential to reduce implementation costs.

Reduced data duplication

Two systems with replicated data may result in double bookings due to synchronization constraints. Using real-time integration between those two systems would allow you to query the current status of a record or execute a booking directly on a central booking API. Integration would allow a single system to be responsible for bookings, reducing the scope of double bookings.

Improved build times through reuse

Integrating Power Platform applications with existing systems or components previously built makes additional functionality available to the application, saving the team from having to recreate it from scratch. The project may benefit from connecting to these existing services, a third-party system, a Microsoft service, or a service created by the Power Platform team.

One such example may be an address search service or a company search facility. Attempting to connect to a raw data source or host the data within Power Platform can be more costly than connecting to a service that performs the desired function.

Conclusion

Now that we understand the key benefits that integrations may bring to a solution, it is worth being aware of the risks and challenges surrounding the implementation of Power Platform integrations.

Power Platform integration challenges

Integrations between two or more systems have inherent challenges that solution architects must overcome for a successful rollout. Being aware of the potential integration hurdles helps us ask the right questions up-front, pre-empting implementation problems. The typical Power Platform integration challenges are as follows.

Security

Integrating with a third-party system means a connection is required to or from a service. Managing and storing credentials brings its own set of challenges. Securely storing and transporting data form a vital part of the security modeling exercise. As a solution architect, you will lead security assessment and planning for Power Platform integrations.

No real-time access

Implementing integrations with real-time access to data may not always be possible or practical. A typical scenario could be a system that exposes invoice records as a flat file generated at midnight on a daily schedule.

When assessing the need for integration, solution architects analyze the constraints presented and arrange for the functionality to work within those constraints. Continuing from the example given earlier, given that the invoice data is downloaded nightly, the Power Platform system would be planned accordingly, alerting users that the invoice data may be a day behind.

Incompatibility

Solution architects must work with numerous compatibility issues, and integrations are no exception. There will be times when services will be unable to connect to Power Platform's APIs due to protocol or authentication restrictions. Third-party systems may find themselves unable to comply with Dataverse authentication requirements. Power App portals may be unable to connect to a select API for user authentication. The types of incompatibilities vary in scope and severity. Solution architects validate potential compatibility issues and propose alternative integration strategies or an overall rethink of the functionality.

Connectivity

Integrating with intranet or on-premise systems brings its own set of challenges. Connecting a cloud-based solution to a sealed-off internal network means navigating through a set of hoops to connect the two domains. Solution architects work with the organization's security experts and platform owners to resolve connectivity challenges.

Company policies

Power Platform solutions that connect to company systems may be subject to company policies presenting additional constraints. Solution architects work with compliance teams to understand the company restrictions and work with the relevant team members to design an integration strategy that complies with company policy.

A typical example may be a company policy that states that all Microsoft 365 user accounts require two-factor authentication. Access to Power Platform systems is restricted using **Conditional Access rules**, preventing authentication from non-authorized devices. Any integrations into Power Platform applications would need to bear that in mind and identify whether the constraints pose a risk to the implementation. You can then mitigate those risks (for example, propose using **Application User** access to the DataVerse API).

As a solution architect, you are responsible for understanding and documenting company policies that may impact the delivery of the Power Platform solution and designing solutions that work within those constraints.

Regulatory and legal requirements

Organizations are often bound by regulatory or legal requirements. As a solution architect, you will work with the organization's business analysts and legal experts to identify any such requirements that may impact the implementation. These regulatory requirements may differ across regions and countries within the same organization.

An example of one such requirement is data privacy. The solution may be required to restrict access to personal data and store it for a minimum or maximum period. Solution architects identify these regulatory constraints and plan the implementation accordingly.

Legacy systems

Large organizations quite often have **legacy systems**, sometimes built decades earlier. These systems tend to have quite different integration capabilities compared to more modern platforms. Integrating with legacy systems can prove challenging, and solution architects often have to find creative ways to solve integration problems.

You may integrate with mainframe systems, where the only means of ingress is through a particular flat file format. Legacy systems may also present non-standard APIs that require bespoke connections.

Solution architects work with administrators and SMEs within the organization to identify the best integration strategy to connect legacy systems with Power Platform solutions.

High volumes of data

Specific integrations may involve transferring and processing large amounts of data. This may be in the form of a large number of records to be processed, a large amount of data throughput, or dealing with spikes in either. Solution architects analyze these non-functional requirements and propose integration strategies capable of performing to the specification. This may mean using high-capacity messaging services such as Azure Service Bus or Azure Event Hub, or using all standard Power Platform facilities such as Dataflow.

High volume integrations also require special consideration when it comes to licensing and API limits management. Processing and inserting a large number of records into Dataverse may result in high API request usage. This high throughput may require additional capacity to be purchased to manage the load. Solution architects consider the technical and licensing implications of handling large datasets and design a solution that best fits the organization's technical and commercial requirements.

Data quality

When integrating with external third-party systems or managing how data is imported into Power Platform applications, you may sometimes find that the quality and integrity are below the standard required by the solution. Performing a preliminary assessment of the quality and integrity of the source data will help you plan for the data transformation and normalization tasks to come.

Solution architects work with business analysts and system owners to understand the normalization and data cleansing that's required to incorporate, import, or access this data from within Power Platform processes.

Orphaned systems

When embarking on a new Power Platform implementation, you may find systems that require integration, with no apparent owner or understanding of how they work. Staff turnover may mean subject matter experts are no longer available to answer questions. Documentation may also be sparse. The team may be required to reverse engineer or decompile applications to understand their inner logic and analyze databases to understand their structure.

Solution architects work with stakeholders, business analysts, and system administrators to unearth the details of these orphaned systems, decide on the best integration strategy, and identify if there is sufficient value to warrant the costs associated with integration builds.

Skills gaps within the team

The Power Platform framework sets out a clearly defined set of skills that consultants and developers are required to have to complete an implementation. Integrations with third-party systems or APIs may require additional skills not currently available within the team. For example, a system built on non-Microsoft programming languages such as Java may require integration with the Dataverse API. The organization may not have the skills to develop or extend the application, and the Power Platform team may be called on to provide the development expertise to extend the Java application.

Solution architects work with the business to identify any skill gaps and put in place mitigations to ensure the delivery of the project is not impacted. This may mean either resourcing additional team members with the required skill sets or identifying alternative implementation routes that do not require the missing skills.

Conclusion

The first step is awareness. Knowing the potential challenges that a team may face when implementing Power Platform integrations will help you ask the right questions from the right teams to identify upcoming hurdles. Armed with this knowledge, you can develop a plan of action, creating POCs integrations where required to de-risk the implementation.

Integration layers

Power Platform integrations can be thought of as consisting of three layers:

- **Data:**

  Integrations provide users with a single view of the data. While the information may be initially stored in multiple systems, integrations offer a seamless user experience, with a single application to view all the necessary data.

- **Application:**

  At the application layer, integrations provide functionality that enriches the existing Power Apps feature set.

- **Process:**

  Business processes may span multiple systems. Integrations combine two or more of these systems, extending each other's capabilities and enriching data.

Let us now understand how to manage the implementations in the next section.

Managing Power Platform integration implementations

Power Platform implementations require planning to be successful. Solution architects lead the evaluation, design, and implementation of integrations, providing structure and support to the build team. The implementation of Power Platform integrations can be split into the following five phases:

The Power Platform integration design process

1	2	3	4	5
Identify need	Evaluate options	Design	Build	Release
• Is an integration needed? • Cost of doing nothing? • What are the benefits?	• Would an out-of-the-box integration do? • What integration mechanism would suit? • Where will the data live? • Is real-time integration needed?	• Would a POC help identify best strategy? • Any outstanding technical queries that need confirmation? • Would users benefits from a preview? • Any 3rd party components that need validation?	• Develop or configure integration • Procure integration components where applicable	• Test the integration • Deploy to target environments

Table 10.1 – Five steps to completing a Power Platform integration

Let's work through the five steps to implementing a Power Platform integration while using this book's case study to illustrate the methodology that will be used at each stage.

Identifying the need for integration

One key question that solution architects ask themselves when considering an integration is the cost of doing nothing. Discussions around business requirements and user experience often lead to the desire for process automation via integration with other systems. You will, at times, find the cost of doing nothing is considerably lower than the cost of designing, building, and maintaining an integration. Hiring additional full-time staff to process the information manually may turn out to be a better solution than integrating the system to perform the task automatically.

Solution architects work with business analysts and product owners to identify a real need for integration, present the business with options and proposals that provide the most value to the organization, and fulfill the business goals.

In the following example, we are assessing a Power Apps portal, identifying the impact and benefits of not going ahead with an address search integration:

Integration		
Portal integration with an address search service.		
Evaluation		Assessment
Cost of doing nothing	Not implementing the integration would mean the customer would need to enter address data manually, resulting in poor UX, data errors, and back-office staff overheads.	
	Reputational cost: High	✓
	Data quality cost: Medium	
	Additional staff cost: Medium	
	Following an initial assessment, doing nothing is not considered an option.	

Table 10.2 – Example of an initial integration assessment

Evaluating integration options

When planning an integration, you will want to assess the technical feasibility of the requirements. You can then flag any risks to the implementation early in the project. The implementation team can then take action to mitigate the risk or find an alternative. Solution architects assess integration data volumes, regulatory restrictions, and licensing requirements.

The following is a typical integration assessment. This scenario evaluates the technical and operational risks associated with an address search integration for Power Apps portals:

1. **Integration overview**:

    Provide Power Apps portal users with advanced address search functionality by integrating with the organization's existing address search API.

2. **Integration strategy**:

    Use Power Apps portal browsers to communicate with the portal server's Liquid templates, triggering a Dataverse plugin that authenticates and communicates with the organization's address search API.

3. **Integration assessment:**

Security	**Leveraging the Power Apps portal's authentication capabilities and DDOS prevention features provides a layer of protection as standard. Securing the address search API credentials in Azure Key Vault using a key rotation strategy will help secure the connection to the service.**	✓
Data volatility	Address data is stable and does not change regularly.	✓
Data volume	The system is expected to perform up to 10 address searches per second at peak times, get 36 K requests per hour, and use 360 Mb per hour of data. API limits may be exceeded. Additional capacity requirements must be factored into the risk assessment.	!
Real-time	Yes, the user expects a real-time response to a search request. Potential risks might be identified in response times to user requests. The target average response time for an address search is 1 second.	!
Batching	Not applicable as the data will be searched in real time from the source.	✓
Regulatory restrictions	None identified.	✓
Licensing	Address Search API requires a license. Costs to be assessed.	✓
Push versus Pull	Power Platform will pull data from the address search API.	✓
Event vs Batch	Not applicable to integration as the address data will be retrieved in real time when the user requests it.	✓
Connectivity	Access to the address search API will require application gateway access to be configured by the organization, and the technical design authority will need a security assessment.	!
Production downtime	A new connection to the address search service means no downtime is required for existing services.	✓

Table 10.3 – Object diagram for onboarding an application

4. **Integration assessment conclusion**:

    The integration is technically feasible. Risk assessment has identified the data volumes and peak requests per hour as areas that require verification and potential POC to prove the infrastructure can handle the load.

    The target average response times of 1 second will also need to be tested under load.

Finally, the connectivity from Dataverse to the organization's API management gateway will need to be planned and configured, potentially adding to the implementation timescales.

Conclusion

Solution architects lead the evaluation of integration strategies, software trials, and POC implementations. The aim is to identify the best solution for the business, with the best implementation route, given the available resources.

POC implementations can help answer outstanding questions and are helpful when identifying the best integration strategy. They are also helpful when users would benefit from an early preview of the functionality that a particular integration route would deliver. POC implementations are valuable tools when validating third-party components.

Design

Having identified the need for integration and validated one or more implementation routes, solution architects start the task of design. Creating a high-level plan for each integration option allows you to visualize the path for technical implementation, making it easier to anticipate any issues or risks associated with the various options.

Power Apps portal integration strategies

The following diagram illustrates an example of a high-level integration design, presenting two options for implementing a Power Apps portal address search integration:

Address search integration
Option 1 – Virtual Tables

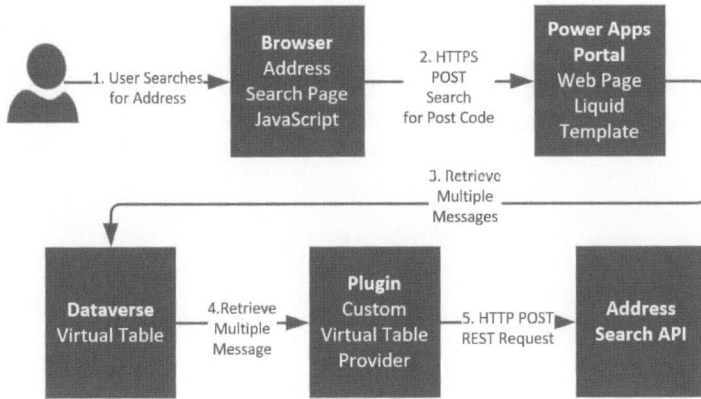

Address search integration
Option 2 – Power Automate

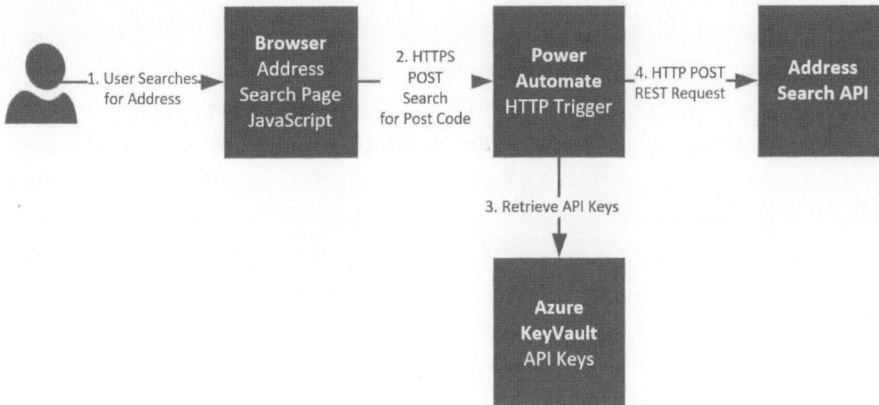

Figure 10.1 – Example of a high-level integration design presenting two options

Reviewing the integration route for each option will offer answers to questions such as security and authentication strategies, technology to be used, and the potential performance bottlenecks that may be found on each option.

> **Integration Tip**
> Power Automate Cloud Flows are often excellent candidates for user interface-level integrations. Model-driven apps may benefit from the wide range of connectors available in Cloud Flows and the seamless integration with Dataverse messages and data structures.

Later in this chapter, we will delve deeper into activities and documentation that solution architects create to help the implementation team create robust Power Platform integrations.

An important part of the integration design phase is identifying who will be responsible for carrying out the various administration and development tasks required to complete an integration. The following section discusses this subject in detail.

Identify responsibility for the implementation

When planning an integration, you will want to clearly define who will be responsible for each area or task to be completed. Power platform integrations typically involve coordinating and collaborating with at least two teams to ensure the respective system owners complete the relevant groundwork, credentials, and security setup.

As a Power Platform solution architect, you are uniquely positioned to understand the technical implications of integrations to/from the platform's components and the various APIs and services. This clarity in the distribution of responsibilities will facilitate the implementation, providing the relevant teams and individuals with advanced notifications and oversight over the upcoming tasks.

The following table illustrates a sample distribution of responsibility for three integrations in a Power Platform limitation:

Integration	Team Responsibilities	
	Power Platform Team	Customer Team
Portal address search	<ul><li>Combined integration security assessment</li><li>Portal configuration and development</li><li>Dataverse plugin integration development</li><li>Secure storage for API credentials</li><li>Power Platform performance analysis</li></ul>	<ul><li>Combined integration security assessment</li><li>Configuration of the API gateway</li><li>Provisioning of API credentials</li><li>API performance analysis</li></ul>
Portal company search	<ul><li>Combined integration security assessment</li><li>Portal configuration and development</li><li>Secure storage for API credentials</li></ul>	<ul><li>Provisioning of API credentials</li></ul>
Power Apps Exchange integration	<ul><li>Power Platform configuration of email integration</li></ul>	<ul><li>Creation of shared mailboxes</li><li>Exchange administrator or global administrator to enable mailboxes in Power Platform</li></ul>

Table 10.4 – Object diagram for onboarding an application

Having agreed on the split of responsibilities for each integration, each team is aware of the high-level tasks they need to complete, lowering the risk of surprises and delays.

Designing robust Power Platform integrations through retry and fallback strategies

Integrations benefit from having a disaster recovery strategy as part of the design phase. The design focuses on mitigating factors that would help a system recover from a failure in the connected systems. Solution architects consider fallback functionality if integration is temporarily unavailable, and system recovery once the integration is back up.

Defining a solid retry orchestration strategy will help the implementation team build highly resilient integrations that can recover from transient errors. The design approach will need to adapt to the technology in use.

Cloud Flow integration retry orchestration

Various Cloud Flow actions provide a means of configuring their retry policy. Power Automate designs include the relevant retry specifications for critical components and Cloud Flow.

Supplementing the built-in retry features within Power Automate, solution architects design solutions with fallback retry strategies, catering to scenarios where transient connectivity issues prevent connecting to an external system for extended periods.

The following diagram illustrates a Power Platform application that automatically sends account updates to an external API. An automated flow attempts to send the account update instantly, while a second scheduled flow is in charge of retrying pending requests:

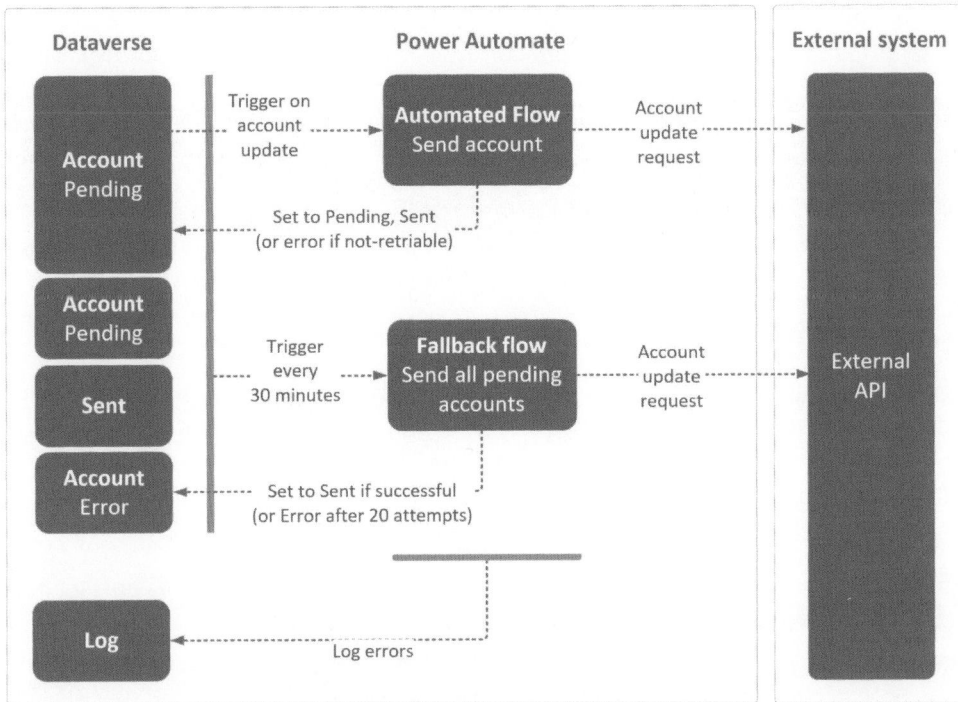

Figure 10.2 – Example Cloud Flow retry orchestration

The sample integration process implements the following functionality:

- **Immediate integration of data**: An attempt to send updated account data is triggered immediately at the point the data changes.

- **Management of non-transient error**: The integration recognizes responses from the external API that should not be retried (for example, missing mandatory data), and marks the integration status for the record as **Error**, preventing further attempts to send the same invalid data.

- **Management of transient faults**: If the integration fails due to a temporary issue (for example, a network connection fault), the record's integration status is set to **Pending** so that it may be retried later.

- **Automated retry strategy**: A fallback flow is responsible for retrieving any accounts pending integration at scheduled intervals (for example, every 30 minutes). The integration is re-attempted up to a configurable number of times (for example, 20 attempts), giving the integration a chance to recover from temporary network issues or downtime in the target system.

- **Fault logging**: Integration errors are recorded in a Log table where administrators may review them. Automated notifications may also be triggered from these Logs to alert the system owners of critical issues that need urgent attention.

Incorporating disaster recovery strategies within integration designs

Integrations benefit from having a disaster recovery strategy as part of the design phase. The design for disaster recovery focuses on mitigating factors that would help a system return to a functional state in the event of a failure in the integration routes. Solution architects consider implementing fallback functionality if the integration is temporarily unavailable, and the recovery of processes and data once the integration is back online.

The following table outlines a disaster recovery strategy for the Power Apps portal address search service integration discussed earlier:

Area	Disaster Recovery Strategy	Assessment
Fallback	If the address search service API fails, the user will be presented with a prompt to enter the address manually.	✓
Recovery	Addresses entered manually during an outage of the address search service will be flagged for the back-office admin staff to verify their validity. A manual correction process will be defined to make the necessary amendments in coordination with the customer.	✓

Table 10.5 – Example of integration fallback and disaster recovery assessment

The build activities are broken down into tasks with sufficient detail for developers to be able to action them. Depending on the skill level of the implementation team, solution architects may need to include additional detail in the build tasks, and you will learn to gauge the team's needs. Investing extra time detailing each component to be built may save weeks worth of work if the integration needs to be rebuilt or refactored due to a lack of understanding of the technical issues that may come up and how to solve them.

Once the integration design is completed, validated by the project's technical design authorities, and broken down into manageable tasks, the implementation can progress to the build stage.

Implementation

Depending on the project's size, the creation of the integration components may fall on the solution architect to complete. However, it is more often the case that technical and functional consultants assist with the integration build. Solution architects provide support to the build team via the following activities:

- **Defining the implementation and development guidelines**:

  They set out the general principles to be used by the implementation team when configuring or developing Power Platform components. This may involve setting out the retry strategies for integration components, down to table and column naming conventions.

  A clear set of guidelines that have been published and are used by the project team members will help create a consistent system that is easier to build and maintain.

- **Defining ways of working**:

  Solution architects work with project managers and the team to define the ways of working. It is often helpful to set out how the team will peer review each other's work, code review, perform unit testing, and take part in release strategies.

- **Supporting the team with technical expertise**:

  Solution architects have a wide range of technical knowledge. They can often support the implementation team by setting up base frameworks for plugin development, configuring flows, and creating Power apps. Solution architects often fill the gaps in technical expertise to keep Power Platform projects moving in the right direction.

- **Carrying out implementation reviews**:

  Solution architects work with the implementation team to review the development and configuration work as it progresses, aligning the technical build to published best practices.

  Power Platform solutions are typically deployed to test environments (for example, integration, test, and user acceptance test environments). Solution architects play a vital role in the smooth implementation of Power Platform applications.

Releasing the integration into production

In preparation for deployment, end-to-end integration validation is key to a successful rollout into production. Lining up all the integrated systems in a test environment is usually complex and time-consuming, often leading to cut corners (for example, target systems may not have a test environment available). Partially testing the solution may leave integration issues undetected, which surface in the production environment.

Your role, as the solution architect, is to ensure systems are available for end-to-end integration testing. The following activities will help ensure the integrated solution is ready for production rollout:

- Request a test environment from the owners of integrated external systems.

- Define or review that the test strategy includes end-to-end testing of the integration.

- Validate the outcome of the end-to-end tests.

Once the integration build and tests are complete, the features that rely on integration may be deployed onto the production environments. At this point, the integrated solution is formally incorporated into the overall disaster recovery plans for the organization.

Designing integrations between Power Platform and Microsoft 365

Power Platform and Microsoft 365 go hand in hand, and seamless integrations between the two services are available as standard. Solution architects leverage these Microsoft 365 components, presenting users with a rich feature set with relatively low implementation effort.

The following Microsoft 365 integrations are considered during the analysis, design, and implementation phases.

Designing for Exchange integration

Power Platform applications benefit from Exchange integration as standard, allowing inbound and outbound email communications and appointments, tasks, and contacts to be synchronized between Dataverse and user Exchange accounts. An overview of the server-side sync architecture between Power Platform and Exchange is shown in the following diagram:

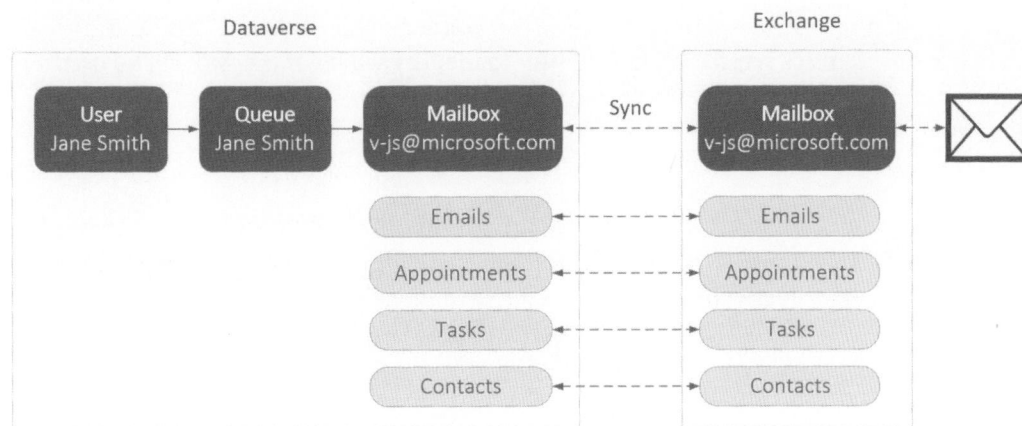

Figure 10.3 – Architecture overview for the Exchange server-side sync integration

Defining the components that make up a Power Platform exchange integration involves identifying various aspects. Let's take a look.

Who or what will send and receive emails?

Both users and non-user mailboxes may send and receive emails within the Dataverse platform. Dataverse users have a queue and corresponding mailbox. Specific scenarios require inbound and outgoing notifications from a Dataverse mailbox that aren't linked to a user. A typical use case for a non-user mailbox is sending automated messages to users or customers from a generic email address.

The integration design will likely identify any non-user mailboxes across the development, test, and production environments. Each Power Platform environment will require non-user Exchange mailboxes (server-side sync integration may only be enabled from one Power Platform environment to a given Exchange mailbox at a time).

What type of Exchange mailboxes will be required?

Power Platform server-side sync can connect to standard Exchange user mailboxes and Exchange shared mailboxes. Shared mailboxes can be used by non-user Dataverse queues, allowing the system to send and receive messages from a service email address without a Microsoft 365 user account or license. When creating an integration strategy, you will want to define the names and number of shared mailboxes used by the system.

Where is the Exchange server?

The Power Platform server-side sync feature can connect with Exchange Online and Exchange on-premises services. You will want to identify which of the two will be used and the version number of any on-premises Exchange servers.

> **Note**
>
> Power Platform allows you to integrate it with other mail servers via POP3, SMTP, and IMAP protocols.

Power Platform server-side sync is compatible with specific on-premises exchange servers. The documentation linked here will contain the most up-to-date compatibility list.

> **Further Reading**
>
> For more information on configuring server-side sync integration with Exchange, please go to `https://docs.microsoft.com/power-platform/admin/integrate-synchronize-your-email-system`.

Designing Power Platform integrations with Outlook

The Dynamics 365 app for Outlook combines familiar email, appointment, and task management features with Power Platform business process automation capabilities. Together, they make up an effective tool for users on the move. Outlook integration relies on the server-side sync feature discussed in the previous section. Server-side sync supports the synchronization of appointments, tasks, and contacts between Dataverse and Exchange accounts.

An overview of the Dynamics 365 for Outlook app architecture is illustrated in the following diagram:

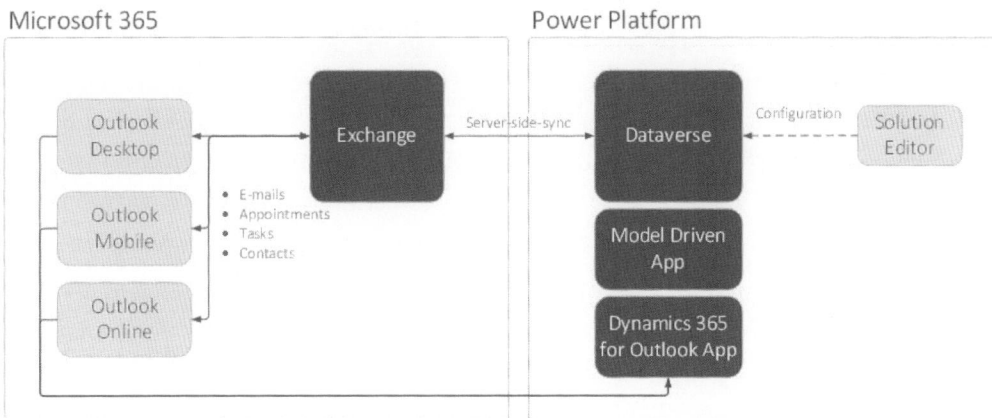

Figure 10.4 – Architecture overview for the Dynamics 365 for Outlook app

When designing an integration between the Power Platform and Outlook, the business needs are matched to product capabilities. The integration design will typically include the types of records and features and the direction of data flow. The following table outlines a feature selection exercise, where the types of data and integration direction are specified:

Design Feature	Designs Details	To Dataverse	To Outlook
Appointments	Appointments to be synchronized automatically between Dataverse and Outlook.	✓	✓
Email	Users will be able to select the emails that are tracked to Dataverse and link them to an application record.	✓	✓
Email templates	Outlook users will be able to select from email templates.	✓	✓
Knowledge articles	Outlook users will be able to reference Dynamics 365 knowledge articles when sending emails to customers.	✓	✓
Delegate access	Outlook users who have been granted delegate access to an Exchange account will be able to send emails and arrange appointments on behalf of another Outlook user. This functionality will be restricted to the Outlook clients that support this functionality.	✓	✓
Contact	Users will be able to select Outlook contacts to be tracked to Dataverse. Contacts within Dataverse associated with applications linked to the Outlook user will be synced with Outlook for that particular user.	✓	✓
Tasks	Users will be able to track tasks from Dataverse onto their Outlook task list and vice versa.	✓	✓

Table 10.6 – Planning the configuration of a Dynamics 365 for Outlook app

The available features depend on the Outlook client in use, the Dynamics 365/Power Platform setup, and the Microsoft Exchange installation type. An overview of the constraints to each deployment type and client follows.

Microsoft Exchange and Dynamics 365/Dataverse installations and their impact on Outlook capabilities

There are three types of Microsoft Exchange installations – online, hybrid, and on-premise. The Dataverse integration capabilities for each of the installation types are as follows:

- **Online installation**:

  When Dynamics 365 Online or Dataverse are combined with Microsoft Exchange Online, users gain the broadest feature set. This type of installation provides access from/to Outlook mobile apps and delegates access, depending on the Outlook client.

- **Hybrid installation**:

  When either one of the services is on-premises, the features that are available to users are reduced. Outlook mobile apps will no longer be able to track emails, contacts, and other records related to Dynamics 365/Dataverse, and delegate tracking is not available in this configuration.

- **On-premise installation**:

  This configuration provides the least number of available features and does not apply to Power Platform applications (as it is an online-only service). Outlook mobile clients are not supported, and contact tracking is further reduced for specific Outlook desktop clients.

Features available on various Outlook clients

Let's look at the feature list:

- **Outlook C2R**: Provides the broadest feature set. When combined with an online-only Dataverse/Exchange architecture, users are granted the fullest access to the Dynamics 365/Power Platform application's capabilities, including delegate access record tracking facilities.

- **Outlook 16 or later**: Access to features such as delegate record tracking is not available when this Outlook client is used. Features such as contact tracking are further reduced if you're using a fully on-premises installation.

- **Outlook 2013**: The feature set is further reduced when using Outlook 2013. Contact tracking, task tracking, and delegate user record tracking are not available in this version of Outlook.

- **Outlook for Mac**: This is the Outlook client that offers the least number of features. Tracking and composing appointments and meetings is further reduced.

- **Outlook web access**: When running on Edge or Chrome browsers, the Outlook web client provides a rich feature set that includes tracking emails, appointments, and meetings while acting as a delegate. Contact and task tracking are not available in this configuration.

- **Outlook mobile apps**: The Outlook iOS and Android mobile apps provide a selection of features that synchronize with Dynamics 365/Dataverse. Full email tracking, including through delegate access, is supported by the Outlook mobile apps. These features are only available in a fully online configuration. Hybrid or on-premises installations of Dynamics 365/Dataverse and Microsoft Exchange do not support synchronization with Outlook mobile applications.

> **Documentation on Dynamics 365 for Outlook Features Available per Configuration**
>
> For full details on the features available for the various combinations of Dynamics 365/Dataverse, Microsoft Exchange, and Outlook clients, please refer to the following documentation: `https://docs.microsoft.com/dynamics365/outlook-app/user/support-matrix`.

When defining the Outlook integration design, you must consider the constraints that are inherent to each deployment type. Please review the following documentation for full details on the Outlook capabilities when integrating with Power Platform Dynamics 365.

> **Dynamics 365 for Outlook Documentation**
>
> Please visit the following documentation page for full details on the capabilities and implementation of the Dynamics 365 for Outlook app: `https://docs.microsoft.com/dynamics365/outlook-app/overview`.

Designing Power Platform SharePoint integrations

The Power Platform and Dataverse include seamless integration with SharePoint as standard, available for SharePoint Online and SharePoint 2013 on-premises (with service pack 1) or later. The **Document Management** section of the Dataverse administration settings provides a portal for the configuration SharePoint integration and is illustrated in the following screenshot:

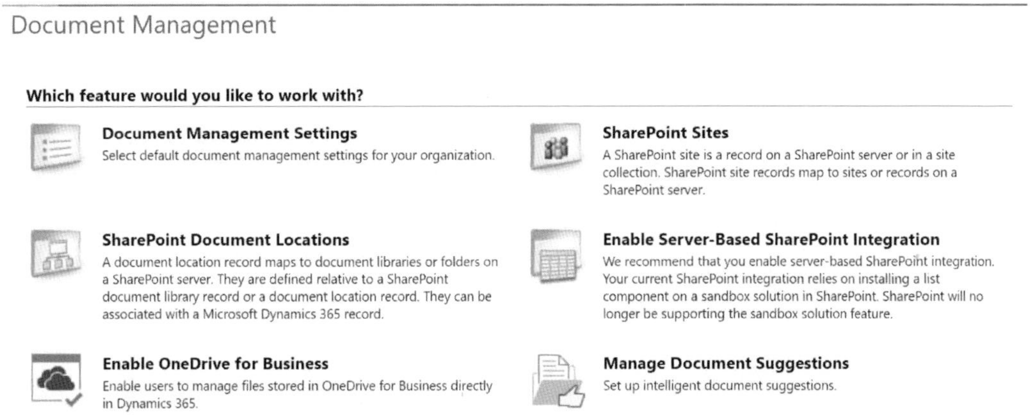

Figure 10.5 – Dataverse SharePoint configuration screen

The standard SharePoint integration dramatically enhances Power Platform's document management capabilities. Now, let's discuss design considerations when implementing SharePoint's document management strategy.

Designing model-driven app integrations with SharePoint

Model-driven apps may be configured to present a SharePoint document management interface within forms. Both standard and custom tables may be linked to a SharePoint folder structure, allowing users to upload and manage documents related to a wide variety of records.

Let's cover the areas to be addressed during the design phase.

Which tables and forms require document management capabilities?

SharePoint integration may be configured for standard tables and custom tables. The design document will define the tables and forms that allow users to upload documents. The following screenshot illustrates the selection of tables to be integrated with SharePoint:

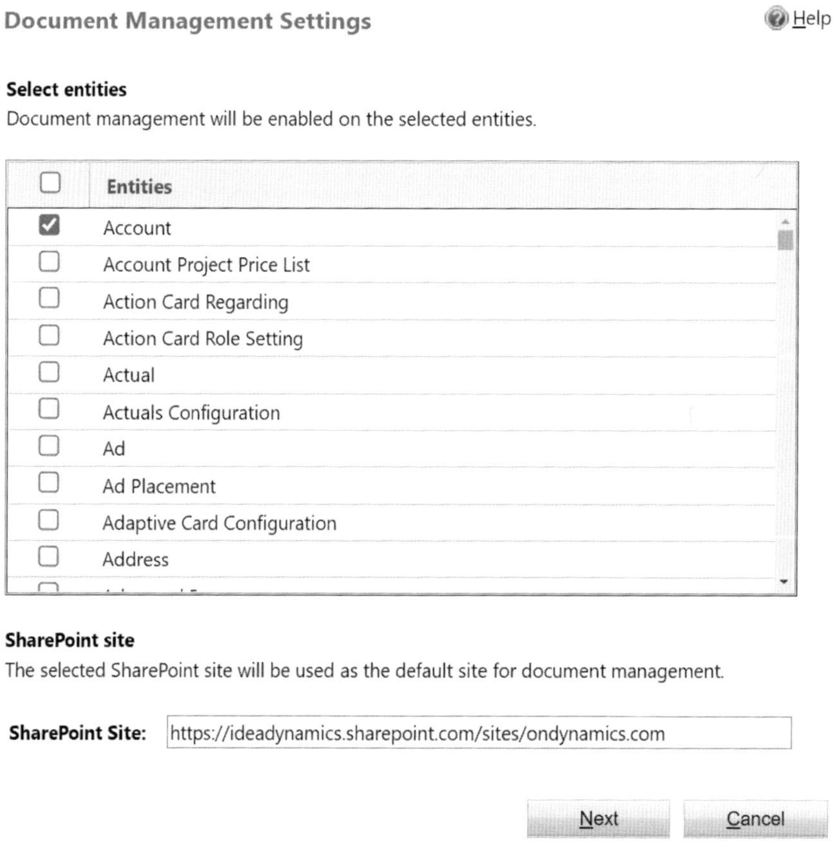

Figure 10.6 – Dataverse SharePoint table selection screen

What SharePoint document management folder structure should you choose?

The standard SharePoint integration allows the administrator to select a flat SharePoint folder structure, with one folder for each table, or a hierarchical folder structure where the parent folder may be a Contact record or an Account.

The following screenshot illustrates this option:

Select folder structure

To create a folder structure based on a specific entity, click the check box, and select an entity. Folders will be created on SharePoint in the context of your Microsoft Dynamics 365 records.

☑ **Based on entity**   Account   ⌄

For entities related to a specific Acc[   ]ounts" folder.
Folder path: **../account/<account n[Account   ]name>**
                                      [Contact   ]

Figure 10.7 – Dataverse SharePoint folder structure selection screen

Who will access SharePoint documents?

Users uploading, reading, and changing documents in SharePoint will require access to be configured on the site. In addition to the Power Platform users, other staff members may need direct access to the SharePoint site. Enabling SharePoint integration would allow a broader range of users to manage the documents without them requiring a Power Platform or Dynamics 365 license.

The added flexibility provided by the SharePoint integration brings a new set of security risks. Members of a SharePoint site that's been integrated with a Power Platform application will have access to all documents within the site by default. While the Dataverse security roles or security groups do not apply to SharePoint sites, several third-party solutions exist to replicate Dataverse access restrictions to SharePoint (please see App Source "SharePoint Permissions Replicator" search results for details).

> **Pillars of Great Architecture – Security**
>
> Enabling the standard Power Platform SharePoint integration can vastly expand the access to application documents. As a solution architect, you will closely review the SharePoint site user list, security model, and data retention policies to ensure that documents are accessible only to authorized users.

Designing Power Apps portal integrations with SharePoint

Using the standard DataVerse server-side integration, the Power Apps portal includes the option of integrating with SharePoint. Portal users are presented with standard portal controls for uploading and managing SharePoint documents linked to a DataVerse table. The functionality mirrors the model-driven app's access to SharePoint documents.

Solution architects answer the following questions during the Power Apps portal design phase:

- **What Portal Web Roles, or types of users, should be granted access to upload and manage SharePoint documents?**

    Identifying and locking down the Portal Web Roles that will be granted access to SharePoint document management is crucial for the platform's security.

- **What level of document security and scanning is required when a user uploads a document?**

    When a user uploads documents to SharePoint via a Power Apps portal, these files are transferred directly to the SharePoint site. SharePoint Online provides a degree of virus detection, which may be leveraged to a certain extent. For more advanced vetting of uploaded files, alternative solutions may need to be considered.

> **Further Reading on SharePoint Online Virus Detection**
>
> Please refer to the following document for detail on the virus detection offered by SharePoint Online: `https://docs.microsoft.com/microsoft-365/security/office-365-security/virus-detection-in-spo`.

SharePoint is a powerful tool for Power Apps portals that require advanced document management capabilities. Please refer to the following documentation for full details on configuring Power Apps portals.

> **Further Reading**
>
> To learn more about configuring Power Apps portals to use SharePoint document management, go to `https://docs.microsoft.com/powerapps/maker/portals/manage-sharepoint-documents`.

Designing integrations with on-premise and cloud-based customer systems

When a Power Platform implementation needs to be integrated with an external system, one of the key questions is how the connection to/from that external system will be routed. Thankfully, Azure and Power Platform include components that facilitate connections to cloud and on-premise systems. This section will discuss the main options available for such scenarios.

Options for connecting on-premise systems and Power Platform

Connecting an on-premise system or interface with a cloud-based solution such as Power Platform means identifying the best possible connectivity route while complying with the organization's security policies and technical constraints. The following options leverage Microsoft's Dataverse and Azure and API management capabilities to connect a Power Platform solution to on-premise services.

Option 1 – push/pull from the Dataverse API

An on-premise application or service that can create an internet connection to the Power Platform application and authentication domains can also connect to the Dataverse API. The on-premise application can then proceed to retrieve Dataverse data, update records, and call actions to perform business logic. This solution does not require Power Platform or Azure gateways to be installed within the internal network.

The owners of the on-premise client application will be responsible for sending the correct sequence of messages to the Dataverse API. Solution architects aim to simplify the interface by creating custom APIs or actions for the on-premise client to consume. The following diagram provides an overview of the typical integration routes for applications looking to push/pull data to/from the Dataverse API:

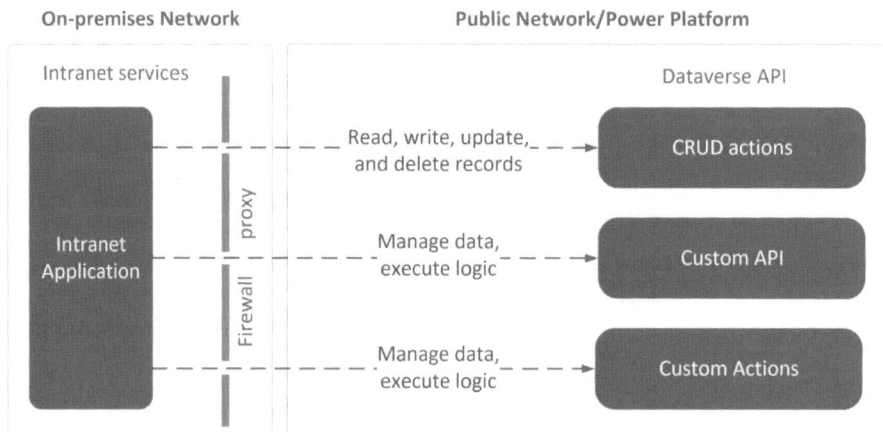

Figure 10.8 – An on-premise application integrating with the Dataverse API (push/pull integration)

Dataverse custom APIs are powerful tools that can help consolidate one or more operations into a single message and create business logic trigger events for consumption by Dataverse API clients. Dataverse custom APIs may be consumed by third-party applications, Power Automate Flows, and any other service that can conform to the Dataverse API standards.

> **Further Reading on Dataverse Custom APIs**
>
> Full details on how to configure custom APIs are available at `https://docs.microsoft.com/power-apps/developer/data-platform/custom-api`.

Option 2 – use an on-premise data gateway to connect to on-premise services

Power Automate, Power Apps, and Power BI (among other Azure components) may leverage on-premise data gateways, allowing its actions to connect to services or APIs within the on-premise network. An on-premise data gateway installed within the internal network will initiate a communication dialog with the cloud-based gateway services, removing the need to open incoming firewall connections.

A typical example is the implementation of a Cloud Flow that communicates with a REST API hosted within the organization's internal network. Having installed an on-premise data gateway within reach of the on-premise REST API, the Cloud Flow can connect to it via an HTTP request.

The following diagram provides a high-level overview of how on-premise data gateways facilitate communications from Power Platform to intranet APIs:

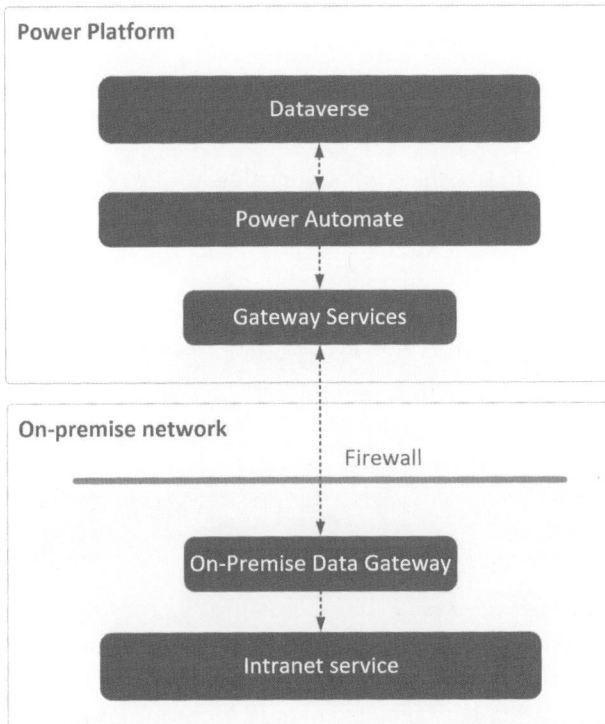

Figure 10.9 – Power Automate connecting to an on-premise network

---

Further Reading on On-Premise Data Gateways

For further details on how to configure on-premises data gateways, please refer to the following documentation: `https://docs.microsoft.com/power-automate/gateway-reference`.

Option 3 – connect to on-premise web applications with an Application Proxy

Web applications hosted within an on-premise environment may be made available for access from a remote client using an **Application Proxy**. The installation follows a similar pattern to on-premise data gateways. An Application Proxy Connector is installed within the on-premise environment at a network location where it has HTTP/HTTPS access to an internal web application. Once configured, the internal web application may be accessed from outside the on-premise network.

Use case scenarios for Application Proxies include linking or embedding internal web applications from a Power Platform model-driven app.

The following diagram illustrates the connection route for Power Apps users also leveraging an on-premise web application using the Application Proxy:

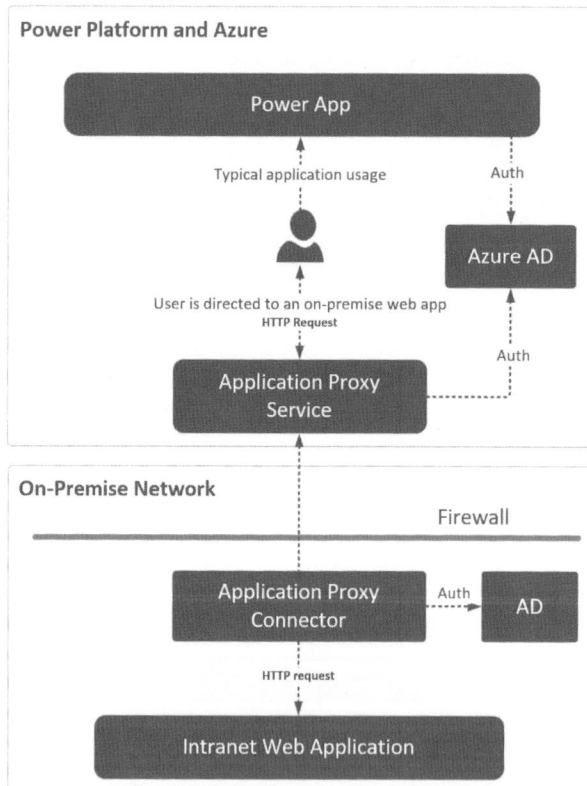

Figure 10.10 – Power Automate connecting to an on-premise network

> **Further Reading on Azure Application Proxy**
>
> For further details on Azure Application Proxy, please refer to the following documentation: `https://docs.microsoft.com/azure/active-directory/app-proxy/`.

Option 4 – bi-directional integration via Azure Service Bus

Azure Service Bus (**ASB**) provides a robust messaging queueing framework that can be leveraged for inbound and outbound integration with on-premise services. Bi-directional integration between Power Platform and an on-premise application may be implemented without opening an inbound firewall rule within the organization's internal network.

The following diagram illustrates an example of bi-directional integration with an on-premise application:

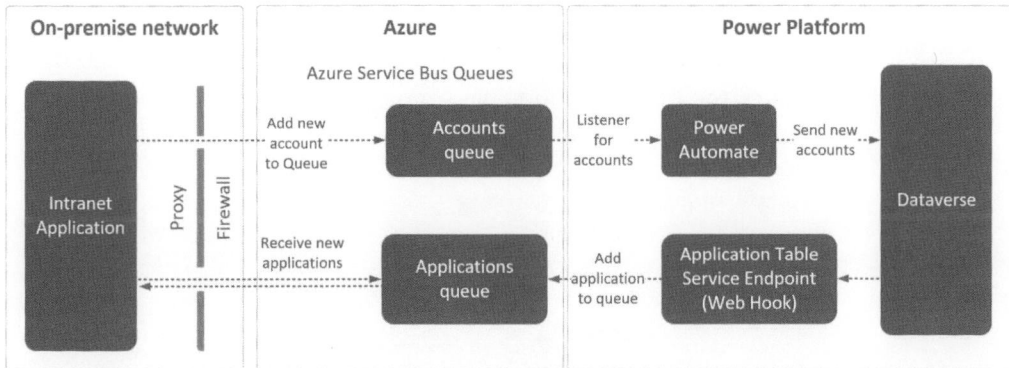

Figure 10.11 – Bi-directional Azure Service Bus integration using Dataverse service endpoints

In the preceding diagram, the integration dialogue is as follows:

- The intranet application sends new accounts to Power Platform via an ASB queue, using an outbound network connection to Azure.

- A Power Automate Flow listens for new ASB messages and updates Dataverse with new account data.

- The Dataverse "Application" table is configured with a service endpoint (webhook), the built-in Dataverse to ASB integration facility. When an Application record is created, the configured endpoint sends the full record context and data to the ASB queue.

- The on-premise application retrieves new Application records from the corresponding ASB queue.

While the proposed ASB integration does not require the inbound firewall rules within the on-premise network to be configured, it requires the intranet application's development or configuration to connect and retrieve messages from the ASB queue.

> **Further Reading on Dataverse Azure Service Bus Integration**
>
> For further details on the standard options available for Dataverse to Azure Service Bus integration, please refer to the following documentation:
> `https://docs.microsoft.com/power-apps/developer/`
> `data-platform/azure-integration.`

The service endpoint functionality that's available for Dataverse tables is a great option that leverages the standard asynchronous message processing functionality. The data that's posted into the ASB queue contains the full record context. The structure of the context message may be cumbersome to consume for services outside the Microsoft stack. An alternative option is to post the message to ASB using Power Automate, where you have greater control over the message contents.

In the following diagram, the ASB integration has been updated to send Application records via a Cloud Flow. When an Application record is created, a custom JSON message is posted to the queue containing the information required by the recipient:

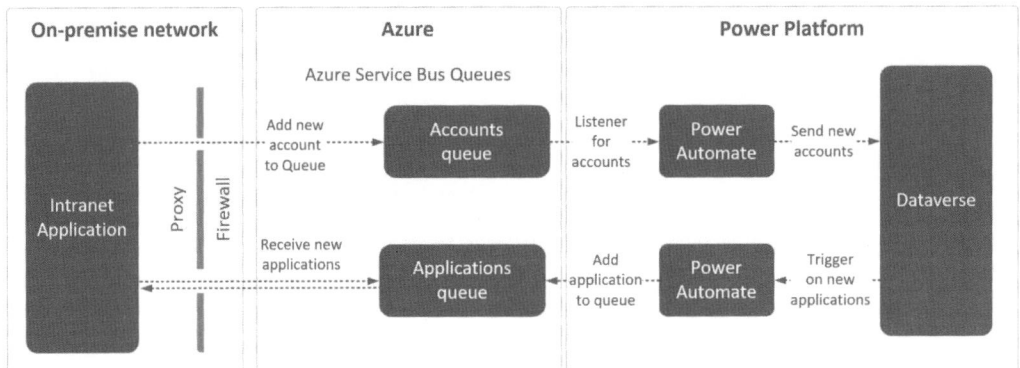

Figure 10.12 – Bi-directional Azure Service Bus integration using Power Automate

Now, let's look at the key features that ASB provides:

- **Retries**: If a listener is unable to process a message, ASB tries to deliver the message later on.

- **Dead letter queues**: If the message is not delivered to the recipient, it can be placed in the dead letter queue for review and processing.

- **Duplicate detection**: This optional feature provides a means of detecting and ignoring messages that have already been posted within a configurable time window.

- **Queues**: Allows a message to be posted that can be read by a recipient.

- **Topics**: If more than one recipient or listener needs to process a message, an ASB topic allows multiple subscribers to receive the same message.

ASB is a robust platform for asynchronous integrations and a valuable tool for Power Platform solution architects.

> **Further Reading on Dataverse Azure Service Bus Capabilities**
>
> For further details on API management, please refer to the following documentation: `https://docs.microsoft.com/azure/service-bus-messaging/service-bus-messaging-overview`.

Option 5 – connect to on-premise services via the API Management Gateway

Microsoft's API Management Gateway offering provides a means of orchestrating APIs within an organization, including on-premise interfaces, to standardize access, security, and protocols. It is a feature-rich service, deserving of a book to cover its capabilities alone.

Self-hosted gateways may be configured to provide access to on-premise APIs. Power Platform solution architects are aware of the capabilities within API Management as the platform may be in use by the organization. The following diagram illustrates the connection route from a Power Platform solution to an on-premise API via a self-hosted API Management Gateway:

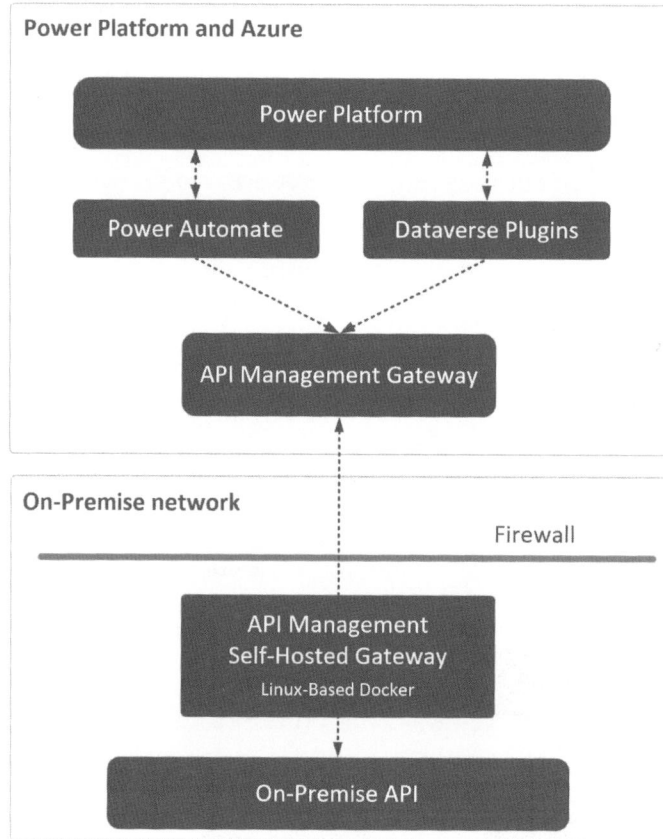

Figure 10.13 – Power Platform solution connecting to an on-premise service via an API Management Gateway

---

Further Reading on API Management

For further details on API Management, please refer to the following documentation: `https://azure.microsoft.com/services/api-management/`.

Integrating Power Platform applications with cloud-based services

The options that are available for connecting on-premise systems can usually be applied to cloud-based integrations. Cloud applications may push and pull data using the Dataverse API. The wide range of Power Automate connectors creates almost unlimited integration opportunities with Microsoft cloud-based systems and beyond.

Let's look at a few additional options that are available when connecting Power Platform solutions to other cloud-based services.

Integrating with external systems and Dataverse Virtual Tables

As far as the users are concerned, Dataverse Virtual Tables look like any other Dataverse table. Their data, however, is stored elsewhere and retrieved in real time via OData v4 or Azure Cosmos DB data providers (with the option of developing custom providers if required). The following diagram illustrates how Power Platform applications leverage Dataverse virtual entities to seamlessly integrate with external OData v4 services:

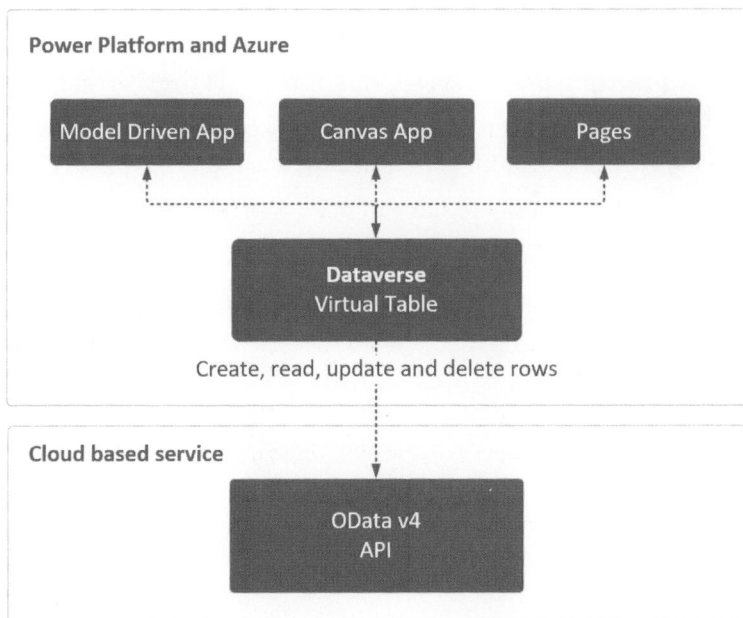

Figure 10.14 – Power Platform integration with an OData v4 API using Virtual Tables

Virtual Tables are created via the standard Power Platform solution editor, by selecting the corresponding table type. They are yet another powerful real-time integration tool that provides seamless integration with the Power Platform's application user interfaces.

> **Further Reading on Dataverse Virtual Tables**
>
> For further details on Dataverse Virtual Tables, please refer to the following documentation: `https://docs.microsoft.com/power-apps/developer/data-platform/virtual-entities/get-started-ve`.

Integrating external data sources into Dataverse using Dataflows

Dataflows are cloud-based services that can be configured to ingest, transform, and load data from various data sources into Dataverse and Azure Data Lake Storage.

The key considerations when selecting Dataflows for Power Platform integrations are as follows:

- They load data into Dataverse (and Azure Data Lake Storage) only. Bidirectional synchronization of data is not supported.
- There are 48 different types of data sources available at the time of writing, catering to a wide range of use cases.
- Advanced data transformations can be achieved using Power Query.
- The data loads may be configured to run manually, scheduled, or at a specific frequency.

The following diagram provides an overview of how Dataflows load data into Dataverse:

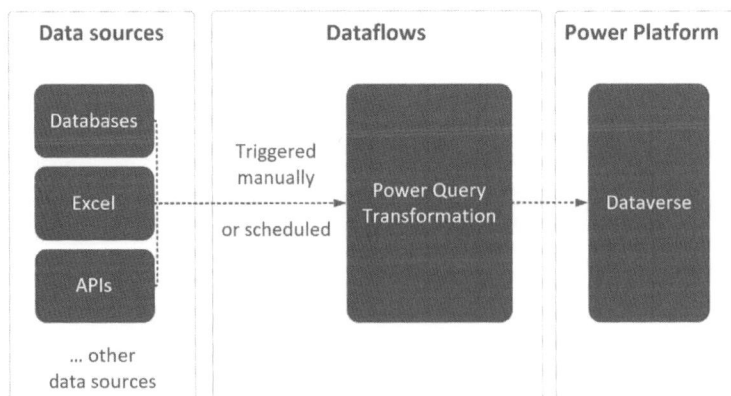

Figure 10.15 – Loading data into Dataverse using Dataflows

Dataflows may be created from the Power Apps menu, as shown in the following screenshot:

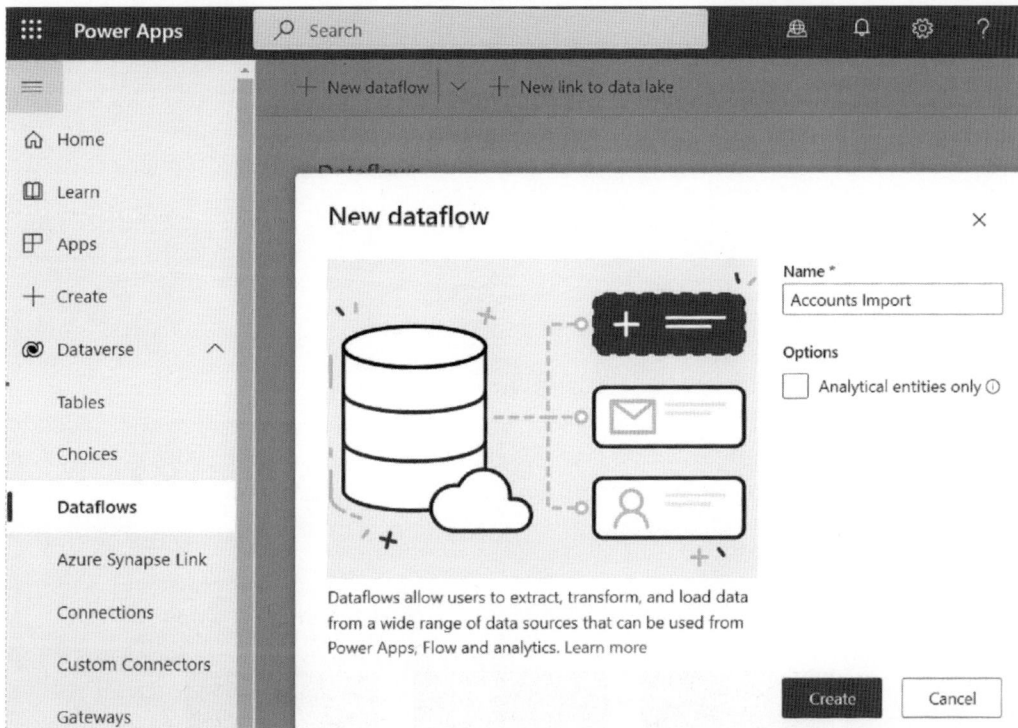

Figure 10.16 – The Dataflows creation page

Immediately after the Dataflow creation page, the user will be prompted to select a data source. Once the data source is selected, transformations may be configured via Power Query as illustrated in the following screenshot:

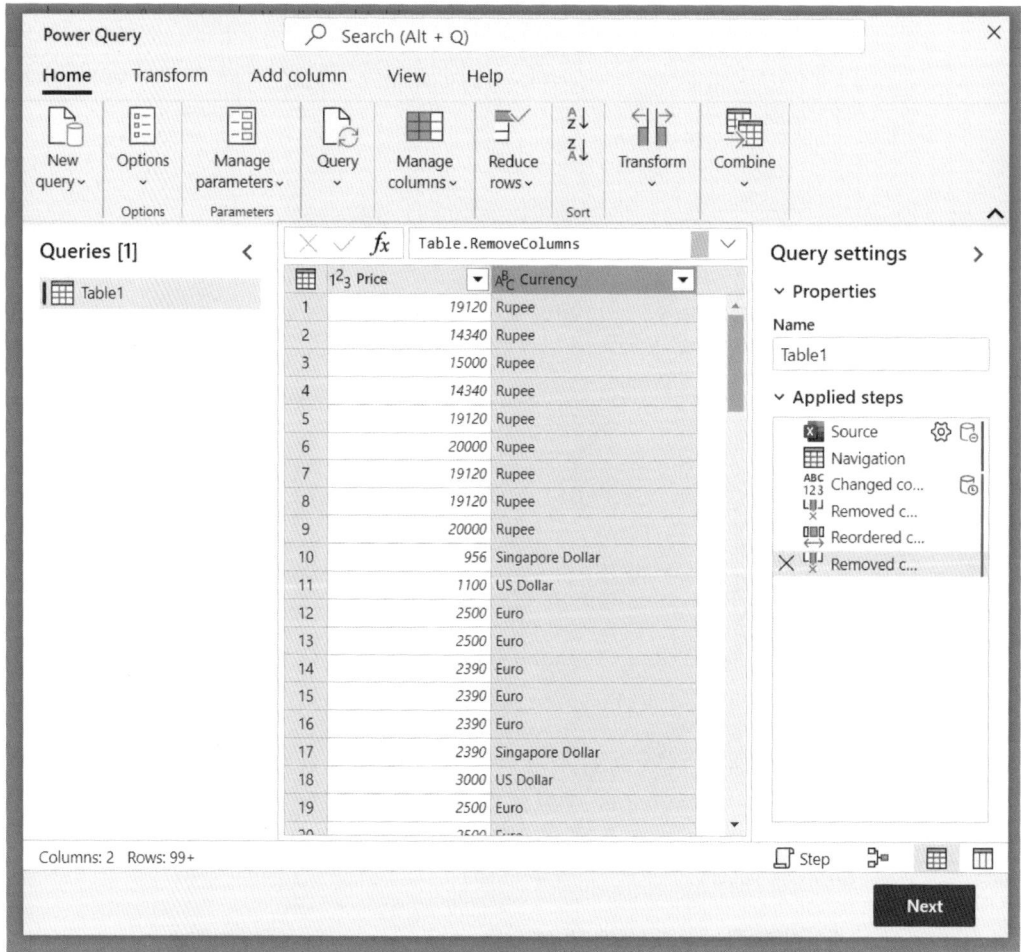

Figure 10.17 – Dataflow transformations using Power Query

Finally, the Dataflow load frequency is specified, allowing for scheduled runs, frequency-based refreshes, or manual triggers:

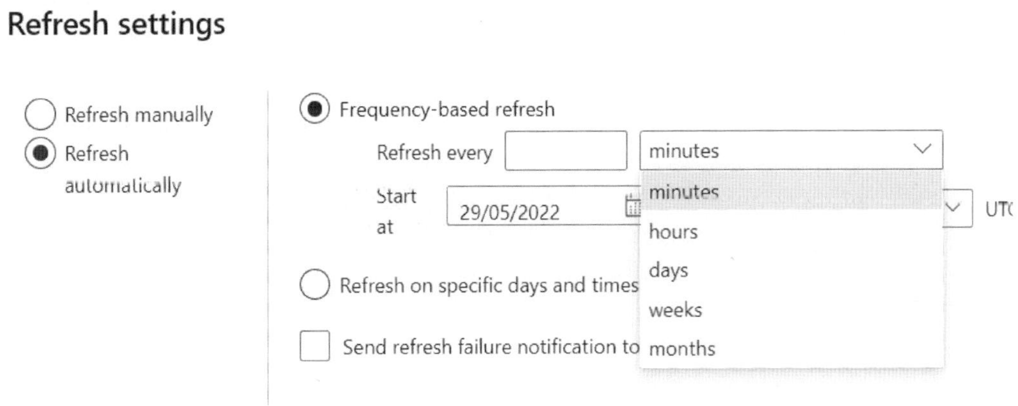

Refresh settings

Figure 10.18 – Refresh settings

Dataflows is a powerful yet easy-to-use integration tool that makes keeping Power Platform application data up-to-date close to effortless.

> **Further Reading on Dataflows for Power Platform Solutions**
>
> For more information on Dataflows for Power Platform solutions, please refer to the following documentation: `https://docs.microsoft.com/power-query/dataflows/overview-dataflows-across-power-platform-dynamics-365`.
>
> For step-by-step instructions on creating Dataflows, please go to `https://docs.microsoft.com/power-apps/maker/data-platform/create-and-use-dataflows`.

Defining inbound and outbound authentication strategies

Authentication is a key consideration when designing Power Platform integrations. The storage, retrieval, and life cycle of credentials are defined in the design documentation to ensure the implementation adheres to the best practices and the organization's security requirements.

The authentication of Power Platform integrations may be split into two areas. The first concerns itself with inbound authentication, granting access to clients wishing to connect to the Power Platform APIs. The second is outbound authentication against external services or APIs and securely managing the credentials for those services.

Designing Power Platform inbound authentication strategies

Clients looking to connect to the DataVerse API must authenticate before being granted access. Two of the main ways of authenticating are by using standard Microsoft 365 users with access to a Power Platform environment and Azure application users:

- **Option 1 – Authenticating using Azure applications users**:

    Azure application users may be configured with access to Power Platform Dataverse-based applications. These users may then be used to connect to the Dataverse APIs. Azure application users do not require a Microsoft 365 user to function. Client ID and secret pairs are generated for each application user, allowing clients to connect using these credentials.

    Azure application users provide additional features beyond standard Microsoft 365 users, including the ability to manage the expiry and rotation of secrets. Therefore, they are considered a secure solution for integrating external systems with Power Platform applications.

    Application users are configured via the Azure portal by following the **App registrations** section of the **Azure Active Directory** page, as shown in the following screenshot:

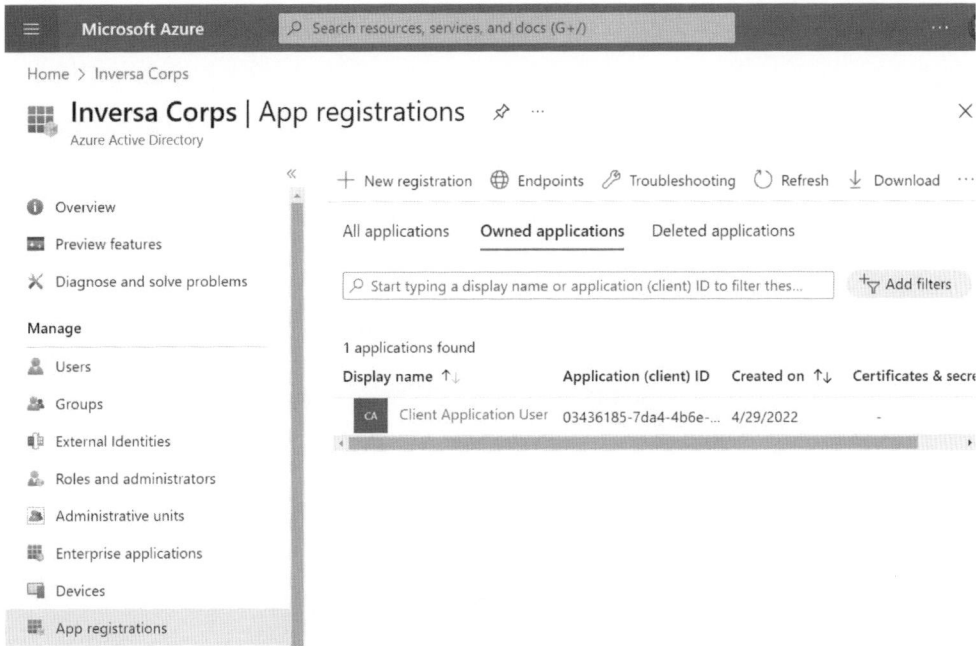

Figure 10.19 – App registrations configuration page

> **Further Reading on Creating Application Registrations to Use with Power Apps**
>
> The following documentation provides detailed instructions on how to create Azure application registrations to connect to Dataverse: `https://docs.microsoft.com/power-apps/developer/data-platform/walkthrough-register-app-azure-active-directory`.

- **Option 2 – Authenticating using Microsoft 365 Power Platform Users:**

  Clients can authenticate with the Dataverse API using Microsoft 365 user credentials. The Microsoft 365 user will require a valid Power Apps or Dynamics 365 license to access Dataverse.

> **Pillars for Great Architecture – Security**
>
> While it is possible to integrate external clients with Dynamics 365 using Microsoft 365 user credentials, Azure application users are better suited for the task. Their secret expiry and rotation capabilities make Azure application users the ideal candidates for inbound integrations into Dataverse and are the recommended option.

Designing Power Platform outbound authentication strategies

Power Platform components looking to connect to external systems or APIs are usually required to authenticate using a set of credentials or secrets. The secure storage and retrieval of these secrets are critical to the safe operation of the solution. Power Platform components manage credentials for connecting to external systems using the following mechanisms.

Azure Key Vault managed credentials

Azure Key Vault provides a secure location for storing, managing, and retrieving secrets and certificates. Power Automate Cloud Flow and Power Apps may be granted access to Key Vault secrets and certificates, allowing them to connect to external systems.

Secrets stored within Azure Key Vault may be configured for expiry and rotation. Azure Key Vault may be accessed from Cloud Flow, Dataverse plugins, and other Power Platform components.

The following screenshot illustrates a Key Vault secret being used to store credentials for an on-premise API:

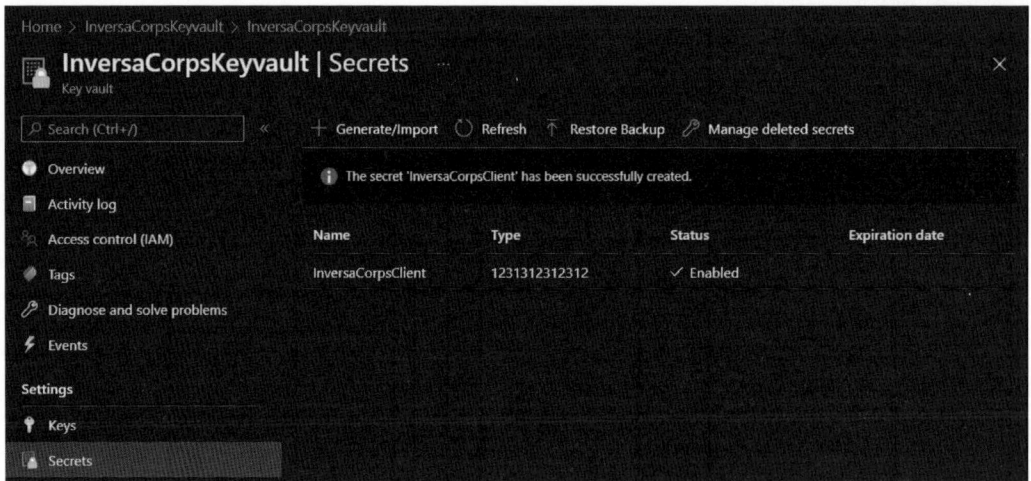

Figure 10.20 – Configuration of Azure Key Vault secrets

Access to read the Key Vault secrets is then granted to an integration user, allowing the solution to query the Key Vault at runtime, reading the credentials that will, in turn, be used to authenticate with an external application or API. Key Vault may also be used to store authentication or encryption certificates via the **Certificates** option. The following screenshot illustrates a Key Vault configuration granting an integration user access to read Key Vault secrets:

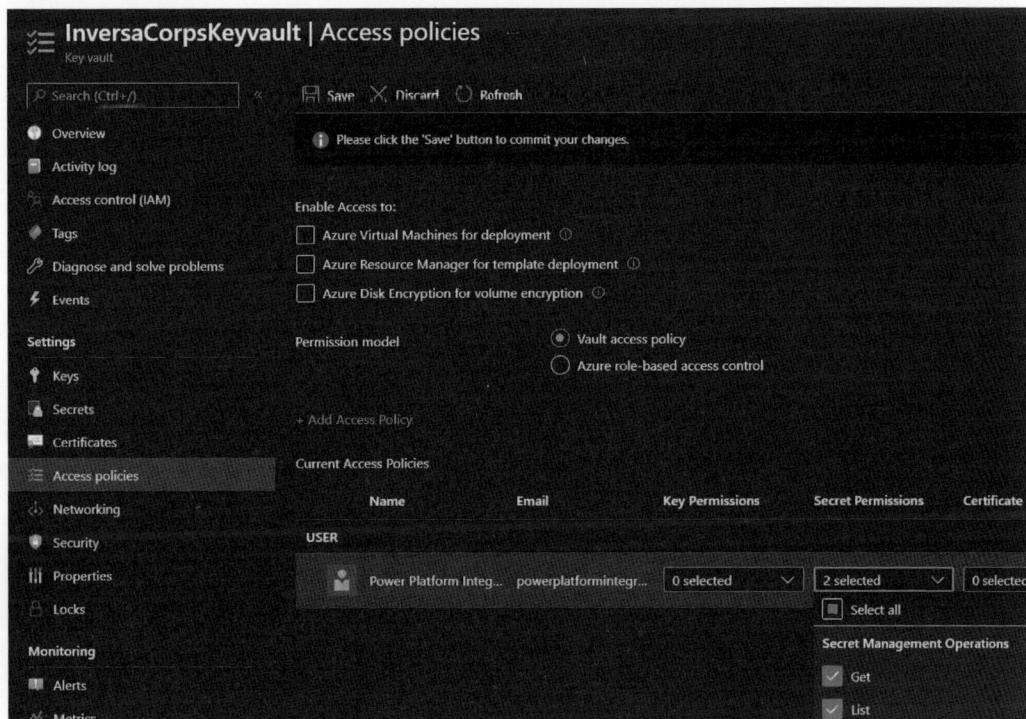

Figure 10.21 – Configuration of Azure Key Vault secrets

Further Reading on Azure Key Vault

For further details on Azure Key Vault, please refer to the following documentation: `https://docs.microsoft.com/azure/key-vault/`.

Storing credentials within Dataverse plugin secure configuration strings

Dataverse plugins allow you to define a secure configuration string where credentials may be stored for use by the plugin code. Although this feature does provide a means of storing and managing credentials for external systems, it does not offer the same rich feature set and security features as Azure Key Vault:

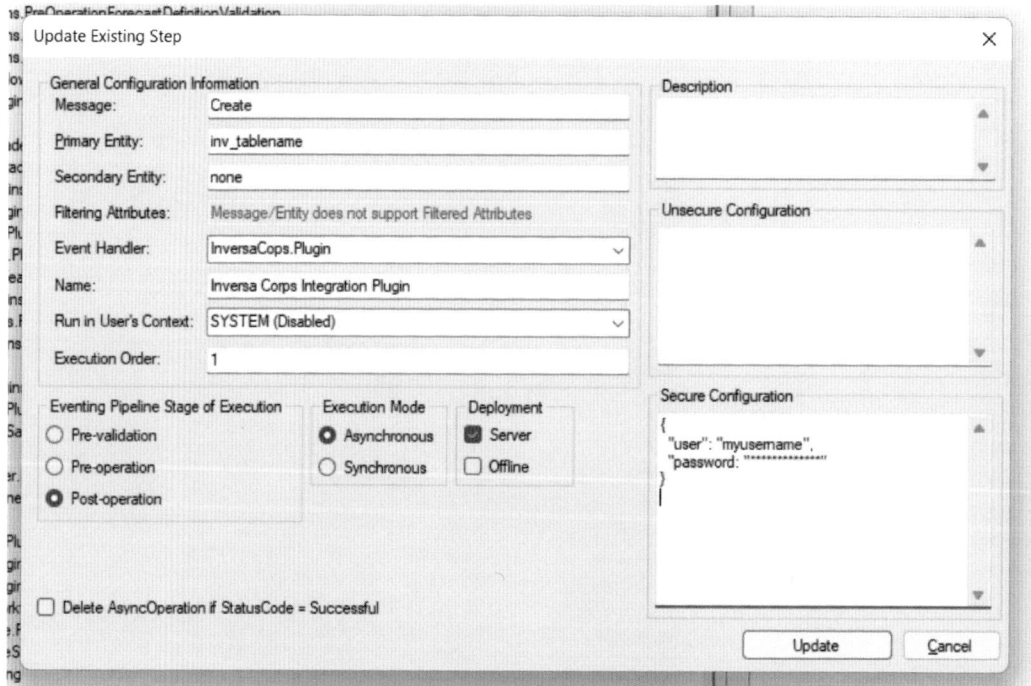

Figure 10.22 – Granting access to Azure Key Vault secrets

> **Further Reading on Registering Plugin Configuration Data**
>
> For more information about plugin configuration data, please go to
> `https://docs.microsoft.com/power-apps/developer/`
> `data-platform/register-plug-in#set-configuration-`
> `data`.

With the secure configuration in place, the Dataverse plugin can read a username and password (or other types of credentials). Certificates and encryption/decryption keys may also be stored in the plugin's secure configuration string. These are typically stored in Base64-encoded format. The plugin code is then passed the secure and unsecure configuration strings as per the following definition:

```
public IntegrationPlugin (string unsecure, string secure){}
```

All Power Platform system administrators with access to a Dataverse environment can read the secure configuration strings for all plugins.

> **Further Reading on Accessing Secure Configuration Data from Within a Plugin**
>
> Please read the following documentation for details on accessing secure plugin configuration data from within a plugin: https://docs.microsoft.com/power-apps/developer/data-platform/write-plug-in#pass-configuration-data-to-your-plug-in.

Designing a business continuity strategy for Power Platform integrations

When designing Power Platform integrations, it is vital to consider continuity strategies to maintain the smooth operation of the solution. A Power Platform continuity strategy may be broken down into three parts – monitoring and alerts, recovery, and exception handling.

Monitoring and alerts

When a system administrator is alerted of any downtime, errors, or transient disconnections, they can act to rectify any issues. Designing and building integrations that present a view of their current and past operational status is key to smoothly running a Power Platform solution. A solid application and integration logging strategy will help provide that transparency to system administrators, allowing them to act quickly in the event of a fault, maintaining optimal system operation.

This level of transparency may be achieved through a three-prong strategy.

Step 1 – Log errors in a table:

Creating and using a **Log** table provides an easy-to-use logging mechanism for integrations, business processes, plugins, and custom code to report any issues that are encountered. The following Dataverse table may be used for this purpose:

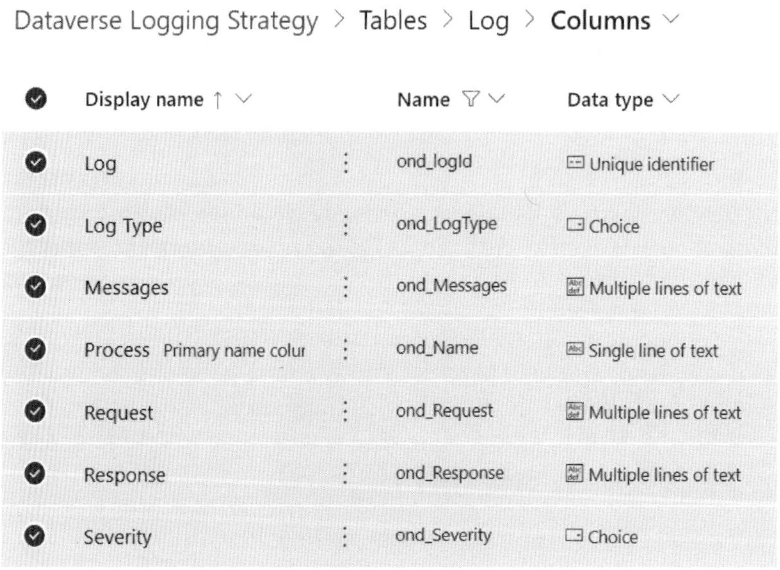

Dataverse Logging Strategy > Tables > Log > **Columns** ∨

	Display name ↑ ∨		Name ∇ ∨	Data type ∨
✓	Log	⋮	ond_logId	⊡ Unique identifier
✓	Log Type	⋮	ond_LogType	▢ Choice
✓	Messages	⋮	ond_Messages	⬚ Multiple lines of text
✓	Process Primary name colur	⋮	ond_Name	⬚ Single line of text
✓	Request	⋮	ond_Request	⬚ Multiple lines of text
✓	Response	⋮	ond_Response	⬚ Multiple lines of text
✓	Severity	⋮	ond_Severity	▢ Choice

Figure 10.23 – Example Dataverse logging table columns

An error log is recorded whenever a fault occurs within an integration or process. Information messages may also be saved to facilitate integration review activities (for example, confirming the response from third-party systems).

The result is a table that records faults and critical information related to integrations and business processes and their severity (ranging from **Info**, **Warning**, to **Error**) and process type. The following is a sample set of log data:

Log Type	Severity	Process	Messages	Request	Response	Status
Integration	Info	SAP Integration	Connectivity restor...	{ "id": "123...	{ "result": ...	Pending
Integration	Error	SAP Integration	Invoice is required	{ "id": "123...	{ "result": ...	Pending
Automation	Warning	Onboarding Proce...	Unable to complet...	{ "id": "456...	{ "result": ...	Pending
Automation	Error	Onboarding Proce...	The Flow failed wit...			Pending
Integration	Error	Website Integration	API not responding	{ "comman...	{ "result": ...	Pending
External System	Info	Inbound Products	Catalog updated			Pending
UX	Error	Application Form	User experienced ...			Pending
Automation	Error	Onboarding Proce...	The Flow failed wit...	request	Response	Pending

Figure 10.24 – Example log table listing integration and business processes faults

Step 2 – Provide a monitoring tool for integration faults:

Administrators and system owners need concise information to make decisions and take corrective actions when a fault occurs. A model-driven app dashboard displaying the logged errors over time and errors pending review gives administrators visibility over the past and current state of the various integrations and processes.

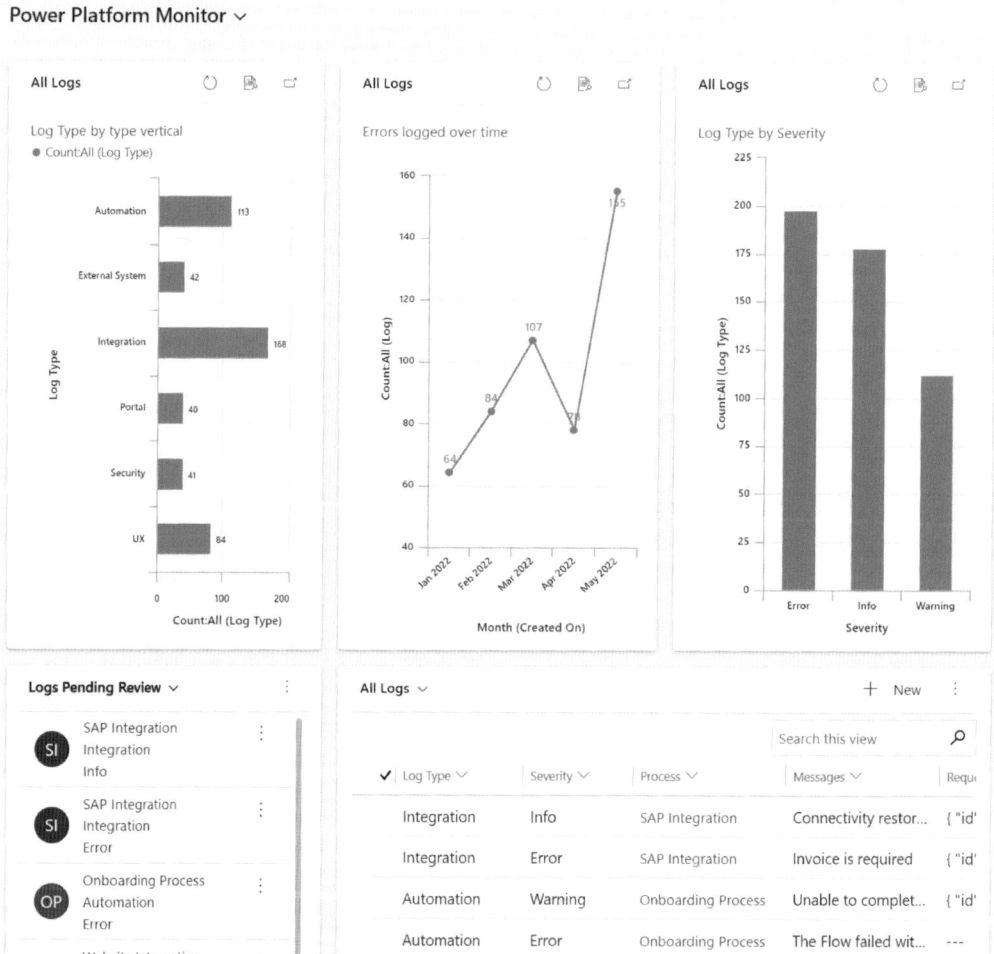

Figure 10.25 – Example Power Platform integration status monitoring dashboard

Administrators can mark the Log records as completed (deactivated) once the issue has been addressed. The action of completing a log entry in this instance removes the log entry from the **Logs Pending Review** section, allowing administrators to focus on new and pending faults.

Step 3 – Create automated fault notifications for administrators:

Notifying administrators when a fault of sufficient severity is logged can help expedite its resolution. Notifications may be in the form of an email message or in-app notifications.

> **Further Reading on In-App Notifications**
>
> Model-driven apps provide a valuable means of notifying model-driven app users via in-app notifications. Please refer to the following documentation for details: `https://docs.microsoft.com/power-apps/developer/model-driven-apps/clientapi/send-in-app-notifications`.

Recovery

Power Platform solution architects aim to design integrations that can auto-recover from transient errors. As we mentioned earlier in this chapter, Power Platform components that integrate with external systems should be designed with retry orchestration to overcome transient errors, as well as a recovery strategy where a process runs on a schedule, addressing failed attempts and integrating with external systems. Through this strategy of retry and recovery, manual intervention and operational costs are reduced, and system uptime is increased.

Please see the *Cloud Flow integration retry orchestration* section in this chapter for an example of an auto-recovering integration strategy.

Exception handling

There will be instances where an outage or error occurs where the solution may not automatically recover. In those instances, it is important to have a clear exception handling strategy so that administrators and support staff can identify components that require attention. Dashboards and views designed explicitly for this purpose will help users take the proper action to rectify the data, allowing the system to continue through its normal process.

The fault logging strategy discussed earlier in this chapter can be used to present system owners with an up-to-date view of the current status of the solution. These logs may be presented graphically to alert administrators when high severity issues arise or to help them identify a surging number of cases, as illustrated in the following visualizations:

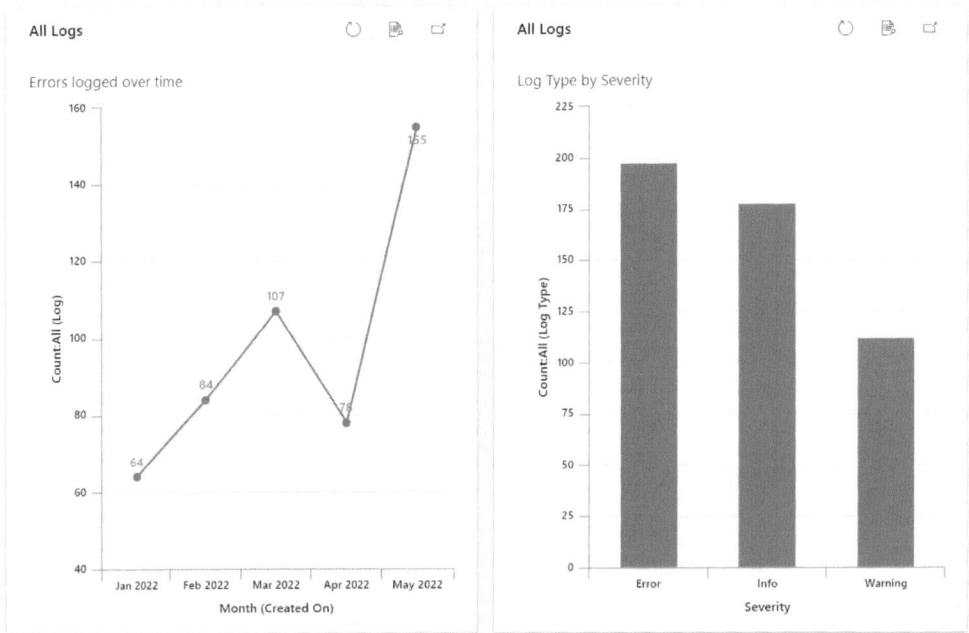

Figure 10.26 – Example real-time integration fault dashboard visualizations

These logging and monitoring tools allow administrators to handle exceptions effectively, enabling early remedial action, increasing service uptime, and reducing operational costs.

Summary

In this chapter, we reviewed the options that are available when integrating Power Platform applications with external systems. You learned how to design integrations with Microsoft 365's key components, including SharePoint and Exchange. You should now understand the options available when connecting to on-premise systems.

Understanding the integration options available to Power Platform applications and the authentication strategies that underpin a secure implementation is crucial for the successful rollout and operation of Power Platform solutions.

In the next chapter, we will look at the concepts and design patterns that make up a secure Power Platform solution.

11
Defining Power Platform Security Concepts

Securing customer and operational data is a key concern of organizations embarking on a digital transformation journey. In this chapter, you will learn how to design a **Power Platform security** model that facilitates the implementation by defining the business unit and team structures, security roles, and column security. You will also define the **Azure Active Directory** configurations required to support a secure authentication process, alongside **data loss prevention (DLP)** policies.

We will define **Power Apps Portal**, **Power Automate**, and **Canvas apps security mode** to support the customer's requirements. You will design management policies to control changes to the security model.

In this chapter, we're going to cover the following topics:

- Designing the Power Platform core security model
- Identifying data loss prevention policies for Power Platform solutions
- Securing Dataverse-based applications
- Defining access routes for external Power Platform users

Designing the Power Platform core security model

Designing a Power Platform core security model involves tackling access to data and systems from three vectors:

- **Authentication:** This vector helps provide a means for users or other systems to validate their right to access Power Platform applications. Authentication is generally handled by the Microsoft 365 user management processes.

- **Network:** We know that connecting to Power Platform systems requires access at the network level. Power Platform solutions are SaaS cloud-hosted. Network access to those cloud-hosted services is, therefore, part of the solution architects' design remit.

- **Authorization:** Once a user is authenticated, they are granted access to Power Platform resources and/or systems based on the permissions associated with their account. Solution architects define the authorization strategies that grant user access.

Understanding an organization's security requirements

During the discovery phase, solution architects work with the business to identify the security infrastructure currently in place. The implementation of a Power Platform solution is unlikely to be the guiding factor for an organization's security and authentication strategy. Power Platform solutions architects look to work with the policies and framework currently in place.

Security infrastructure discovery checklist

To understand an organization's existing security framework, solution architects work with business analysts and systems owners to complete a **security baseline checklist**, similar to the one described in the following table:

Security Infrastructure Discovery Checklist	
1	Do you use Azure Active Directory?
2	Do you use Active Directory On-Premise?
3	Do you use directory solutions from other sources?
4	Do you use multi-factor authentication?
5	Do you use conditional access?
6	Do you need to access other Microsoft 365 tenants?
7	Do you need to provide access to external users or organizations?

Table 11.1 – Example security infrastructure discovery checklist

These questions will help you get a base understanding of the current security and authentication infrastructure. The answers may warrant further questions and investigation to pinpoint the detailed security framework. Once you understand the security systems in place, you are ready to find out how they are managed.

Security management discovery

Once the existing security framework has been identified, you can proceed to discover its management and change processes. The following set of questions can help solution architects understand the security processes to be followed when implementing a Power Platform solution:

Security Management Discovery Questions	
1	How is security managed?
	For example, how are Microsoft 365 users created, as well as the product licenses associated with them?
2	What security policies must be followed?
3	Is there an approval process for security architecture?
4	How is access to applications managed?
5	Is there a specific team that will be responsible for controlling Power Platform security?
6	What is the process for granting users access to applications?

Table 11.2 – Example security management discovery questions

The answers to these questions will dictate the process to be followed during the design and implementation of the Power Platform security concepts.

Power Platform security guidelines and best practices

The following are a set of guidelines and best practices you should follow when designing and implementing the Power Platform security concepts:

- **Grant access to data as needed**: This concept means to grant access to the data that's required for users' roles while providing read-only access to related data for context. Deleting data is to be limited, in favor of deactivating records.

- **Keep it simple**: When defining a security strategy, solution architects consider how difficult it would be to manage on a day-to-day basis, and the effort involved in making changes to the security model. Hence, it is a good idea to keep it simple.

- **Use the features provided by the platform**: Customer requirements may sometimes lead to a custom security implementation. These requirements may be born out of apprehension that's inherent to moving to a cloud-based solution. Custom security implementations are often expensive to build, and difficult to change and maintain. Solution architects work to understand the real need behind complex security requirements and propose a solution that leverages the standard Power Platform and Microsoft 365 security features.

- **Implement security at the platform layer**: This concept helps leverage the platform's security features rather than bespoke application security. Standard platform layer security is usually easier to implement and maintain.

- **The security model is a living document**: Organizations evolve and so do requirements and Power Platform implementations. Solution architects design a security model and make the designs accessible to the system owners. As the usage of the system grows, the security model may require updates as the original requirements and the decisions that were made around them may no longer apply.

Securing Power Platform environments

There are several ways users may gain access to Power Platform environments. Solution architects understand all the access vectors and define a security model that defines how each of them will be configured.

Controlling access via security groups

Power Platform environments may be associated with a Microsoft 365 or Azure AD group, effectively restricting access to the environment to members of that group. During the initial environment definition, solution architects define the security groups that are required to control access to each environment level.

Once an environment is associated with a group, only members of that group can access the system (except for Microsoft 365 global admins, Power Platform admins, and delegate admins).

The following diagram illustrates a typical Power Platform environment and security group configuration:

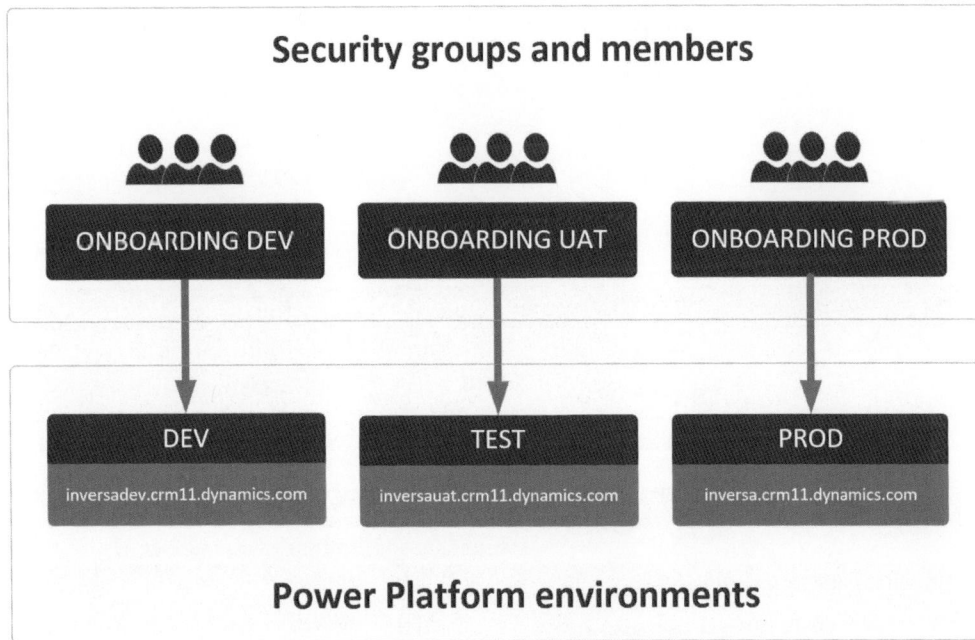

Figure 11.1 – Example Power Platform security group environment configuration

Having configured the environments and security groups, administrators can control the users that have access to each Power Platform environment level by adding and removing users from each group. Environments may be configured to use security groups via the Power Platform administration portal, as illustrated in the following screenshot:

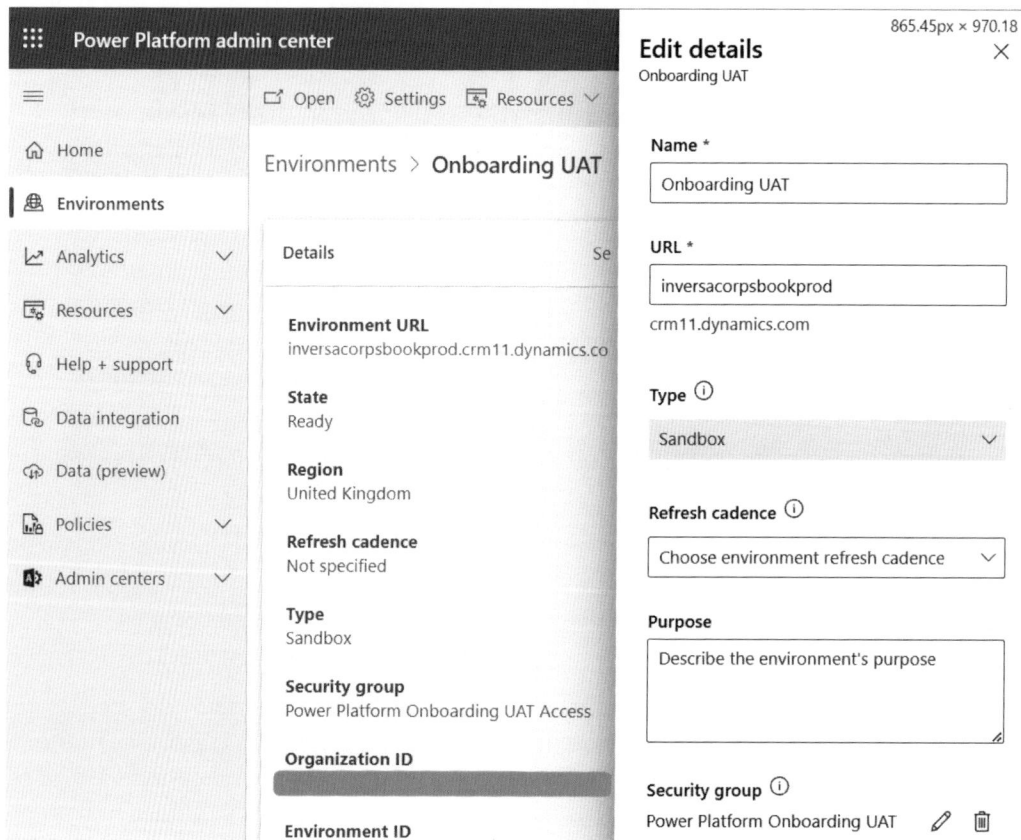

Figure 11.2 – Setting security group access for a Power Platform environment

If a Power Platform environment is not associated with a security group, all users with the appropriate license will be automatically added to the environment. When a Microsoft 365/AD user is added to a security group, they are automatically added to the *Dataverse environment*. Conversely, when a user is removed from a security group, their corresponding Dataverse user is deactivated.

> **Note**
>
> When a security group is associated with a Power Platform environment, all the users that were previously active within the system will be deactivated unless they are already in the security group (or they have a Microsoft 365 admin role granting them access to the environment).

Microsoft 365 roles and admin accounts

Microsoft 365 includes specialized roles that automatically grant system administrators access to Power Platform environments. These Microsoft 365 roles are as follows:

- **Global Administrator**: Users with this role have the highest level of control over a Microsoft 365 tenant, and they are automatically granted system administrator access to all Power Platform environments within it. These users are granted access regardless of the security group configuration.

- **Microsoft Power Platform Admin**: Users with this Microsoft 365 role are granted access to all Power Platform environments. They can manage Power Apps, Power Automate, and data loss prevention policies. These users are granted access regardless of their security group configuration.

- **Delegated Admin**: Used by **Microsoft Cloud Solution Provider program (CSP)**, partners, this role grants users access to all services within a tenant. Users with this role will also have system administrator access to Power Platform environments.

Environment roles

Users may also be granted roles within a Power Platform environment. If a Dataverse database does not exist with an environment, the following two roles may be used:

- **Maker**: Users with this environment role can create and manage Power Apps within a Power Platform environment

- **Admin**: Users can manage the Power Platform environment's configuration and settings

Once a Dataverse database has been created within a Power Platform environment, the Dataverse security model takes over.

Providing Dataverse API access to external applications

External applications looking to access the Dataverse API will need to authenticate themselves. Two types of users exist for this purpose.

- **Users**: Licensed users with a Microsoft 365 account. While external clients can authenticate with a Microsoft 365 username and password, it is not the recommended access route. A Power Platform or Dynamics 365 license will be required, and standard users do not provide the same means of security afforded by application users.

- **Application users**: Users registered in Azure AD as application registrations. These types of users do not consume a Power Platform or Dynamics 365 license.

Please refer to *Chapter 10*, *Power Platform Integration Strategies*, for instructions on creating application users.

> **Further Reading**
>
> The following documentation provides full details on managing application users within a Power Platform environment: `https://docs.microsoft.com/power-platform/admin/manage-application-users`.

Defining data loss prevention policies for Power Platform solutions

Data loss prevention (**DLP**) policies help prevent data from being released unintentionally. They help protect the security of a tenant.

When configuring and implementing a Power Platform solution, it is important to be aware of the following DLP features and restrictions that may be in place.

Key DLP considerations

The following are some key DLP considerations:

- DLP controls the combination of connectors that may be used
- DLP policies are not enabled by default
- Tenant administrators may define DLP policies for all environments within a tenant

- DLP policies may be implemented at the tenant or environment level
- Environment DLP policies may not override tenant DLP policies
- DLP policies are cumulative, with the most restrictive policy being applied

Data loss prevention best practices

The following is a list of guiding principles when defining DLP policies:

- It is a good idea to define the minimal number of policies.
- Avoid applying multiple policies to an environment if possible.
- Apply DLP policies across all environments, block unsupported non-Microsoft connectors, and classify Microsoft connectors as "business data."
- Define a policy for Power Platform default environments and other non-production environments, with additional restrictions on connectors classified as business data.
- For specific environments that require additional access, create additional policies or exclude them from the more restrictive ones.
- Establish policies early and create exceptions later.

Deployment of data loss prevention policies

When deploying DLP policies, solution architects consider the following:

- When a DLP is rolled out, it may disable existing Power Apps or Cloud Flows.
- Policies may take minutes to propagate to all environments.
- Policies may be applied at the tenant or environment level only, not at the user level.
- Users may view the DLP policies that have been applied.

If an existing process is found to be in breach of the DLP policies, it will be automatically disabled, and the owner will receive the following email notification:

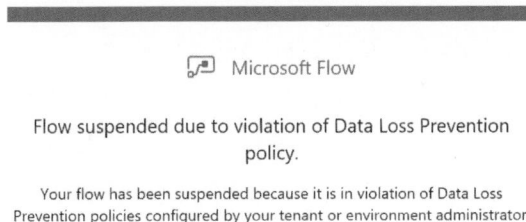

Figure 11.3 – Notification received by owners of processes restricted by DLP policies

DLP deployment checklist

Before DLP policies are configured, it is important to validate the rollout by running through a DLP deployment checklist that includes the following aspects:

- **Confirm feasibility**: Confirm that the Power Platform solution can be delivered and configure DLP to allow the Power Platform solution to function.

- **Confirm owners**: Understand what the Power Platform team has control over, and what is controlled by other teams or groups.

- **Confirm lead time**: The lead time required for configuring DLP policies so that it can be taken into account during the rollout of the solution.

Configuring and updating DLP policies

Depending on the size of the organization, there may be individuals or teams dedicated to configuring DLP policies. Power Platform solution architects either configure or provide input for configuring DLP policies to ensure the Power Platform solution is secure, while at the same time being able to perform.

DLP policies may be configured via the Power Platform admin center by selecting the **Data policies** option, as illustrated in the following screenshot:

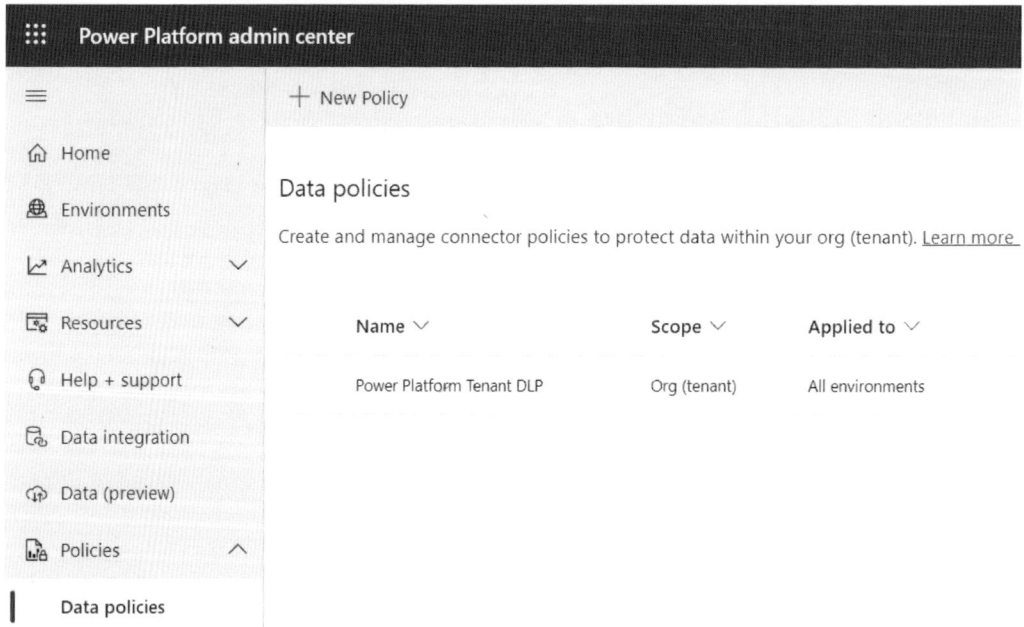

Figure 11.4 – Configuring Power Platform DLP policies

The DLP configuration pages allow you to categorize connectors into one of three areas:

- **Non-business (default)**: Connectors for non-sensitive data
- **Business**: Connectors that will handle sensitive business data
- **Blocked**: Connectors that may not be used

The following screenshot illustrates the DLP connector configuration page. Note that custom connectors may also be configured and restricted via a DLP policy using an API/connector host URL pattern:

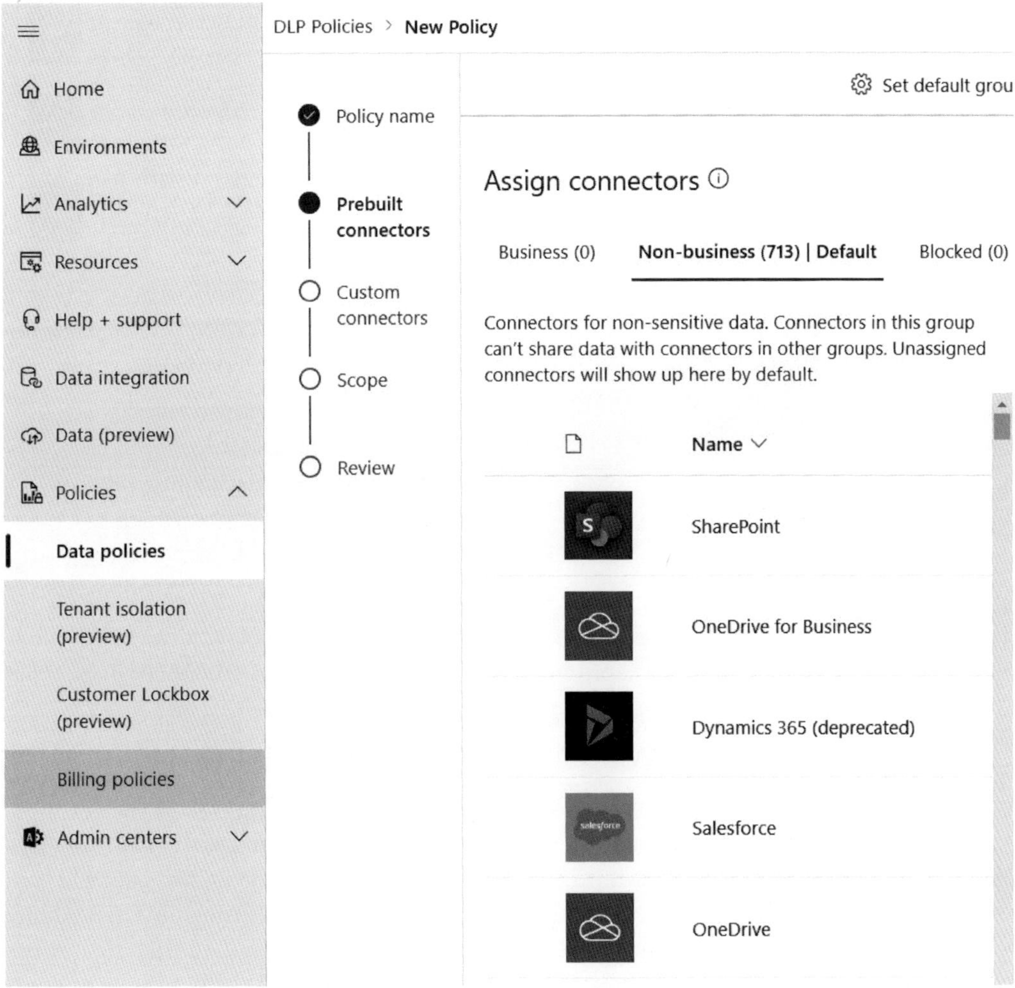

Figure 11.5 – DLP connector restriction options

And finally, once the connectors have been assigned to their appropriate DLP restriction categories, the policy itself may be associated with all Power Platform environments or specific environments, as illustrated in the following screenshot:

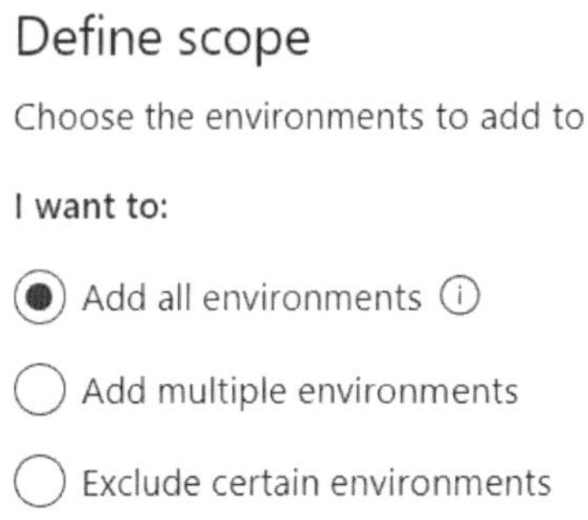

Define scope

Choose the environments to add to this policy. Learn more

I want to:

◉ Add all environments ⓘ

◯ Add multiple environments

◯ Exclude certain environments

Figure 11.6 – Defining the scope of DLP policies

DLP policies are powerful tools that can help prevent the unauthorized distribution of business data. Solution architects work with organizations to define and configure DLP policies to ensure the Power Platform's data is secure.

> **Further Reading**
>
> Please refer to the following documentation for detailed instructions on how to configure DLP policies: `https://docs.microsoft.com/power-platform/admin/prevent-data-loss`.

Securing Dataverse-based applications

In this section, we will discuss how to secure Dataverse and the applications that use its security framework. We will start by looking at how users interact with the solution, tailoring the security settings to enable authorized tasks and restrict other activities.

Common usage patterns for security design

When defining the security model, solution architects assess how the system will be used. The following table lists the key patterns for users looking to access Power Platform applications:

Usage Pattern	Description	Usage Examples
Active involvement	Direct interaction with the data or the customer.	Sales staff
Secondary involvement	Providing cover for absence, providing specialist advice.	Interim staff and legal teams
Transactional interaction	Responding to requests, actioning, no ongoing engagement.	Contact center staff
Management oversight	Oversight over the business or an area. Providing direction to others and reviewing.	Sales manager and finance director
Reporting	Viewing aggregated data, preserving anonymity, no direct access to customer data.	Contact center manager
Compliance	Read access to all records for the business area, to assure compliance.	Compliance and legal departments

Table 11.3 – Common usage patterns for Dataverse applications

When defining the security model, solution architects analyze how users interact with data and whether they work by themselves or interact with other team members.

Best practices

Power Platform solution architects secure Dataverse solutions with the following best practices in mind:

- Design security to cater to the majority of access patterns, and treat exceptions as such.

- Use **Dataverse Business Units** as security boundaries for controlling access to data, rather than as a replica of the organizational structure.

- Use the simplest security model that meets the requirements while still being performant.

- Access to a single record may not be revoked when access to a broader dataset containing the record has been granted. The security model must be defined accordingly.

Leveraging Dataverse security features

Dataverse provides a rich feature set for managing data access privileges. The following list outlines the main Dataverse security concepts:

- Users

- Teams

- Business Units

- Table ownership

- Security roles

- Column-level security

- Sharing

- Azure AD security groups

- Auditing

- Hierarchical security

The following subsections describe each of these security concepts.

Users

Users looking to access Dataverse data require a **user record**. Privileges are configured for that user, granting access to tables, columns, and rows. These user records are automatically created when a Microsoft 365 user account is granted access to Dataverse by assigning the corresponding licenses and security groups (where appropriate; see **Azure AD Groups** security configuration for Dataverse teams, as described in the following section).

The two main types of Dataverse users are as follows:

- **Licensed Users**: Users with a Microsoft 365 user account

- **Application users**: Users configured for applications and external services to communicate with Dataverse

Licensed Users

Users with the appropriate license and group membership will appear on the Power Platform admin center page, as follows:

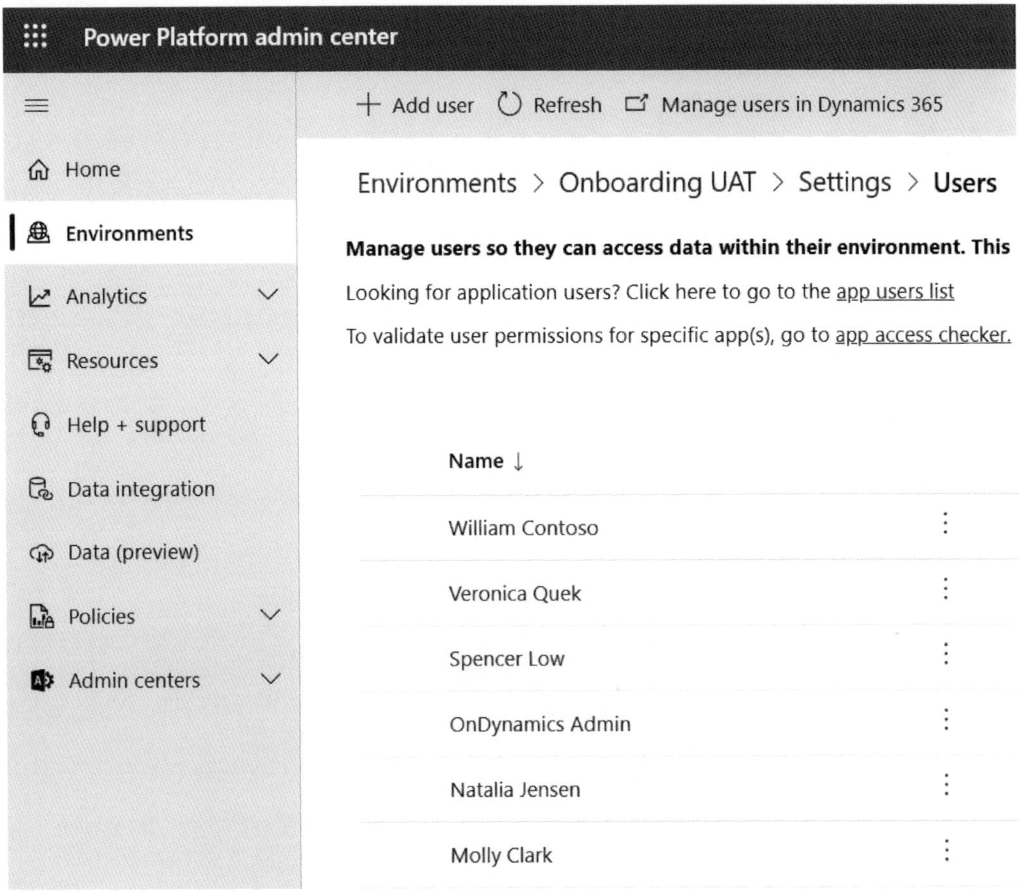

Figure 11.7 – Power Platform admin center page listing active users

Application users

New application users can be registered via the **App registrations** section of the Azure Active Directory page in the Azure portal. The following screenshot illustrates an example application user registered in Active Directory:

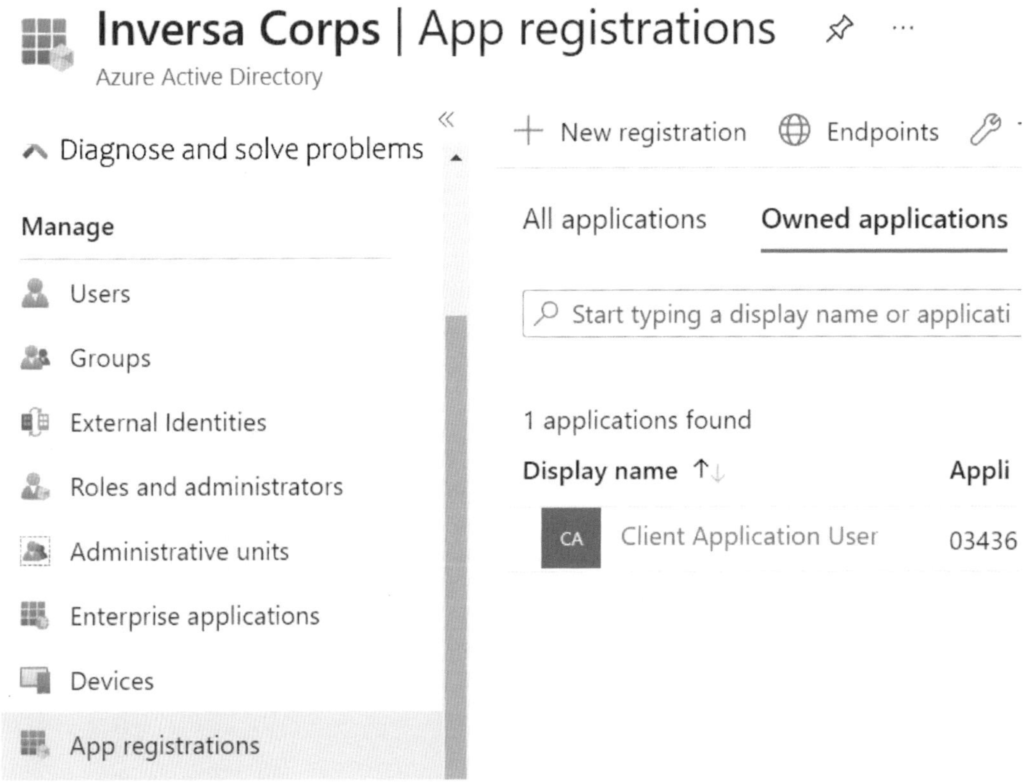

▦ Inversa Corps | App registrations ⚲ ⋯
Azure Active Directory

«

⌄ Diagnose and solve problems ▲

＋ New registration	⊕ Endpoints	🔧

Manage

👤 Users

👥 Groups

🕮 External Identities

👥 Roles and administrators

👥 Administrative units

▦ Enterprise applications

🖳 Devices

▦ App registrations

All applications   **Owned applications**

🔍 Start typing a display name or applicati

1 applications found

Display name ↑↓		Appli
CA	Client Application User	03436

Figure 11.8 – The Azure portal page listing App registrations configured in AD

Once the application registration is complete, the application user may be created in the Power Platform admin center. The resulting application user is illustrated in the following screenshot:

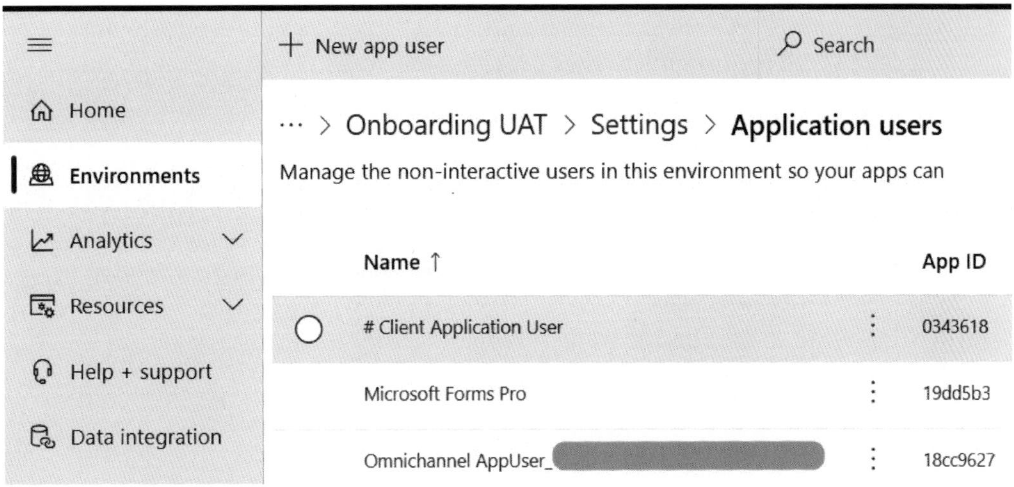

Figure 11.9 – Power Platform admin center listing configured application users

Standard users and application users can then be given security roles and assigned to teams.

> **Further Reading**
> Please refer to the following documentation for additional details on Power Platform application users: https://docs.microsoft.com/en-us/power-platform/admin/manage-application-users.

Teams

Dataverse Teams provide a means of grouping users. Grouping users into teams reduces or removes the need for managing rights for each user, and provides a mechanism for granting row access to the entire group.

There are four types of Dataverse teams:

- **Owner Teams**: These teams may own (or be assigned) rows. As a result, members of that team are granted access to those rows.

- **Access Teams**: Used for easily sharing access to records, access teams are not associated with security roles. They provide a mechanism for associating and granting access to users and specific records.

- **Azure AD Security Group Teams**: These teams work the same as Owner Teams. Membership is managed in Azure AD security groups.

- **Azure AD Office Group Teams**: The same as Azure AD Security Group Teams, except they are associated with a Microsoft 365 group, which may be created by users with lesser privileges.

When creating a Dataverse Azure AD Security or Office Group team, it is possible to define whether members, guests, or owners of the group will be replicated as Dataverse users. The following screenshot illustrates the available options:

Membership type *

| Members and guests | ⌄ |

Members and guests

Members

Owners

Guests

Figure 11.10 – Group member replication options available when creating an Azure AD Security or Office Group team

Solution architects review the organization's functional and security requirements and define a team strategy that leverages the different types of teams. The following diagram illustrates various use cases for the different types of Dataverse teams:

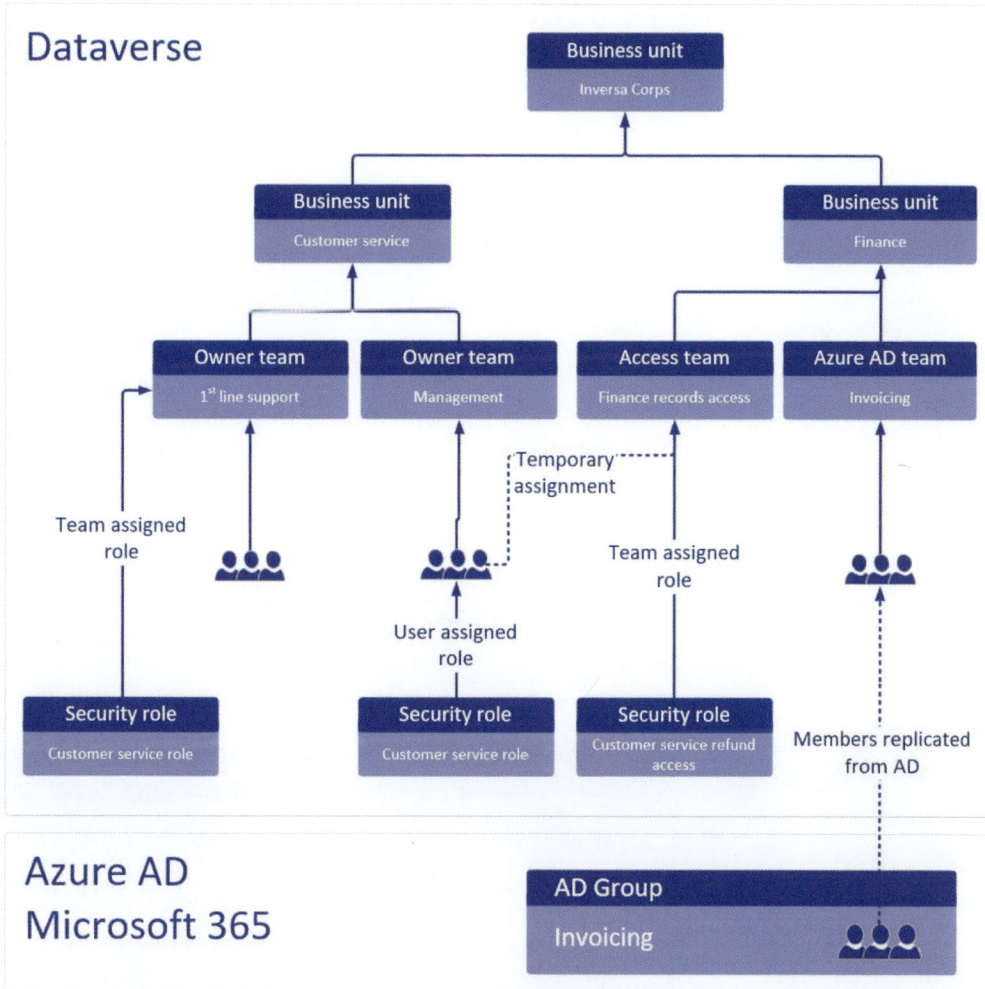

Figure 11.11 – Diagram illustrating various use cases for the different types of Dataverse teams

Business units

Dataverse **business units** contain teams and users. They are key components in the Dataverse security model, as they allow data to be partitioned within tables. Combining business units with security models allows users and their data to be segmented.

When designing the Dataverse security model, solution architects define a business unit hierarchy that matches the security requirements, rather than the organizational structure,

Consider the following when defining Business Units:

- Dataverse Business Units are there to facilitate the segmentation of data.

- As their primary function is to secure data, they should be defined and created with that purpose in mind.

- Since they mirror an organization's structure directly, Dataverse Business Units are likely to hinder the security modeling process as they will create additional unnecessary complexity to be worked around.

- It is the combination of security roles and business units that control the segmentation of data.

The following diagram illustrates a typical business unit structure:

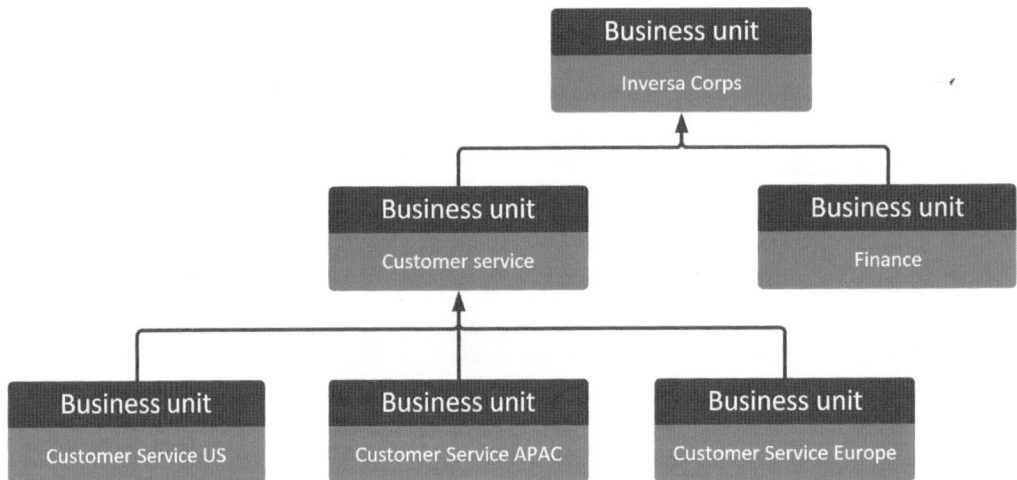

Image 11.12 – Example Dataverse business unit structure

> **Note**
>
> Most of the time, you will want to define a business unit hierarchy based on security requirements. There are exceptions to this rule, where the organizational structure may, at times, match the needs of the Dataverse security model.

Table ownership

Dataverse tables are configured on creation using one of two ownership modes:

- **User and Team Owned**: Rows within the table will be owned by either a user or a team. This ownership mode provides more granular control over access to data rows. Security roles associated with the teams and users can control the level of access on a record based on its owner.

- **Organization Owned**: Rows are owned by the organization as a whole, and do not have a specific user or team owner. Using **Organization** table ownership simplifies the security model, as table ownership is not a factor in the configuration. This configuration trades the ability to control user/team-level access to rows for simplicity.

> **Note**
>
> Once a table has been created using organization-level ownership, it can't be changed. The table would need to be recreated, resulting in potential migration and refactoring efforts. Solution architects should only select organization-level table ownership when it is confirmed that there will never be a need to control access to its rows based on the user or team that owns it.

Security roles

Dataverse security roles provide granular control over the level of access granted to users and teams. They are the central mechanism for controlling who has access to Dataverse data, the level of access, the features may use, and the actions they may perform.

Security roles may be assigned to teams (and therefore granted to the team's members) or directly assigned to individual users.

Record-level privileges

Security roles can specify the level of permissions to be granted to users and teams. The following screenshot illustrates the eight available privileges:

Table	Create	Read	Write	Delete	Append	Append To	Assign	Share
Article	●	●	●	○	○		●	
Article Template	●	●	○	○			●	
Bookable Resource	○	◐	◐	○	◐		◐	◐	◐

Figure 11.13 – Security role privileges

Solution architects review the business requirements and define the minimum level of access required by users. The eight record-level privileges are as follows:

- **Create**: Grants users the ability to create rows

- **Read**: Grants users the ability to view rows

- **Write**: Grants users the ability to update rows

- **Delete**: Grants users the ability to delete rows

- **Append**: Grants users access to link a row to another record (for example, linking a contact record to an account by setting the contact record's account lookup)

- **Append To**: Grants users the ability to associate a record from another row (for example, from the account record, associate existing contacts with the account)

- **Assign**: Grants users the ability to assign rows (available in team/user-owned tables)

- **Share**: Grants users the ability to share rows

Levels of access

Row-level privileges may be further configured by the five levels of access illustrated in the following screenshot:

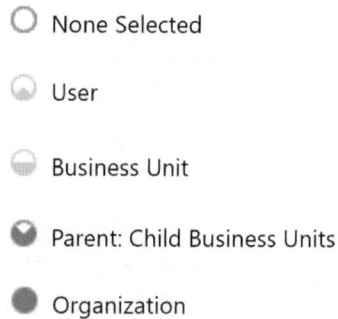

○ None Selected

◔ User

◑ Business Unit

◕ Parent: Child Business Units

● Organization

Figure 11.14 – The five levels of access for a row-level security role

The five levels of access are as follows:

- **Global/Organization**: Organization-level access to rows. The highest level of access is usually restricted to managers and individuals that require full dataset access.

- **Deep**: Business Unit and child Business Unit-level access to rows. This grants access to rows owned by users/teams within the business unit and business units below. This level of access is usually restricted to managers with oversight over a business unit and its subordinates.

- **Local**: Business Unit-level access to rows. This grants access to rows owned by users/teams within the same business unit. This level of access is usually restricted to managers with oversight over a specific business unit.

- **Basic**: User/team-level access to rows. This grants access to rows owned by the user, or a team the user belongs to, rows that are shared with the user, and rows that are shared with a team the user belongs to. This is the typical level of access that's granted to sales and customer service staff.

- **None**: Grants no access to data.

Security roles member privilege inheritance

Security roles may be configured for member privilege inheritance. The two inheritance options are as follows:

- Team privileges only

- Direct user (Basic) access level and team privileges

As the name implies, the key difference between these two application modes is that, when a security role is assigned to a team, the team's user has the security role assigned as if it has been directly associated with their user. This removes the need to assign security roles directly to users and allows administrators to manage Dataverse access using solely user team memberships.

When selecting **Direct User (Basic) access level and Team Privileges**, the team's members will receive the security role privileges as if the role had been assigned directly to the user. This removes the need to assign at least one security role to the user record, simplifying the user management and onboarding process:

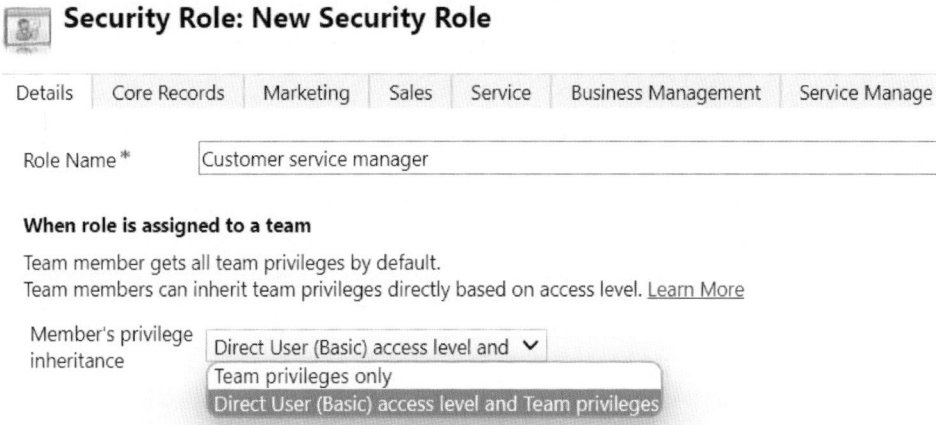

Figure 11.15 – Security role member's privilege inheritance options

> **Note**
>
> Using **Direct User security** roles in combination with **Azure AD Group Teams** is a great way to streamline the creation and management of Dataverse users. New users may be added to a Microsoft 365 group and have their accounts created in Dataverse. Any necessary security roles are assigned automatically.

Layering security roles

The effect of security roles is cumulative. When a user is granted multiple security roles, they gain access to rows by aggregating all the permissions granted by the assigned roles. This aggregation of security roles provides a means of defining security design strategies that leverage security role layers.

The four main Dataverse security role layering strategies are as follows:

- **Position role**

  Position-specific roles include all the permissions a user requires. Roles will typically be named after the position that it caters for (for example, *Sales Person* or *Customer Service Manager*). While this strategy provides a clear set of self-contained roles, each fully defining all the privileges a position requires, it may result in a higher maintenance overhead, as the various roles are likely to have a common set of permission across them. Adding a new custom table may mean editing all the roles to include access to the new table:

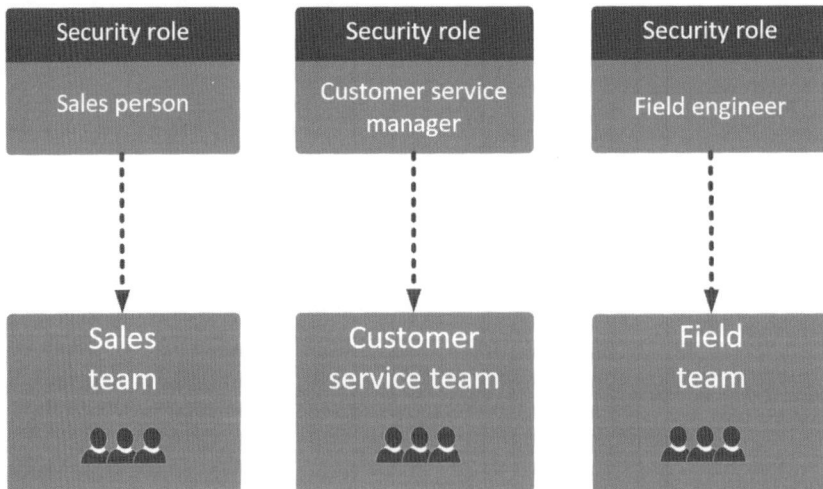

Figure 11.16 – Example of a position role-based security model

- **Base role and position role**

   This security role strategy adds a base layer to the position role. The base security role includes permissions that are common across the board (for example, all users will need a basic level of create/read/write access to contact records). The position role can then focus on complementing the base role, including permissions that are specific to the position in question. An example set of base and position roles are as follows:

   - *Contoso – Baseline*: Grants base access to all common tables

   - *Contoso – Sales*: Grants basic level read/write access to leads and opportunities

   A member of the sales team could then be assigned the Baseline and Sales person roles, thus completing their access to Dataverse:

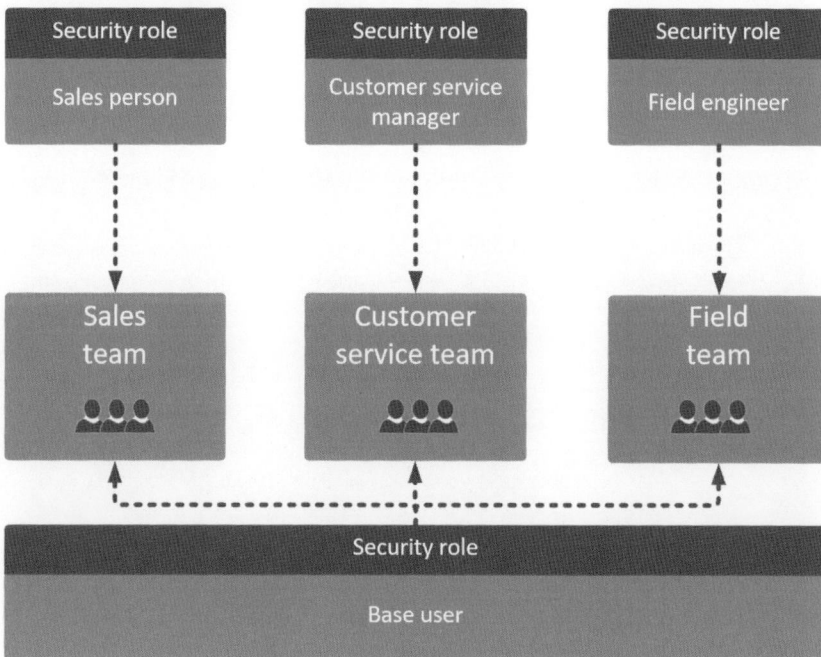

Figure 11.17 – Example of a base role and position role security model

- **Base role and capability role**

  This strategy is similar to the base role and position role strategy. The main difference is that the specialized roles are built around capabilities rather than staff member positions. An example set of base and capability roles are as follows and shown in the *Figure 11.18*:

  - *Contoso – Baseline*: Grants base access to all common tables

  - *Contoso – Surveys*: Allows you to manage surveys sent to customers

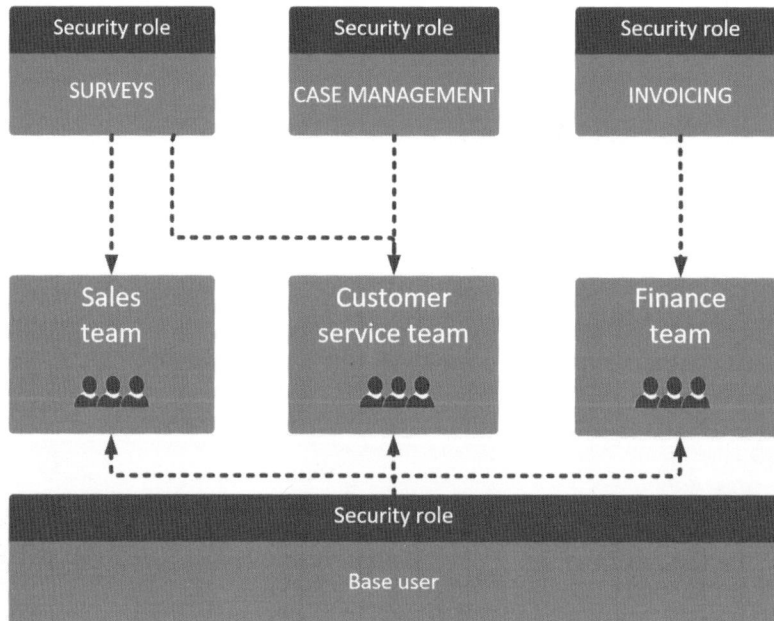

Figure 11.18 – Example of a base role and capability role security model

- **Base role + position role + capability role**

  This strategy combines the position and capability roles, providing greater flexibility when defining and assigning permissions. An example set of roles is as follows and shown in the *Figure 11.19*:

  - *Contoso – Baseline*: Grants base access to all common tables

  - *Contoso – Sales*: Grants basic level read/write access to leads and opportunities

  - *Contoso – Surveys*: Allows you to manage surveys sent to customers

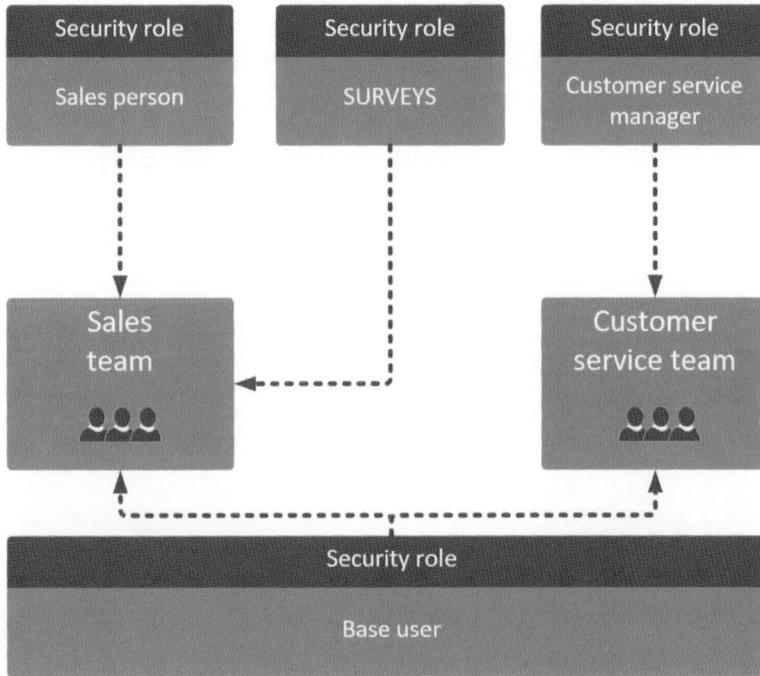

Figure 11.19 – Example of a base role + position + capability role security model

Column-level security

Dataverse columns may be configured for column-level security, allowing administrators to specify the user and/or teams that will be granted access. Column-level security works separately from security roles and is designed to provide further control over who can see and update data within specific fields. This may be used to control access to personal data within a contact record, granting read access to only a select group of people or teams.

Sharing

The **sharing** feature within Dataverse allows rows to be shared with a user or team that would not normally have access.

> **Note**
> Sharing a large number of records will result in performance degradation as sharing creates a *sharing record* per row per user, resulting in a potentially large dataset that needs to be checked by Dataverse every time a user attempts to access a row. Therefore, sharing is used when the volume of data to be shared is expected to be low.

Auditing

Auditing is configured at the environment, table, and column levels. When auditing is enabled, it logs data changes performed by Dataverse users.

Read actions are not monitored by the Dataverse auditing facility. They may, however, be captured using activity logging, which is monitored via the Microsoft 365 Security and Compliance Center. Activity logging must be enabled before use.

Defining a Dataverse permissions matrix

Both implementation consultants and stakeholders will benefit from a high-level permissions matrix. This is typically a table that presents the different roles (or teams) and the actions they can perform in the system. From the requirements captured so far, solution architects list the various activities and the users that perform them in a matrix, as follows:

#	Action	Project Initiator	Practice Manager	Resource Manager	Project Resource	System Administrator
	Opportunity to quote to project					
1	Create opportunity	●				●
2	Convert opportunity into a quote		●			●
3	Define quote resourcing requirements			●		●
4	Soft book resources			●		●
5	Substitute resources			●		●
6	Convert quote to project		●	●		●
7	Hard book resources			●		●
	Maintenance of master data and general administration					
8	Maintain master data catalog		●			●
9	Maintain pricelists		●			●
10	Onboard new Power Platform users		●			●

Table 11.4 – Example of a high-level Dataverse permissions matrix

The Dataverse permissions matrix allows you to quickly review and compare roles. It also serves as a discussion point with stakeholders, who will be able to visualize the separation of roles. The security design may then be adjusted based on these discussions.

Defining access routes for external Power Platform users

External users may access Power Platform applications via several routes. The following is a summary of the main routes through which external users may access the Power Platform:

- **Power Pages**

  Power Pages (previously Power Apps Portals) may be configured to authenticate external users through a variety of authentication protocols, including AD and Azure AD B2C.

- **Connected tenants**

  Microsoft 365 tenants may be connected, granting access to users from one tenant to the other. This implementation route allows users from another organization or Microsoft 365 tenant to access Model-Driven Apps, Canvas Apps, and Dataverse using the credentials from the external tenant.

- **Custom applications**

  Custom applications may implement any number of authentication strategies. While the connection from the custom application to Power Platform and Dataverse may be through an application user or service account, external users may authenticate any number of bespoke protocols with the custom application, thus allowing external users access to Power Platform data.

As a solution architect, you will work with the business to identify the optimal access route for external users.

Summary

In this chapter, you learned how to work through the security architecture discovery process, and you learn about how to define security concepts for Power Platform applications, and, more specifically, the Dataverse security concepts. A solid security solution design is crucial for the successful implementation and ongoing operation of Power Platform applications.

In the next chapter, you will learn how to manage the implementation of Power Platform solutions, including how to validate compliance with security concepts and how to resolve automation and integration conflicts.

Part 4:
The Build – Implementing Solid Power Platform Solutions

In this section, you will learn about the key role solution architects play during the implementation process. Navigating through our fictional case study at Inveriance Corps, you will employ a framework for evaluating detailed designs and the resulting implementation, learn how to resolve automation and integration conflicts, and define strategies for a successful go-live transition. This section contains the following chapters:

- *Chapter 12, Validating the Solution Design and Implementation*
- *Chapter 13, Power Platform Implementation Strategies*
- *Chapter 14, Leveraging Azure DevOps for Power Platform*
- *Chapter 15, Go-Live Strategies and Support*

12

Validating the Solution's Design and Implementation

In the previous chapters, you learned how to lead the Power Platform solution design process. Using descriptive visual designs, component reuse patterns, and time-tested automation strategies, you can build a solid foundation for your implementation. You also learned how to translate complex requirements into effective data models, develop resilient integration strategies, and define the solution's security concepts.

In this chapter, you will review the output from the solution design stages and evaluate its implementation for compliance with Microsoft Power Platform best practices and its close alignment to the organization's requirements.

The implementation will be regularly assessed for adherence to security concepts and conformance with API limits. You will also learn how to resolve integration and automation conflicts through a systematic approach to problem-solving.

In this chapter, we are going to cover the following main topics:

- Continuous review of detailed designs and their resulting implementation
- Validating compliance with the defined security requirements
- Implementing solutions that work within Power Platform API limits
- Resolving business automation conflicts
- Resolving integration design conflicts

Continuous review of detailed designs and their resulting implementation

As the implementation progresses, detailed designs are created to cover the functional and technical areas. Solution architects review these technical designs to ensure adherence to best practices and the design principles set out at the beginning of the project.

Validating the Power Platform detailed designs

Validating Power Platform designs typically involves running several reviews, including best practices, company policy, and regulatory considerations. Solution architects ensure the designs are compliant, working with various teams within the organization to ensure the designs are ready for implementation.

The following diagram illustrates the various stages in a solution design and review process:

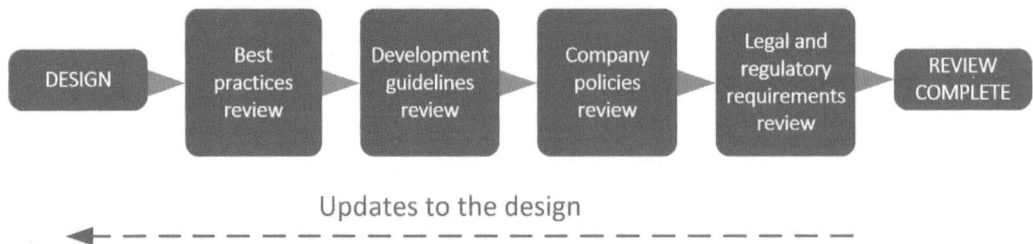

Figure 12.1 – Example Power Power Platform design validation process

The order in which these reviews take place is flexible and subject to change, depending on availability. Depending on the solution's size and complexity, some review stages may not apply. Solution architects work with the business to drive the following solution design stages through to completion.

1 – adherence to best practices

The design documentation is reviewed to ensure it adheres to published Power Platform best practices. The review process aims to identify any design elements that do not meet best practice standards and need to be adjusted, changed, or replaced.

Design documents are also reviewed to ensure they take into account the *nine pillars for great Power Platform architecture* (please refer to *Chapter 1, Introducing Power Platform Solution Architecture*, for details).

Reference Documentation

The latest Microsoft Power Platform best practices are available in the following documentation:

Power Platform Best Practices and Guidance: `https://docs.microsoft.com/power-platform/guidance/`

Dynamics 365 Development Best Practices: `https://docs.microsoft.com/en-us/dynamics365/customerengagement/on-premises/developer/best-practices-sdk`

---

2 – adherence to development guidelines

In the initial phases of a Power Platform project, solution architects define and release the development guidelines to be used by the build team. This document is usually published on a *Team Wiki page* for ease of access. The following screenshot illustrates the location of an Azure DevOps Wiki created as a source of reference for consultants and developers:

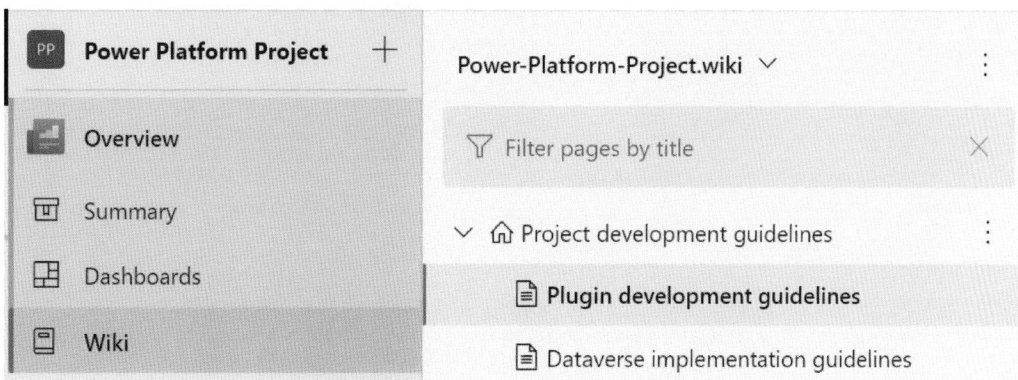

Figure 12.2 – Example development guidelines Wiki in Azure DevOps

For details on setting up an Azure DevOps Wiki, please refer to the following online documentation: `https://docs.microsoft.com/azure/devops/project/wiki/wiki-create-repo`.

Design documents produced by the team are reviewed for adherence to the project's development guidelines. Deviations from the defined standards can then be corrected, resulting in a cohesive implementation.

A development guidelines review is typically carried out by someone other than the main author for a given design document. A solution architect or consultant with sufficient knowledge of the technology in question to make an informed assessment.

3 – compliance with company policies

During the requirements capture phase, **company policies** affecting the Power Platform implementation would have been identified. The detailed design documentation is reviewed to ensure that all company policies have been taken into account. This covers areas such as storing and processing personal information and user access restrictions.

Solution architects work with business analysts and system owners to understand how to identify the company policies that apply to the solution and ensure the design complies with those policies.

4 – compliance with legal requirements

Similar to the review for adherence to company policies, any **legal requirements** that are identified during the requirements capture and analysis phase are taken into account during the detailed design process. The design review aims to ensure the legal requirements are catered for and address any gaps in the design.

Conclusions on the design validation process

Solution design reviews help get the project off on the right foot, provide a level of confidence in the solution, and reduce the risk of refactoring if a component is found to be non-compliant with a regulatory requirement at a later stage in the project. Now, let's look at the process of reviewing the actual implementation of a Power Platform solution.

Validating and reviewing the Power Platform implementation

Solution architects define the implementation review process early on in the project. The review process may include peer reviews, unit test requirements, code reviews, and source code pull request strategies. Depending on the project's size, solution architects may be directly involved in carrying out the implementation reviews.

The following subsections describe the typical implementation review processes for a Power Platform implementation.

1 – peer reviews

The larger the implementation team, the more comprehensive the range of skills and expertise the team members will have. **Peer reviews** provide a means of managing the build process, reducing the risk of implementing a solution that requires rework or refactoring to meet industry best practices and the project's development guidelines. Solution architects define the peer review process that consultants and developers use when completing a task or component.

Using this process, functional team members review each other's work on completion, cross-checking it with the following:

- Compliance with the project's development guidelines and naming conventions for tables, columns, views, and forms
- Adherence to the detailed designs

The reviewer will typically reference the Development Guidelines Wiki that was created at the beginning of the project to ensure the implementation follows it closely. The following screenshot illustrates a typical Development Guidelines Wiki built using Azure DevOps:

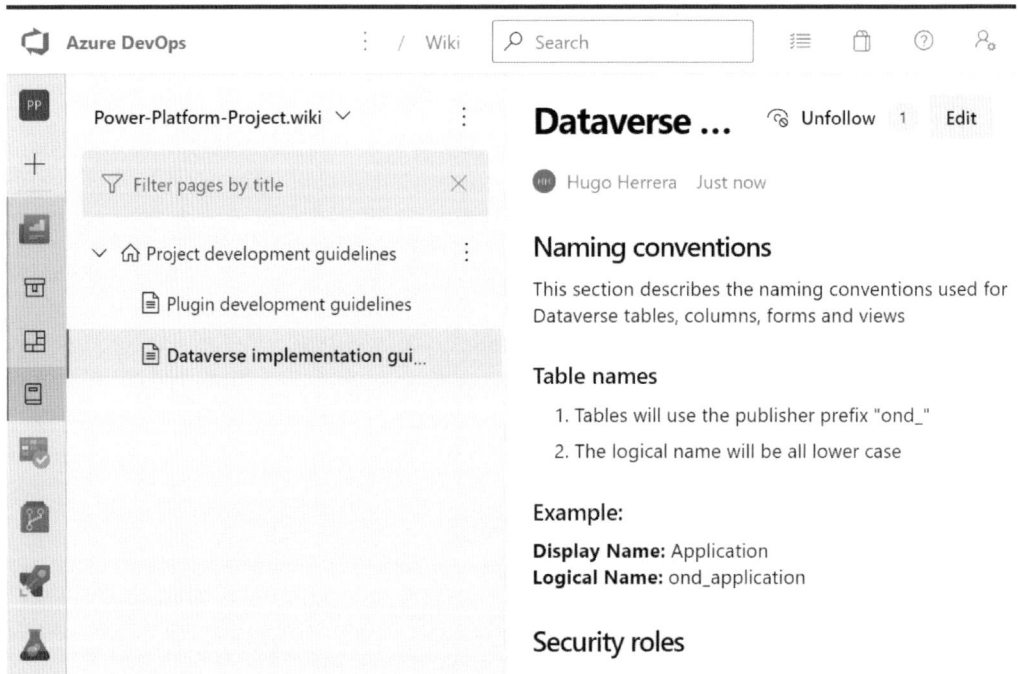

Figure 12.3 – Example Development Guidelines Wiki built using Azure DevOps

2 – code reviews and pull requests

Code reviews serve a similar purpose to functional peer reviews, helping to identify areas of the build that require changes to meet development guidelines and best practices. Solution architects define the code review and pull request (where applicable), helping developers build supportable and extendable code.

The following areas are typically covered in the code review process:

- The code is necessary. Identify if the functionality could be implemented without code and favor the low-code option.

- The code is structured following project guidelines and a recognized development standard (for example, SOLID development; please search for *.NET SOLID development* for details).

- The code meets project guideline style conventions.

- The code's logic is sound.

- Code duplication is kept to a minimum, if at all.

The peer reviewer will typically place comments on a pull request. When using Git as a source control repository, you will likely want to define a branching and pull request strategy. The following diagram illustrates an adaptation of GitFlow tailored for Power Platform development (please search for *GitFlow* for details on the concept behind the GitFlow branching model for Git):

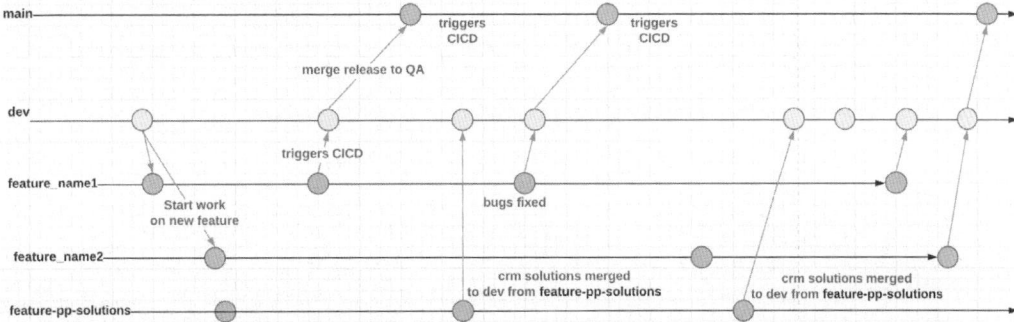

Figure 12.4 – Example Git branching and merging strategy for Power Platform development

The Git branching and merging strategy in the preceding example leverages feature branches for parallel implementation of Power Platform components, together with Power Platform's solution-specific branch, to reduce/remove the risk of merge conflicts. While this is not always the ideal source control solution for all Power Platform projects, the development team must have a clear directive so that code is developed, managed, and reviewed consistently.

3 – unit test coverage

As the application grows, so will the unit test requirements. Depending on the nature of the application, the code base may grow. In addition, specific projects will benefit from UI unit tests on Model-Driven Apps and **Power Apps Portals**.

Solution architects review the implementation regularly, ensuring a sound unit test strategy is followed throughout the build.

Solution architects and test managers compare the current testing process against the test strategies defined during the design process (please refer to *Chapter 8, Leading the Power Platform Design Process*) and recommend adjustments or additional coverage if necessary.

4 – overall implementation review

Carrying out an overall implementation review at specific checkpoints in the implementation helps solution architects steer the solution toward the design envisioned at the beginning of the project.

These checkpoints involve taking stock of all the components that have been configured in the following areas:

- **Dataverse configuration**: Review the tables, columns, processes, and plugins that have been built to date, and steer any areas that may need adjustments.

- **Dataverse security**: Review the security roles that have been configured to match the designs and use cases.

- **Model-Driven Apps**: Review the configuration of Model-Driven Apps forms, views, menus, and related functionality, confirming that the application is easy to use and fulfills the objectives.

- **Canvas Apps**: Similar to Model-Driven Apps, reviewing the applications is easy and fulfills the objectives.

- **Power Automate**: Review the implementation for compliance with implementation guidelines and best practices.

- **Power Pages**: Review the configuration of Power Apps Portals.

- **Power BI**: Review the configuration and integration of Power BI to meet the implementation guidelines.

Conclusions on the implementation review process

Reviewing how the Power Platform solution is being implemented is critical to the success of the project. Regular health checks help keep a solution on track and reduce the risk of refactoring and defects.

In the next section, we will review how technical designs may be reviewed for compliance with security requirements.

Validating compliance with the defined security requirements

Solution architects revise Power Platform's detailed designs to address security requirements. This involves reviewing authentication strategies, storing credentials and secrets, and conditional access rules, all of which will be discussed in the following sections.

Validating Dataverse security for compliance with best practices and guidelines

The security concept document will have defined the model that describes the security within a Dataverse environment. Solution architects review the implementation of the security model to ensure compliance.

Validating authentication strategies

This involves reviewing connections from Power Platform applications and services to systems that require authentication. The security and integration designs will set a standard for the authentication protocols and minimum requirements for outbound connections.

Connections from external systems to Power Platform services will also require authentication. These connections are reviewed for compliance with the minimum authentication security strategy set out in the designs.

Users or services using an authentication strategy that is not compliant with the designs need to be closely reviewed and potentially updated to use an approved authentication method.

Validating storage and processing secrets

Authenticating with external systems typically requires storing secrets or credentials that are used for authentication purposes. Safely storing, retrieving, and managing these credentials is critical for the secure operation of Power Platform applications.

Solution architects validate the following areas of the implementation:

- **Securely storing credentials**: The location that's used to store credentials and secrets is carefully selected during the design stages. These decisions bear in mind the current and future estate within the organization and restrictions imposed by company policies (for example, the availability of an Azure subscription and Azure Key Vaults). Solution architects validate that the solution has been built using the selected credential storage locations.

- **Securely retrieving credentials**: Power Platform applications that integrate with external systems may need to access credentials stored in a safe location. The action of retrieving those credentials may compromise the security of their storage location unless proper care is taken during the implementation. Retrieving credentials using an application key/secret that is accessible to a wide range of users can result in all the credentials in the accessed store being compromised. Solution architects review the detailed designs and ensure that their implementation complies with the overall project security concepts.

- **Securely managing and rotating credentials**: The project security concept will have defined processes for rotating credentials and secrets if appropriate. Solution architects validate that the Power Platform solution has been built to facilitate the cyclical update of these credentials. The normal functions of the application are unaffected by this process.

Monitoring for security compliance

As the implementation moves forward, new components will be built by the various team members. These components are typically developed while following the principles defined in the design documentation. An important part of the solution architect's role is to review the implementation of these security concepts and ensure the following:

- **Outbound integrations are stored securely**: Connections from Power Automate, Dataverse plugins, and **Canvas Apps** store and retrieve credentials for target systems securely (using Key Vault where applicable).

- **Plugin configuration security**: If credentials are stored in Dataverse plugin-secure configuration strings, these are only accessible to authorized staff members. Note that all Dataverse system administrators can read the plugin's secure configuration settings.

- **Adherence to data loss prevention policies**: Changes to data loss prevention policies may result in processes being deactivated without notice. Solution architects are aware of upcoming DLP policy changes and can assess the impact they would have on Power Automate processes.

Implementing solutions that work within Power Platform API limits

Power Platform applications are required to work within a set of API limits. These limits are in place to prevent the cloud-based platform from being overused and to provide a reliable service to all its users. You will typically assess the projected consumption during the design stage. Solution architects review detailed designs to identify areas that may lead to a Power Platform component breaching API limits.

User API limits

Users interact with Dataverse either via a Power App (for example, a Model-Driven App) or via the Dataverse API, as is the case with application users. The published request limits change from time to time (please visit `https://docs.microsoft.com/power-platform/admin/api-request-limits-allocations` for the latest allocation limits).

Licensed user request limits

Depending on the type of license, users will be presented with different API limit allocations. Solution architects review the licensing strategy to ensure the standard allowance will be sufficient to cater to the projected API requests during the regular operation of the Power Platform application.

Non-licensed user request limits

Non-licensed application users have a different set of allocation limits. Solution architects and implementation consultants use non-licensed application users when connecting external services or applications to Dataverse to benefit from the added flexibility and security they provide.

Dataverse service protection API limits

The Dataverse API is bound by service protection limits that are designed to maintain a reliable service for all users. Solution architects review the detailed designs to identify areas where these limits may be breached (for example, integrations that require millions of records to be created/updated in a short space of time may be throttled by the Dataverse API's limits). Solution architects review the detailed designs and identify components (or groups of components) likely to breach the API limits. The plans are then adjusted to work within limits (for example, distributing the API requests across multiple licensed users, extending the data import load window, or changing the load altogether to reduce throughput).

> **Reference Documentation**
>
> The latest Dataverse service protection API limits are available in the following documentation: `https://docs.microsoft.com/power-apps/developer/data-platform/api-limits`.

Power Automate limits

Cloud Flows are bound by a set of API and action limits. Solution architects review detailed designs to ensure the resulting processes perform within the purchased API capacity.

For example, a Cloud Flow containing a loop that typically runs 1,000 times per execution and results in 20 actions per loop cycle, which would result in 20,000 action steps, potentially breaching the daily allocation. They may be subject to throttling.

> **Reference Documentation**
>
> The latest Power Platform API limits are available in the following documentation: `https://docs.microsoft.com/power-automate/limits-and-config`.

Resolving business automation conflicts

Business automation processes may conflict with each other, especially as the application grows in size and complexity. Solution architects review the business automation design, identify areas where these conflicts may occur, and make adjustments to the designs to prevent these.

A typical example would be a business process that relies on a record moving through a sequence of statuses. Individual processes may guide the record's status, depending on their triggers and logic. As the application grows, so does its processes. The implementation team may lose visibility over the processes controlling the status of the record. In those instances, solution architects define a business automation process that is coherent and consistent throughout. A potential solution could be to implement state-machine business logic that ensures a record is always in the correct status.

Systematically problem-solving automation conflicts

Business automation conflicts can be difficult to troubleshoot due to the number of moving parts involved in a typical Power Platform business application.

Identifying race conditions

When more than one process or multiple instances of the same process run in parallel to update a given data item, this gives rise to what is known as a race condition. These, in turn, can result in unexpected results or data that is out of date.

To resolve race conditions, you must systematically review each process that writes to a given data item (for example, check all processes that update a given column). These may be Power Automate processes, plugins, or external systems updating Dataverse.

The asynchronous nature of Power Automate Cloud Flows can often lead to such scenarios if they're left unchecked. There are instances where controlling the concurrency of the Cloud Flow is the only way to prevent a race condition. In those instances, you may look to change the Cloud Flow trigger, setting the degree of parallelism to 1, as shown in the following screenshot:

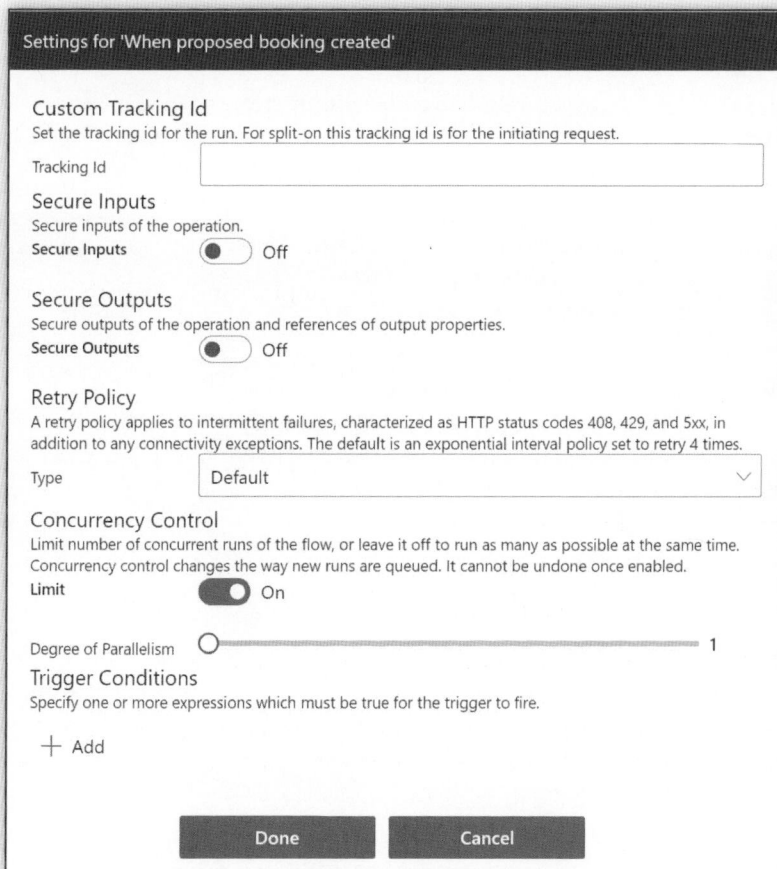

Figure 12.5 – Setting the Cloud Flow degree of parallelism to 1

> **Note Regarding Cloud Flows and Their Degree of Parallelism**
>
> Once a Cloud Flow trigger's degree of parallelism is set, it cannot be unset. You will, however, still be able to change its value from 1 to 100.
>
> Another important consideration when setting the degree of parallelism is that setting it to 1 will considerably reduce the Cloud Flow's performance, as it will only be able to service one instance at a time.

Review processes for updating a table or column

Running a dependency check on a column will typically list processes that are either reading or writing to that column.

For plugin-based processes, a scan of the code base for column usages can also yield a list of potential components that may be at fault.

> **Note**
>
> Using EarlyBound code generation to automatically create a type-safe Dataverse structure in .NET code can be an invaluable tool for identifying columns are tables used by plugins. The type-safe nature of the code will make it easy to find all references to a column.
>
> Please refer to the following documentation for details on Early Bound classes `https://docs.microsoft.com/power-apps/developer/data-platform/org-service/generate-early-bound-classes`.
>
> The following XRM Toolbox plugin provides an easy means of generating an Early Bound class structure: `https://dynamics-chronicles.com/article/xrmtoolbox-presentation-early-bound-generator`.

Resolving integration conflicts

Solution architects review the designs and implementation of Power Platform integrations to identify areas where they may be a conflict between them or other business processes. The actions and domain for each integration are reviewed individually and in combination with different integrations to identify potential clashes.

A typical example of an integration conflict is enriching contact data from two different sources:

- One integration may be responsible for updating a contact's address and contact details.

- A second integration may also update contact details, overwriting the first integration's data.

The result is a Dataverse contact with data in an inconsistent state.

The following steps will help you identify and resolve integration conflicts:

- Review the integration designs to identify which interfaces interact with the affected data item.

- Review the actual implementation, scanning for Power Automate Cloud Flows, workflows, plugins, and actions (and possibly JavaScript custom code) that interact with the affected data items. This may be done via a Dataverse dependency check on a column or table and by scanning the source code for the relevant columns if applicable.

- Update the design, making adjustments to ensure conflict does not occur. For example, suppose two interfaces are writing to the same contact address field. In that case, a process could be put in place, providing priority to interface A, which would result in updates from interface B being ignored. Alternatively, the design could be changed in agreement with the product owners, resulting in only one interface updating contact addresses, thus removing the conflict.

The integration designs and their resulting implementation are adjusted to ensure the domain and reach of each integration are clearly defined, and that any overlaps in data jurisdiction are addressed.

Systematically problem-solving integration conflicts

One key tool in resolving integration conflicts is a log. When an integration logs every request and response sent to and from an external service, it is possible to identify integration problems much more quickly than examining the changes to a dataset.

Chapter 10, Power Platform Integration Strategies, discussed the benefits of using a custom log table to audit the dialogue between Power Platform and external applications. This logging mechanism can be used to ascertain the events that took place leading to an incident and help guide a solution, which may be any of the following:

- Updating the outbound integration process

- Updating the calling integration client

- Applying a data fix if the issue is understood as an isolated one-off incident

This section provided a high-level overview of Power Platform integration conflict resolution. Please refer to *Chapter 10, Power Platform Integration Strategies*, where we discussed integration strategies in detail, for more information.

Summary

This chapter taught you to review the detailed designs and implementation for compliance with best practices, development guidelines, security requirements, and legal requirements. You also learned how to assess the API request usage for a Power Platform implementation and the adjustments that can help reduce the risk of over-consumption. These review tasks are essential for steering the implementation toward the vision set out in the early phases of the project.

In the next chapter, you will learn how to define solid Power Platform implementation strategies, including configuring Power Platform tenants and organizations, leveraging Azure DevOps, optimizing team output, and defining effective test strategies.

13
Power Platform Implementation Strategies

As we move along in this chapter, you will learn to follow industry best practices and strategies for successfully implementing Power Platform applications. You will learn how to consider the deployment options available and learn to select the Power Platform topologies and environment strategies that are best suited to an organization's needs.

Defining strategies to optimize the output of cross-functional development teams will also be explored here. Finally, you will review the test strategies and frameworks available to ensure high-quality control throughout the implementation process.

In this chapter, we are going to cover the following main topics:

- Power Platform environment and tenant configurations
- Optimizing output of cross-functional Power Platform development teams
- Implementing effective test strategies for Power Platform solutions

Power Platform environment and tenant configurations

Power Platform environments and tenants are the base containers that host the databases, applications, and processes that make a solution. As a solution architect, you will help shape the Power Platform environment strategy. By understanding the current and future business needs and the capabilities afforded by the Power Platform infrastructure, you will propose the creation of environments to help the organization fulfill its requirements.

A **tenant** can host one or more Power Platform environments. A *Default* environment with a base Power Platform database is automatically created when a tenant is instantiated.

Selecting a geographical location for the environments

When an environment is created, a geographical location is selected. Based on regulatory requirements and the geographical location of users, the appropriate location is selected. A typical set of options presented to users when creating an environment is as follows:

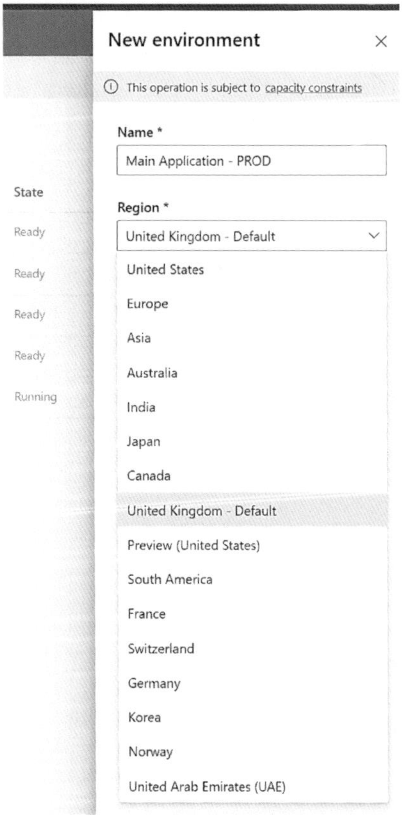

Figure 13.1 – Geo-locations available when creating a new environment

In consultation with the organization's legal and compliance teams, solution architects select the most appropriate location.

The following restrictions apply when creating new Power Platform environments:

- The *India* and *Australia* regions are restricted to organizations whose tenant is based in the same location due to tax laws. An exception may be requested for *Australia*.

- The **US Government (GCC)** is restricted to US government-associated organizations only.

Once an environment is created, you may review its geographical location within the Power Platform environment list.

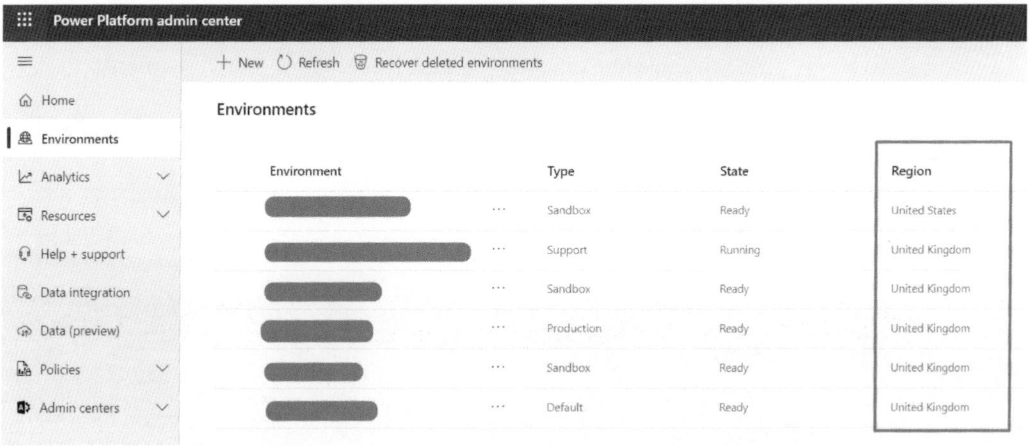

Figure 13.2 – Viewing the geographical location of environments

Solution architects work with the business to select the geo-location for environments based on the following criteria:

- **Geographical proximity to the uses** – the closer the users are to the environment's location, the lower the latency and the faster the system performs.

- **Compliance with regulations and company policies** – the organization may be bound to store its data within specific geographical boundaries.

Once an environment is created, it is not possible to change its location using the Power Platform admin center. Migration of an environment's geographical location may be requested. However, this process is not generally available and may take over ten days to complete. For that reason, it is essential to carefully select the location when the environment is created.

Deciding on a Power Platform environment strategy

Power Platform implementations tend to use multiple environments to separate components under development from the user testing and production systems. Additionally, Power Platform solutions may split environments by functional area, business applications, and geographical distribution.

A typical Power Platform implementation may be distributed across environments.

Separation of development, test, and production activities

The minimum recommended set of Power Platform implementation environments are development, test, and production instances.

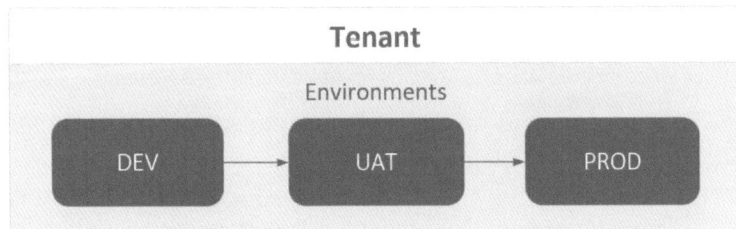

Figure 13.3 – Minimum recommended set of environments

Having these three base environments allows for development and support activities without affecting production systems. Testing can also be performed in a controlled production-like environment separate from the development instance.

Separating the development environment from the main deployment base is sometimes helpful, depending on the size of the implementation team. A deployment master environment that only contains components ready for deployment prevents unwanted or unfinished functionality from entering the test and production environments. This environment strategy is illustrated in the following diagram:

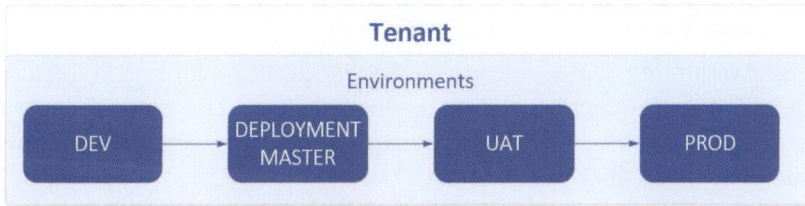

Figure 13.4 – Using a deployment master environment to manage work in progress

When a project is working on multiple streams of functionality, it can sometimes be beneficial to split the development environments, allowing different teams to work on their own functional area, unit testing, and deploying as and when the features become available. The following diagram illustrates two workstreams developing in two separate environments, which then merge functionality into the deployment master environment:

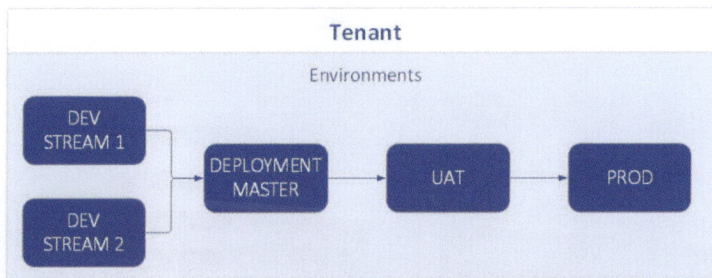

Figure 13.5 – Splitting work streams across development environments

Deciding on the best environment strategy for managing the development and deployment phases will very much depend on the team size and the functionality being built. Solution architects weigh the benefits additional environments bring to the project versus the deployment and dependency management overheads they present, and then select the simplest option that will fulfill the goals of the project.

Opting in for Early Upgrades in Development Environments

It is often helpful to test upcoming Power Platform updates in a development or test environment before release into production. Separate development and test environments allow solution architects to select these for early access to updates, enabling the organization to pre-empt any capability or upgrade issues and carry out any required changes before release into production. The following document describes the steps to allow early access updates: https://docs.microsoft.com/en-us/power-platform/admin/opt-in-early-access-updates.

Separating business applications across environments

When an organization requires a wide range of applications built using Power Platform (and Dynamics 365) components, splitting applications into separate environments is sometimes helpful. You would look to split applications across environments where sharing by these applications is minimal.

Their business requirements and domains vary sufficiently to warrant a clear distinction in their functionality and data.

The following diagram illustrates different business requirements that have been split across two sets of environments. The first set covers the customer **Onboarding Application**, while the second set of environments includes a separate **Sales Application**.

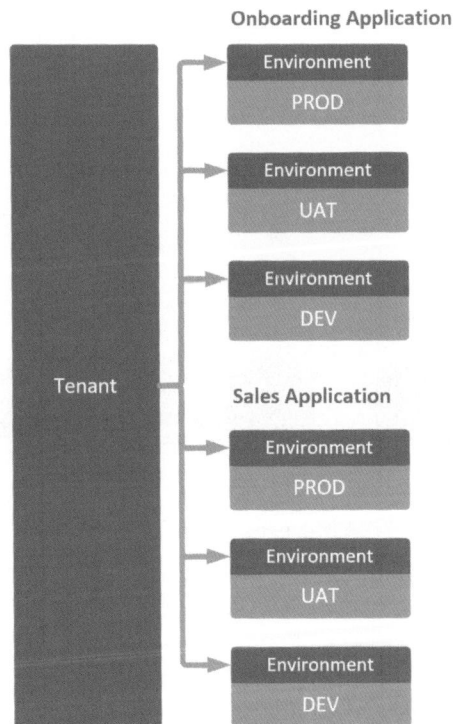

Figure 13.6 – Splitting business requirements and applications across environments

This split of functionality across environments simplifies the deployment and support processes and reduces the risk of functional changes from one application affecting the other.

Separating master data environments

Organizations may look to manage a specific set of data in a centralized database, often titled **master data**. The data may be a product catalog, a collection of price lists, a central customer database, or various other types of data. When there is a clear requirement and mandate for the business to manage this data centrally within a purpose-built data and application, Power Platform can put forward a solution in the shape of an environment dedicated to the hosting and management of master data.

This master data environment may then be used by various other applications (Power Platform-based or otherwise). The following diagram illustrates two Power Platform applications using a central master data environment as a source:

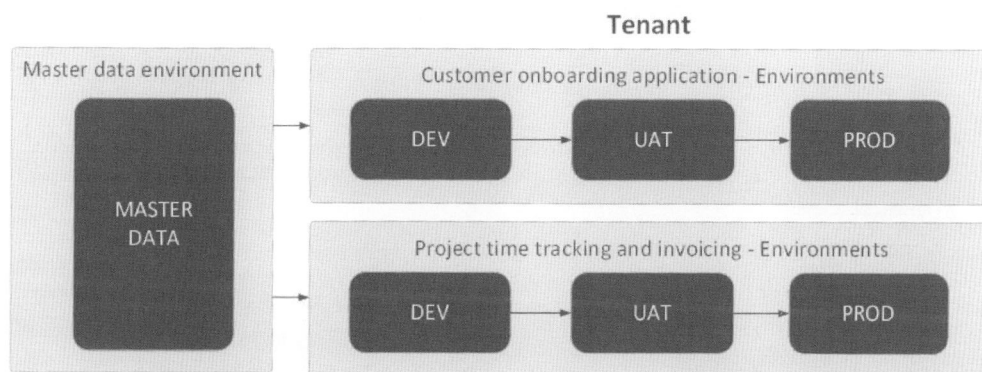

Figure 13.7 – Using a master data environment within a Power Platform implementation

A connection with a master data environment may be carried out using the various integration capabilities within the Power Platform framework, including virtual tables, Power Automate cloud flows, and the Dataverse API.

Using multi-environment strategies to secure Power Platform applications

Using multiple environments to separate applications or business domains provides an additional layer of security. Each environment hosts its own Dataverse database, and access is controlled through separate AD security groups, and security roles.

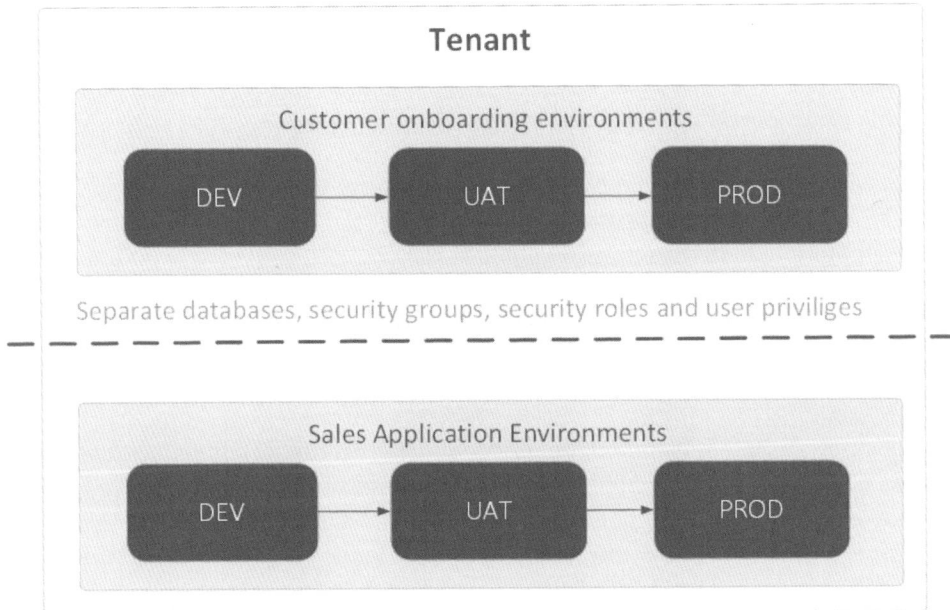

Figure 13.8 – Increasing security by separating applications across multiple environments

Deciding whether to enhance security by creating additional environments usually considers the type of user accessing the system; for example, an organization may want to separate systems accessed by the public from their internal backend applications. Solution architects weigh the benefits that additional security would provide versus the build and maintenance overheads of having additional environments to take care of.

Using multiple environments for scalability

Power Platform environments are bound by service protection and database limits. When working with high-volume or high-throughput solutions, solution architects consider the benefits of having a separate environment to handle these activities that push the platform to its limits. Separating these demanding services from the organization's other Power Platform applications helps reduce the risk of impacting users with high-throughput loads of data.

Sandbox versus Production

Power Platform environments may be configured at either Sandbox or Production level. Typically, non-production environments are configured using the **Sandbox** configuration to reduce operational costs. Production environments offer enhanced capabilities, including automated backups going back for a month. It is possible to switch between a Production configuration and a Sandbox configuration, but note that changing from Production to Sandbox will result in losing backups older than a week.

Managed versus unmanaged solutions

As a general rule, managed solutions should be restricted to development environments as using them in target environments could result in orphaned components being left behind when deleted from the source. Managed solutions are therefore recommended when importing into target environments such as QA, UAT, preproduction, and production.

For additional details on the differences between managed and unmanaged Power Platform solutions, please refer to the following document: `https://docs.microsoft.com/power-platform/alm/solution-concepts-alm#managed-and-unmanaged-solutions`.

Optimizing the output of cross-functional Power Platform development teams

Solution architects have a pivotal role within a Power Platform implementation. Their wide range of knowledge and experience can be leveraged to guide team members to deliver a project through the most optimal route possible. To successfully deliver a project, solution architects engage in the following activities.

Understanding the team's capabilities

Solution architects identify the team member's core competencies. These may be either functional, technical, knowledge in a specific type of Power Platform application, or a focus on integration-related activities.

Understanding the key capabilities facilitates the following activities:

- **Distributing work optimally across team members**

  Once the team's core skills are understood, solution architects work optimally with the business to help distribute the implementation work. This allows experts on a specific subject area to focus on delivering the solution.

  In consultation with the business, work will sometimes be distributed to team members that are being up-skilled in a particular implementation area (for example, training junior team members to work on Power Apps Portals applications). These team members would typically require support to complete the implementation tasks, which is the subject of the next section.

- **Supporting team members where needed**

  Team members will often benefit from the support of a solution architect or one of their peers to complete implementation tasks. Solution architects identify team members who need assistance, typically through daily standup or implementation reviews.

- **Adjusting as needed**

  There may be instances where the original work allocation may not be suitable. Team members may find specific tasks beyond their capabilities or desired career path. Solution architects identify areas that need adjustment and re-route the work to alternative team members to maintain overall team efficiency.

Implementing effective test strategies for Power Platform solutions

Testing Power Platform implementations is another crucial part of the development life cycle. Solution architects work with test managers to ensure a test strategy is in place, including one or more of the following activities.

Manual testing

Manual validation of a solution is often the simplest form of testing and the most frequently used as it is easily accessible to standard Power Platform users. The system is put through its paces by running through the application, website, or process to validate its performance and compliance with the business requirements.

Solution architects work with test managers to ensure tests are carried out systematically. Azure DevOps test plans help teams drive internal quality by providing a test management solution where user acceptance criteria, test cases, and results may be tracked. Please refer to the following document for full details on using Azure DevOps test plans: `https://docs.microsoft.com/azure/devops/test/overview?view=azure-devops`.

Automated tests

Automated testing requires the configuration of tools that simulate the steps carried out by users on an application. The following are a few examples of how automated tests may be configured for Power Platform applications:

- **Model-driven apps automated testing**

  Model-driven app testing may be automated using frameworks like EasyRepro. These tools allow testers to create scripts that run the application user interface, simulate user actions, and validate that the application's output matches the business requirements.

  The following link provides additional details on the EasyRepro framework for automated testing of model-driven apps: `https://github.com/microsoft/EasyRepro`.

- **Power Apps portals automated testing**

  Power Apps portals are websites that may be tested using standard web application test tools available in the market. Typical automated tests will focus on simulating user interaction with the application frontend and performance benchmarking of the portal.

- **Canvas apps automated testing**

  Power Apps Test Studio provides a means of performing automated testing. The following link provides additional details on Test Studio for canvas apps: `https://docs.microsoft.com/power-apps/maker/canvas-apps/test-studio`.

Load tests

Load testing involves the generation of traffic or actions on an application to validate its performance under load. Typically, load tests are carried out on public-facing portals to ensure the user experience will be acceptable to customers and end-users.

Power Pages and model-driven apps may be tested using web application testing tools available on the market. Note that you may need to notify Microsoft before running load tests on Power Platform applications.

Penetration tests

Penetration tests (pen tests) aim to detect security gaps in an application or service. These tests are typically carried out by specialist teams dedicated to the task. The results of pentests are usually a set of items graded by severity. Solution architects review the pentest results and action the areas that fall within the implementation team's control. Product-related security gaps are typically reported to Microsoft support for resolution.

Summary

This chapter has taught you the benefits of having a multi-environment strategy, from development to production environment considerations, through to the security and scalability benefits of having separate environments per application or domain. You have also learned about optimizing team output and general Power Platform testing considerations. This understanding will help you make the right decision when creating the base environments and give the project the best chance of success thanks to an optimal development stratcgy.

In the next chapter, you will learn how to leverage Azure DevOps's task management, source control, and release management capabilities.

14
Leveraging Azure DevOps for Power Platform

Azure DevOps is the one-stop solution that encompasses task and test management, source control, and pipelines for the build, unit test, and deploy solutions. Using Azure DevOps provides Power Platform projects with a framework through which implementation activities may be managed and monitored. In this chapter, you will learn how to implement task management, source control, and **application life cycle management (ALM)** using Azure DevOps.

In this chapter, we are going to cover the following topics:

- Leveraging Azure DevOps for task management
- Leveraging Azure DevOps for source control
- Leveraging Azure DevOps for application life cycle management (ALM)

Leveraging Azure DevOps for task management

Power Platform solution architects are often responsible for creating a base structure that holds requirements, tasks, and bugs. Azure DevOps includes four work item models:

- Agile
- CMMI
- Scrum
- Basic

You will typically work with product owners and business analysts to select the most appropriate model for the project. The project's work items are created and distributed across the team for implementation. The following screenshot illustrates a set of work items for a Power Platform Portal and Model-Driven App backend solution:

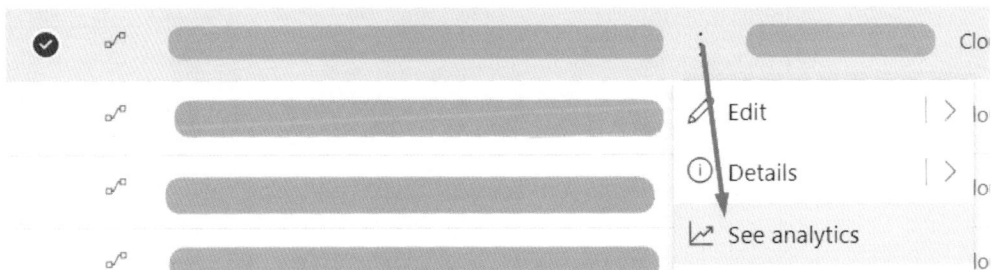

Figure 14.1 – Example Azure DevOps task management backlog view

Azure DevOps's work item processes allow the business to track and manage the work being carried out by the implementation teams and provide a compass and clear directives for each team member to work on.

Leveraging Azure DevOps for source control

Azure DevOps provides two types of source control: Git and Team Foundation Version Control (previously known as TFS). A source control repository is created by default when a new Azure DevOps project is instantiated, where the user is presented with the aforementioned version control options:

Actions   Usage   Errors   Select range   Last 30 days   ⌄

‹ Back to report

Export data
Show as a table
Get insights
Sort axis   ›

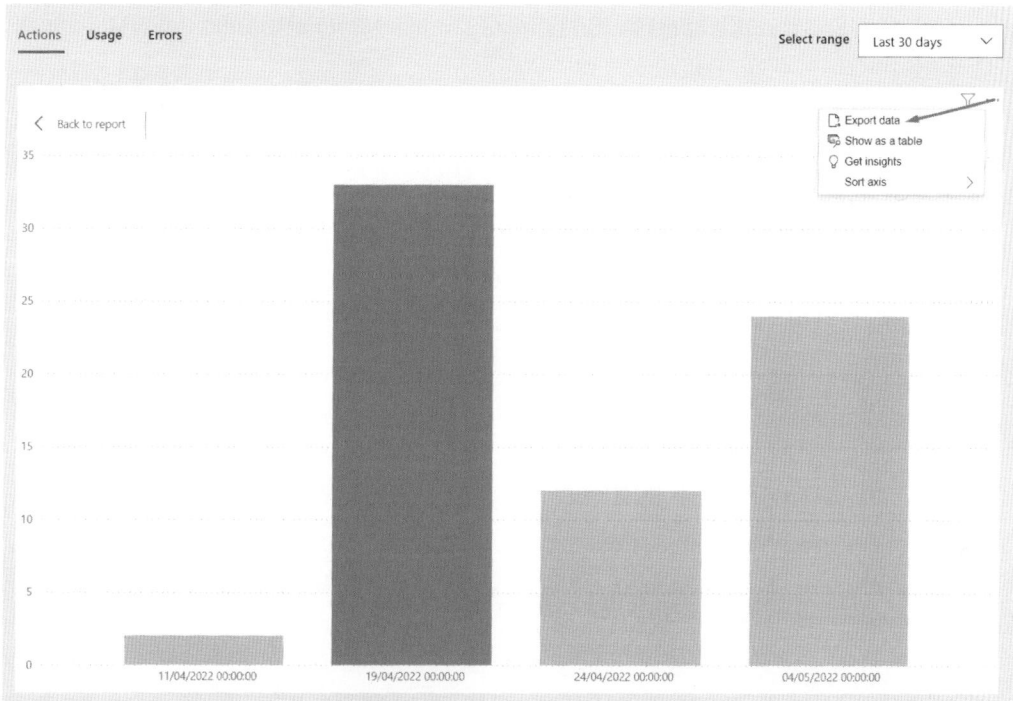

Figure 14.2 – Azure DevOps source control repository options

Additional repositories may be added, which may differ from the default. The following screenshot shows an additional repository being created within an existing project:

AggregationDateMakerDailyActions	Sum of BillableActionsMakerDailyActions
11/04/2022 00:00	2
19/04/2022 00:00	33
24/04/2022 00:00	12
04/05/2022 00:00	24

Figure 14.3 – Creating additional repositories within Azure DevOps

Source control is an essential part of the Power Platform implementation process, typically storing the following artifacts:

- Dataverse plugin source code

- Model-Driven Apps customization source code (PCFs, web resources, and images)

- Dataverse exported solutions

- Data (master data, reference data) to be deployed to target environments

- Azure component source code (for example, Azure Functions)

Solution architects define the project's *ways of working* to ensure all team members develop and manage sources within the Azure DevOps repositories.

Manual and automated source control of Power Platform solutions

Power Platform solutions contain the definition for tables, processes, apps, forms, and other components used to define the Power Platform configuration. These solutions are exported from a source/development environment as ZIP files and then imported into target environments (for example, QA and production environments).

Storing Power Platform solutions in a source control environment provides a means of recording and versioning the system's configuration. Deployments to target environments may also be carried out from solution files stored in source control. Automated deployments will be discussed in more detail in the upcoming sections.

Solution files may be stored either as ZIP files or extracted to a file and folder structure using the Power Platform SolutionPackager tool (please refer to the SolutionPackager tool's docs for additional details: `https://docs.microsoft.com/power-platform/alm/solution-packager-tool`).

The following screenshot illustrates a typical source control folder structure that's used to store Power Platform solutions:

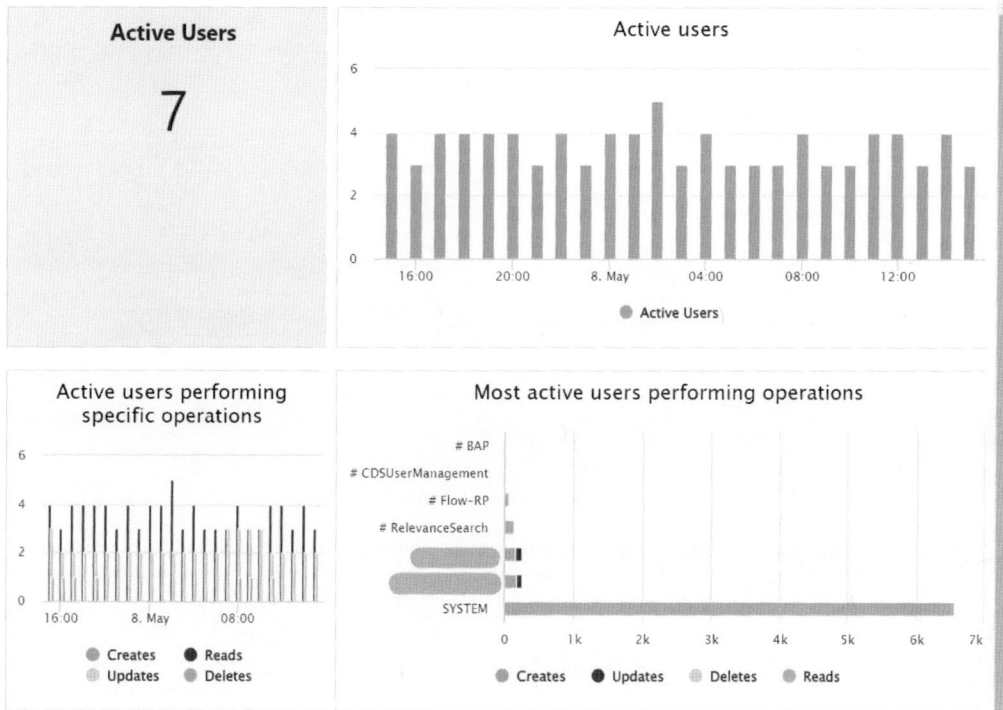

Figure 14.4 – Storing Power Platform solutions in source control

Solution files may be checked into source control manually or via an automated process such as an Azure DevOps pipeline. Manually submitting solution files may be carried out using standard source control tools (for example, the Azure DevOps web portal itself). The next section discusses the options available for automated source control of Power Platform solutions.

Automated source control of Power Platform solutions

Azure DevOps pipelines provide a mechanism for automated source control of Power Platform solutions. Solutions may be exported, validated, extracted, and checked into a source control repository. The following diagram illustrates a typical Azure DevOps pipeline that automatically checks solutions into a repository:

Capacity

| Summary | Dataverse | Microsoft Teams | Add-ons | Trial |

See where your org (tenant) is using storage, add-ons, and Microsoft Power Platform requests that could impact your capacity.
Learn more

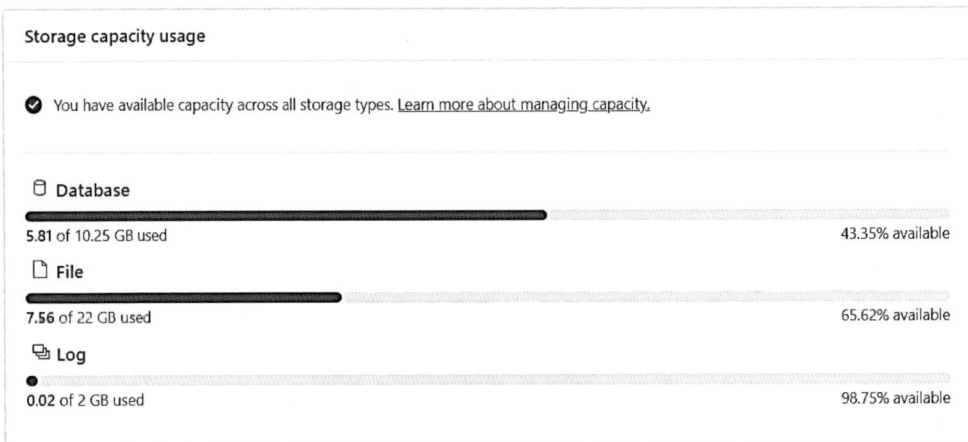

Storage capacity usage

✓ You have available capacity across all storage types. Learn more about managing capacity.

🗄 **Database**

━━━━━━━━━━━━━━━━━━━━━━━━━━━━━━━━━━━━━━━

5.81 of 10.25 GB used   43.35% available

📄 **File**

━━━━━━━━━━━━━━━━━━━━━━━━━━━━━━━━━━━━

7.56 of 22 GB used   65.62% available

🗂 **Log**

●━━

0.02 of 2 GB used   98.75% available

Storage capacity, by source   View self-service sources

Source	Database	Log	File
Org (tenant) default ⓘ	10 GB	2 GB	20 GB
User licenses ⓘ	256 MB >	N/A	2 GB >
Additional capacity	0 MB	0 MB	0 MB
Total	10.25 GB	2 GB	22 GB

Figure 14.5 – Azure DevOps pipeline for automated Power Platform solution source control

The Azure DevOps pipeline shown in the preceding diagram can be created by following these steps:

1. **Create an Azure DevOps pipeline**

   Navigate to the **Pipelines** option within the Azure DevOps project:

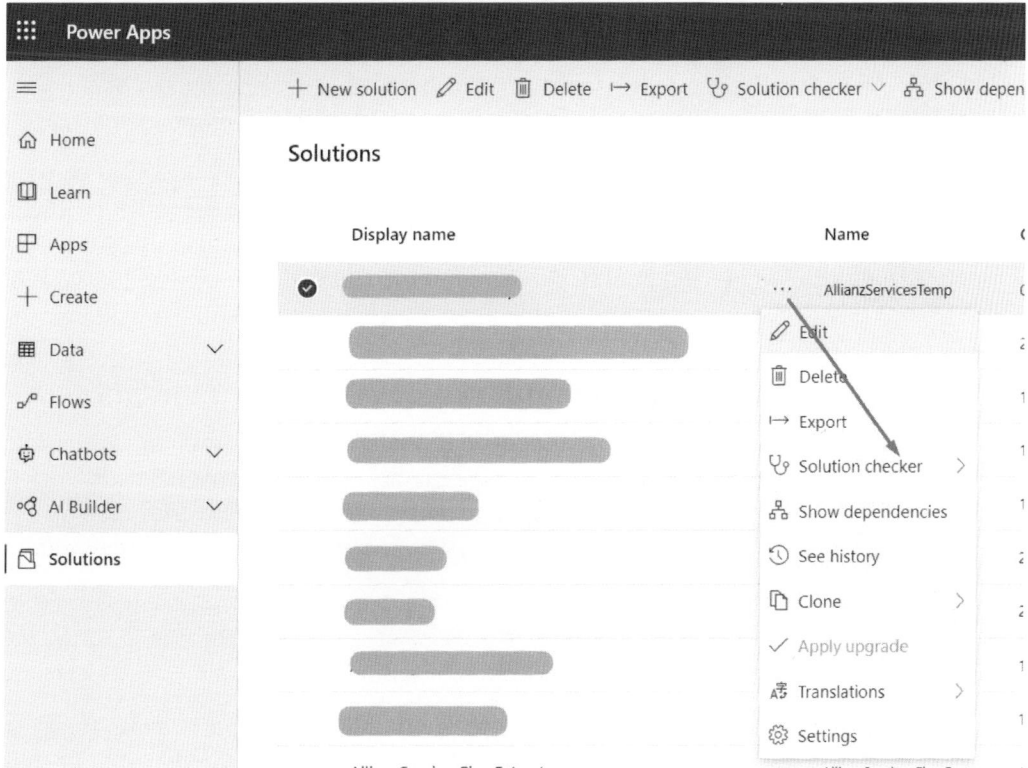

Figure 14.6 – Creating an Azure DevOps pipeline

2. **Select the classic editor option**

   In the **New pipeline** screen, select the **Use the classic editor** option. Selecting this option will allow you to create DevOps tasks using an editor UI:

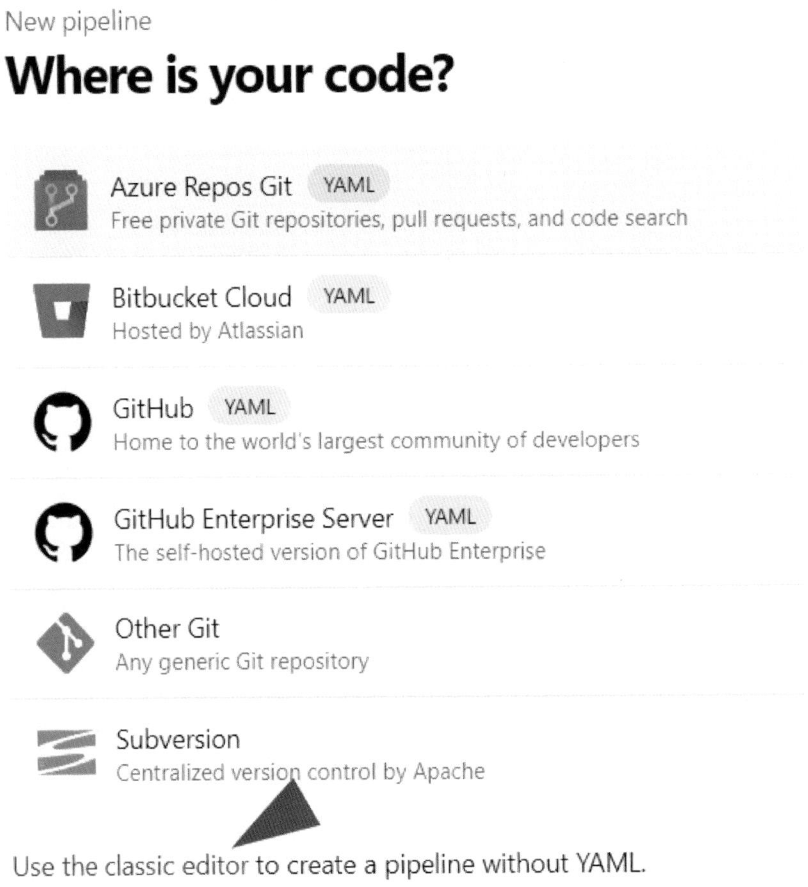

   New pipeline

   # Where is your code?

   Azure Repos Git   YAML
   Free private Git repositories, pull requests, and code search

   Bitbucket Cloud   YAML
   Hosted by Atlassian

   GitHub   YAML
   Home to the world's largest community of developers

   GitHub Enterprise Server   YAML
   The self-hosted version of GitHub Enterprise

   Other Git
   Any generic Git repository

   Subversion
   Centralized version control by Apache

   Use the classic editor to create a pipeline without YAML.

   Figure 14.7 – Selecting the classic editor option to manage pipelines using a UI rather than a YAML script

3. **Select a source control repository**

   Selecting the source control repository and branch where Power Platform solutions will be checked into Azure DevOps provides both Git and TFVC options for version control.

In this example, we will be using the **Azure Repos Git** option:

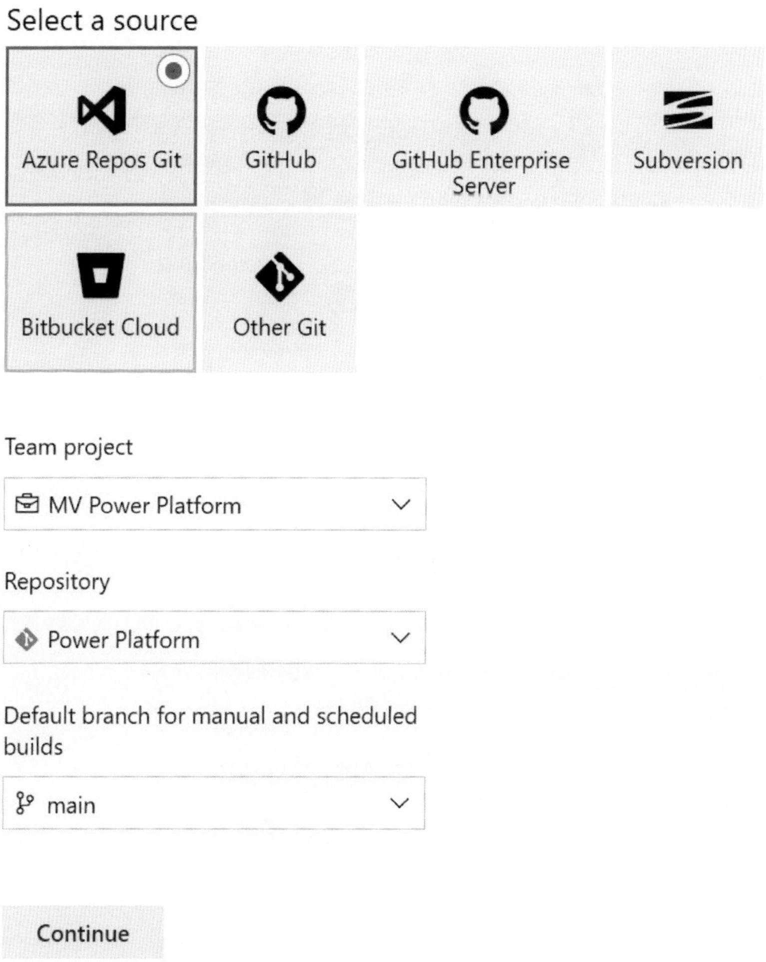

Select a source

Azure Repos Git   GitHub   GitHub Enterprise Server   Subversion

Bitbucket Cloud   Other Git

Team project

MV Power Platform   ⌄

Repository

Power Platform   ⌄

Default branch for manual and scheduled builds

main   ⌄

Continue

Figure 14.8 – Selecting the repository and branch where Power Platform solutions will be checked in

After that, select the **Empty job** option to start from a clear pipeline:

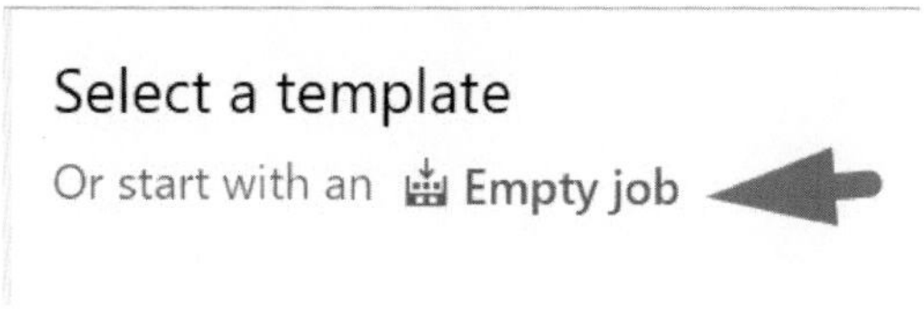

Select a template

Or start with an   Empty job   ⬅

Figure 14.9 – Selecting the Empty job option to start with a clear pipeline

4. **Add the Power Platform Tool Installer task**

    I. Click the + button on the first task placeholder, search for **Power Platform Tool Installer**, and press the **Add** button:

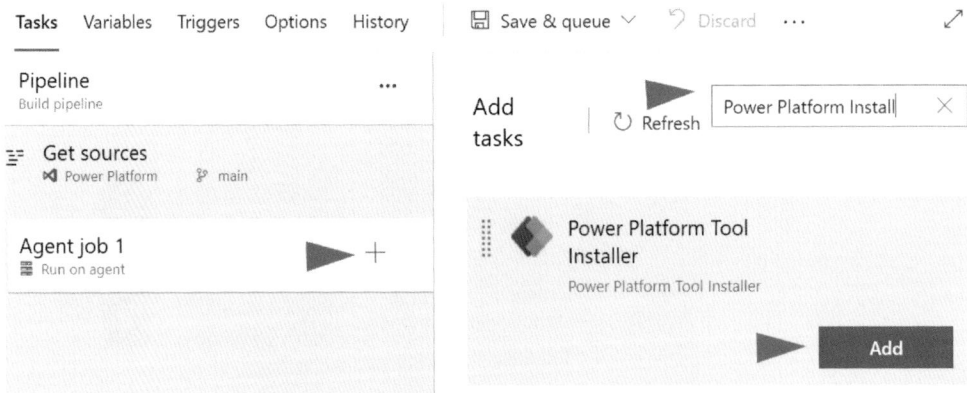

Figure 14.10 – Adding Power Platform Tool Installer

    II. If the **Power Platform Tool Installer** option does not appear in the search results, please search for **Power Platform** on the same screen, and add the free Azure DevOps **Power Platform Build Tools** extension by pressing the **Get it free** button:

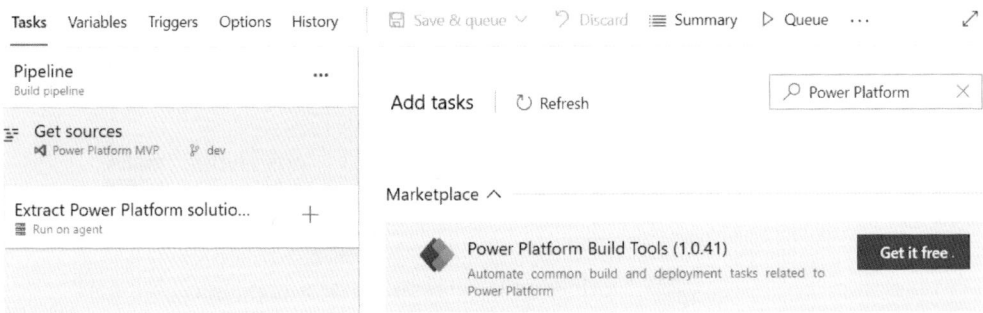

Figure 14.11 – Getting Power Platform Build Tools for your Azure DevOps organization if it's not already installed

III. Once **Power Platform Tool Installer** has been set as the first task, the task itself may be given a name, as follows:

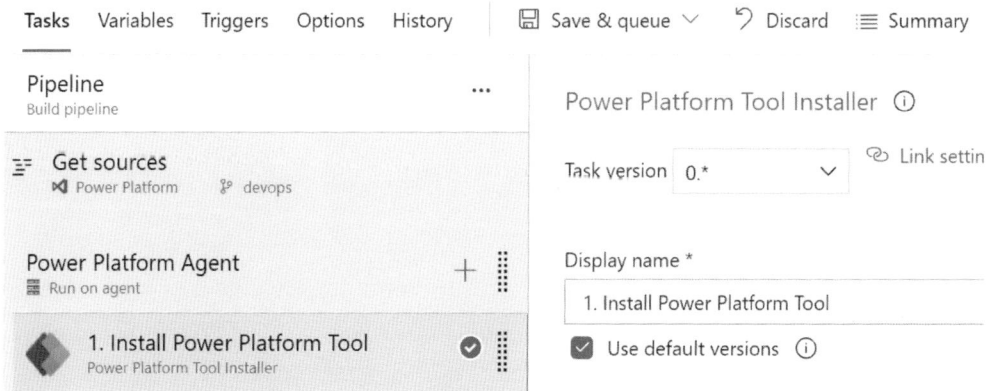

Figure 14.12 – Naming tasks in Azure DevOps pipelines

5. **Add the Power Platform Export Solution task**

   Search for and add the **Power Platform Export Solution** task using the same method when adding the **Power Platform Tool Installer** task and set the following key fields:

   - **Display Name**: This allows you to give the task a descriptive name, which could include the name of the solution being exported.

   - **Authentication type**: Two options are available. The first allows for standard username/password credentials to be used when connecting to the Power Platform environments and will require an AD user for authentication. While useful under certain circumstances, the second authentication type option is recommended as it does not require a full Power Platform user and leverages the application user functionality. If this is the first time that a service connection is being used within an Azure DevOps project, you will be required to create one at this point by pressing the **+ New** button.

   - **Solution Name**: The name for the solution to be exported. Note that this is not the display name for the solution. You may obtain the name from the solution list in the make.powerapps.com portal.

   - **Solution Output File**: The path and filename for the Power Platform solution ZIP file. You may want to create the repository folder structure in advance. The following example illustrates a solution being exported to the PowerPlatform. Solutions/Packed/CoreComponents_managed.zip source control path.

- **Export as Managed Solution**: Solutions may be exported as managed or unmanaged. In this example, we are exporting a managed solution. However, we will add a second task to export an unmanaged version later.

The following screenshot illustrates a task that's been configured to export a managed solution:

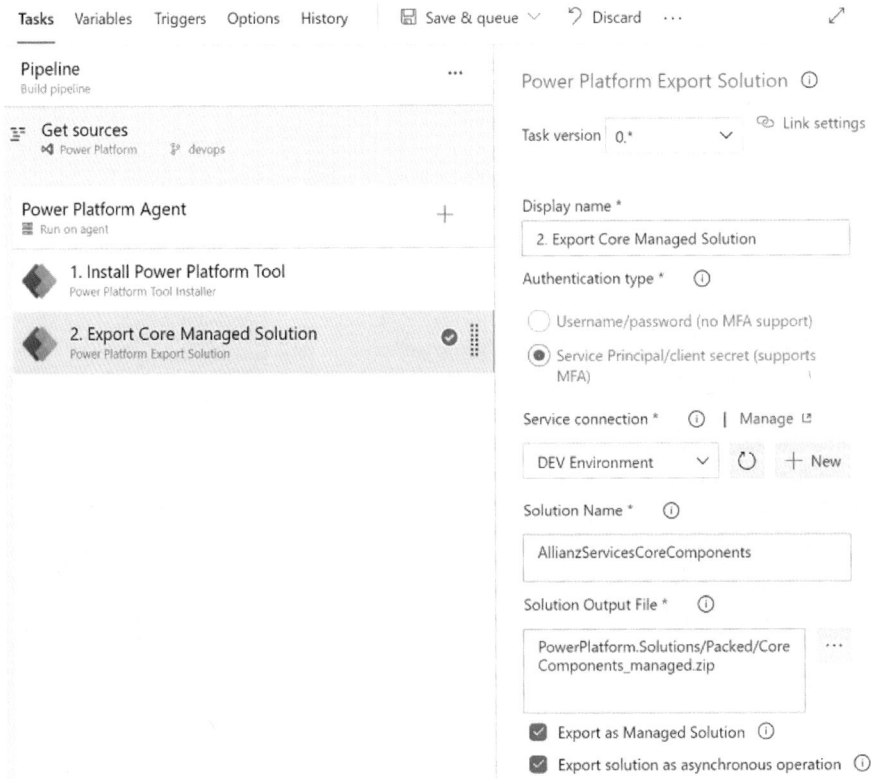

Figure 14.13 – Configuring the Power Platform Export Solution task in an Azure DevOps pipeline

Now, let's look at creating a new service principal.

6. **Adding a new service principal**

   I.   Click on the + **New** button to add a new Azure DevOps service principal:

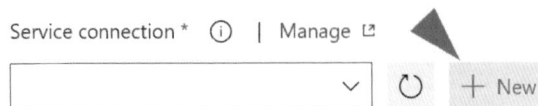

Figure 14.14 – Adding a new Azure DevOps service principal

You will be presented with a form similar to the following:

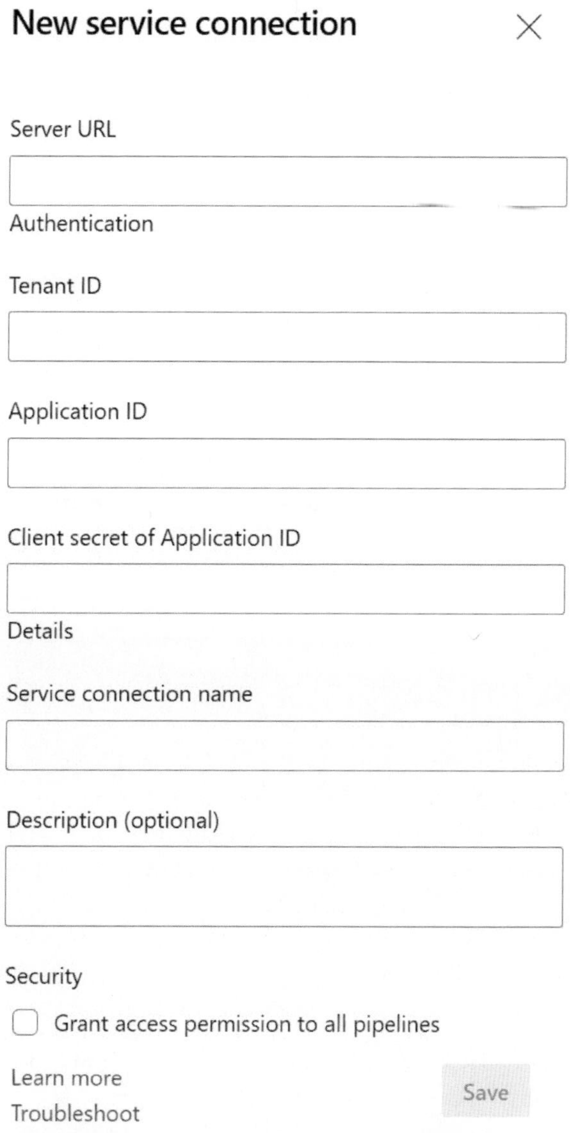

New service connection   ✕

Server URL

Authentication

Tenant ID

Application ID

Client secret of Application ID

Details

Service connection name

Description (optional)

Security

☐ Grant access permission to all pipelines

Learn more
Troubleshoot

Save

Figure 14.15 – New service connection form

If an **Azure Application Registration** and corresponding Power Platform Application User have already been created, you can proceed to fill in the **New service connection** form. Alternatively, the steps required to create these are as follows.

> **Note**
> Application registrations may be created via the Azure portal/Power Platform admin center or a PowerShell script. For details on creating service principals using PowerShell, please refer to `https://docs.microsoft.com/power-platform/alm/devops-build-tools#configure-service-connections-using-a-service-principal`.

II. Open the **Azure Active Directory** page within the Azure portal (`portal.azure.com`):

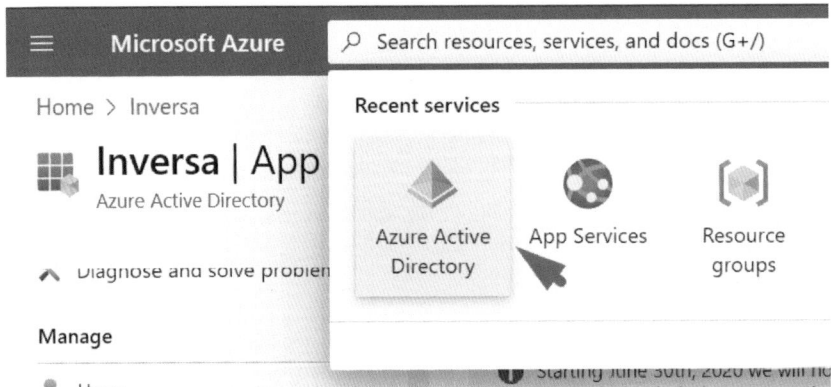

Figure 14.16 – The Azure Active Directory configuration page

Add a new app registration:

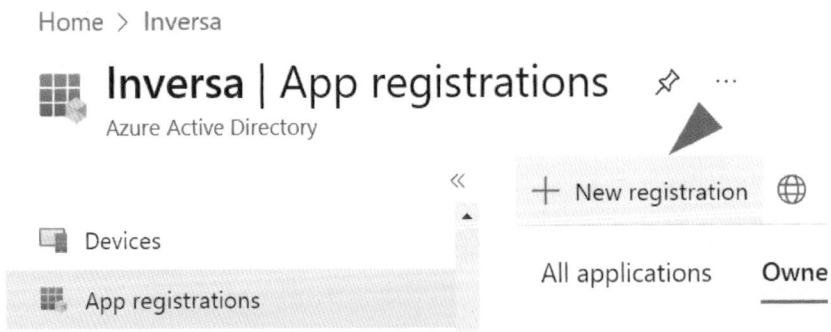

Figure 14.17 – Adding a new app registration

III. Set the app registration's name and select the **Single tenant** option:

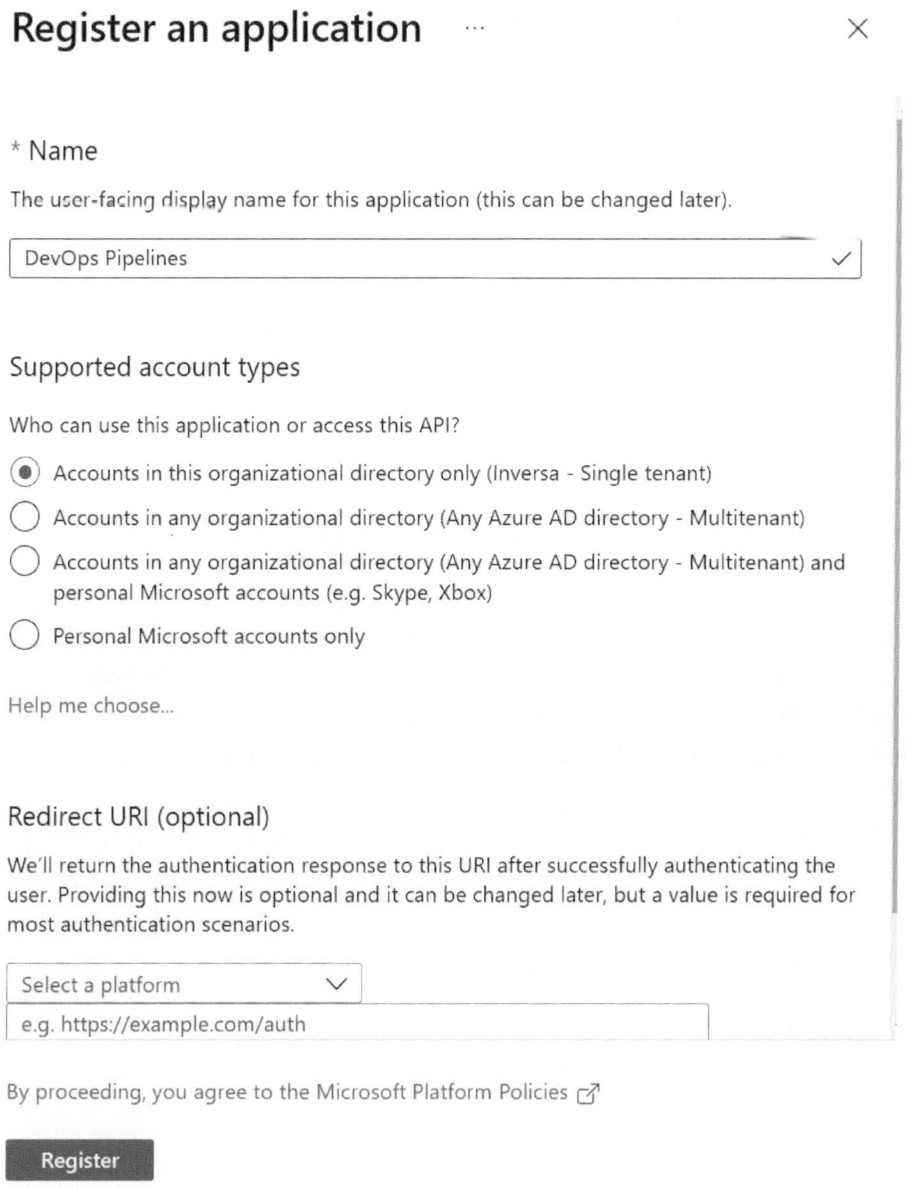

Register an application ···   ✕

* Name

The user-facing display name for this application (this can be changed later).

| DevOps Pipelines | ✓ |

Supported account types

Who can use this application or access this API?

- ◉ Accounts in this organizational directory only (Inversa - Single tenant)
- ○ Accounts in any organizational directory (Any Azure AD directory - Multitenant)
- ○ Accounts in any organizational directory (Any Azure AD directory - Multitenant) and personal Microsoft accounts (e.g. Skype, Xbox)
- ○ Personal Microsoft accounts only

Help me choose...

Redirect URI (optional)

We'll return the authentication response to this URI after successfully authenticating the user. Providing this now is optional and it can be changed later, but a value is required for most authentication scenarios.

| Select a platform | ∨ |

e.g. https://example.com/auth

By proceeding, you agree to the Microsoft Platform Policies ⌃

Register

Figure 14.18 – Configuring the app registration options

IV. Once app registration has been added, you need to note down the application (client) ID and the directory (tenant) ID, as these will be required when you configure the service principal in Azure DevOps:

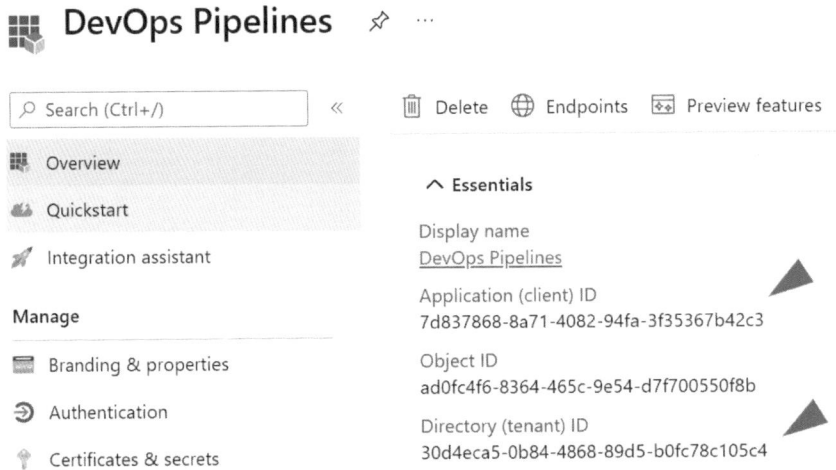

Figure 14.19 – The application ID and tenant IDs for an Azure app registration

Next, we will generate a secret for the app registration via the **Certificates & secrets** menu, selecting the validity period as required. After the secret expires, a new secret will need to be generated and the Azure DevOps service principal updated. The following screenshot shows an app registration secret being generated with an expiry period of 12 months:

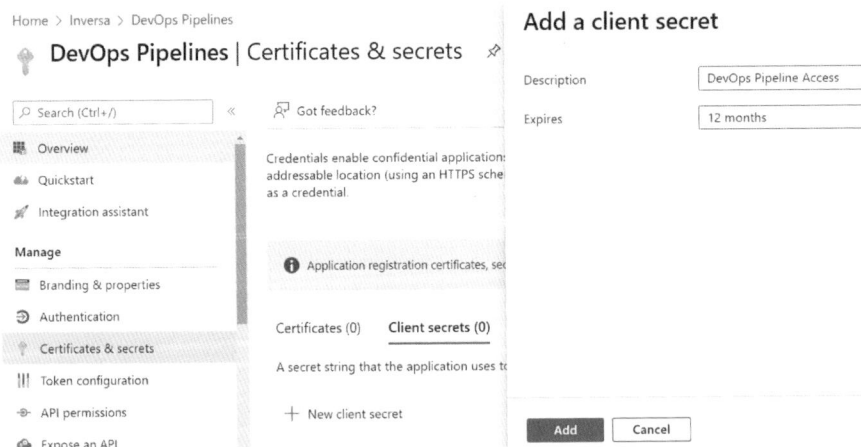

Figure 14.20 – Generating an authentication secret for an app registration

The app registration secret is used instead of a password when authenticating using a service principal. It is important to note the automatically generated secret at the point it is created, as it is not possible to retrieve it from the Azure portal at a later date. The app registration secret is displayed as follows:

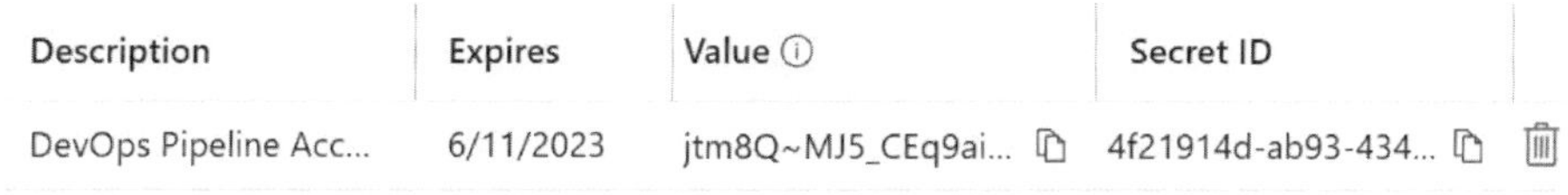

Description	Expires	Value ⓘ	Secret ID
DevOps Pipeline Acc...	6/11/2023	jtm8Q~MJ5_CEq9ai... ⧉	4f21914d-ab93-434... ⧉ 🗑

Figure 14.21 – App registration secret

Now that we have the application ID, tenant ID, and application secret, we can complete the Azure DevOps Power Platform service connection form:

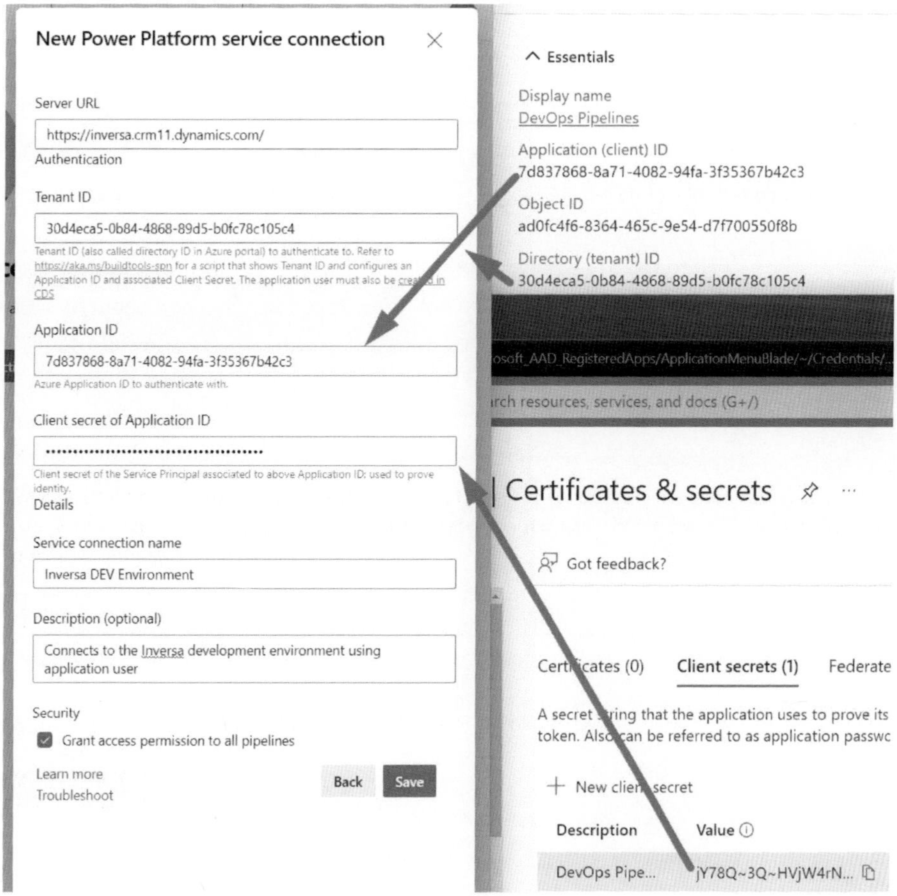

Figure 14.22 – Completing the Azure DevOps power Service connection with the app registration details

Once the app registration is in place, you can create a matching Power Platform Application User. From the Power Platform admin center, navigate to the environment that requires the service principal connection and open the **Application users** screen:

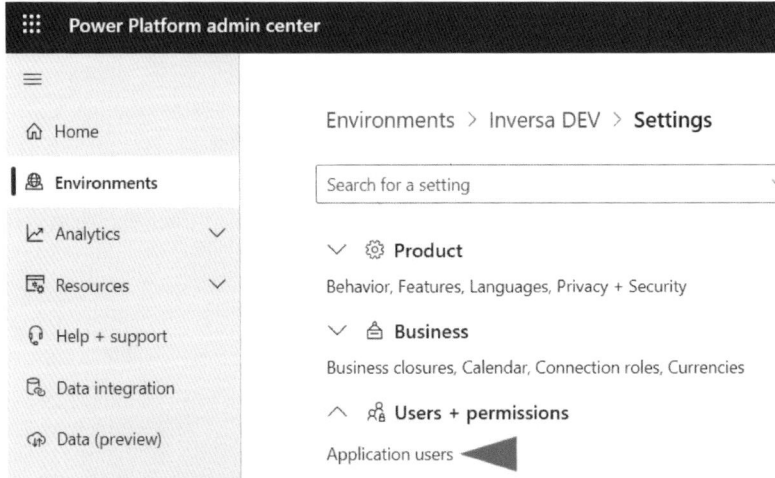

Figure 14.23 – Adding a Power Platform application user

From the **Application users** screen, select **New app user**. Select a security role with sufficient administrative privileges to export solutions (in the following screenshot, we have selected a custom security role called DevOps that will provide enough privileges):

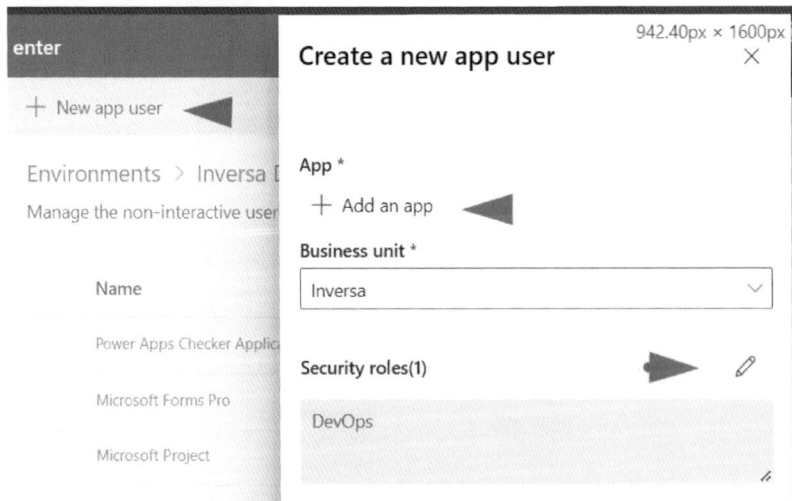

Figure 14.24 – Selecting a security role for the application user

Pressing the + **Add an app** button will bring up all the app registrations that exist in the tenant. Select the app registration you created for this particular Application User:

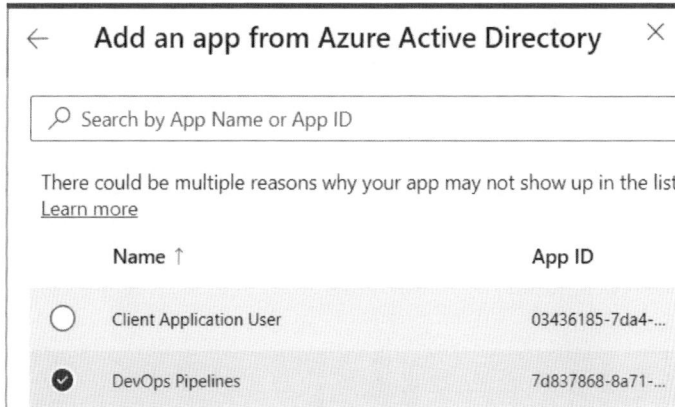

Figure 14.25 – Linking a Power Platform application user to an app registration

Once the app registration and security roles have been set, click the **Create** button:

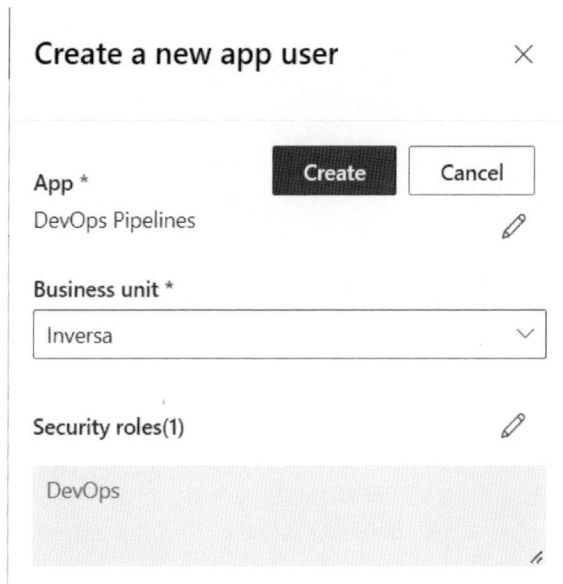

Figure 14.26 – Power Platform application user ready for creation

Once the application user has been created, they can be managed via the Power Platform **Application users** view:

Figure 14.27 –Application users list

We have now configured the following:

- Azure app registration

- A Power Platform application user

- An Azure DevOps service principal

With these three components in place, the Azure DevOps pipelines are ready to communicate with the Power Platform environment.

7.   **Set the service principal on the Azure DevOps export task**

With the Azure DevOps service principal in place, we can set the corresponding field on the **Power Platform Export Solution** task:

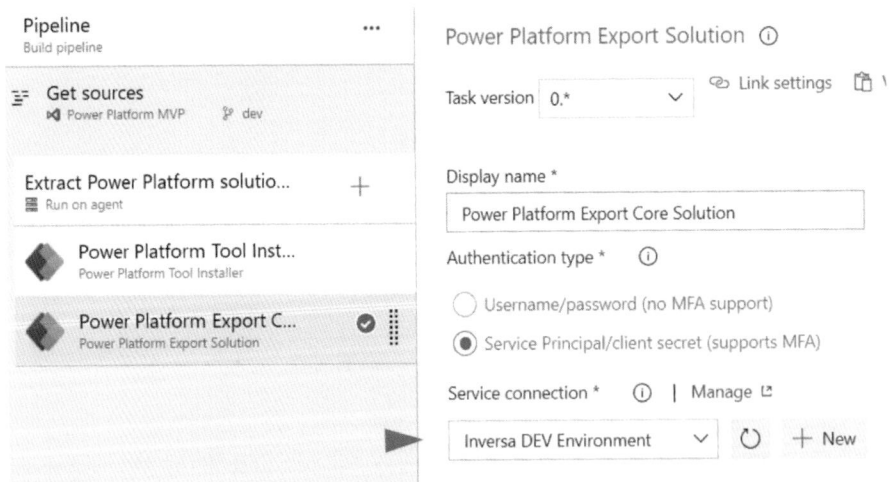

Figure 14.28 – Setting the service principal for the Power Platform Export Solution task

8. **Testing the Azure DevOps Service Principal connection**

    Now is a great time to validate the connection from Azure DevOps to the Power Platform environment. Pressing the **Save and Queue** button (or just **Queue** if the save option is not available) will run the pipeline tasks in sequence:

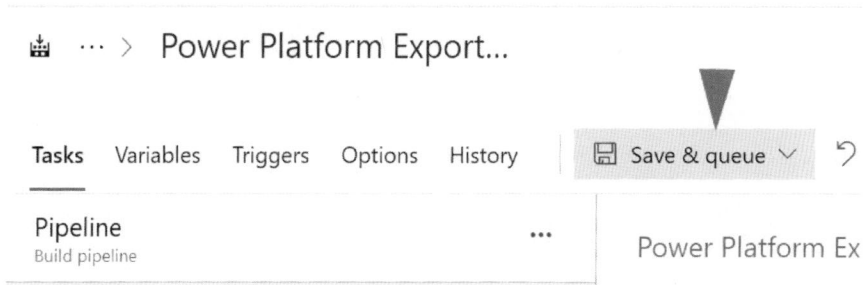

Figure 14.29 – Running the Azure DevOps pipeline

    If this is the first pipeline you've created within an Azure DevOps organization, you may find that the parallelism capacity for Microsoft-hosted pipeline agents is 0. If that is the case, the pipeline execution will exit with the following error:

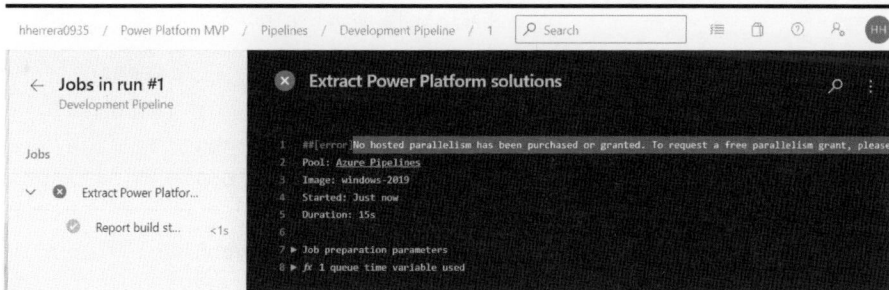

Figure 14.30 – Azure DevOps pipeline error displayed when no hosted agent capacity is available

    There are three options to resolve this pipeline capacity issue:

- **Request a free parallelism grant**: Completing the following form will typically increase capacity by 1: `https://aka.ms/azpipelines-parallelism-request` within two business days.

- **Install a self-hosted Azure Pipeline agent**: Please refer to the following document for details on self-hosted agents: `https://docs.microsoft.com/azure/devops/pipelines/agents/agents?view=azure-devops&tabs=browser#install`.

- **Purchase additional capacity**: Linking the Azure DevOps project to an active Azure subscription means additional Microsoft-hosted jobs may be added. The **Parallel jobs** menu within the Azure DevOps **Project Settings** page provides a means of increasing capacity. One parallel job is required to run pipelines. Selecting the **Change** option will allow you to select an appropriate Azure subscription and increase the capacity:

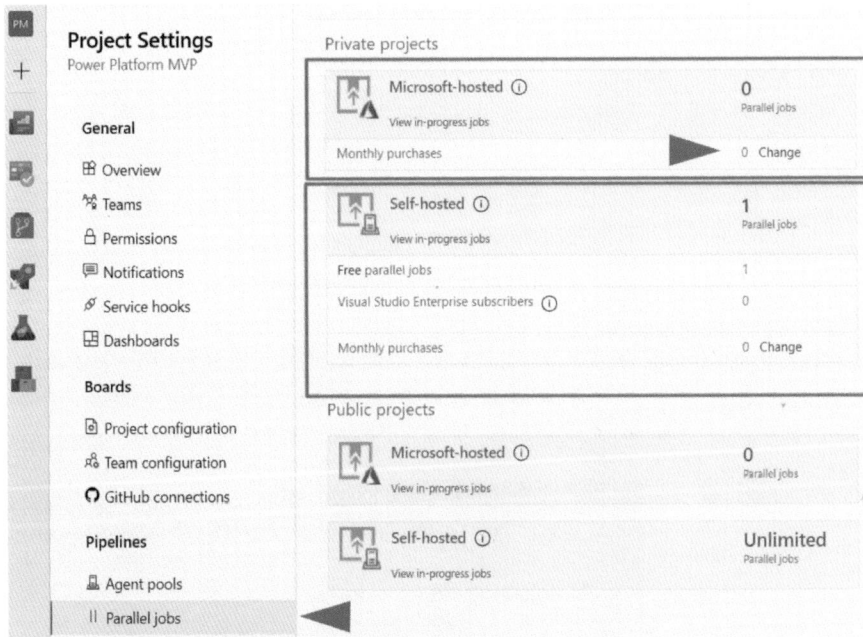

Figure 14.31 – Increasing Microsoft-hosted parallel jobs capacity in the Azure DevOps Project Settings page

Once capacity has been increased, pipelines will run without displaying a capacity error.

9. **Add pipeline tasks to export any other required solutions**

   We have created a task to export a Power Platform solution and validated it as functional and able to connect to Dataverse. At this point, you may wish to extract any other solutions that make up the implementation. A managed version of the solution may also be exported for safe-keeping in source control.

Adding **Power Platform Export Solution** tasks will be the same as the first export – that is, changing the source solution to be exported and deciding whether to export a managed/unmanaged solution. The following screenshot shows four Power Platform Export Solution tasks, where a core solution and a flows solution are being exported in both managed and unmanaged formats:

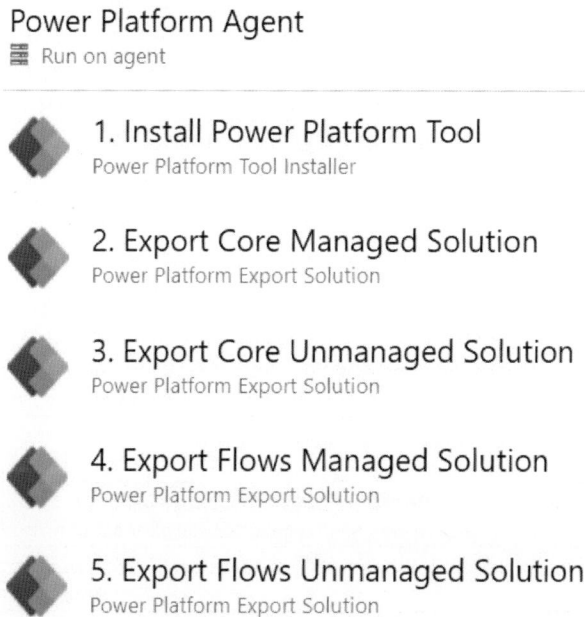

Power Platform Agent
Run on agent

1. Install Power Platform Tool
Power Platform Tool Installer

2. Export Core Managed Solution
Power Platform Export Solution

3. Export Core Unmanaged Solution
Power Platform Export Solution

4. Export Flows Managed Solution
Power Platform Export Solution

5. Export Flows Unmanaged Solution
Power Platform Export Solution

Figure 14.32 – Adding export tasks for all the required solutions

10. **Add a task to run the Power Platform solution checker**

An Azure DevOps pipeline is ideal for running an automated Power Platform solution checker. Once the solution files have been exported, running a solution check can help ensure only solutions that meet the project's specific quality criteria are checked into source control and deployed to target environments.

Add a task by searching for **Power Platform Checker** and configuring the following key fields:

- **Service connection**: The environment that will run the solution checker. This is typically the same as the source environment.

- **Local Files to Analyze**: A path and file wildcard search for solution ZIP files to be checked. We will be checking all the managed solutions in our example.

- **Error Level**: The minimum solution checker entry that will be considered an error, stopping the pipeline's execution and preventing the solution from entering source control. The following options are available:

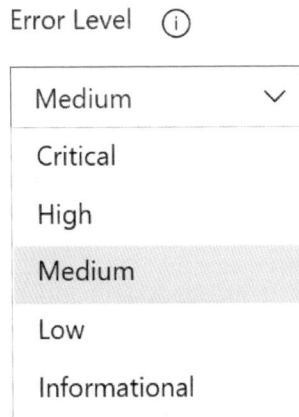

Figure 14.33 – Solution checker Error Level options

- **Error threshold**: The number of errors that will stop the execution of the pipeline.

The following screenshot illustrates the Power Platform solution checker options:

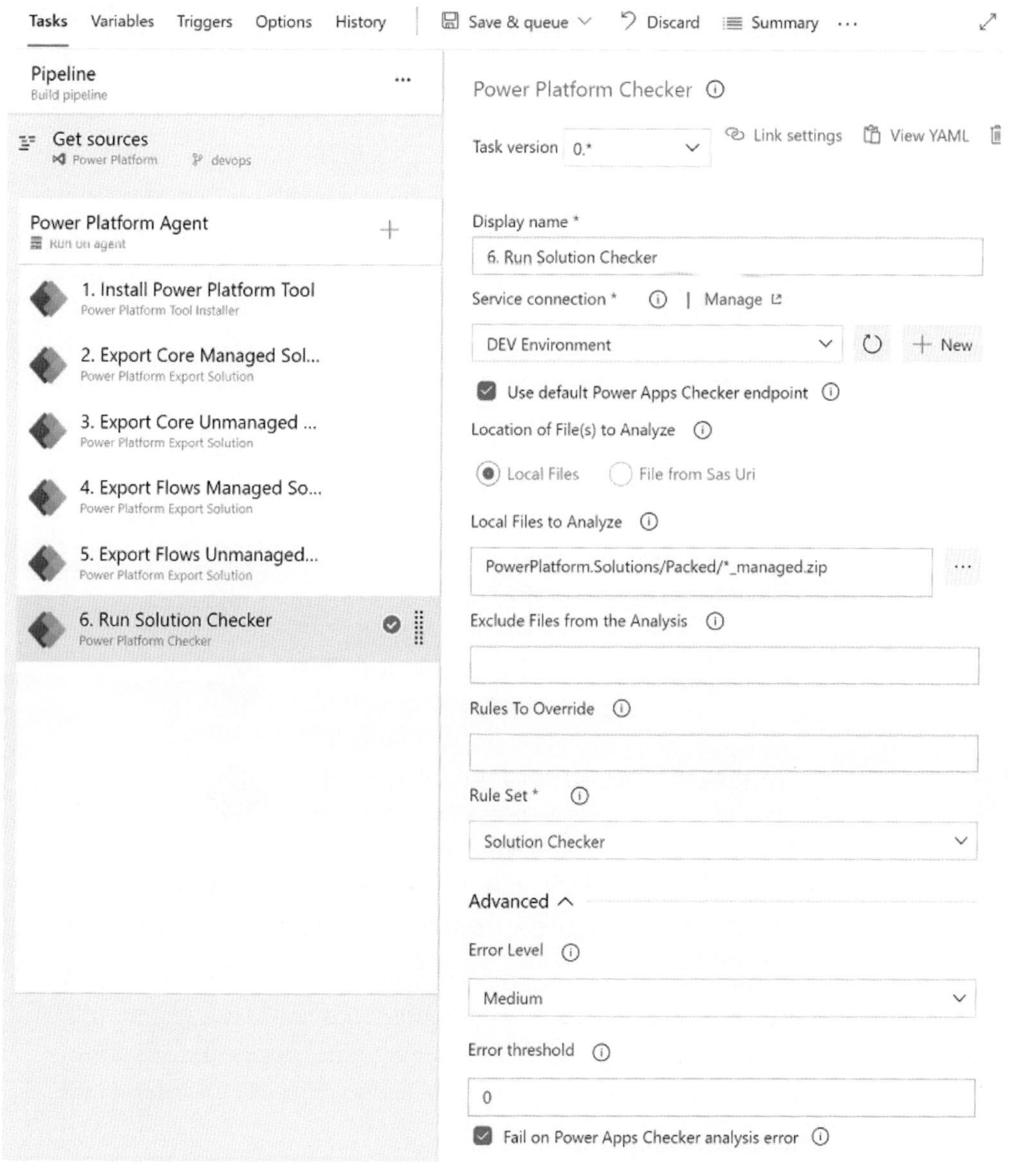

Tasks Variables Triggers Options History | 💾 Save & queue ∨ ↺ Discard ≡ Summary ⋯ ↗

Pipeline
Build pipeline ⋯

≣ **Get sources**
⋈ Power Platform   ⅋ devops

Power Platform Agent   +
▦ Run on agent

◆ **1. Install Power Platform Tool**
Power Platform Tool Installer

◆ **2. Export Core Managed Sol...**
Power Platform Export Solution

◆ **3. Export Core Unmanaged ...**
Power Platform Export Solution

◆ **4. Export Flows Managed So...**
Power Platform Export Solution

◆ **5. Export Flows Unmanaged...**
Power Platform Export Solution

◆ **6. Run Solution Checker** ✓ ⋮
Power Platform Checker

Power Platform Checker ⓘ

⮾ Link settings 📋 View YAML 🗑

Task version 0.* ∨

Display name *
> 6. Run Solution Checker

Service connection * ⓘ | Manage ↗
> DEV Environment ∨ ↻ + New

☑ Use default Power Apps Checker endpoint ⓘ
Location of File(s) to Analyze ⓘ
◉ Local Files   ○ File from Sas Uri

Local Files to Analyze ⓘ
> PowerPlatform.Solutions/Packed/*_managed.zip ⋯

Exclude Files from the Analysis ⓘ
>

Rules To Override ⓘ
>

Rule Set * ⓘ
> Solution Checker ∨

Advanced ∧

Error Level ⓘ
> Medium ∨

Error threshold ⓘ
> 0

☑ Fail on Power Apps Checker analysis error ⓘ

Figure 14.34 – Pipeline options available in the Power Platform Checker task

11. **Add a task to extract the Power Platform solutions for source control**

Extracting a Power Platform solution into its individual components results in a folder and file structure that is better suited for source control and versioning than a ZIP file.

In this example, we will clear the folder where the extracted solution components live (as a previous check-in would have filled the folder already) before extracting our freshly exported Power Platform solutions. The sequence of tasks is illustrated in the following screenshot:

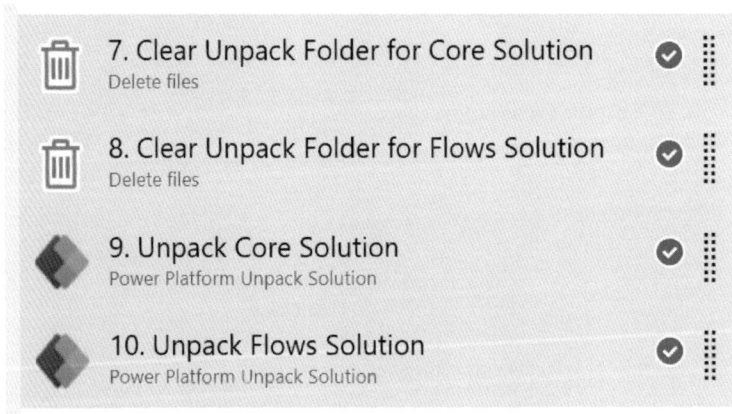

Figure 14.35 – A sequence of pipeline tasks that clear the previously extracted folders and proceed to extract the new solutions

First, we must add an action to **Delete files** that were previously extracted and checked into source control. The following example clears the **PowerPlatform. Solutions/Extracted/Core** folder, ready for the new set of components to be extracted:

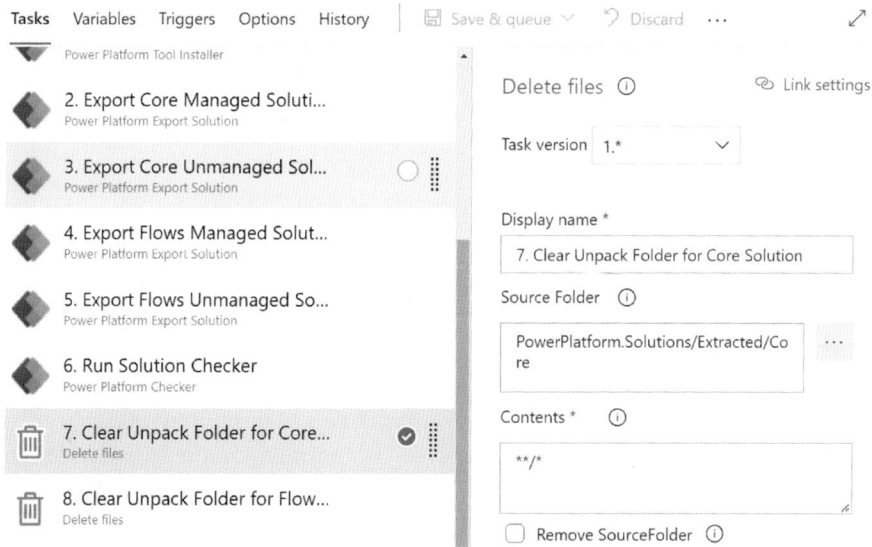

Figure 14.36 – Adding a Delete files action to clear previously checked-in solution components

You must repeat the **Delete files** action for as many folders as required to ensure all previously extracted solution components have been cleared. This prevents deleted Power Platform components from resurfacing unexpectedly.

We are now ready to add a **Power Platform Unpack Solution** task to the pipeline. The key configuration parameters to be completed are as follows:

- **Solution Input File:** The path to the solution ZIP file that was exported in the previous pipeline steps.

- **Target Folder to Unpack Solution:** The path in the source control folder structure where the extracted components will be saved.

- **Type of Solution**: The available options are **Managed**, **Unmanaged**, and **Both**. Selecting **Both** requires unmanaged and managed file versions, with the managed version having a filename ending in _managed.zip:

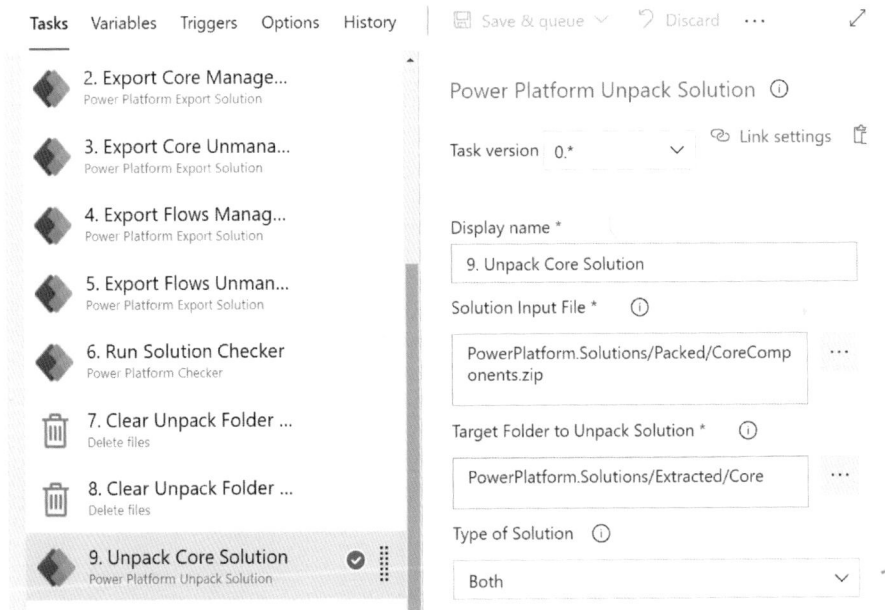

Figure 14.37 – Options available for the Power Platform Unpack Solution task

The following link provides additional details on the solution packer options related to this task: https://docs.microsoft.com/power-platform/alm/solution-packager-tool.

You must then repeat the **Power Platform Unpack Solution** task for any other solutions that have been extracted in the previous pipeline steps.

12. **Check the solutions into source control**

Once the solutions have been exported, verified, and unpacked, they are ready to be checked into source control. There are various ways of checking in files from a DevOps pipeline. In our example, we will be using Git as our source control repository and a **Command line** task to carry out the necessary Git commands.

The following screenshot illustrates a **Command line** task that checks all updates into a Git repository, including solution ZIP files and extracted solution components:

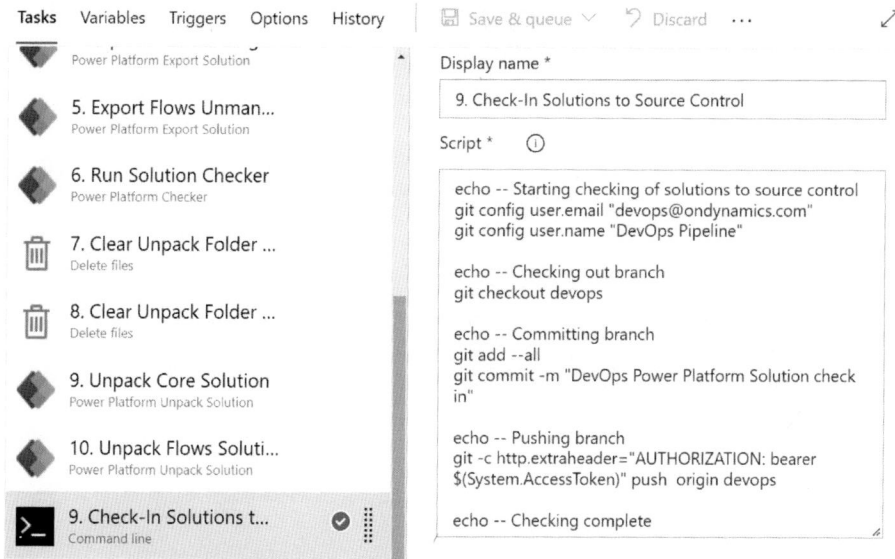

Figure 14.38 – An Azure DevOps Command line task, configured to
check changes into a Git repository

The command-line script that's been used in the example pipeline task is as follows:

```
echo -- Starting checking of solutions to source control
git config user.email "devops@ondynamics.com"
git config user.name "DevOps Pipeline"


echo -- Checking out branch
git checkout devops


echo -- Committing branch
git add --all
git commit -m "DevOps Power Platform Solution check in"


echo -- Pushing branch
git -c http.extraheader="AUTHORIZATION: bearer $(System.
AccessToken)" push  origin devops


echo -- Checking complete
```

Note that the command-line script references a `System.AccessToken`, a variable that's automatically populated by the pipeline to facilitate authentication. The following pipeline agent setting must be ticked for `System.AccessToken` to be accessible to the script:

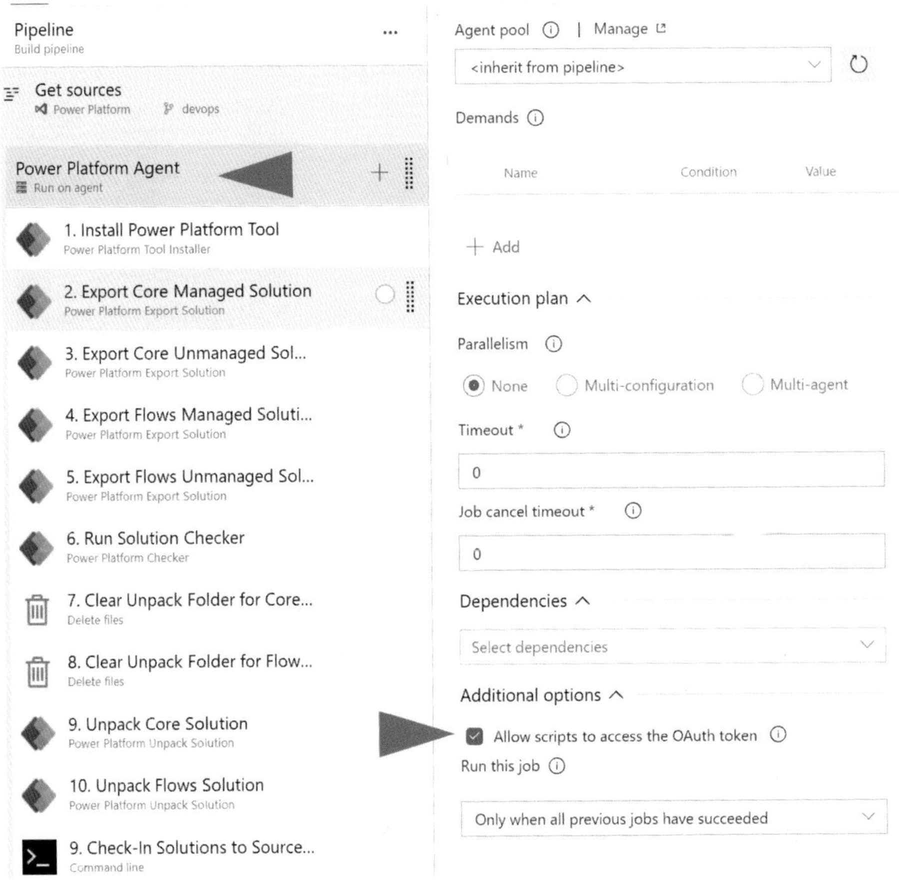

Figure 14.39 – The pipeline agent setting that allows scripts to use System.AccessToken for authentication

Finally, the project user needs **Contribute** permissions to be able to check the solution files into the repository. Permission may be assigned to the project user via the **Repository** menu on the project's settings page, as shown in the following screenshot:

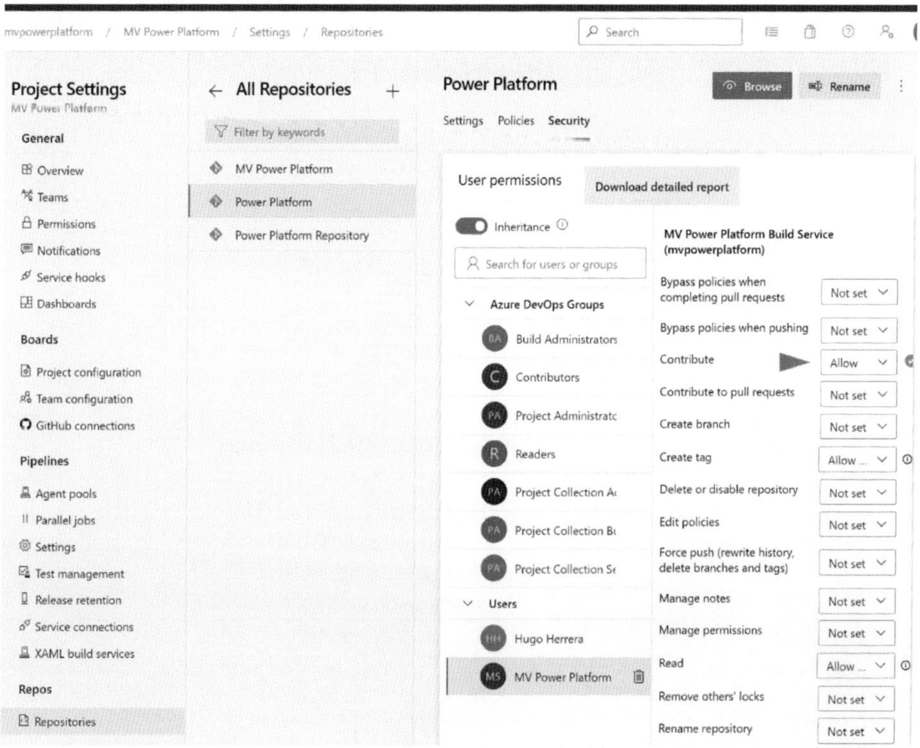

Figure 14.40 – Granting the project user permission to check files into the repository

13. **Test the pipeline**

Once the pipeline tasks have been completed, the entire process can be validated through a sequence of test runs. The runtime logs provide a means of troubleshooting any issues that are encountered by the steps until the pipeline configuration runs through to completion, as shown in the following screenshot:

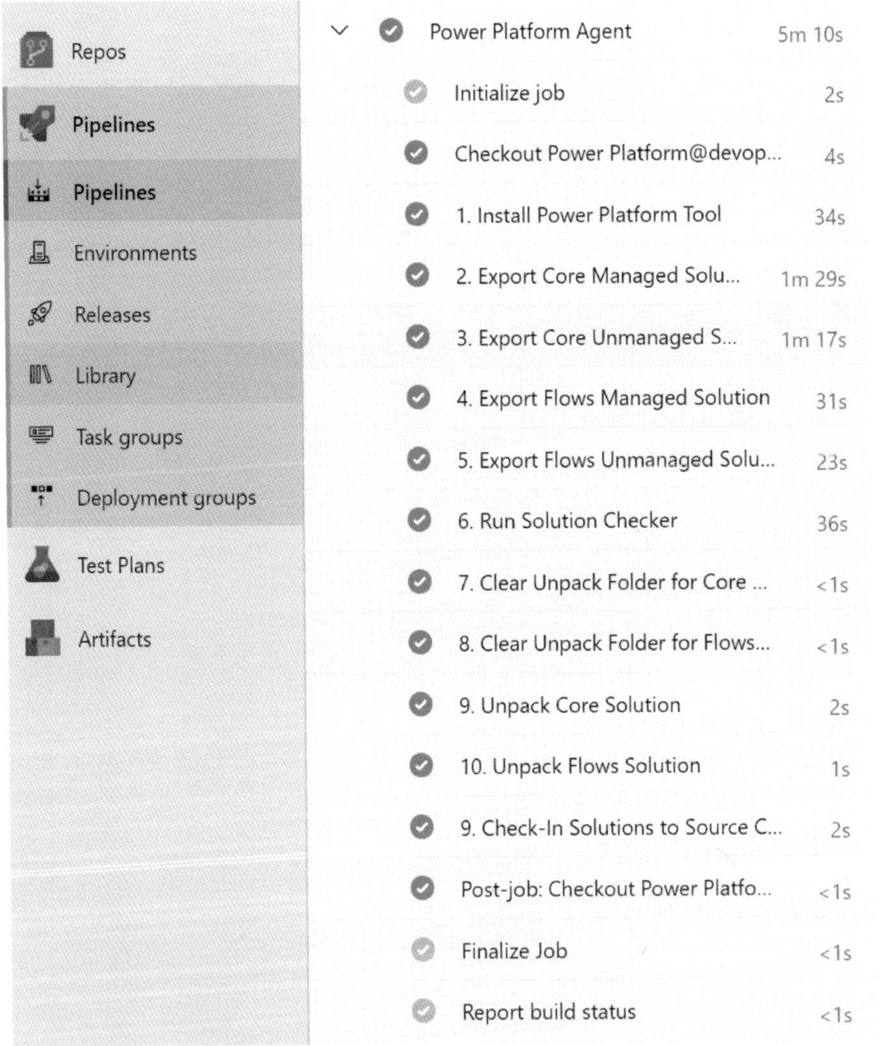

Repos	✓	✓	Power Platform Agent	5m 10s
Pipelines		✓	Initialize job	2s
Pipelines		✓	Checkout Power Platform@devop...	4s
Environments		✓	1. Install Power Platform Tool	34s
Releases		✓	2. Export Core Managed Solu...	1m 29s
Library		✓	3. Export Core Unmanaged S...	1m 17s
Task groups		✓	4. Export Flows Managed Solution	31s
Deployment groups		✓	5. Export Flows Unmanaged Solu...	23s
Test Plans		✓	6. Run Solution Checker	36s
Artifacts		✓	7. Clear Unpack Folder for Core ...	<1s
		✓	8. Clear Unpack Folder for Flows...	<1s
		✓	9. Unpack Core Solution	2s
		✓	10. Unpack Flows Solution	1s
		✓	9. Check-In Solutions to Source C...	2s
		✓	Post-job: Checkout Power Platfo...	<1s
		✓	Finalize Job	<1s
		✓	Report build status	<1s

Figure 14.41 – A successful DevOps pipeline execution

14. **Decide whether to schedule the pipeline for regular check-ins to source control**

Unless configured otherwise, DevOps pipelines are triggered manually. Depending on the project team's ways of working, performing a daily check-in of the Power Platform solution may be beneficial. Scheduled check-ins also have the added benefit of alerting the DevOps team of any issues with the solutions. The process will fail if the solution checker finds problems with the exported solutions.

The following screenshot shows the pipeline configured for execution every night at 23:00 hours:

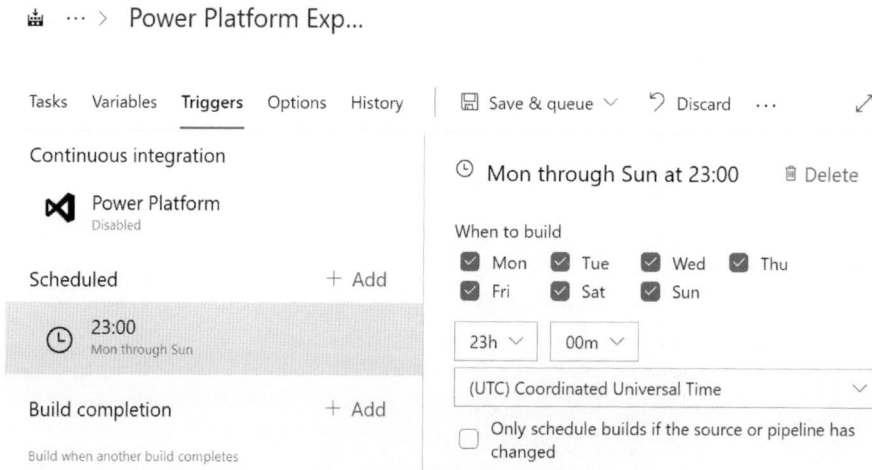

Figure 14.42 – A DevOps pipeline configured to run every night at 23:00 hours

With that, we have created an Azure DevOps pipeline that extracts solutions from a development environment, runs the Power Platform solution checker, extracts the solution components, and checks the results into source control. In the next section, we will look at source control for Power Pages.

Managing source control for Power Pages

Power Pages store their configurations in Dataverse tables. As a result, configuration for Power Pages can be exported and deployed using standard tools such as the Configuration Data Migration tool or XRMToolbox plugins such as Portal Records Mover.

The Portal Records Mover plugin provides a mechanism for exporting Power Page configurations to files and for direct transfer from one environment to another. It has handy features that enable/disable system plugins that would otherwise conflict with the import process. The following screenshot illustrates the main screen of Portal Records Mover:

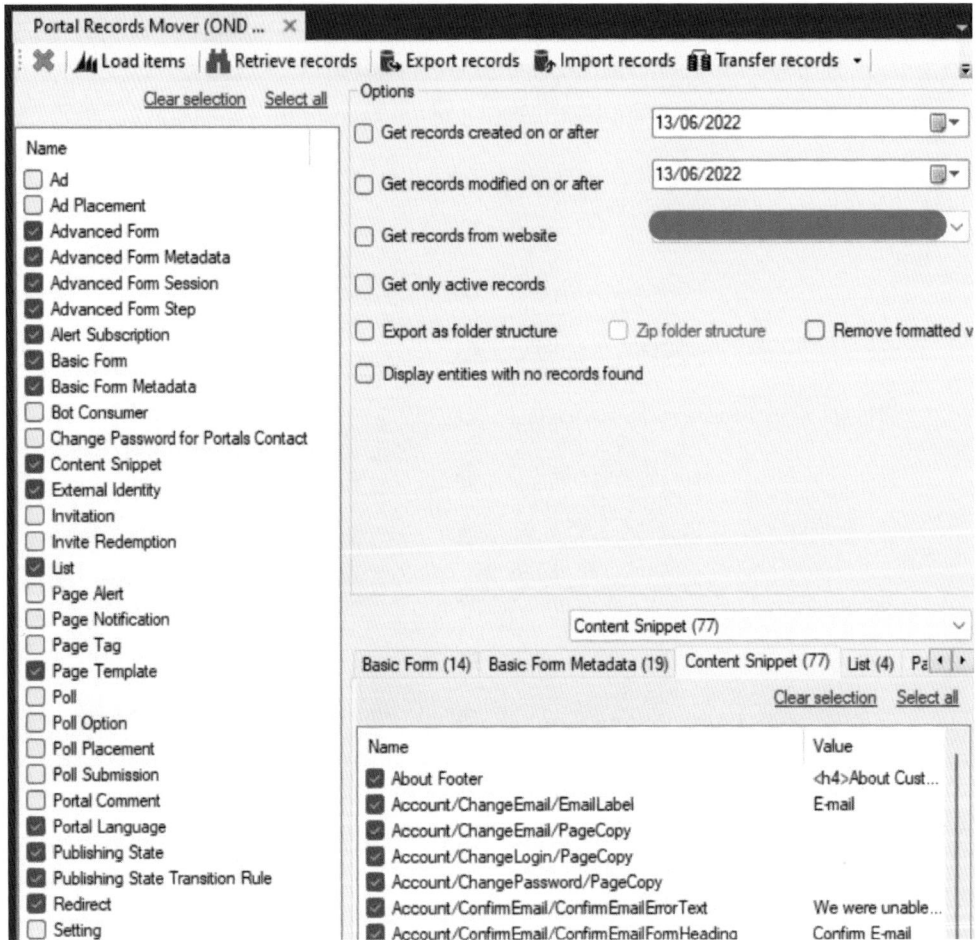

Figure 14.43 – The Power Portal Records Mover main screen

The Portal Records Mover configuration files may be exported and stored in source control alongside its setting files, as follows:

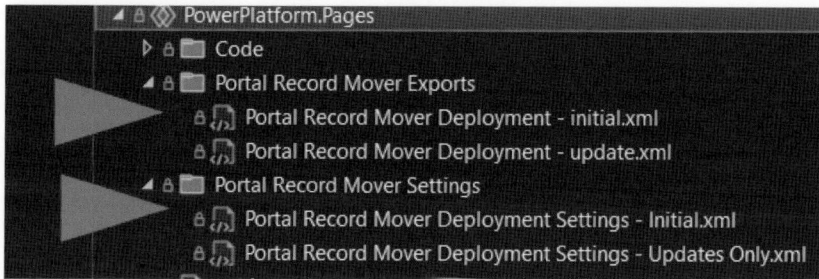

Figure 14.44 – Power Pages configuration files saved in a file structure for source control

---

Reference Documentation on the Portal Records Mover Plugin

For further details on the Portal Records Mover plugin for XrmToolbox, please go to `https://www.xrmtoolbox.com/plugins/MscrmTools.PortalRecordsMover/`.

Storing Power Page JavaScript and CSS configurations in source control will also provide a means of versioning and tracking changes. These files can be managed manually or exported into a folder structure similar to the one shown in the following screenshot by using the Portal Code Editor plugin for XrmToolbox:

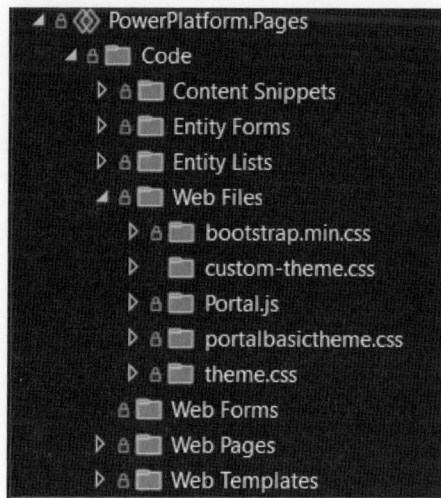

Figure 14.45 – Power Page JavaScript and CSS files saved in a folder structure and checked into source control

The Portal Code Editor export facility is shown in the following screenshot:

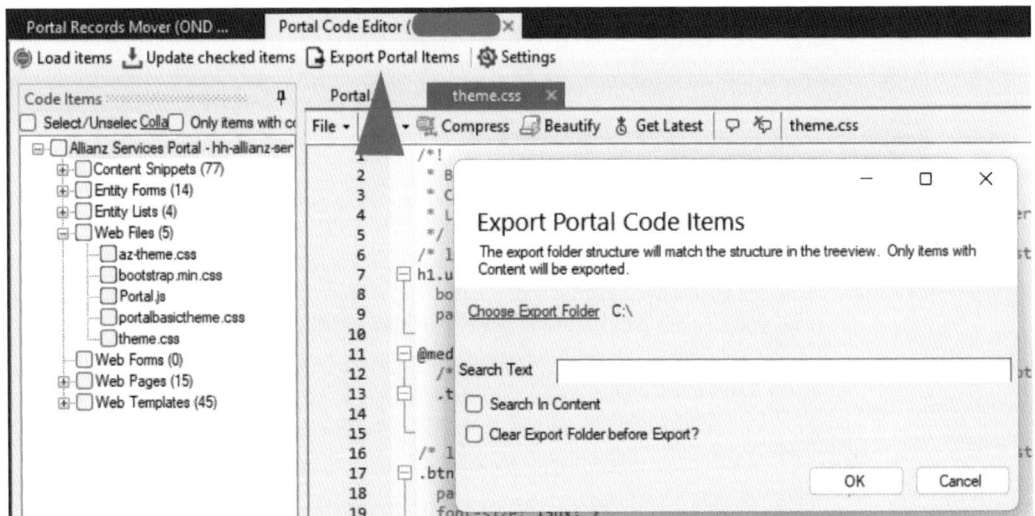

Figure 14.46 – Using the Portal Code Editor plugin to export code items to a folder structure

> **Reference Documentation on the Portal Code Editor Plugin**
>
> For further details on the Portal Code Editor plugin for XrmToolbox, please go to `https://www.xrmtoolbox.com/plugins/MscrmTools.PortalCodeEditor/`.

The Power Pages extension for Visual Studio Code also downloads and edits portal code, including Liquid templates. For further details, please go to `https://docs.microsoft.com/en-us/power-apps/maker/portals/vs-code-extension`.

Managing source control of Dataverse plugins

Dataverse plugins are built using the .NET Framework and follow standard C# source control practices. All Dataverse plugins should be checked into source control, where they will be used for future enhancements and bug fixes:

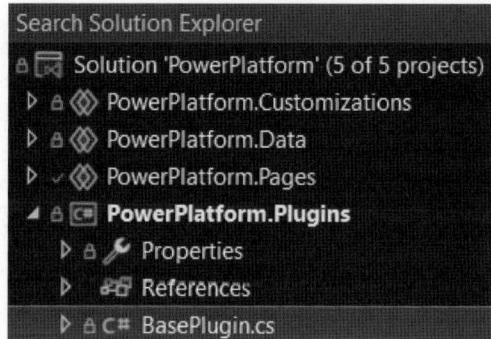

Figure 14.47 – A Dataverse plugin within a Visual Studio project structure checked into source control

Conclusion

In this section, we reviewed the options available for storing and managing Power Platform configurations in source control. The next chapter discusses automated Power Platform deployments. But for now, let's learn how to leverage Azure DevOps for ALM.

Leveraging Azure DevOps for application life cycle management (ALM)

Releases in Azure DevOps effectively manage the application life cycle for Power Platform solutions. The concept of Releases revolves around a set of source artifacts (for example, Power Platform solution files) and a sequence of **release pipelines** that deploy those artifacts to target environments (for example, QA and PROD Power Platform environments).

Solution architects configure release pipelines, setting up a framework for continuous delivery that provides the following benefits:

- Reduce delivery risks via a sequenced and controlled deployment strategy.
- Reduce the risk of errors caused by manual deployments.
- Increase productivity and release capacity through automation.

In this section, we will create a Release Pipeline that deploys to QA and production environments from source control.

Configuring release pipelines for automated deployments

In this section, we will create a release pipeline that retrieves Power Platform solution files stored in source control, validates the solution files by testing the deployment to a validation environment, and then proceeds to deploy the solution to QA if valid. The deployment to the production environment can then be triggered manually, using precisely the same solution files deployed to QA.

The following diagram illustrates the Release Pipeline we are about to create:

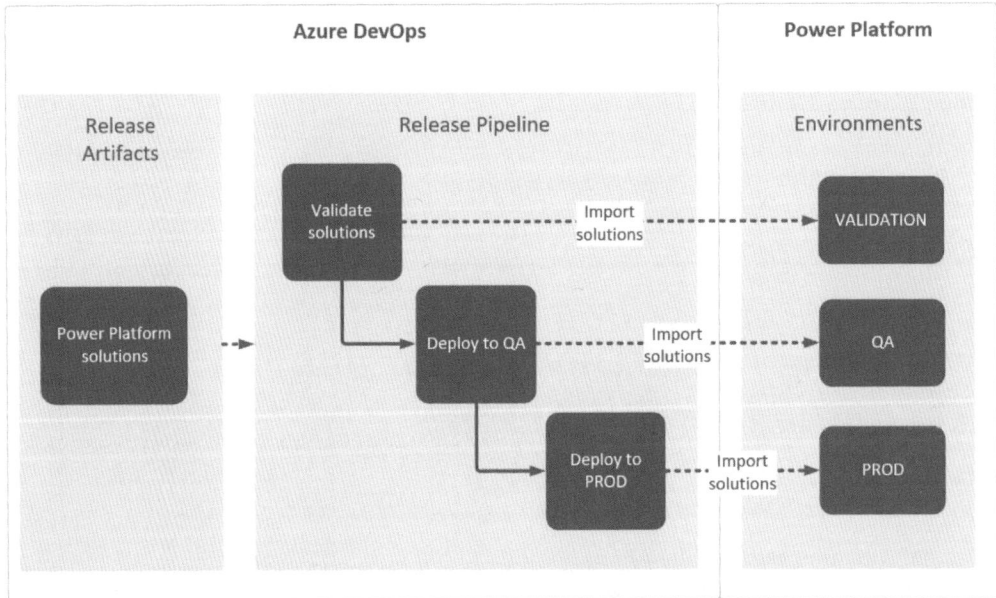

Figure 14.48 – Example Release Pipeline deployment to QA and production Power Platform environments

Follow these steps to create an Azure DevOps Release Pipeline:

1. **Open the New Release Pipeline page**

    Navigate to the **Azure DevOps Pipelines** | **Releases** menu and select the **New release pipeline** option:

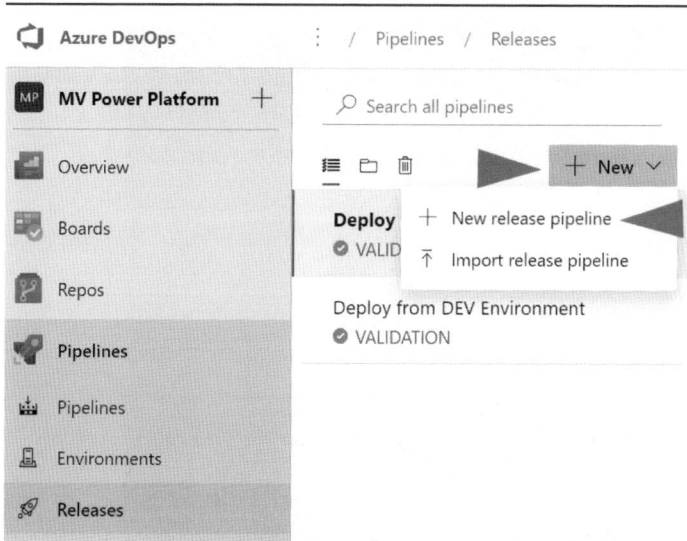

Figure 14.49 – Opening the New release pipeline editor

2. **Start from an empty job**

When asked to select a template, select the **Empty job** option to create a Power Platform deployment release:

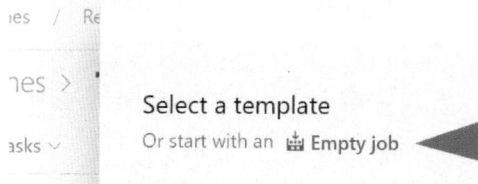

Figure 14.50 – Creating a Power Platform Release Pipeline from a clear template

3. **Label the first stage in the release**

A stage is automatically added when the release is created. In our scenario, we will label the stage **VALIDATION** as it will check the solution and run a test deployment to a VALIDATION environment:

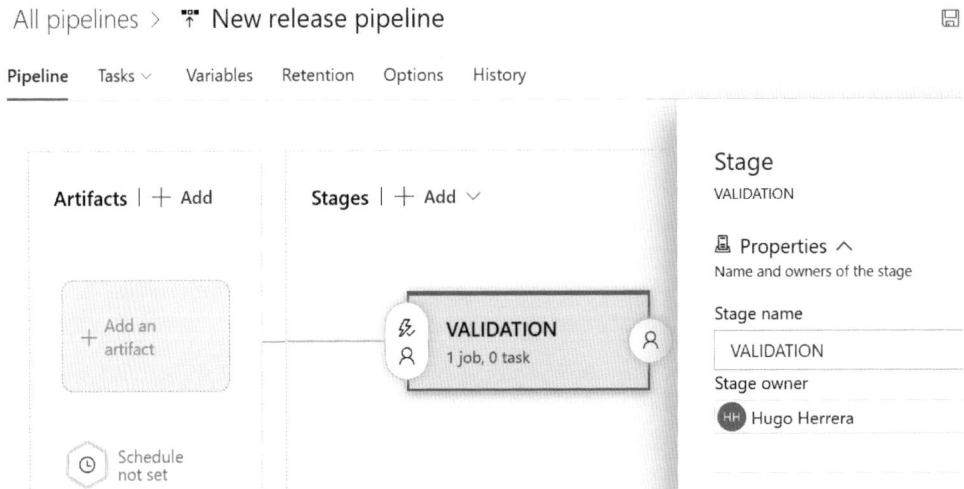

Figure 14.51 – Naming the Release stage

4. **Select the Power Platform solutions as source artifacts**

Select the **Add an artifact** option and select the repository and branch that holds the Power Platform solution files (please see the previous section for details on creating a build pipeline that automatically checks Power Platform solutions into source control):

All pipelines >   ⚑ New rele

ipeline   Tasks ∨   Variables   Ret

Artifacts | + Add

⬥
Add an artifact

🕐 Schedule
not set

Add an artifact

Source type

⬇️   ⬥
.▫.   ✓ Azure Re…
Build

5 more artifact types ∨

Project *   ⓘ

MV Power Platform

Source (repository) *   ⓘ

Power Platform

Default branch *   ⓘ

devops

Default version *   ⓘ

Latest from the default branch

☐ Checkout submodules ⓘ

☐ Checkout files from LFS ⓘ

Shallow fetch depth ⓘ

Source alias *   ⓘ

_Power Platform

Add

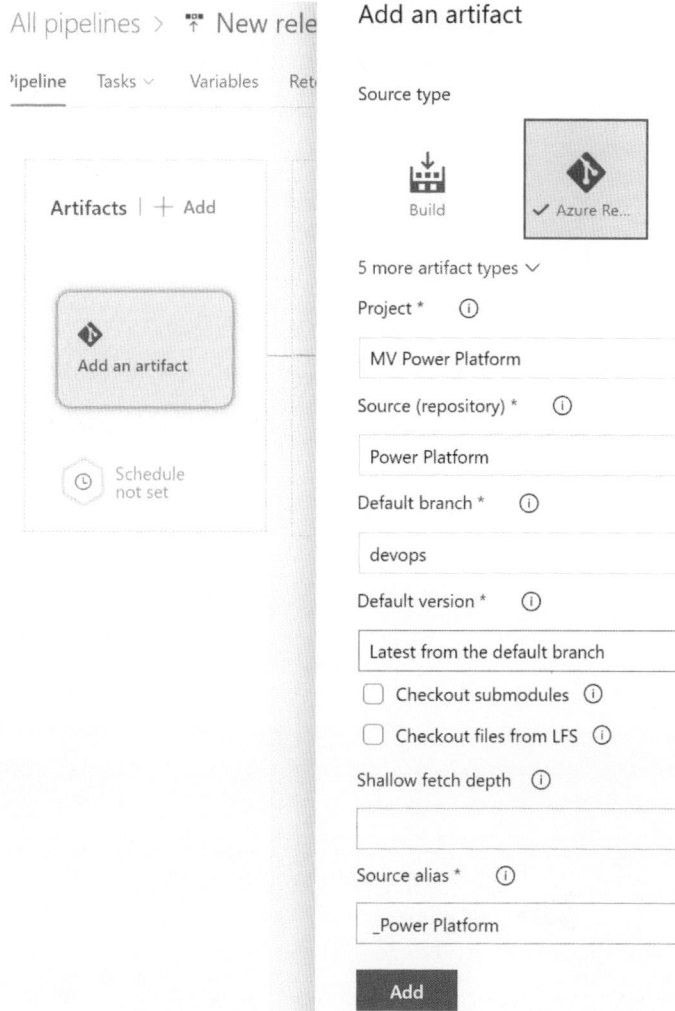

Figure 14.52 – Selecting the location of the source Power Platform solution files

5.   **Add the Power Platform deployment tasks to the VALIDATION stage**

The newly created **VALIDATION** stage is currently empty. Clicking on the job/task option highlighted in the following screenshot will bring up the stage editor:

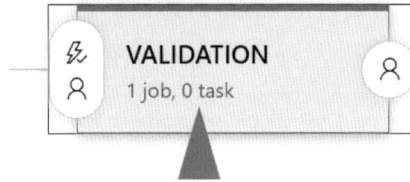

Figure 14.53 – Opening the stage editor

The first task to add will be the Power Platform Tool Installer task (please see the previous section for details on installing Power Platform Tools on a new Azure DevOps organization):

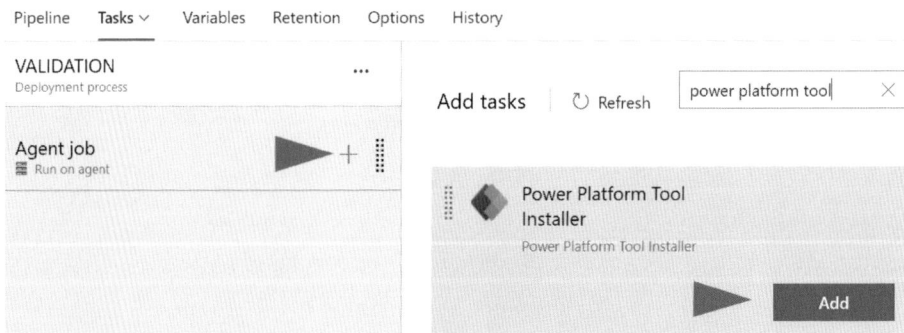

Figure 14.54 – Adding the Power Platform Tool Installer task to a Release stage

6. **Add the Power Platform Checker task to the VALIDATION stage**

    Add the **Power Platform Checker** task to the stage:

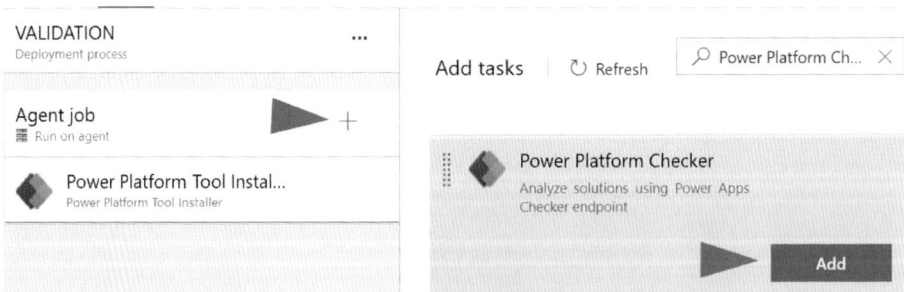

Figure 14.55 – Adding the Power Platform Checker task to a Release stage

Proceed to configure the **Power Platform Checker** task to validate the solutions that are about to be imported into the target system. In this scenario, we will be checking all the managed solutions in the **Packed** folder, as shown in the following screenshot:

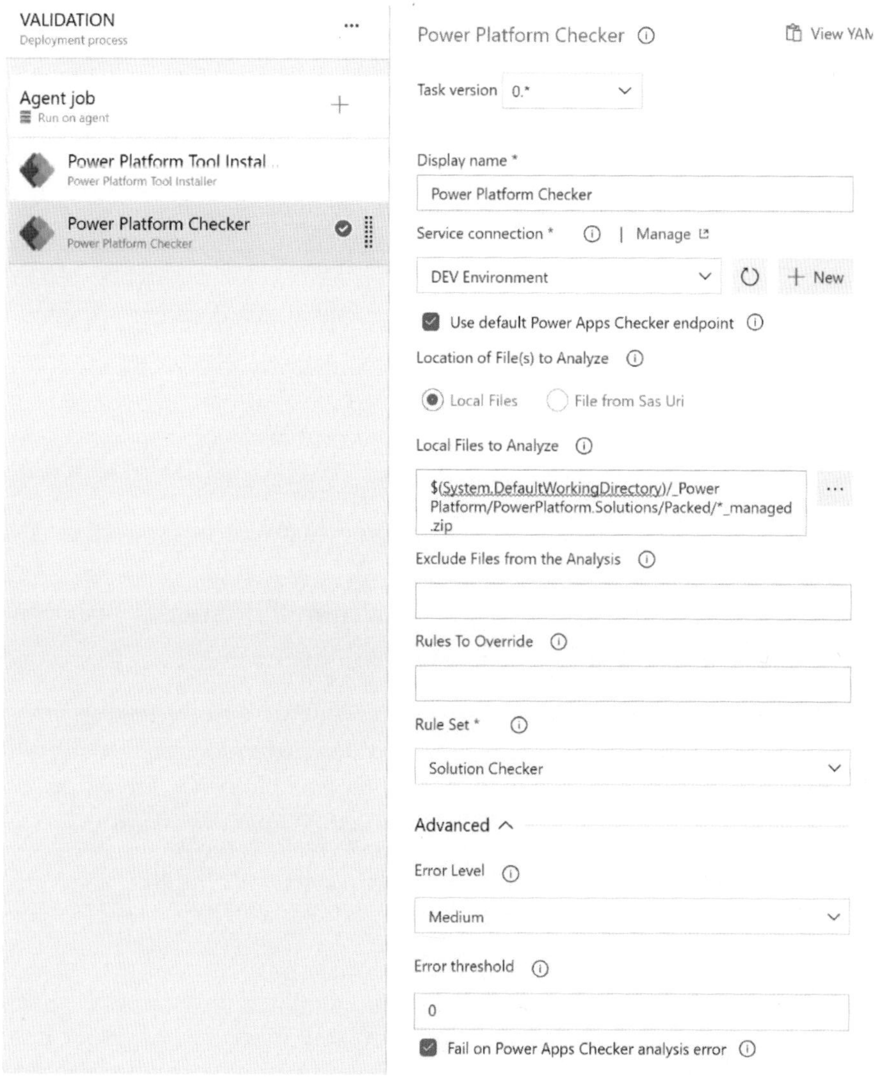

Figure 14.56 – Adding the Power Platform Checker task to a Release stage

The service connections we set up in the previous section may be used for this exercise.

7. **Add the Power Platform Backup Environment task to the VALIDATION stage**

The **Power Platform Backup Environment** task will create a backup of the **VALIDATION** environment before the solutions are imported, which can later be used to restore the environment to the state before the solutions were imported:

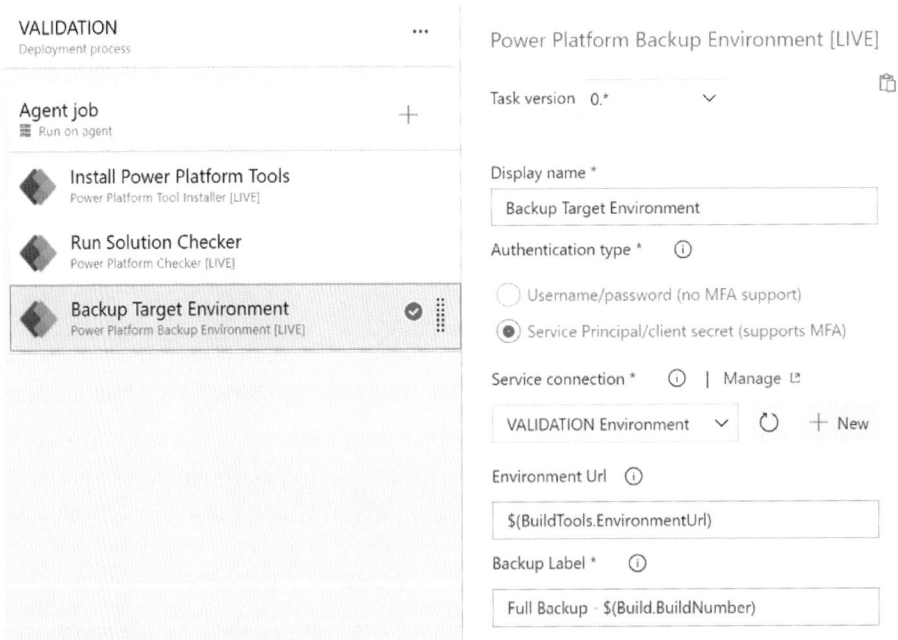

Figure 14.57 – Adding the Power Platform Backup Environment task to the VALIDATION stage

> **Note**
> When using a service principal connection, the Power Platform Backup Environment task requires additional privileges to perform the backup. The following document provides details on how to set up the service principal using PowerShell: https://docs.microsoft.com/en-us/power-platform/admin/powerplatform-api-create-service-principal.

8. **Add the Power Platform Import Solution task to the VALIDATION stage**

Search for the **Power Platform Import Solution** task and configure it to import the first Power Platform solution to a target environment. The process is the same as the solution import tasks we completed in the previous section:

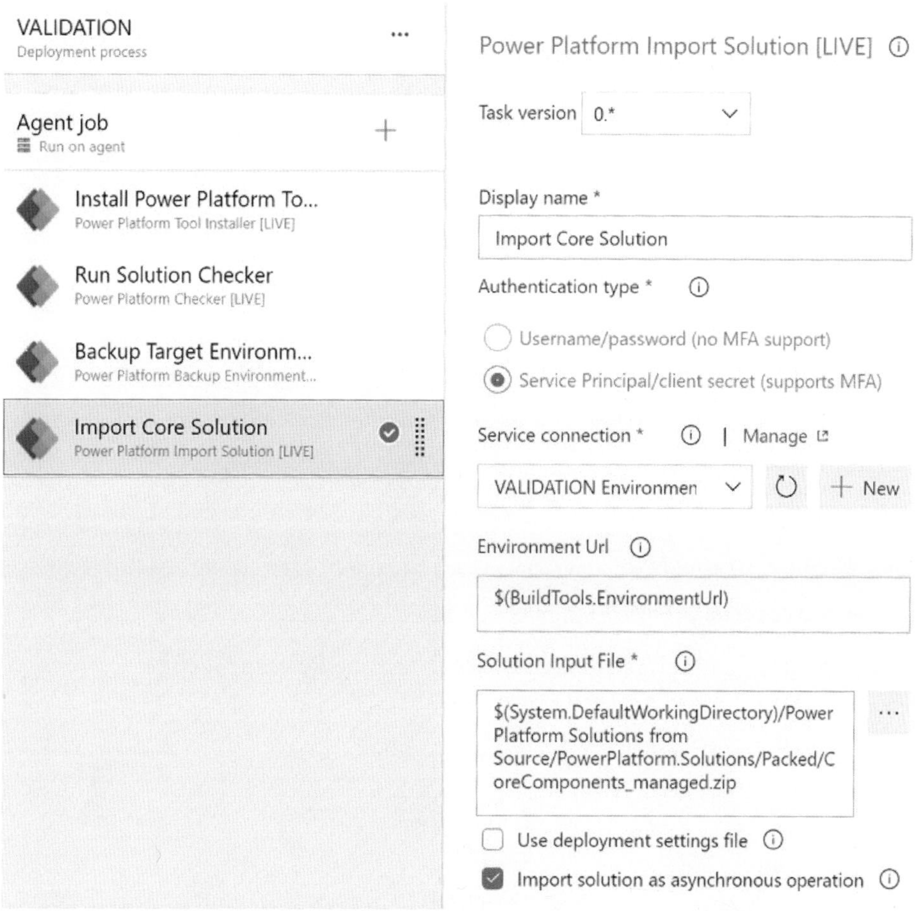

VALIDATION
Deployment process   ...

Agent job   +
Run on agent

Install Power Platform To...
Power Platform Tool Installer [LIVE]

Run Solution Checker
Power Platform Checker [LIVE]

Backup Target Environm...
Power Platform Backup Environment...

Import Core Solution
Power Platform Import Solution [LIVE]

Power Platform Import Solution [LIVE] ⓘ

Task version   0.*   ⌄

Display name *

Import Core Solution

Authentication type *   ⓘ

◯ Username/password (no MFA support)

◉ Service Principal/client secret (supports MFA)

Service connection *   ⓘ | Manage ↗

VALIDATION Environmen   ⌄   ↻   + New

Environment Url   ⓘ

$(BuildTools.EnvironmentUrl)

Solution Input File *   ⓘ

$(System.DefaultWorkingDirectory)/Power Platform Solutions from Source/PowerPlatform.Solutions/Packed/CoreComponents_managed.zip   ...

☐ Use deployment settings file   ⓘ

☑ Import solution as asynchronous operation   ⓘ

Figure 14.58 – Adding a Power Platform Import Solution task to the VALIDATION stage

Any other solutions that need to be imported into a target system must be added as additional tasks in the Release stage. We added a second Flows solution import task in the following screenshot:

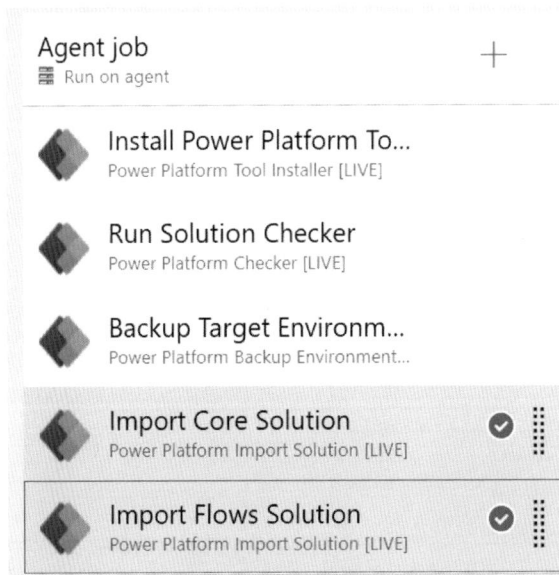

Figure 14.59 – Adding other solutions that need to be imported during the VALIDATION stage

9. **Save and test the pipeline stage**

    Save the stage and select **Create release** to test the Release pipeline:

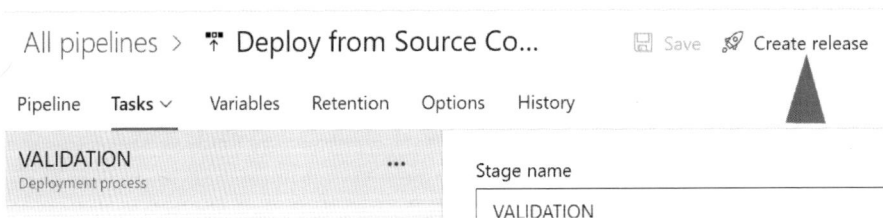

Figure 14.60 – Running the Release pipeline

Any issues that are raised during the execution of the release may be resolved in the same way as standard pipelines.

10. **Add a QA Deployment Stage**

Now that the **VALIDATION** stage has been completed and tested, we can create a QA deployment stage:

Select the **Clone** option below the **VALIDATION** stage to replicate the stage:

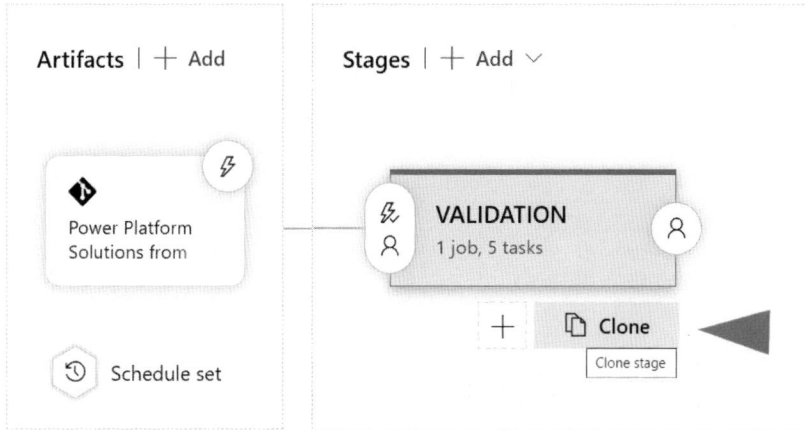

Figure 14.61 – Adding the QA deployment stage after the VALIDATION stage

11. **Configure the QA deployment stage name and target**

Name the stage appropriately (for example, QA) and update all the Power Platform-related tasks, ensuring they point to the correct target environment:

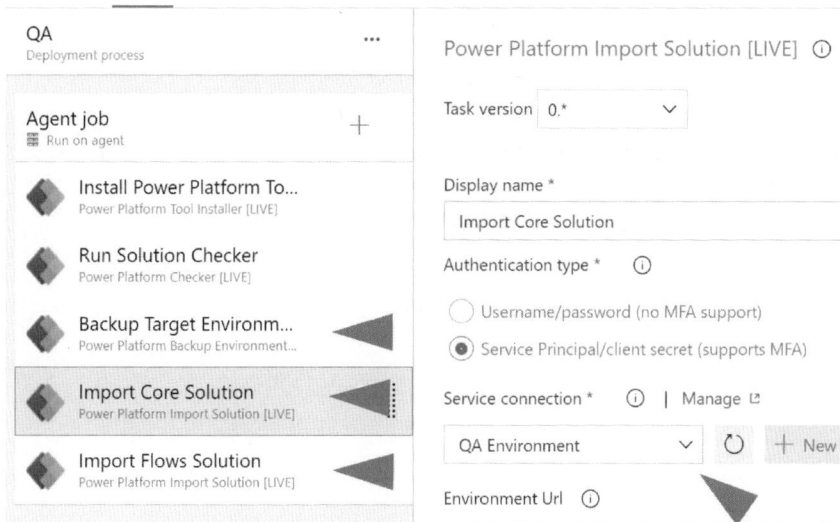

Figure 14.62 – Updating the Power Platform tasks to ensure they point to the QA environment

12. **Configure the PROD deployment stage name and target**

Clone the QA stage, naming the new stage appropriately (for example, PROD), and update all the Power Platform-related tasks, ensuring they point to the production Power Platform environment:

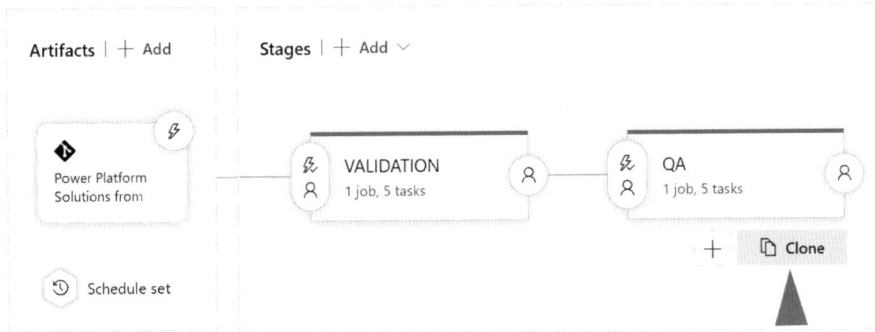

Figure 14.63 – Creating a production Release stage as a clone of the QA stage

On the newly created **PROD** stage, select the trigger option:

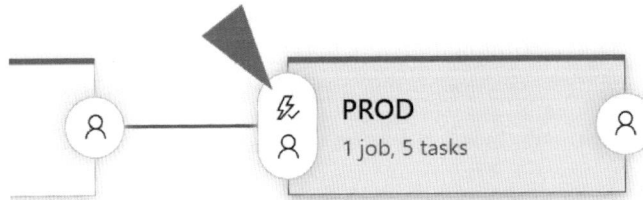

Figure 14.64 – Editing the trigger for the production Release stage

Configure the trigger for the **PROD** stage to be manual, providing additional control over the deployment:

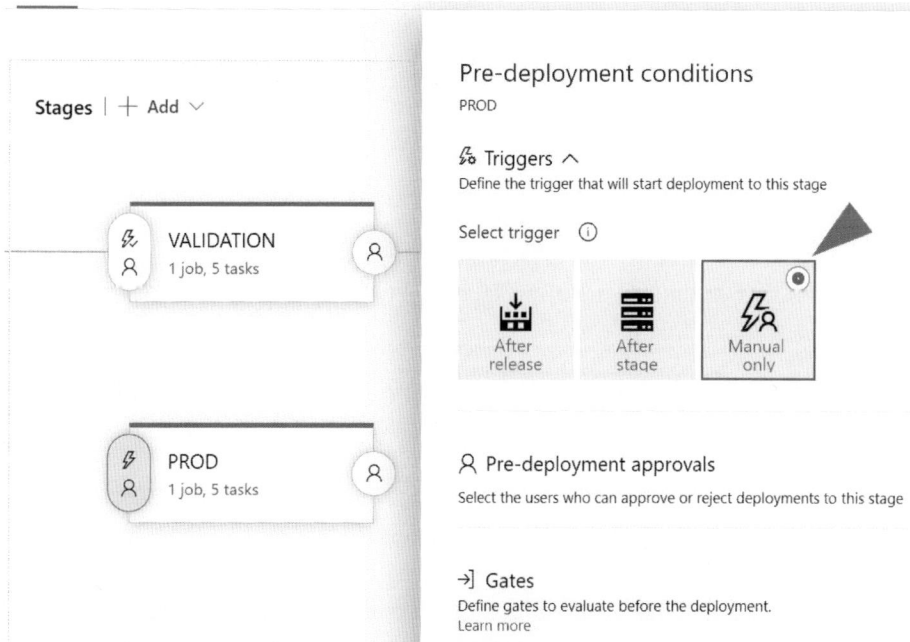

Figure 14.65 – Configuring the PROD deployment stage to trigger manually

The Power Platform-related tasks in the **PROD** stage should now also be updated, with each one pointing to the corresponding production Power Platform environment.

13. **Test the Release process**

   Now that we have a process in place, we are ready to test the release cycle end-to-end. Selecting the **Create release** option will kick off the deployments:

Figure 14.66 – Initiating a release

The Release starts with all stages pending execution:

Figure 14.67 – Release with all stages pending execution

As the release progresses, the **VALIDATION** stage will run through to completion. If successful, it will automatically trigger the QA deployment stage:

Figure 14.68 – Release progressing through to the QA deployment stage

Once the QA deployment is complete, the release will update the status of the stages accordingly. The **PROD** stage has been configured to be triggered manually. Once the QA deployment has been validated, the release into production may be initiated by selecting the release instance, as shown in the following diagram:

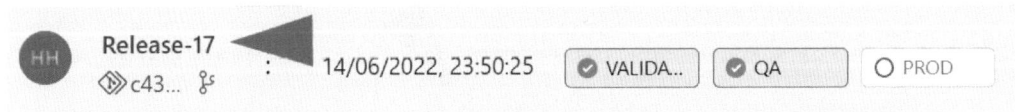

Figure 14.69 – Release with the VALIDATION and QA deployment stages completed

On the **Release instance** page, the **PROD** deployment may be initiated by selecting the **Deploy** option below the corresponding stage:

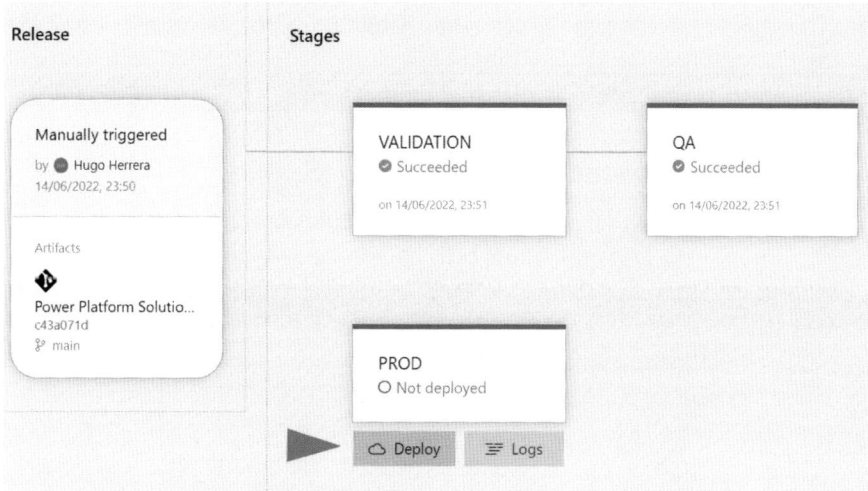

Figure 14.70 – Triggering the deployment to production

Once the deployment to production is complete, the stages will be marked accordingly:

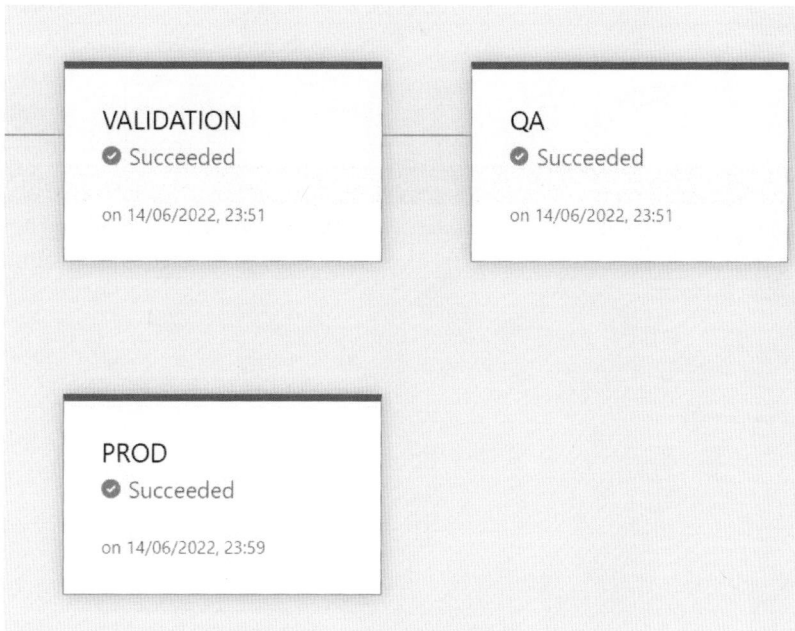

Figure 14.71 – Example of a completed Release in Azure DevOps

The Azure DevOps Release we configured in this section is an example of how a Power Platform application life cycle can be implemented. As a solution architect, you will assess the level of automation and controls required by the project.

Deploying configuration data as part of a pipeline

Azure DevOps pipelines may also be configured to deploy configuration data onto target environments. The **Power DevOps Tools** provide just such facilities, extending Azure DevOps capabilities. Reference data and Power Pages configuration may be automatically deployed to target environments using the **Import Config Migration Data** task. Please reference the following Azure DevOps Marketplace page for details: `https://marketplace.visualstudio.com/items?itemName=WaelHamze.xrm-ci-framework-build-tasks`.

Conclusion

In this section, we worked through the Azure DevOps pipeline and release management process.

Summary

In this chapter, you learned how to leverage Azure DevOps's task management, source control, and release management capabilities. You are now ready to set up the ALM source control and release processes for Power Platform implementations.

In the next chapter, you will learn how to define go-live strategies, resolve performance bottlenecks, troubleshoot data migrations, and ensure the go-live readiness of your Power Platform projects.

15
Go-Live Strategies

In this chapter, you will roll out a phased go-live strategy for our fictional digital transformation project at **Inveriance Corps**. You will learn how to anticipate potential performance issues and resolve performance bottlenecks across the full range of Power Platform components. By doing so, you will understand how to troubleshoot data migration and resolve identified deployment issues.

Solution architects tend to understand Power Platform implementations better than most project members. It is essential to leverage this knowledge to push the project through to completion, educating the testing team on the architecture so that all areas are validated, helping triage issues, and helping define a go-live strategy.

In this chapter, we are going to cover the following topics:

- Selecting a go-live strategy
- Preparing for go-live
- Rolling out the production environment

By the end of this chapter, you will be able to identify factors that impact go-live readiness and take the appropriate remedial actions for a successful Power Platform go-live.

Selecting a go-live strategy

Power Platform projects range from solutions that provide the business with brand-new functionality or systems that partially or fully replace existing services within the organization. Brand-new services tend to have fewer dependencies and a more straightforward go-live rollout, as users do not need to migrate or "move" from one system to another. When the time comes to switch on the lights, having defined a go-live strategy, activities, and readiness checklists will help you preempt potential hurdles.

Whether releasing a brand-new application or replacing an existing service, Power Platform solution rollouts use either a phased approach or a single go-live release. This section will discuss the benefits of a phased rollout versus what is often called the **big-bang approach**.

Selecting a phased go-live strategy

Power Platform solutions lend themselves to phased releases due to the modular nature of their components, databases, and automation capabilities. A phased go-live strategy usually involves an initial release containing a subset of the full functionality, including the minimum set of features that make the solution viable. The initial release is followed by subsequent releases that further enhance the solution and provide users with additional functionality.

Let's look at the benefits and drawbacks of a phased go-live strategy.

Pros and cons of a phased go-live strategy

The main pros and cons phase Power Platform releases are summarized as follows:

Pros:

- **Earlier return on investment (ROI)**: Releasing smaller portions of a solution while the rest of the application is developed and tested means the business can benefit from Power Platform sooner.

- **Reduced operational risk**: Multiple phased releases result in a lower operational risk level from each release than a single-release approach.

  For example, when rolling out a new customer onboarding solution, the first release may include personal customers, while the second phase may cater to business customers. In this example, the business customer base is unaffected by the initial release, thus reducing the risk to the business.

- **Reduced complexity per release**: Each phase concerns itself with a subset of the target capabilities. Therefore, the implementation of each release is more manageable, allowing the team to focus on functionality specific to each release.

Cons:

- **Potential refactoring cost risks**: Demanding release timescales may lead to design decisions in the earlier phases of the project that are incompatible with requirements raised in a subsequent stage. While solution architects aim to design extendable solutions and cater to upcoming needs, a phased release approach adds the element of *surprise* to a certain extent. These surprises may result in refactoring costs and additional implementation time in the project's later phases.

- **Co-ordination of parallel work streams**: Phased releases typically result in parallel work streams, where portions of the implementation team are focused on delivering a given release. At the same time, another group may be required to start work in the release that follows. It typically falls on the solution architect to devise a framework that allows multiple workstreams to work in parallel. Source control, testing, development environments, and release management of each parallel workstream will need to be coordinated, adding to the complexity of the project rollout.

  Phased rollouts have become the preferred approach for Power Platform projects, and they provide clear benefits to the business in minimizing operational risk and earlier ROI. As a solution architect, you will balance the benefits to the organization against the additional overheads inherent in coordinating parallel work streams.

You will also aim to reduce the need for refactoring in later phases of the project by understanding the overall set of requirements for upcoming project phases. You may then allocate the time to design a solution that will cater to known forthcoming business needs, architecting an extensible solution that can handle *surprise* requirements.

Minimizing risks with a phased go-live roadmap

A **phased rollout** is effectively a promise to deliver a full set of functionality, in stages, to the business. A schedule usually backs up this promise for when each feature will be made available. Solution architects work with the business to agree on the release roadmap for a Power Platform solution while considering implementation and testing estimates and business priorities.

The release roadmap allows solution architects to focus on specific feature sets for the earlier phases. It also provides an overarching view of the full capabilities to be delivered. The architectural design can then prioritize the delivery of the project's earlier stages while still being extendable to include the functionality required by the complete feature roadmap.

Phased go-live strategy conclusions

Phased go-live rollouts tend to be the preferred release strategy for Power Platform solutions thanks to their ability to minimize operational risk to the business and quicker ROI. They are well suited for larger implementations that could typically take over 6 months to deliver in their entirety.

The benefits of a phased rollout also come with the potential for additional mid-project refactoring costs and overheads while managing parallel work streams. If the benefits of a phased rollout do not outweigh the risks, a single-release implementation may be the most suitable approach.

Selecting a big-bang go-live strategy

A single release into production may be the most suitable strategy when the project's size and complexity do not warrant a phased approach. There are also instances where dependencies between deliverables mean a phased rollout is not technically feasible.

Pros and cons of a big-bang go-live strategy

The pros and cons of adopting a big-bang go-live strategy are as follows:

Pros:

- **A focused delivery stream**: All implementation team members have a clear target in mind, and all workstreams are focused on delivering a single go-live target. The solution architect can define a simplified development framework that doesn't need to coordinate parallel work streams and multiple phases.

- **Resolves inter-deliverable dependencies**: Dependencies between deliverables can sometimes make it difficult or technically unfeasible to deploy these in phases. In those instances, the big-bang approach would help resolve those inter-deliverable dependencies, as they are all deployed into production at the same time.

Cons:

- **Longer lead time to ROI**: Delivering all required functionality as part of one large release usually means the lead time to go live is greater than if the project had been released in stages. The business must wait for all the functionality to be built before getting an ROI.

Big-bang go-live strategy conclusions

Opting for a single large release into production versus a phased approach reduces the complexity of the team's implementation dynamics. All team members are focused on a single goal and one large go-live target. This approach is often used for lower complexity projects spanning less than 6 months from initiation to go-live.

The next section discusses the preparation activities required for a successful go-live.

Preparing for go-live

Planning the launch of a Power Platform application is crucial to its success. A wide range of systems, users, and business areas must be coordinated and aligned for a solution to go live without a hitch. Solution architects work with product owners, IT teams, business analysts, and key stakeholders to identify the resource needed for go-live, define responsibilities during the cutover period before launch, and define a go-live checklist.

This section discusses each area to be planned before the product launch.

Identifying the resources required to go live

Launching a Power Platform solution requires the support of several resources within the implementation team, third-party suppliers (where applicable), and groups within the organization itself. Solution architects understand the makeup of the Power Platform solution better than anyone. They can identify the individuals/teams whose actions will be required during the cutover stage, go-live day, and post-launch.

The following resources are typically required for go-live:

- **The Power Platform implementation team**: The individuals involved in the solution's development and implementation will be ideally placed to facilitate the smooth transition of the system into production.

- **The Power Platform test team**: The team responsible for validating the requirements are implemented correctly is also ideally placed to validate the production environment is ready for the big switch-on. They will typically validate that production functionality and integrations are fully functional.

- **The procurement team**: The organization's procurement team is in charge of purchasing the Power Platform licenses needed for production use.

- **The Active Directory administration team**: The team or individual that will be responsible for provisioning Microsoft 365 users for access to the Power Platform applications and services, including license assignment. The team will require instructions on which AD security groups to assign licenses.

- **The legacy system administration team**: When a Power Platform application replaces an existing legacy system, the administrators or owners of the current system will typically be involved to ensure the migration process goes smoothly.

- **The integrated systems owners**: Power Platform applications often integrate with other systems inside and outside the organization. The owners and administrators of these integrated systems will be responsible for ensuring production instances are ready and accessible and ready to be connected on go-live day.

- **The key stakeholders**: The individuals whose day-to-day activities will be transformed with the introduction of the new Power Platform applications. These users will be instrumental in facilitating the transition into production and coordinating the user base to access the newly launched system.

- **The change advisory board**: If the organization has an active change management team or a **change advisory board (CAB)**, they will be involved in reviewing the upcoming Power Platform product launch. Solution architects typically work with the CAB, preparing a rollout and rollback strategy for the solution and meeting with the change management team to get a sign-off for the system's launch.

- **The business-as-usual support team**: The team that will be responsible for supporting the new Power Platform solution once it's live. They will need to be brought up to speed on the general support actions and typical troubleshooting steps. An operational support guide document may be created, guiding the team on the regular maintenance tasks and day-to-day user support.

- **The IT network team**: Depending on the types of Power Platform integrations, the organization's IT network management team may need to change the internal and perimeter network systems.

- **The pentest team**: Typically outsourced to an external organization, the penetration testing team is responsible for identifying any vulnerabilities in Power Platform applications and integrations. The results of the penetration tests will be used to make adjustments to the configuration as needed.

- **The IT security team**: Where applicable, the organization's security team will be involved in validating the storage and management of credentials, the strategy for rotating secrets, and ensuring any the results of the penetration tests are reviewed and that any gaps in the security of the system addressed before launch.

- **The users**: These are the individuals and teams that will be using the new Power Platform applications and services. The training materials and the communication strategy, which will be discussed later in this chapter, will help ensure the users are ready to use the application on day one.

Depending on the complexity of the Power Platform solution and the size of the organization, additional individuals and teams may need to be brought into the go-live plan. Solution architects understand each of the components that make up a Power Platform solution and the individuals that can make each area of the system work. They then collaborate with them to make the launch happen.

Training users and maximizing adoption

Power Platform applications are typically designed with their target users in mind. Solution architects coordinate the creation of training materials to help users get the most out of their newly launched system. The following activities will help provide users with a clear understanding of the system, helping the solution get off to a good start.

Activities to maximize user understanding of the system and its adoption

The following list describes the typical activities and artifacts that are used by a Power Platform implementation project to facilitate understanding and adoption of the system:

- **Training documentation**:

    Typically, this is a PowerPoint or Word document listing step-by-step instructions. Depending on the size of the solution and the number of teams working on the system, creating separate targeted training documents for each team will help focus the material and make it more relatable to each team's day-to-day activities.

- **Recorded training videos**:

    This is a recorded video walking through each of the activities users will have to perform during a typical day. This will also help cement their understanding of the system. Typically, short videos targeted at specific tasks will allow individuals to use these recorded videos as a training catalog they can refer to quickly when a question arises.

- **Hands-on training sessions:**

    Live training sessions with the users before go-live will help solidify the user's understanding of the system. These training sessions are typically carried out in a pre-production environment and improve user adoption by allowing users to try out the application. Through these hands-on training sessions, users can carry out tasks in a safe environment.

These training activities are typically coordinated or performed by solution architects. They aim to help users make the most of their new Power Platform application and cement user adoption, which is critical to the project's success.

Defining the post-go-live capacity management and monitoring plan

During the project's analysis, implementation, and testing stages, Power Platform capacity management must be considered at every step. The consumption of Power Automate Cloud Flows, the Dataverse API's usage, and database storage capacity are key factors that will require continuous management and monitoring before and after go-live.

Capacity management considerations and actions before go-live

Solution architects reassess the following capacity allocations for a Power Platform solution before go-live.

Monitoring Power Automate Cloud Flow consumption

Solution architects closely monitor the consumption of Power Automate billable actions to ensure their usage does not breach the licensed capacity limits during the design phase.

Step 1 – export the Cloud Flows billable actions analytics

Each Cloud Flow analytics may be viewed via the **See analytics** menu option:

Figure 15.1 – Viewing Cloud Flow analytics

The analytics can be exported to Excel via the **Export data** menu:

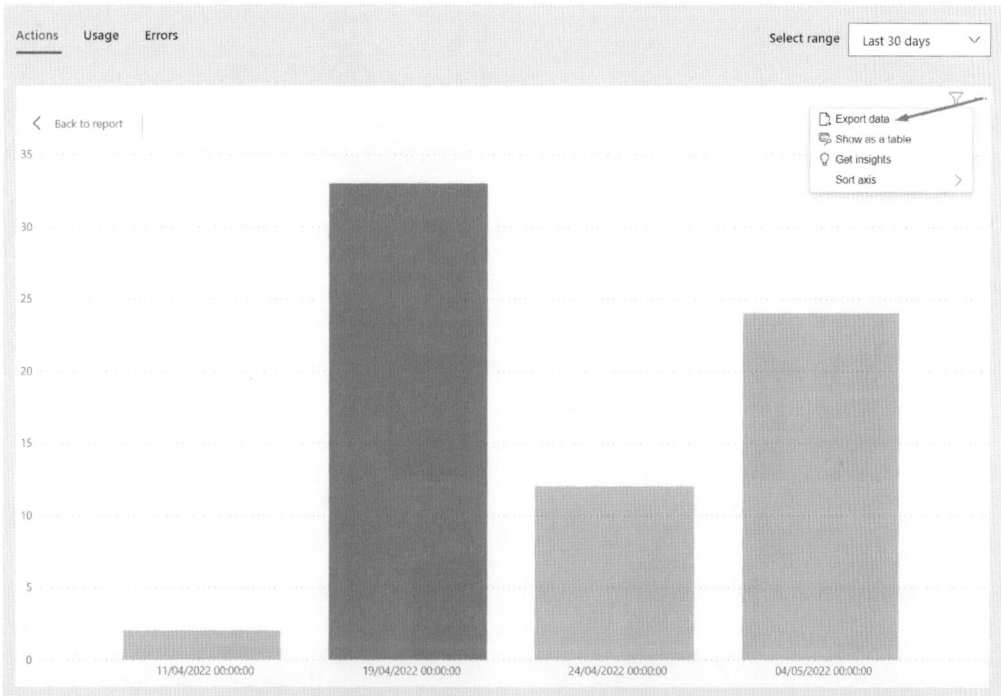

Figure 15.2 – Exporting cloud-billable action analytics

The exported spreadsheet contains the billable actions for a specific flow for the previous days:

AggregationDateMakerDailyActions	Sum of BillableActionsMakerDailyActions
11/04/2022 00:00	2
19/04/2022 00:00	33
24/04/2022 00:00	12
04/05/2022 00:00	24

Figure 15.3 – The exported Cloud Flow billable action statistics

Step 2 – combine the billable flow counts for all flows onto a pivot table

The exported flow billable action statistics can then be collated into a worksheet that can be analyzed using an **Excel Pivot Table**. The resulting pivot table can then present a summarized analysis of the total Cloud Flow billable actions consumption per day:

Flow Actions by Date	14-Sep	15-Sep	16-Sep	17-Sep	Total
Flow 1	3,122	2,965	2,846	3,175	90,272
Flow 2	6,255	3,212	12,074	12,763	175,361
Flow 3	15	30	211	214	3,427
Flow 4	2	2	20	22	62
Total	9,394	6,209	15,151	16,174	269,122

Table 15.1 – Pivot table listing the total Cloud Flow billable actions consumption per day

Step 3 – project the daily billable flow action count based on expected production loads

The information from the spreadsheet can then be used to project the total Cloud Flow billable actions consumption per day:

Base Statistics			Projected Flow Actions for the Number of Applications Per Day		
Date	Billable Flow Actions	Applications Created on Date	100	200	400
14-Sep	32,899	80	39,729	73,876	142,171
15-Sep	18,332	33	44,220	82,860	160,139
16-Sep	50,261	99	50,712	95,844	186,106
17-Sep	53,556	98	54,535	103,489	201,397

Table 15.2 – Pivot table listing the total Cloud Flow billable actions consumption per day

Step 4 – propose a licensing strategy that supports the projected Cloud-billable action load

Having identified the projected Cloud Flow billable action consumption per day, you can propose a licensing structure that will cover the capacity demands of the application once it's in production:

Projected Applications Per Day	100	200	400
Projected API call usage per day	54,535	103,489	201,397
Single enterprise user base API Call daily allowance	0	0	0
Additional capacity required	54,535	103,489	201,397
10K capacity add-ons required	6	11	21
Cost $	240	440	840

Table 15.3 – Example of the proposed Power Automate capacity add-ons required

The preceding table illustrates the proposed Power Automate capacity add-ons required to cater to a Power Platform application that processes a projected 100, 200, and 400 applications per day.

Monitoring Dataverse API usage

The Power Platform Dataverse API has strict usage and service protection limits. Solution architects monitor API usage using the **Dataverse analytics** page to identify processes that might potentially breach these limits and degrade the application's performance:

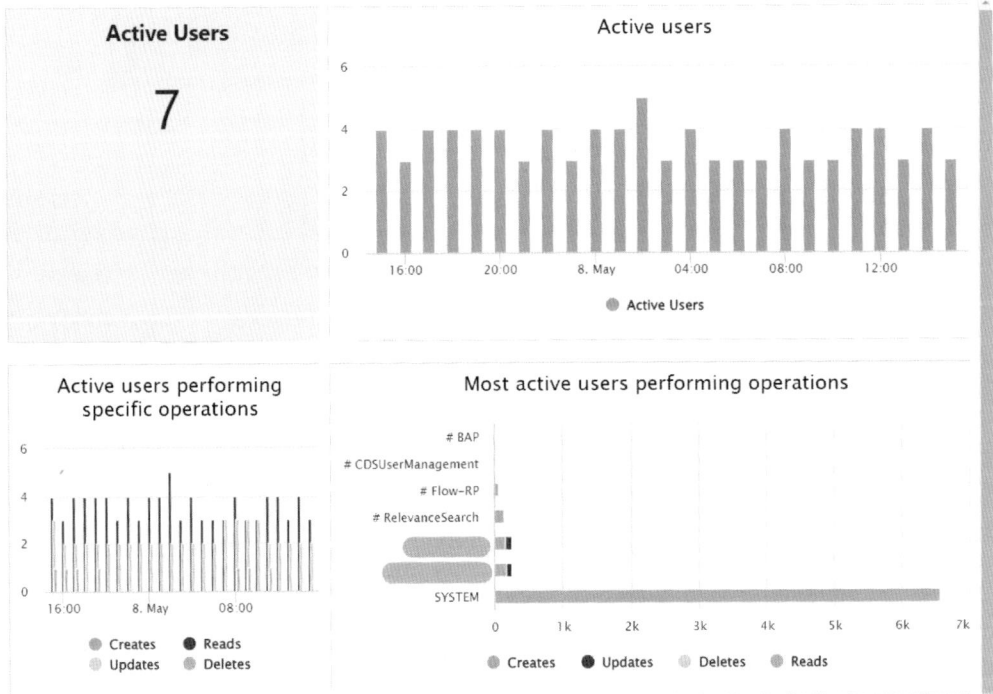

Figure 15.4 – Dataverse API analytics page

Monitoring available storage capacity

The available storage is regularly monitored to ensure sufficient capacity for the system's operation. Monitoring the storage capacity is particularly important as we approach the solution's launch day. The **Capacity** page in the Power Platform admin center provides an overview of the storage used by the various environments:

Capacity

Summary   Dataverse   Microsoft Teams   Add-ons   Trial

See where your org (tenant) is using storage, add-ons, and Microsoft Power Platform requests that could impact your capacity.
Learn more

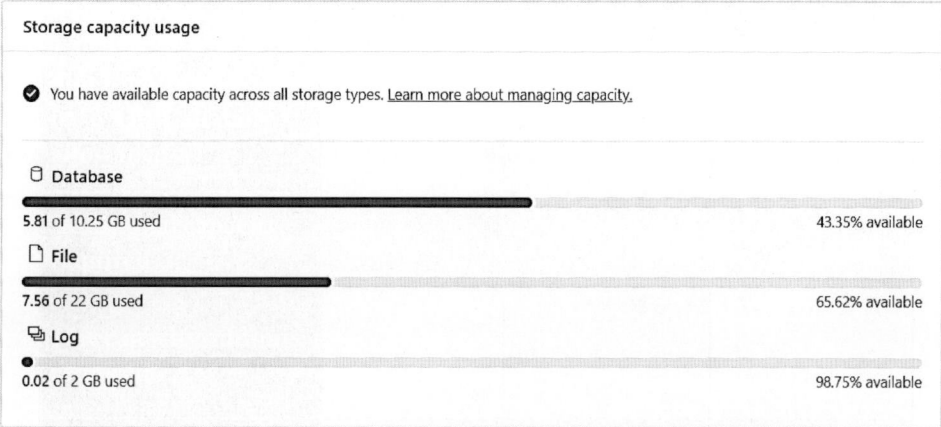

Storage capacity usage

✓ You have available capacity across all storage types. Learn more about managing capacity.

⬡ **Database**

5.81 of 10.25 GB used   43.35% available

🗋 **File**

7.56 of 22 GB used   65.62% available

🗖 **Log**

0.02 of 2 GB used   98.75% available

Storage capacity, by source   View self-service sources

Source	Database	Log	File
Org (tenant) default ⓘ	10 GB	2 GB	20 GB
User licenses ⓘ	256 MB >	N/A	2 GB >
Additional capacity	0 MB	0 MB	0 MB
Total	10.25 GB	2 GB	22 GB

Figure 15.5 – Power Platform storage capacity monitoring

Based on the current and projected usage of the system, solution architects can identify whether additional storage capacity should be purchased for the production environment to perform without reaching its capacity limits.

Defining a post-launch capacity monitoring plan

Having reviewed the system capacity requirements and resulting licensing needs during the implementation and go-live preparation stages, solution architects define a plan for continued monitoring. This continuous monitoring strategy will form part of an operation support guide discussed later in this chapter, which the business-as-usual support team will reference.

Planning the go-live cutover (who will do what and when)

Launching a Power Platform solution usually requires a carefully scripted set of actions to be carried out in sequence. Solution architects work with the teams and individuals to define a cutover strategy, a schedule for the pre-go-live activities, and perform a dry-run to iron out any issues.

Defining a cutover strategy

The cutover strategy identifies the following:

- **What will be done?**

  The high-level functionality that will be delivered (Power Pages onboarding an application for new retail customers and supporting a Model-Driven app backend)

- **Who will do it?**

  The roles, individuals, and teams that will be involved in the cutover. The following table shows an example of this:

Team	Tasks
Power Platform implementation team	Will be responsible for the deployment to production
Power Platform test team	Will be responsible for validating the production environment
Procurement team	Will be responsible for purchasing the production licenses for all users
Active Directory administration team	Will be responsible for assigning users to the corresponding security and license groups
The legacy system administration team	Will be responsible for migrating data to the new production environment
Integrated system owners	Will be responsible for validating the connection from the integrated systems
Key stakeholders	Will be responsible for the go-live communication to the broader user base
Business-as-usual support team	Will be responsible for supporting user access queries from go-live day
IT network team	Will be responsible for configuring access for on-premise integrations
The users	Will be responsible for validating access to the new production environment and reporting any issues to the business-as-usual team

Table 15.4 – Distribution of go-live responsibilities

- **When will it be done?**

  The date when the Power Platform solution will go live. The cutover strategy also defines when and how a rollback will take place. Having defined the general cutover strategy, we can create a cutover plan.

Creating a cutover plan

The cutover plan lists the various steps that need to be completed before go-live, when they will be carried out, and by whom. The following is an example cutover plan:

Power Platform go-live date: 01-03-2022

#	Step	Est. Start		SME	Owner	Status
1	Deploy Dataverse solution	1st Mar 22	1	Jane	Power Platform Team	Pending
2	Deploy Power Pages configuration	1st Mar 22	1	Jane	Power Platform Team	Pending
3	Backup production environment	1st Mar 22	1	Mark	BAU Team	Pending
4	Migrate customer data to production	2nd Mar 22	1	Susan	Legacy App Team	Pending
5	Allocate users to production security groups	2nd Mar 22	1	Mark	AD Admin Team	Pending
6	Assign Power Platform licenses to users	2nd Mar 22	1	Mark	AD Admin Team	Pending
7	Validate production environment	3rd Mar 22	2	Jenny	Test Team	Pending
8	Communicate go-live launch to users	4th Mar 22	0	Sam	Sales Team Lead	Pending

Table 15.5 – Sample cutover plan

Rehearsing the cutover to go-live

Once the cutover strategy and rollout schedule have been defined, the plan is put through its paces. This test run helps identify any issues or gaps in the rollout of the Power Platform process.

Ramping up the operational support activities

Once the Power Platform solution is live, the organization's support teams will play a role in the day-to-day maintenance and management of the system. Depending on the size and complexity of the implementation, solution architects may create an operational support guide document to facilitate this transition.

The operational support guide will typically cover the following topics:

- Introduction to the Power Platform solution
- Environment list
- An itemized list of all architectural and functional components to be supported
- Regular maintenance, including scheduled activities and rotation of secrets
- Managing product updates
- User onboarding and removal
- Typical support activities and a troubleshooting guide

The organization's support team then uses the operational support guide to service the user base and perform ongoing maintenance tasks.

Preparing a communication plan

The Power Platform user base and its impacted business units are typically notified of the upcoming launch of Power Platform applications. The timing and format of this communication are agreed upon with the business and key stakeholders to prepare the user base.

Common go-live issues and how to preempt them

During the rollout of a Power Platform solution, a set of common issues may arise. Let's look at the most common problems and how to identify them:

- **Insufficient testing**: A lack of testing may lead to areas of the Power Platform applications and integrations underperforming. A thorough test strategy and executing these test cases will help reduce the risk of the application failing to perform to specifications.

- **Incorrect assumptions**: These may be simple assumptions (for example, expecting the production user licenses to be in place on go-live) to more complex considerations regarding the connectivity to external systems and network access to on-premise services. A solid review of the cutover plan, including the distribution of responsibilities, will help reduce the number of assumptions that adversely impact the go-live plan.

- **Missing rollback strategy**: Without a defined rollback strategy, the business may find itself in a limbo state if the application go-live can't be completed. Solution architects work with the business and system experts to define a solid rollback strategy, allowing the business to restore operations in the event of a fault during the rollout process.

Preempting rollout complications and de-risking the application go-live

Let's understand the issues, as follows:

- **Identify issues that will be present at go-live**: Depending on the project timescales and delivery constraints, a Power Platform project may need to go into production before all the issues that have been identified during testing can be resolved. Identifying these issues and alerting users of their existence and when they are scheduled to be fixed will help reduce their impact on the production rollout.

- **Perform a pre-deployment**: Preparing the production environments and integrations ahead of time will help de-risk the rollout of the solution. Any component that's prepared ahead of schedule will help identify issues in advance and provide more time for resolution. For example, a pre-deployment of the Power Platform solution may identify a problem with the available storage capacity, allowing more time to either clear resources or purchase additional storage.

- **Perform data migration early**: Data migration is often left to the later stages of the project. Performing early data migration test runs and running a mock production data migration before go-live will help iron out any issues with the process.

- **Validate access for production users**: Ensuring users have access to the production environment before go-live will remove one potential issue and de-risk the rollout of the application.

- **Run the old and new systems in parallel**: For Power Platform applications that replace legacy systems, the ability to run the old system in parallel will de-risk the rollout of the new application. Users can still perform their day-to-day tasks while the new application is brought online and users start moving to the new system.

- **Automate the production rollout**: Removing the scope for human error will further decrease the go-live risks. Whether through an Azure DevOps deployment pipeline or other means of automation, solution architects aim to automate the deployment of the following items:

  - User, teams, and business units

  - Reference data

  - User configuration

  - Data migration

Validating the solution before rolling it out to production

There are several tools available within the Power Platform framework that help solution architects validate the production-readiness of an implementation. Let's take a look:

- **Power Apps Solution checker**: This tool is built into Power Platform solutions. It helps validate Model-Driven apps by checking the components within a Dataverse solution. The checkers validate processes, table configurations, plugins, and JavaScript web resources for deprecated functionality and development best practices. The following screenshot illustrates how the Power Apps **Solution checker** can be triggered:

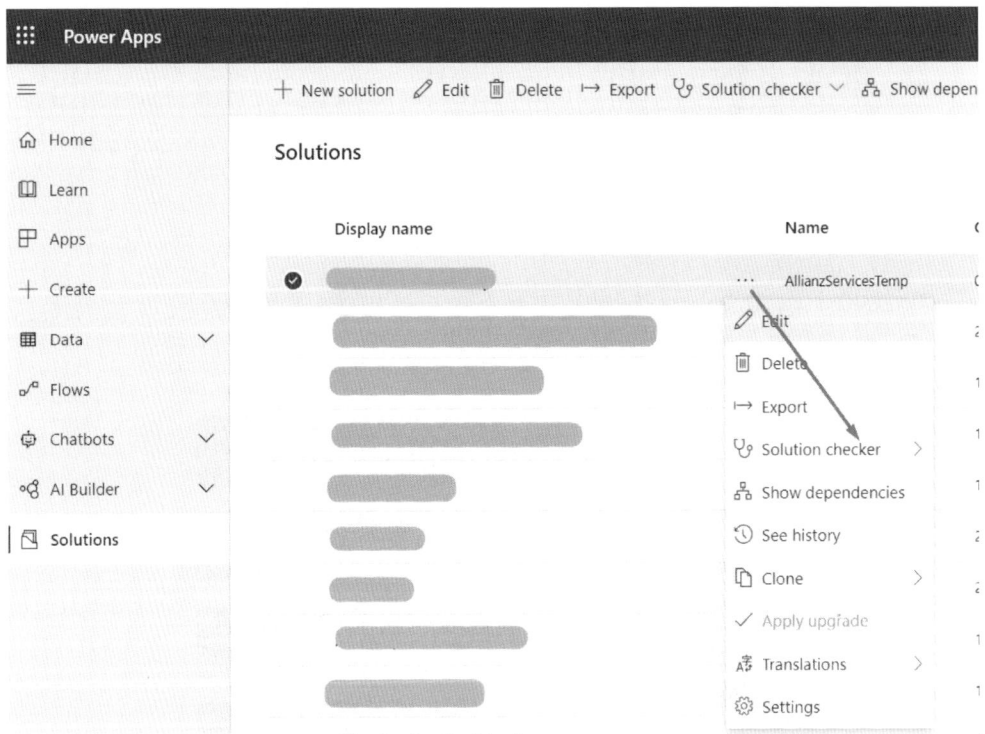

Figure 15.6 – Using the Power Apps Solution checker

Solution architects aim to resolve all issues raised by the Power Platform Solution checker before deploying to production.

- **Dataverse analytics**: We discussed this tool in the capacity monitoring sections of this chapter. Dataverse analytics provides invaluable insights into the Dataverse APIs, allowing solution architects to spot areas that require attention before go-live (for example, spikes in API calls that may result in throttling of the application).

> **Reference Documentation**
>
> The following links provide additional documentation on the features within Power Apps Checker and Dataverse Analytics, respectively:
>
> `https://docs.microsoft.com/powerapps/maker/data-platform/use-powerapps-checker`
>
> `https://docs.microsoft.com/power-platform/admin/analytics-common-data-service`

Taking into account the Power Platform product release schedule

Power Platform receives regular maintenance updates and feature upgrades. As these updates are applied automatically, solution architects need to understand the impact they may have on a production environment.

Solution architects review the release schedule to ensure upcoming updates do not impact the rollout of an application into production.

> **Power Platform Release Schedule**
>
> The following document lists the Power Platform release schedule: `https://docs.microsoft.com/en-us/dynamics365/get-started/release-schedule`.

In addition to the release schedule, solution architects regularly review the upcoming Power Platform features and enhancements to plan for new functionality and deprecations.

> **Power Platform Release Plans**
>
> The following document lists the Power Platform release plans: `https://docs.microsoft.com/en-gb/dynamics365/release-plans/`.

To preempt go-live rollout issues, solution architects first apply upcoming updates to a development or test environment using the early access facility within the Power Platform application.

> **Power Platform Early Access Updates**
>
> The following document describes the options available for early access to Power Platform updates: `https://docs.microsoft.com/en-us/power-platform/admin/opt-in-early-access-updates`.

Running through the go-live checklist

The following checklist lists the various implementation milestones that must be completed before go-live can proceed:

Area	Items to Check	Check Outcome
Agreed scope	The scope for the release into production has been agreed upon with all involved parties. Key stakeholders and product owners are aware of the functionality available for users on go-live. The release schedule and scope for each phase are also agreed upon for phased rollouts.	✓
Acceptance	The requirements have been accepted as delivered (taking into account any known issues).	✓
UAT completion	Users have validated the solution, and it is ready for production deployment.	✓
Performance	Performance tests have been carried out, and any improvements have been completed.	✓
Pentest	Pentesting has been completed, where applicable, and any issues raised have been addressed.	✓
External dependencies	All dependencies with external systems have been identified and confirmed ready for production use.	✓
Licensing	Production licenses have been procured and are ready for assignment to the user base.	✓
Training	The users have received training materials or training sessions and are familiar with the upcoming functionality.	✓
Support readiness	The support team has been briefed on their responsibilities. They have an operational support guide in place and are ready to service user queries and issues on go-live day.	✓

Table 15.6 – Go-live checklist in action

Solution architects run through a readiness checklist, which can be used to inform a go/no-go decision.

The go/no-go decision

Product owners, key stakeholders, and the implementation team will typically meet before the cutover date to decide whether the solution is ready to be put into production. This decision will be informed by the go-live checklist. Depending on the outcome of the meeting, further work may be required to ensure the readiness of the solution for go-live.

Rolling out the production environment

Once the go-live checklist is completed, and the go-ahead is given to proceed to production, the solution is ready to be deployed. This section will discuss the various activities that are carried out by solution architects to ensure the successful completion of the Power Platform rollout.

The cutover

The cutover plan that was prepared in the earlier sections of this document is used during the actual rollout into production. With their deep understanding of the implementation, solution architects are well suited to help coordinate the rollout steps. The following table illustrates how a cutover plan might be checked through to completion:

Power Platform Go-live date: Date: 1st April 2022

#	Step	Start		SME	Owner	Status
1	Deploy Dataverse solution	1st April 22	1	Jane	Power Platform Team	COMPLETE
2	Deploy Power Pages configuration	1st April 22	1	Jane	Power Platform Team	COMPLETE
3	Backup production environment	1st April 22	1	Mark	BAU Team	COMPLETE
4	Migrate customer data to production	2nd April 22	1	Susan	Legacy App Team	COMPLETE
5	Allocate users to production security groups	2nd April 22	1	Mark	AD Admin Team	COMPLETE
6	Assign Power Platform licenses to users	2nd April 22	1	Mark	AD Admin Team	COMPLETE
7	Validate production environment	3rd April 22	2	Jenny	Test Team	COMPLETE

Table 15.7 – Production rollout

Deciding when to roll back

Rolling back a deployment into production is typically a last resort. Let's look at the reasons for initiating a rollback.

Unavailability of an external dependency critical to the implementation

Power Platform solutions may depend on external systems, and some of these dependencies may be critical to the normal functioning of the application. For example, a Power Pages application may depend on an external API to perform address searches or company lookups. Source systems may unexpectedly become unavailable, requiring the go-live to be postponed.

Unexpected deployment or migration errors

This could be the failure of a deployment or migration task that can't be recovered within the agreed-upon timescales for the go-live rollout.

Under these circumstances, solution architects will work with the product owners to carry out the rollback and restore business operations.

Troubleshooting data migration issues

Solution architects work with the implementation team to identify and resolve data migration issues. Some typical data migration issues are as follows:

- **Breaching the service protection limits**:

  High throughput may result in the Dataverse APIs being overrun, resulting in pushbacks from the platform's service protection limits. A potential solution is to include the distribution of API requests across multiple license accounts.

  An alternative solution is to change the data migration mechanisms by using data flows instead of direct access to the Dataverse API to import data.

  Another solution may be to throttle the rate of imported data so that it works within the advertised limits or respect the pushback messages returned by the API when a limit is breached.

  The following document details the service protection limits that may impact the capacity to import large amounts of data into Dataverse: `https://docs.microsoft.com/power-apps/developer/data-platform/api-limits`.

- **Over-consumption of Power Platform request limits:**

    When Cloud Flows are used to import data, they consume billable actions. Breaching the licensed allocation of billable actions may result in the throttling of Cloud Flows. Depending on the configured retry strategy for these flows, they may fail to perform or trigger.

    The following document details the API request limits and allocations that may impact the capacity to process large amounts of data:

    `https://docs.microsoft.com/en-us/power-platform/admin/` `api-request-limits-allocations`.

Handing over operational support

Once the Power Platform solution has been successfully deployed into production and the system has been validated as ready to go live, operational support is typically handed over to its IT support teams. The operational support guide discussed earlier in this chapter is used from that point onwards to service user queries, resolve user issues, and perform scheduled maintenance tasks.

The Power Platform solution is now ready for business-as-usual.

Summary

This chapter taught you about the benefits of a phased go-live versus the big-bang approach to production rollouts. You learned how to prepare a Power Platform implementation for go-live by defining a cutover process and a production readiness checklist. Finally, you learned how to proceed with the rollout into production, identify and resolve data migration issues, and hand it over to operational support.

You are now a fully versed Power Platform solution architect able to take a project from its conception through to completion.

The next chapter will help you prepare for the Power Platform Solution Architect Expert certification.

Part 5:
Power Platform
Solution Architect
Certification Prep

Prepare for the PL-600 exam and validate your knowledge of Power Platform solution architecture through a set of practice exam questions.

This section contains the following chapter:

- *Chapter 16, Microsoft Certified: Power Platform Solution Architect Expert Practice Exams*

16
Microsoft Certified: Power Platform Solution Architect Expert Certification Prep

Having gone through the implementation of our digital transformation scenario right from initial analysis to architectural design, implementation, and successfully going live, you are now armed with a wealth of knowledge that will help you become a Microsoft Certified Power Platform Solution Architect.

This chapter provides insights that will help you prepare for the PL-600 exam that leads to the Microsoft Certified: Power Platform Solution Architect certification, including references to additional learning materials and further reading.

You will also get to test your knowledge with mock PL-600 Microsoft Certified Power Platform Solution Architect certification exam questions.

In this chapter, we are going to cover the following main topics:

- The benefits of being a Microsoft Certified: Power Platform Solution Architect Expert

- Preparing for the PL-600 – the Microsoft Certified: Power Platform Solution Architect Expert Microsoft exam

- Tips for the day

- PL-600 example questions

- Recommended further reading and additional learning materials

- Final thoughts

The benefits of being a Microsoft Certified: Power Platform Solution Architect Expert

Undertaking the Power Platform Solution Architect Expert certification can help bring about several personal benefits and help your organization achieve Microsoft competencies. Some of the main reasons for taking the PL-600 certification exam are as follows:

- The motivation to learn the full range of Power Platform capabilities.

- The Microsoft Certified Professional badge improves the standing of your CV.

- It can help your organization achieve its Microsoft competencies (please visit `https://docs.microsoft.com/partner-center/learn-about-competencies` for more details).

- You can validate your Power Platform solution architecture knowledge and identify areas that require improvement.

The next section lists several activities that will help you prepare for the PL-600 exam.

Preparing for the PL-600 – the Microsoft Certified: Power Platform Solution Architect Expert Microsoft exam

A Power Platform solution architect aims to listen to an organization, interpret its needs, create a solid blueprint for its current and future aspirations, and guide the implementation through to going live and beyond. The PL-600 exam helps you validate your understanding of the technology, techniques, and best practices that help you achieve this goal.

The PL-600 exam is, for the most part, a test of common sense. Given a series of hypothetical scenarios, you will be asked to provide solutions to problems using your knowledge of Power Platform capabilities.

The following tasks will give you the best chance of success in the examination:

- **Review the exam skills** – review the skills measured in the examination. The following link leads to the PL-600 examination page, listing the topics covered: Error! Hyperlink reference not valid.https://docs.microsoft.com/learn/certifications/exams/pl-600.

- **Revise the relevant chapters** – revise the chapters in this book related to the skills measured in the exam.

- **Practice** – practice these skills, either in real-life projects or in hypothetical scenarios, to hone your knowledge of Power Platform's capabilities.

- **Additional reading** – review the recommended further reading and additional learning materials reference in the next section of this chapter.

- **Take the mock exams** – take the practice exams at the end of this book to confirm your readiness.

- **Further revision** – revise any areas that require further attention based on the result of the practice exams.

Tips for the day

The PL-600 is a timed exam that tests your knowledge of Power Platform solution architecture. These are a few tips that can help you get the best result on the day.

- **Read the actual question** – the question may ask, "*What should you recommend?*" This could mean that there may be other answers that are technically feasible but are not recommended and, therefore, shouldn't be selected.

- **Peek ahead at case study questions** – peek ahead at the questions when reading through the background and requirements for a case study. The questions will give you some context and save time when reading through the case study.

- **Save tough questions for the end** – if the answer is not apparent, answer to the best of your knowledge and save it for review later. If time allows, at the end of the exam stage, you can go back and review those answers in more detail.

The following section includes example questions to help you prepare for the PL-600 exam.

PL-600 example questions

The PL-600 is a timed exam where you will be asked to answer multiple-choice questions. This section includes a set of example questions that will help you prepare for the examination, followed by answers and their reasoning.

Question 1 – Dataverse column types

An organization is looking to provide staff members with a means of registering customer requests received over the phone. The requests need to be stored in a database. The staff members must be able to do the following:

- Select one or more preferred contact methods for the customer

- Select the product related to the request

Which two column types could you use to implement the requirement?

    A. A calculated column

    B. A choices column

C. A lookup column

D. A rollup column

Answers

The correct answer is **B** and **C**:

A. **Incorrect** – a calculated column cannot be used for data entry. It is used to calculate a value based on the content of other fields or formulae.

B. **Correct** – the choices column would be a good candidate, allowing the staff member to select one or more preferred contact methods for the customer.

C. **Correct** – a lookup column in a product table would allow the staff member to select from a catalog of products.

D. **Incorrect** – a rollup column cannot be used for data entry as they are read-only fields. They may, however, be used to aggregate data from related tables.

Question 2 – Dataverse security

Your task is to define a security model that allows for easy onboarding of new Power Apps users, granting them the following:

- A Power Apps license

- Access to the Power Platform environment

- Full read/write access to the contact and account tables

The requirement is to onboard new users onto the system with as few steps as possible. Which two Power Platform features would best fulfill the requirement?

A. Dataverse **AAD Security Group** teams

B. Dataverse **Access** teams

C. A security role configured for *direct user (Basic) access-level* and team privileges

D. A manager hierarchy security model

Answers

The correct answer is **A** and **C**:

A. **Correct** – a team configured as an AAD Security Group can be used to associate a Microsoft 365 user to a Dataverse team automatically. The AAD Security Group may also be used to assign a Power Apps license to group members automatically.

B. **Incorrect** – a team of type **Access**, while helpful in granting users access to specific records, does not provide features that expedite the onboarding of new users onto a Power App.

C. **Correct** – security roles configured for direct user (Basic) access-level and team privileges remove the need to assign a security role directly to the user to enable them to access the system, thus removing one step from the onboarding process.

D. **Incorrect** – a manager security model does not provide features that expedite the onboarding of new users onto a Power App.

Question 3 – Select a Power Platform component

Your task is to design an application form where users can change the priority of a record from 1 to 10. The users will be able to change the rating using a slider. The organization would like to be able to reuse the slider field functionality in other forms and tables.

What Power Platform component or feature would be best suited to fulfill the requirement?

A. A slider column

B. **Power Control Framework (PCF)**

C. An HTML web resource

D. A canvas app

Answers

The correct answer is **B**:

A. **Incorrect** – at the time of writing, Dataverse does not include slider columns as standard.

B. **Correct** – a PCF component can be used to drive a whole number column that can be reused in other forms and tables.

C. **Incorrect** – an HTML web resource alone would not provide a means of updating the underlying Dataverse column. PCF components are an evolution of web resources and are the preferred solution.

D. **Incorrect** – while an inline canvas app can be used to implement a slider on a form, its reusability across tables would be limited.

Question 4 – Identify functional and non-functional requirements

An organization is looking to implement a public-facing customer self-service portal with a Power Apps backend to manage customer requests. The **requirements capture** sessions resulted in the following four requirements. Mark each requirement as either functional or non-functional. Each correct answer contributes toward the total score:

#	Requirement	Functional or non-functional?
A	The self-service portal needs to handle 100 concurrent users.	
B	Customer requests must be automatically assigned to the team responsible for the request type.	
C	The portal and backend application must have at least 99% uptime.	
D	A confirmation email notification will be sent to the customer when a request is resolved.	

Answers:

A. **Non-functional** – concurrent user capacity does not require specific functionality to be built

B. **Functional** – the automatic assignment of requests is functionality, requiring implementation

C. **Non-functional** – system uptime requirements do not specify functionality to be implemented

D. **Functional** – automated email notifications require functionality to be implemented

Question 6 – Select the most appropriate feature

Users require a simple way of searching for accounts, both from form lookups and via account views in a model-driven app. The requirements are as follows:

- Users can search for accounts via a unique identifier.
- For longer account names, users would like to search by a shorter name without using the * sign in their search.

Which three Power Platform capabilities would fulfill the requirements?

    A. Canvas apps

    B. A quick-find view

    C. Alternative-find forms

    D. An additional **short name** text column

    E. An autonumber column

Answers

The correct answer is **B**, **D**, and **E**:

    A. **Incorrect** – canvas apps do not change the way model-driven app search functionality works.

    B. **Correct** – columns configured in quick-find views are used by search functionality. Adding an auto-number column and a "short name" text column to this view would let users search by those two fields.

    C. **Incorrect** – alternative-find forms are not a Power Platform feature.

    D. **Correct** – an additional **short name** column can be populated with a portion of the original account name. When users enter the short name without a * wildcard, the account will be listed in the results.

    E. **Correct** – an autonumber column will generate a unique identifier for the account that can be used when searching.

Question 7 – Power Apps portal (Power Pages) security features

Team leaders using a Power Apps portal must be able to view and edit their own cases and the cases created by members of their team. The data structure is illustrated in the following object model diagram:

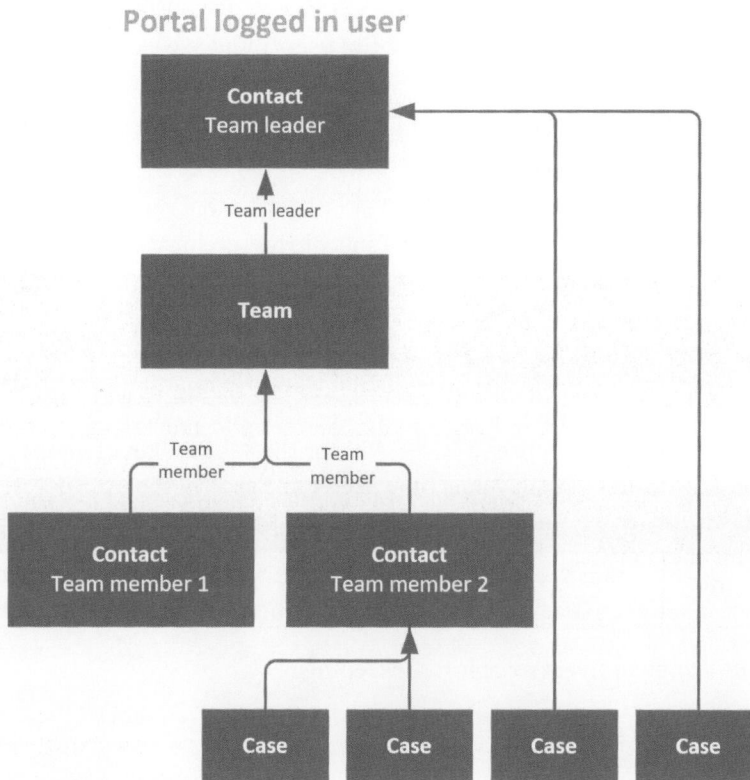

Figure 16.1 – The Power Apps portal contact, team, and case data structure

Which two Power Platform security features would provide the required functionality?

    A. A security role

    B. A web role

    C. Table permissions

    D. AAD

Answers

The correct answer is **B** and **C**:

A. **Incorrect** – security roles control access to tables within model-driven apps, canvas apps, and the Dataverse API. Portals have security capabilities that sit on top of security roles, managing permissions for users logged in using the contact table.

B. **Correct** – web roles allow certain portal users to have elevated data access privileges.

C. **Correct** – table permissions provide granular control over the data accessible to portal users and can traverse hierarchies of data.

D. **Incorrect** – while AAD may be used as an authentication method for Power Apps portals, it does not address the specific hierarchical data access needs presented by the requirements.

Question 8 – Retry strategies

An organization requires the integration of a Power Platform solution with an external service. The external service exposes a REST API for the submission of invoices. When invoice records are created in Dataverse, they need to be sent to the external API in near real time, and the invoice data must reach the external service in 2 hours at the most. The integration is business-critical:

Select three actions in sequence the integration might perform to fulfill the requirement.

A. Create a copy of the invoice for safekeeping.

B. On failure, retry the integration at a predetermined frequency.

C. Switch the Power Automate flow off and back on.

D. If failures exceed an agreed threshold, store the invoice data in a fallback storage area, alert the administrators, and add a failure notification to the administrator's dashboard.

E. Trigger the integration to the REST API when an invoice is created.

Answers

The correct action sequence is **E**, **B**, and **D**:

E – Trigger the integration to the REST API when an invoice is created

B – On failure, retry the integration at a predetermined frequency

D – If failures exceed an agreed threshold, store the invoice data in a fallback storage area, alert the administrators, and add a failure notification to the administrator's dashboard

The first step satisfies the near-real-time integration requirement. The second step adds resilience to the integration. The third step provides fallback and manual intervention to resolve critical integration issues.

Question 9 – Select a suitable Power Platform feature

Customer service staff are tasked with progressing applications from registration to review and completion. Each step of the application process requires the staff members to complete information specific to the stage. The organization wants to ensure staff members complete the application tasks in a predetermined sequence, guided by the application through to completion.

What Power Platform feature can fulfill the requirement?

    A. A Power Automate cloud flow

    B. A workflow

    C. A business process flow

    D. A duplicate detection rule

Answers

The correct answer is **C**:

    A. **Incorrect** – cloud flows do not provide a guided UI for users

    B. **Incorrect** – workflows do not provide a guided UI for users

    C. **Correct** – business process flows guide users step by step through a process, requiring a user action at each stage

    D. **Incorrect** – duplicate detection rules do not provide a guided UI for users

Question 10 – Select a suitable Power Platform feature

The management team within an organization requires real-time reporting on data across two Dataverse environments. The reports require graphical representations of customer application data processed through both environments in a printable paginated output.

What Power Platform feature can fulfill the requirement?

A. Dashboards

B. Dataverse charts

C. Power BI

D. DirectQuery

Answers

The correct answer is **C** and **D**:

A. **Incorrect** – model-driven app dashboards display data on the same Dataverse database. While virtual entities may be able to bring both Dataverse instances together, the requirement for paginated output means dashboards will not fulfill the organization's needs.

B. **Incorrect** – Dataverse charts, used in model-driven app views and dashboards, are bound by the same limitations as answer A.

C. **Correct** – Power BI can retrieve data from multiple environments and fulfills the requirement for paginated output.

D. **Correct** – Power BI DirectQuery satisfies the need for real-time reporting.

Question 11 – Select a suitable application

An organization is looking to implement a solution that can receive customer requests and complaints via email, phone, and online. These requests will then be routed to teams of staff members, who would then use knowledge base articles to help identify solutions. Customers can interact with their requests or complaints and receive status updates online.

What two components or applications should you recommend?

A. Canvas apps

B. A customer self-service portal

C. Power BI

D. Dynamics 365 Customer Service

Answers

The correct answer is **B** and **D**:

A. **Incorrect** – canvas apps, while flexible, would require substantial investment to implement the requirements and will not be suitable for a public-facing customer portal

B. **Correct** – customer self-service portals fulfill the requirement for submission and interaction with complaints and requests

C. **Incorrect** – Power BI is a reporting tool and would not satisfy the case management and customer interaction requirements

D. **Correct** – Dynamics 365 Customer Service satisfies the case management processes in the requirement

Question 12 – Identify functional and non-functional requirements

An organization is looking to implement an insurance broker application, connecting institutional customers to brokers. The **requirements capture** sessions resulted in the following four requirements. Mark each requirement as either functional or non-functional. Each correct answer contributes toward the total score.

#	Requirement	Functional or non-functional?
A	The application needs to handle up to 1 million insurance applications per year.	
B	Insurance applications that do not get a response from a broker within 1 hour will be marked as "late."	
C	Applicants will be able to select from a catalog of insurance products.	
D	Management reports will be emailed to board members every Monday at 9:00.	

Answers:

A. **Non-functional**

B. **Functional**

C. **Functional**

D. **Functional**

Question 13 – Data migration

A customer is looking to migrate 7 million contact records from a legacy SQL database to a hosted on-premises database on go-live day. The migration will be a one-off exercise, and the data needs to be imported within a 3-hour window.

Which two Power Platform features could you use to migrate the data?

- A. Dual-write
- B. DataFlex
- C. Dataflows
- D. Data Import Wizard
- E. Custom import

Answers

The correct answer is **C** and **E**:

- A. **Incorrect** – the dual-write functionality is designed to sync data between Dataverse and Dynamics 365 Finance and Operations (for reference, see `https://docs.microsoft.com/dynamics365/fin-ops-core/dev-itpro/data-entities/dual-write/dual-write-overview`).

- B. **Incorrect** – Data Flex is not a Power Platform feature.

- C. **Correct** – dataflows and an on-premises data gateway will enable data migration directly from the source database (for reference, see `https://docs.microsoft.com/power-query/dataflows/using-dataflows-with-on-premises-data`).

- D. **Incorrect** – given that the migration of data requires 7 million records to be imported within a 3-hour window, the standard Power Platform Data Import Wizard functionality will likely struggle to import the data within the required period of time.

- E. **Correct** – a custom-built data import that leverages the Dataverse web API can be programmed to leverage parallel import threads and concurrent application users to import the data within the required period of time.

Question 14 – API and service protection limits

An organization requires a large number of business automation processes. The processes need to be built using a low-code/no-code approach so that the system administrators can maintain them. Power Automate is selected as an ideal fit for the requirement.

During the design process, you consider that the large number of transactions performed by Power Automate will require additional capacity to operate within the API limits and consider service protection limits.

Which three Power Platform features can you use?

    A. Distribute business processes across more cloud flows.

    B. Purchase Power Automate capacity add-ons.

    C. Implement a retry strategy when connecting to Dataverse.

    D. Enable low consumption mode.

    E. Configure cloud flow triggers to run under the context of the calling user or record owner.

    F. Set the scope of the cloud flow trigger to the organization.

Answers

The correct answer is **B, C,** and **E**:

    A. **Incorrect** – creating additional cloud flows does not directly reduce the consumption of API requests or provide recovery from service protection limit breaches.

    B. **Correct** – Power Platform capacity add-ons allow cloud flows to perform additional API calls within a 24-hour period (for reference, see `https://docs.microsoft.com/power-platform/admin/capacity-add-on`).

    C. **Correct** – tuning the retry strategy for cloud flow Dataverse actions will result in more resilient automation when there is a potential for the service protection limits to be reached (e.g., a maximum number of API calls per 5-minute sliding window).

    D. **Incorrect** – low consumption mode is not a feature available in Power Automat.e

    E. **Correct** – configuring the cloud flow trigger to run under the context of the calling user (or the record owner) can help distribute the API call consumption across the allocations available across the user base.

    F. **Incorrect** – setting the scope of the cloud flow trigger to the organization does not directly impact the API Call consumption.

Question 15 – External client authentication

An insurance broker is looking to extend their Power Platform implementation, creating an API for external company systems to communicate with and request insurance quotations. The Dataverse Custom API functionality is selected as a fit for the requirement.

Your task is to define the authentication strategy for the external company systems to use when communicating with the API. Which two features and methods should you use?

    A. Create standard Power Platform users and provide credentials to the external company systems.

    B. Create an Azure AD app registration and Power Platform application user, and provide the client with the ID and secret to the external company systems.

    C. Configure anonymous access to the Dataverse API.

    D. Create an HTTP-triggered cloud flow that the external systems can call.

    E. Schedule the expiry and rotation of credentials.

Answers:

The correct answer is **A** and **E**:

    A. **Incorrect** – while technically feasible for applications to use standard Power Platform users to authenticate, they consume a user license and are not recommended for application to application authentication.

    B. **Correct** – Power Platform application users are ideally suited for use by applications looking to connect and authenticate with Dataverse.

    C. **Incorrect** – the Dataverse API does not provide an anonymous feature, and it is unlikely you would want to use one in this scenario.

    D. **Incorrect** – while technically feasible for applications to leverage an HTTP-triggered cloud flow, it would not provide a standard authentication mechanism that leverages Dataverse security roles and would require a custom-built credentials check.

    E. **Correct** – AAD app registrations allow for the scheduled expiry of secrets. An app registration secrets rotation policy would contribute toward the security of the Dataverse API.

Question 16 – Data security

An online bank is looking to implement a Power Platform solution. Potential customers will be able to apply for a bank account via Power Pages, and back-office staff will process the application data via a model-driven app.

Regulatory restrictions require that customer service staff should be able to see all data except the customer's date of birth. Staff members from the legal team will be able to see all customer data.

Which Power Platform features can be used to fulfill the data security requirements?

    A. Power Platform teams

    B. Field-level security/column-level security

    C. Web roles

    D. Security roles

Answers

The correct answer is **A** and **B**:

    A. **Correct** – a Dataverse team, together with field-level security, can be used to secure access to a specific column on a table.

    B. **Correct** – field-level security can be configured to restrict access to specific table columns (for reference, see `https://docs.microsoft.com/power-platform/admin/field-level-security`).

    C. **Incorrect** – web roles are a feature within Power Pages (Power Apps portals) and do not apply to model-driven apps.

    D. **Incorrect** – Dataverse security roles control access at the table level. For column-level permissions, please use field-level security.

Question 17 – Table security

A customer service organization would like to give all staff the ability to see all accounts within a Power Platform environment. However, they should only be able to change accounts owned by their team.

What Dataverse security feature could you use to implement the requirement?

      A. A field-level security role

      B. A security role with organization-level read access and user-level write access

      C. Team restriction

      D. Table permissions

Answers

The correct answer is **B**:

      A. **Incorrect** – field-level security does not control access at the table level.

      B. **Correct** – the security role assigned to a team the user belongs to would provide the required level of access.

      C. **Incorrect** – team restriction is not a Dataverse feature.

      D. **Incorrect** – table permissions are a feature within Power Pages (Power Apps portals) and do not apply to model-driven apps.

Question 18 – Dataverse relationships

You are tasked to build a Power Platform application that allows potential customers to apply for an account. The contact table will be used to store the applicant's details, and a custom "application" table with a link to the contact table will be used to store applications.

When a contact record is assigned to a team, linked applications should also be assigned to the same team as the contact.

What two features can help you configure that behavior?

      A. A 1:N relationship from contact to application, configured with a parental behavior type

      B. An N:1 relationship from contact to application, configured with a parental behavior type

C. A 1:N relationship from Contact to Application, configured with configurable cascading

D. An N:1 relationship from Contact to Application, configured with configurable cascading

Answers

The correct answer is **A** and **C**:

A. **Correct** – parental behavior sets the **Assign** action to **Cascade All**, automatically assigning the applications when a contact is assigned.

B. **Incorrect** – while the parental behavior is correct, the N:1 relationship from the contact to the application table is opposite to the requirement.

C. **Correct** – configurable cascading can be used to refine cascade behaviors further. The Assign action can be set to Cascade All, automatically assigning the applications when a contact is assigned.

D. **Incorrect** – while the parental behavior is correct, the N:1 relationship from the contact to the application table is opposite to the requirement.

Question 19 – Data security

A healthcare organization has multiple Power Platform environments for various applications. One of the environments contains live patient data, and the organization wants to restrict channels so that the data stays within the environment. Automated and manual data exports should be restricted to prevent outbound movement of the patient data.

What two Power Platform features and methods can help to fulfill the requirement?

E. Assign patient data to an administration team

F. Data loss prevention policies

G. Configure live data restrictions

H. Disable the **Export to Excel** permission on security roles

Answers

The correct answer is **B** and **D**:

- A. **Incorrect** – assigning data to a team would not, by itself, prevent it from being exported or sent via connectors.
- B. **Correct** – a Power Platform data loss prevention policy assigned to the corresponding environment can be configured to restrict connector access.
- C. **Incorrect** – live data restrictions are not a Power Platform feature.
- D. **Correct** – the Export to Excel permission grants access to the corresponding feature. Without it, users will not be able to export data to Excel from a model-driven app.

Question 20 – Customer satisfaction surveys

A company wants to send a customer satisfaction survey to all new customers. The survey must be sent 5 days after the customer has completed a purchase, which is recorded in Power Platform as a custom table in Dataverse.

What two components would you recommend?

- A. Power BI
- B. Power Automate
- C. Dynamics 365 Customer Voice
- D. Power Pages
- E. Forms Pro

Answers

The correct answer is **B** and **C**:

- A. **Incorrect** – Power BI does not provide customer survey functionality.
- B. **Correct** – a cloud flow can be run as a schedule, triggering Customer Voice to send a survey 5 days after a purchase is recorded in Dataverse.
- C. **Correct** – Dynamics 365 Customer Voice integrates with Dataverse and is able to send surveys to customers.
- D. **Incorrect** – Power Pages does not provide survey functionality as standard.
- E. **Incorrect** – Forms Pro is now Dynamics 365 Customer Voice.

Question 21 – Integration options

An organization is looking to integrate a model-driven app with an external system as follows:

- Allow model-driven app users to read and write to contact records stored in an external database that supports OData V4.

- Any purchases recorded in the external system are replicated in real time to a custom "Purchases" table within Dataverse.

Select the most appropriate option for each requirement:

Requirement	Solution
Allow model-driven app users to read and write to contact records stored in an external database that supports OData V4.	A. A web resource with JavaScript
	B. Virtual tables
	C. The Dataverse Web API
Any purchases recorded in the external system are sent in real time to a custom "Purchases" Dataverse table.	D. Virtual tables
	E. Dataflows
	F. The Dataverse Web API

Answers:

A – the first requirement is best suited for virtual tables. They provide seamless integration of external OData V4 data sources with read/write capabilities (for reference, see `https://docs.microsoft.com/power-apps/maker/data-platform/virtual-entity-walkthrough-using-odata-provider`).

F – the second requirement can be best fulfilled via a direct push of data from the external system to the Dataverse Web API (for reference, see `https://docs.microsoft.com/en-us/power-apps/developer/data-platform/webapi/overview`). While dataflows can be used to replicate data, they do not provide a real-time integration capability.

Question 22 – Select the ideal components

A water cooler service provider is looking to provide its customers with a website where they can do the following:

- View their existing orders and raise new requests for deliveries
- Initiate a web chat with a virtual agent, which may direct them to customer service staff

Which Power Platform components would you recommend?

A. Dynamics 365 Customer Voice

B. Power Virtual Agents

C. A canvas app

D. Power Pages/Power Apps portals

Answers

The correct answer is **B** and **D**:

A. **Incorrect** – Customer Voice provides survey functionality and does not fulfill the requirements

B. **Correct** – Power Virtual Agents provide chatbot functionality and redirection to customer service staff

C. **Incorrect** – canvas apps are not designed to fulfill the role of a public website

D. **Correct** – Power Pages/Power Apps portals provide an ideal platform for a public-facing website that fulfills the requirements

Question 23 – Select integration options

You have been tasked by an organization to integrate a Power Platform solution with a bespoke API. The integration needs to retrieve the latest currency exchange rates from the external API and update the Dataverse exchange rate table daily.

What solution would you recommend?

A. Virtual tables

B. Power Automate Desktop

C. Power Automate

D. A custom connector

E. Dual-write

Answers

The correct answer is **C and D**:

F. **Incorrect** – virtual tables do not run on a schedule or update data within Dataverse

G. **Incorrect** – while Power Automate Desktop could be used, it would require a dedicated machine to run and is designed to automate user workflows instead

H. **Correct** – a cloud flow can be scheduled to run daily, connecting to the custom API

I. **Correct** – a custom connector can be created to connect with the API and retrieve data for insertion into Dataverse

J. **Incorrect** – dual-write is a Dynamics 365 Finance and Operations integration feature

Question 24 – Functional versus non-functional

You are working on a Power Apps request management solution, and during the requirements capture phase, you need to identify non-functional requirements.

Identify the three non-functional requirements in the following list:

A. Staff members must be able to access the system 24 hours a day.

B. An email must be sent to the owner when a request is assigned.

C. The requests must be stored for 5 years from the date of creation.

D. The solution must be able to handle up to 10,000 requests per hour.

E. The staff members will be able to close requests once resolved.

Answers

The correct answer is **A, C**, and **D**:

A. **Correct** – uptime requirements are considered non-functional

B. **Incorrect** – email automation is a function of the system

C. **Correct** – data retention policies are considered non-functional

D. **Correct** – performance requirements are considered non-functional

E. **Incorrect** – request closure is a function of the system

Question 25 – Table columns

While designing the data model for a Power Platform application, you need to create a solution that satisfies the following requirements:

- Users will be able to select one or more options from a drop-down list.

- Users will be required to provide a signature when closing.

What Dataverse columns can you use to fulfill the requirements?

A. A choice column

B. A signature column

C. A multiline text column

D. A choices column

E. A lookup column

Answers

The correct answer is **C** and **D**:

A. **Incorrect** – choice columns only allow the selection of a single item.

B. **Incorrect** – signature columns are not available in Dataverse. You can create a multiline text column and display a signature control.

C. **Correct** – a multiline text column can be configured to display a signature control.

D. **Correct** – a choices column allows the users to select multiple options.

E. **Incorrect** – a lookup column does not fulfill either requirement.

Question 26 – Connecting external services

An organization is looking to configure application users for use by an external service. The application users will provide read-only access to the contacts table in Dataverse.

Select three components that will require configuration:

A. AAD app registration

B. AAD Security Groups

C. An application user

D. A security role

E. A Power Apps license

Answers:

The correct answer is **A**, **C**, and **D**:

A. **Correct** – an AAD app registration is configured with an application ID and secret for use by Power Platform.

B. **Incorrect** – security groups are not required for the configuration of application users.

C. **Correct** – a Power Platform application user is linked with the app registration application ID.

D. **Correct** – a security role associated with the application user can be configured with the required read-only permissions.

E. **Incorrect** – an application user does not require a Power Apps license.

Question 27 – Dataverse teams

You are currently designing the Dataverse team strategy for an organization looking to implement a new Power Platform solution:

Team requirement	Type of team
Team members will be granted organization-level read/write access to contact records.	A. Owner team
	B. Access team
Users need to be temporarily granted access to records.	C. Owner team
	D. Access team
Newly created accounts will be automatically assigned to the team.	E. Owner team
	F. Access team

Answers:

Team requirement	Type of team
Team members will be granted organization-level read/write access to contact records.	A. Owner team – table-level permissions are granted via security roles associated with owner teams
	B. Access team
Users need to be temporarily granted access to records.	C. Owner team
	D. Access team – access teams can be used to grant access to records temporarily
Newly created accounts will be automatically assigned to the team.	E. Owner team – assignment of records to a team requires ownership
	F. Access team

Question 28 – External users accessing a solution

You are looking to provide external users with access to personal data associated with their contact records. The data is hosted within a Power Platform environment. The users are not part of the tenant hosting the Power Platform database and are not expected to have a Microsoft 365 account.

What solutions can you recommend?

- A. A model-driven app
- B. Power Automate Desktop
- C. Power Pages/Power Apps portals
- D. Dynamics 365 Customer Service

Answers

The correct answer is **C**:

- A. **Incorrect** – model-driven app access requires a Microsoft 365 account.
- B. **Incorrect** – Power Automate Desktop is a workflow automation tool and would not fulfill the requirement.
- C. **Correct** – a Power Pages website can be used to provide access to users through various authentication methods other than Microsoft 365.
- D. **Incorrect** – Dynamics 365 Customer Service on its own does not provide access to external users.

Question 29 – Identify the functional requirements

You are running a session to capture requirements for a new Power Platform implementation and are tasked with identifying functional requirements.

Which of the following are functional requirements?

A. Users must fill in mandatory fields specific to each stage in the case management process before proceeding to the next stage.

B. In the event of an outage, the solution must recover within 5 minutes.

C. Any cases not resolved within 5 minutes will change status to "delayed."

D. User actions should not take longer than 10 seconds.

Answers

The correct answer is **A** and **C**:

A. **Correct** – the requirement defines functionality.

B. **Incorrect** – recovery time requirements do not specify functionality to be implemented.

C. **Correct** – automated changes in case status are a behavior of the system and are considered functional requirements.

D. **Incorrect** – performance-related requirements are considered non-functional.

Question 30 – Fit gap analysis

You are running a fit gap analysis on a set of requirements. The organization is looking to provide management with detailed visualizations of the data hosted within Dataverse in a paginated format.

Which solutions will be a good fit for the requirement?

A. Power Automate

B. Power BI

C. Dashboards

D. Canvas apps

Answers

The correct answer is **B**:

- A. **Incorrect** – Power Automate does not provide visualization capabilities.
- B. **Correct** – Power BI is a good fit thanks to its advanced reporting features and paged output capabilities.
- C. **Incorrect** – dashboards are able to display visualizations but do not provide paginated output.
- D. **Incorrect** – canvas apps are interactive applications rather than reporting tools.

Question 31 – Microsoft 365 integration

An organization is implementing a Power Platform solution. Users will send emails to customers from within a model-driven app.

Which features can be used to implement the solution?

- A. Dynamics 365 for Outlook
- B. Server-side synchronization
- C. Microsoft Exchange on-premises
- D. Microsoft Exchange Online

Answers

The correct answer is **B**, **C**, and **D**.

Dynamics 365 for Outlook is external to model-driven apps. All other components can be used to send emails from a model-driven app (although Exchange on-premises is subject to limitations and minimum versions).

Question 32 – Document management

An organization requires customers to upload documentation via a Power Pages site or Power Apps portal. The total capacity needed for documents is expected to grow by 30 GB per year.

What solution should you recommend?

    A. Server-side synchronization

    B. SharePoint integration

    C. Dataverse notes document storage

    D. Power Automate

Answers

The correct answer is **B**.

Power Pages and Power Apps portals SharePoint integration provides a high-capacity solution for document storage.

Question 33 – Integration options

A Power Platform implementation requires contact creations, updates, and deletions to be sent to an external system. The external system expects to receive data using a queue platform.

What solutions should you recommend?

    E. Cloud flows

    F. Webhooks

    G. Power Automate Desktop

    H. Azure Service Bus

Answers

The correct answer is **B** and **D**.

Azure Service Bus and Power Platform Webhooks can be configured to send the required data actions to a queue (for reference, see `https://docs.microsoft.com/power-apps/developer/data-platform/use-webhooks`).

Question 34 – Solution strategies

You are defining the deployment strategy for Power Platform solutions. What solution type should you recommend when deploying to a production environment?

> A. Unmanaged solutions
>
> B. Instant solutions
>
> C. Managed solutions
>
> D. Power solutions

Answers

The correct answer is **C**.

Managed solutions provide additional controls over unmanaged solutions, making them suitable for production environments. Instant/power solutions are not Power Platform features.

Question 35 – Dataverse features

An organization is looking to implement a request management application. Staff members need to be able to search for a request using a unique identifier number, which will be in the form of an integer.

In addition, external services connecting to the Dataverse API need to be able to retrieve request records easily and quickly using the same identifier number.

What two Dataverse features should you recommend?

> A. A whole number column
>
> B. Autonumbering
>
> C. An alternate key
>
> D. An integer key

Answers

The correct answer is **B** and **C**.

A column configured for autonumbering can automatically generate an integer number for each record. An alternate key can be configured to use the `autonumber` integer as a key for easy retrieval of records via the Dataverse API.

The following chapter provides links to documentation that will help you in your examination.

Recommended further reading and additional learning materials

The following links provide additional details of the Power Platform capabilities and describe the role of a solution architect:

- *Microsoft Power Platform documentation* – the core documentation covers all Power Platform technical capabilities:

    `https://docs.microsoft.com/power-platform/`

- *Learning path – Solution Architect: Design Microsoft Power Platform solutions* – detailed learning path documentation to help you with the PL-600 exam:

    `https://docs.microsoft.com/learn/paths/solution-architect-data/`

- *Microsoft Power Platform Build Tools for Azure DevOps* – application life cycle management and build tool instructions for use with Power Platform implementations:

    `https://docs.microsoft.com/power-platform/alm/devops-build-tools`

- *Learning path – Architect solutions for Dynamics 365 and Microsoft Power Platform* – the Dynamics 365 and Power Platform solution architects certification learning path:

    `https://docs.microsoft.com/en-us/learn/paths/become-solution-architect/`

- *Microsoft Dynamics 365 – Implementation Guide: Success by Design* – the fast-track Dynamics 365 and Power Platform implementation guide:

    `https://www.d365implementationguide.com/books/asvr`

- *Course PL-600T00: Microsoft Power Platform Solution Architect* – course details to help you succeed in your PL-600 exam:

    `https://docs.microsoft.com/learn/certifications/courses/pl-600t00`

The reference material listed in this section will help complete your Power Platform knowledge and keep you abreast of new developments.

Conclusion on practice exams

In this section, you have had the chance to validate your knowledge of Power Platform solution architecture. Good luck with your examination!

Final thoughts

Power Platform solution architecture, in many ways, aims to help people solve their day-to-day business challenges. As a solution architect, you become a leader, a technical authority, a source of knowledge, and a creator. You drive the solution, the team, and the project, bringing those elements together in a synergy that gets results.

What we have discovered so far

This book's primary goal was to help you excel as a Power Platform solution architect. Let's look back at what we have learned:

1. **The Power Platform solution architect's role** – the first few chapters dove right into what it means to be a solution architect. We navigated through the various components that make up Power Platform and introduced the concept of hands-on solution architecture.

2. **Requirements analysis, solution envisioning, and the implementation roadmap** – we then proceeded to work through the processes of requirements analysis, business process mapping, and solution envisioning. You have learned to provide clear direction and focus for a project and solution.

3. **Architecting Power Platform solutions** – in the following chapters, we learned to create architectural designs for Power Platform applications. We covered the areas of data modeling, integration strategies, and all-important security concepts. Understanding these concepts puts you in the unique position of being able to lead the Power Platform design process.

4. **Implementing Power Platform solutions** – implementation is most likely the busiest phase of any project. In these chapters, you learned how to validate solution designs and implementation. We then worked through effective Power Platform implementation strategies and planned for the all-important solution to go live.

5. **Preparing for the Power Platform solution architect certification** – the last chapter focused on helping you prepare for the Power Platform solution architect exam. It was also a chance to validate your understanding of the concepts described in this book.

You now have a comprehensive framework for establishing the architecture of your Power Platform-based solutions.

Where to next?

We embarked on a journey to learn what it means to be a solution architect. In doing so, we discovered the virtually limitless capabilities of the Power Platform ecosystem. You listen to an organization, translate its needs into great solution architecture, and drive your vision of a successful digital transformation to completion.

As a Power Platform solution architect, you are in a unique position. You understand the intricacies of complex business solutions and can drive a solution, delivering on the promises that Power Platform makes. You now know how to leverage Power Platform to your advantage. Leading by example through a hands-on approach to technical leadership, you raise those around you towards a common goal.

Index

Packt>

Subscribe to our online digital library for full access to over 7,000 books and videos, as well as industry leading tools to help you plan your personal development and advance your career. For more information, please visit our website.

Why subscribe?

- Spend less time learning and more time coding with practical eBooks and Videos from over 4,000 industry professionals

- Improve your learning with Skill Plans built especially for you

- Get a free eBook or video every month

- Fully searchable for easy access to vital information

- Copy and paste, print, and bookmark content

Did you know that Packt offers eBook versions of every book published, with PDF and ePub files available? You can upgrade to the eBook version at packt.com and as a print book customer, you are entitled to a discount on the eBook copy. Get in touch with us at customercare@packtpub.com for more details.

At www.packt.com, you can also read a collection of free technical articles, sign up for a range of free newsletters, and receive exclusive discounts and offers on Packt books and eBooks.

Other Books You May Enjoy

If you enjoyed this book, you may be interested in these other books by Packt:

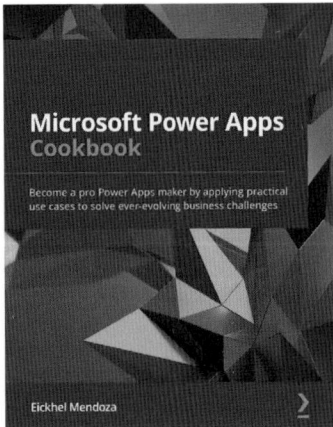

Microsoft Power Apps Cookbook

Eickhel Mendoza

ISBN: 9781800569553

- Build pixel-perfect solutions with canvas apps
- Design model-driven solutions using various features of Microsoft Dataverse
- Automate business processes such as triggered events, status change notifications, and approval systems with Power Automate
- Implement AI Builder's intelligent capabilities in your solutions
- Improve the UX of business apps to make them more appealing
- Find out how to extend Microsoft Teams using Power Apps
  Extend your business applications' capabilities using Power Apps Component Framework

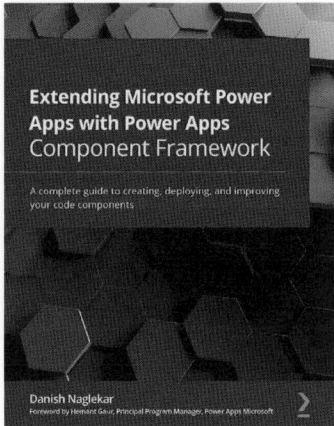

Extending Microsoft Power Apps with Power Apps Component Framework

Danish Naglekar

ISBN: 9781800564916

- Understand the fundamentals of Power Apps Component Framework
- Explore the tools that make it easy to build code components
- Build code components for both a field and a dataset
- Debug using test harness and Fiddler
- Implement caching techniques
- Find out how to work with the Dataverse Web API
- Build code components using React and Fluent UI controls
- Discover different deployment strategies

Packt is searching for authors like you

If you're interested in becoming an author for Packt, please visit `authors.packtpub.com` and apply today. We have worked with thousands of developers and tech professionals, just like you, to help them share their insight with the global tech community. You can make a general application, apply for a specific hot topic that we are recruiting an author for, or submit your own idea.

Share Your Thoughts

Now youve finished *Microsoft Power Platform Solution Architect's Handbook*, we'd love to hear your thoughts! Scan the QR code below to go straight to the Amazon review page for this book and share your feedback or leave a review on the site that you purchased it from.

`https://packt.link/r/1-801-81933-5`

Your review is important to us and the tech community and will help us make sure we're delivering excellent quality content.

Printed in Great Britain
by Amazon

28709243R00284